AN A.K. RICE INSTITUTE SERIES

GROUP RELATIONS READER

edited by

Arthur D. Colman and W. Harold Bexton

GROUP RELATIONS READER
Arthur D. Colman and W. Harold Bexton, Editors

Library of Congress Catalogue Card Number LC 75-24569

International Standard Book Number ISBN (Hard Bound)
0-916050-01-7. (Soft Bound) 0-916050-02-5.

Published by GREX
P.O. Box 1758, Sausalito, California 94965

Printed in the United States of America by
Associates Printing and Publishing Company
132 Woodland Avenue
San Rafael, California 94901

Cover design by W. Harold Bexton

First Edition

AN A.K. RICE INSTITUTE SERIES

GROUP RELATIONS READER

edited by

Arthur D. Colman and W. Harold Bexton

THE A.K. RICE INSTITUTE

The A. K. Rice Institute was established in 1970 for the purpose of furthering the principles and methods of group relations training developed at the Centre for Applied Social Research of the Tavistack Institute of Human Relations in London. The Institute takes its name to honor the late A.K. Rice under whose leadership the work developed.

The Institute is now constituted by seven Centers in the United States, each one of which conducts programs of its own. They are located in: Connecticut, The Center for Education in Groups and Organizations (CEGO); Los Angeles, The Center for Organizational Leadership and Authority (SCOLA); Minneapolis, North Central Group Relations Center; New York, The Institute for the Applied Study of Social Systems (IASOSS); San Francisco, (GREX); Texas, The Texas Group Relations Center; and Washington, D.C., The Washington-Baltimore Center.

The GROUP RELATIONS READER is the first in a series of publications sponsored by the A.K. Rice Institute.

The Board of the A.K. Rice Institute which sponsored the GROUP RELATIONS READER consisted of the following members:

One or more conferences a year are sponsored by the A.K. Rice Institute itself.

Contributors

Astrachan, Boris, M.D. Professor of Clinical Psychiatry, Yale University School of Medicine.

Bexton, W. Harold, M.Arch. Department of Architecture, University of California, Berkeley. Principal, ENRAD, Environmental Research and Design, Berkeley.

Bion, Wilfred, R., M.D. Distinguished Group Theorist.

Colman, Arthur D., M.D. Associate Clinical Professor, Department of Psychiatry, University of California Medical Center, San Francisco. Board of Directors, A.K. Rice Institute.

Flynn, Hulda. Assistant Professor of Psychiatry, Yale University School of Medicine.

Fried, Matt, Ph.D. Research Center for Group Phenomena, New York, N.Y.

Geller, Jesse. Associate Professor of Psychology in the Department of Psychiatry, Yale University School of Medicine.

Harvey, Henry, MPA, Lecturer Psychiatry and Public Health, Yale University School of Medicine.

Hausman, William, M.D. Professor and Head, Department of Psychiatry University of Minnesota Medical School, Minneapolis. President, Board of Directors, A.K. Rice Institute.

Lofgren, Lars B., M.D. Associate Professor of Psychiatry in Residence, University of California School of Medicine, Los Angeles.

Menninger, Roy W., M.D. President, The Menninger Foundation, Topeka, Kansas. Board of Directors, A.K. Rice Institute.

Menzies, Isabel, E.P. Consultant, Centre for Applied Social Research, Tavistock Institute of Human Relations, London

Miller, Eric. M.A., Ph.D. Chairman, Centre for Applied Social Research, Tavistock Institute of Human Relations, London. Board of Directors, A.K. Rice Institute.

Musto, David F., M.D. Associate Professor of Psychiatry (Child Study Center) and Associate Professor of History, Yale University, New Haven.

Redlich, Fritz C., M.D. Professor, Department of Psychiatry, Yale University.

Rice, A.K. Formerly Chairman, Centre for Applied Social Research, Tavistock Institute of Human Relations, London.

Richardson, Elizabeth. Research Fellow, University of Bristol

Rioch, Margaret, Ph.D. Professor of Psychology, The American University, Washington, D.C. Board of Directors, A.K. Rice Institute.

Singer, David L., Ph.D. Williamstown Psychological Consultants. Williamstown, Mass. Board of Directors, A.K. Rice Institute.

Whiton, Mary Beth, Ph.D. Williamstown Psychological Consultants, Williamstown, Mass.

Williams, Dennis, Ph.D. Department of Architecture, University of California, Berkeley.

Acknowledgements

We wish to thank all those who contributed to the *Reader*. In particular we wish to acknowledge the following:

The American Group Psychotheraphy Association, for permission to reprint from the *International Journal of Group Psychotherapy*:

"Group Relations: Rationale and Technique" by Margaret J. Rioch. Vol. 20, pp. 340-355 (pp. 340-347 reprinted in Reader). Copyright 1970.

"The Impact of Group Relations Conferences on Organizational Growth" by Roy W. Menninger. Vol. 22, pp. 415-432. Copyright 1972.

Tavistock Publications Ltd., London, and Basic Books, Inc., New York, publishers, for permission to reprint pages 141-155 of:

"Experiences in Groups" by Wilfred R. Bion. Copyright 1959 and 1961.

The William Alanson White Psychiatric Foundation, Inc., for permission to reprint from *Psychiatry*:

"The Work of Wilfred Bion on Groups" by Margaret J. Rioch. Vol. 33, pp. 56-66. Copyright 1970.

" 'All We Like Sheep—' (Isaiah 53:6): Followers and Leaders" by Margaret J. Rioch. Vol. 34, pp. 258-273. Copyright 1971.

"Strange Encounter: The Use of Study Groups with Graduate Students in History" by David F. Musto and Boris M. Astrachan. Vol. 31, pp. 264-276. Copyright 1968.

Tavistock Publications Ltd., London, publishers, for permission to reprint:

Pages 3-32 of: "Systems of Organization" by E.J. Miller and A.K. Rice. Copyright 1967.

Pages 22-131 of: "Learning for Leadership" by A.K. Rice. Copyright 1965.

Preface

This volume of reprints and original papers represents an introductory interdisciplinary survey of writings in Group Relations theory and practice. The papers fall into two general categories which transcend this volume's organization into Theory, Method, and Application. The first group contains the initial writings of Bion, Rice and Miller from the Tavistock Institute of Human Relations, in London, particularly its Centre for Applied Social Research. In the second group are the "second generation" American studies, largely in the field of application, derived from many intellectual centers throughout the country. The work of Margaret Rioch at the Washington School of Psychiatry who, with a few associates, introduced Group Relations Conferences to the United States, bridges these categories.

The immediate intellectual history of this field is still very much bound up with its institutional origins. A. Kenneth Rice, who first developed the learning model of the Group Relations Conference, was an organizational consultant who used psychoanalytic ideas to enrich his own understanding of organizational process. On the other hand Rioch and her colleagues at the Washington School of Psychiatry were most involved in the field of mental health and education. Many of the writings collected here reflect this split in interest areas. Most recently there has been some broadening of interest areas to include a variety of fields including architecture, history, and philosophy. Some of these new areas are represented. Many others could have been included.

The immediate need for this Reader grew out of the introduction of the Group Relations model into the educational curriculum at the Department of Architecture at the University of California, Berkeley. As students and faculty became interested in the work and came to conferences and workshops, the need for a central reference volume of major contributions in the field became more urgent. Conference brochures list a "selected bibliography" for membership but, remarkably, even in a bibliophilic community such as Berkeley it was actually impossible to find many of the books and articles. At the very best a student and potential member would have to visit departmental libraries in psychology, business administration, education, and design to find representative references. The lack of one journal that publishes writings in this field was a serious hazard to keeping up with the most recent literature.

GREX, the San Francisco Bay Area affiliate of the A.K. Rice Institute, and the Department of Architecture (through a National Institute of Mental Health Grant for Training in Behavioral Factors in Design) initially coordinated their skills and financial resources to develop a prototype volume. Our impression of the need for such a work was confirmed by the rate at which copies were consumed by our local membership and taken from the local libraries. The Board of Directors of the A.K. Rice Institute agreed to sponsor and finance the publication of the Group Relations Reader as the first in an A.K. Rice Series of publications in the Group Relations field. A committee composed of Arthur Colman, James Miller, and David Singer was constituted to work out the practical aspects of publications. Our thanks go to this committee, the entire Board of Directors, and particularly to William Hausman, the first president of the A.K. Rice Institute.

The selections included in this volume are biased towards "classics" and breadth of interest. Selections from the books of Bion, Rice, Miller and Rice, and Richardson stand in their own right but inevitably compromise the total vision of those authors. Readers are heartily encouraged to read these works in their entirety. Work in the field of Design is overrepresented reflecting the editors' immediate training needs. Many important articles have been left out. Our hope is to compile other volumes of important articles in the field as needed.

We wish to thank all those who have contributed to this Reader and many others, who, although not included, contributed by their ideas and experience to the growth of the model.

Arthur D. Colman, M.D.
W. Harold Bexton, M.Arch.

Contents

ILLUSTRATIONS

GROUP RELATIONS READER

part one
THEORY

The papers collected here span developmental, group, and organizational theory as they apply to the Group Relations model. Bion's work in small group theory, particularly his interest in differentiating the Basic Assumption group from the Work group, is critical to Rice's development of an organization theory which takes into account the impact of covert processes. Colman's paper studies the developmental origins of group consciousness using the recent work of Margaret Mahler as his theoretical base. Permission for an excerpt from the writings of Melanie Klein could not be obtained. This is an important deficit; although she does not talk directly about group psychology, her theories about infant fantasies and defense mechanisms underlie the theory advanced by Bion, Rice, and others from the Tavistock Institute.

It is unfortunate that theoretical work in this area has not progressed further. The "great masters" are repeatedly referenced but little has been done to expand or alter their work. This volume quantitatively mirrors the fact that Group Relations application and methodological innovation have advanced far beyond its theoretical bases.

A.D.C.

1.

GROUP RELATIONS: RATIONALE AND TECHNIQUE

Margaret J. Rioch

In June 1965, the Washington School of Psychiatry, the Yale University Department of Psychiatry, and the Centre for Applied Social Research of the Tavistock Institute of London held their first Group Relations Conference in the United States at Mount Holyoke College. With this event began the transplantation of educational methods that had developed within the Tavistock Institute of Human Relations of London to American soil.

These methods of Group Relations Training go back to a two-week residential conference organized by the Tavistock Institute and the University of Leicester in September 1957, which has been described by Trist and Sofer (1959). In the introduction to their book, *Explorations in Group Relations*, these authors speak of the contribution of social psychology, especially the work of Kurt Lewin; of the contribution of group psychotherapy, especially the work of W.R. Bion; and of the influence of Bethel, on the thinking which went into the arrangement of this conference. The primary emphasis at that time was on the study of small groups, with secondary emphasis on the application of this study to the problems that members encountered in their own work. The membership was drawn from a variety of organizations, over half of the participants being from industry or allied fields. The staff were all professional psychologists or members of allied social science disciplines who had had psychological training. The small groups, called Study Groups, were conducted only by those who had had experience in psychoanalysis. The aim of the training offered by this conference was "to encourage in those who participate a constructively analytical and critical approach to the way they perform their roles in the groups to which they belong" (Trist and Sofer, 1959). This conference seems to have been very similar to those being run in the 1950's in the United States by the National Training Laboratories. In fact, during the planning stages, a member of the Planning and Policy Committee of the National Training Laboratories consulted with the Executive Committee.

In the twelve years following the conference described by Trist and Sofer (1959), major changes took place in the theory and practice of the British conferences, which are now under the sponsorship of the Centre for Applied Social Research of the Tavistock Institute, so that when they were transplanted to the United States in 1965 they were no longer very similar to the

3

comparable events of the National Training Laboratories. The British and the American institutions had gone separate ways. The changes in the British conferences will be described in the next sections of this paper. They have been in large part due to the work of A. Kenneth Rice, who directed all of the Tavistock-Leicester Conferences from 1962 through 1968. Until 1968 Rice was Chairman of the Centre for Applied Social Research in which he acted as senior staff member until his untimely death on November 15, 1969. This Centre is one of the divisions of the Tavistock Institute. In developing his particular theory and practice of group relations training, Rice was ably and creatively seconded by Pierre Turquet, who is at present (1969) Chairman of the Adult Department of the Tavistock Clinic. Rice's successor as Chairman of the Centre and as Director of the British core conferences is Eric Miller.

These conferences are held annually in the spring at the University of Leicester. For some time they were under the joint sponsorship of the two institutions, but at present the sponsorship is by the Centre alone. Nonresidential courses have also been held in London. Other institutions in Britain have organized similar conferences and courses, often in collaboration with the Tavistock Institute staff. The Grubb Institute of Behaviorial Studies (formerly called Christian Teamwork Institute of Education) has developed an independent series of courses and several residential conferences a year in which both concepts and methods derive from the Tavistock-Leicester model. The University of Bristol Department of Education, and the Department of the Treasury, Tube Investments, Limited, and other British organizations have either asked the Tavistock to run conferences for them or have developed their own in consultation with Tavistock.

In 1963, two members of the Washington School of Psychiatry faculty (Morris Parloff and Margaret Rioch) attended the Tavistock-Leicester Conference. They formed the opinion that the introduction of this kind of conference into the United States would mean a valuable addition to the methods of group relations training in this country. After having satisfied themselves that this would not be a duplication of methods being used at the time by the National Training Laboratories, they recommended to the Tavistock Institute that a special conference be set up in Britain in the summer of 1964 at a time when a number of Americans could conveniently attend and form their own judgments of the feasibility and desirability of importing the methods to the United States. Accordingly, in July 1964, a special conference was arranged, attended by about 25 British and 25 American members. The latter were recruited with the help and support of the Washington School of Psychiatry. Enough of the participants found it a useful experience so that the decision was taken to run the first American conference in June 1965 under the co-sponsorship of the Washington School of

Psychiatry and the Yale Department of Psychiatry. The Walter Reed Army Institute of Research, as a government agency, could not officially co-sponsor the event, but the Division of Neuropsychiatry under the leadership of David McK. Rioch gave unofficial moral support, supplied members and staff members, and helped in the organizational planning. The Tavistock Institute had no formal responsibility for financing and administering the conference, but as the institution supplying the Director (A.K. Rice) and two other senior staff members (P. Turquet and J. Sutherland) and representing the tradition that was being built upon, it was actually the center of the conference. The Executive Committee of the Conference consisted of the Director and two American members, F.C. Redlich, then Chairman of the Yale Department of Psychiatry, now Dean of its Medical School, and M.J. Rioch, member of the Executive Council of the Washington School of Psychiatry. The conference was held at Mount Holyoke College. This location has now become part of the tradition of the two-week conferences that have been held there every year since 1965 in June. At the end of the 1967 Conference the Executive Committee decided that the joint sponsorship of the two-week conference by the Washington School of Psychiatry and Yale University, which had been maintained for three years, should come to an end. More unified and efficient management, it was thought, could be obtained by the sponsorship being lodged solely in the Washington School of Psychiatry. In order to preserve the inter-institutional and international character of the conference the Washington School of Psychiatry authorized the formation of a board of individuals from a number of different institutions in the United States and Great Britain. This Board carries authority and responsibility for the appointment of Director and Staff and for general policies concerning the conference.

Soon after the conferences were started in the United States, it became clear that there were many people who might profit from membership but who would not be able to spend the time or money for two weeks in residence, especially without having any firsthand knowledge of what was involved and what possible benefits might be derived. Thus, in September 1966, the first one-week American conference was held at Connecticut College in New London. Since then a one-week conference has been held every year in late August at Amherst College. There has been a special effort in these conferences to build an American staff which can function independently. Since 1967, the Director has been an American, and the intention is to maintain and develop American leadership in these conferences.

Beginning in 1968, a number of other events were held in the United States using the Tavistock model. The Joseph Priestley District of the Unitarian-Universalist Association has sponsored a four-day residential conference in February or March annually

5

since 1968. The University of Maryland sponsored a workshop which took place over two consecutive weekends in 1968. The Woodrow Wilson School of Public and International Affairs at Princeton University and John Hopkins University sponsored a two-day Intergroup Workshop in 1969.

While these events represent an enlargement of the activities of the Tavistock-Washington School of Psychiatry group conferences and a spread of the tradition, the growth has been purposefully slow and the institution with its branches is a small one. This permits a homogeneity of method and outlook which is much more difficult to maintain in a very large organization. At present the British Tavistock conferences and the American Washington School conferences are very close in philosophy and method. This close relationship is maintained by the presence of British staff in the American conferences and of American staff in the British events.

For the sake of simplicity, this paper will refer primarily to the residential conferences in this country as the major methods of studying group relations sponsored by the Washington School of Psychiatry. This is merely a short-cut, however, since a number of shorter, nonresidential workshops have been held, along with some longer courses. Although the design of these events necessarily varies, the underlying philosophy and methods are the same.

RATIONALE

In order to understand man in society, it is necessary to shift one's view from the individual and the pair to a larger whole. The thrust of the Washington School of Psychiatry-Tavistock Conferences is the attempt to make this shift.

Nineteenth-century science tended to break things down into smaller and smaller pieces, and great progress was made in this way, but the task now is one of integration and organization of the small pieces into intelligibly patterned wholes. This is true in biology and medicine as well as in the social sciences. One investigator, in the field of medicine, Dr. Thomas McP. Brown of George Washington University, likens the task to that of a person sitting on a merry-go-round in which the horse is not only going around and up and down but also sideways, while the whole thing, mounted on a huge truck, is racing along at 100 miles per hour. In this position the investigator is supposed to describe and understand phenomena which are on a similar merry-go-around proceeding down the road alongside him (Brown, 1969). The usual approach to a situation like this is to try to limit attention to one small aspect which can be encompassed and kept in view all the time, like the one horse in front of us on our own merry-go-round. But this will not yield a solution to complex problems in medicine and biology, and still less so in the social sciences. In order to see the total pattern, attention must shift from the single horse, or, in other words, from the single individual, and we must take in a larger view. This is very easy to say, but in actual practice it is very difficult to do, especially for those who were trained in individual psychology or in looking through a microscope at the individual cell in biology. Even the social psychologist, who by definition is interested in something quantitatively larger than the individual, often finds his task so exceedingly difficult that he opts for something like a study of how individuals differ in their behavior in groups.

The two major changes which have taken place in the Tavistock-Leicester conference model in the years of A.K. Rice's directorship are both related to this shift in perspective. The first has to do with leadership and authority. On Rice's (1965) *Learning for Leadership*, he stated, "I am now working on the assumption that the primary task of the residential conferences with which my colleagues and I are concerned is to provide those who attend with opportunities to learn about leadership." His concept of leadership is a complex one which carries with it all of his very rich thinking about organizational structure and the life of institutions. More recently the conferences have been described as being about authority, and in 1969, the aim of the conference was defined in its brochure as being "to provide members with opportunities to learn about the nature of authority and the interpersonal and intergroup problems encountered in its exercise."

There is no attempt on the part of the conference staff to prescribe how members shall define or use the words authority and leadership. In considering the various meanings of these terms as they are experienced in concrete situations, members sometimes acquire greater clarity in their own thinking about these important topics. In using the word authority the conference staff indicates its concern with this significant issue in present-day society.

By focusing on problems of leadership and authority, it is possible to see the patterns of the group emerging with regard to these concepts. The leader or leadership in a group can be thought of as representing or embodying the function of the group, especially its major function or primary task. "Primary task" is one of Rice's central concepts, and it has been defined and explained in several of his works (Rice, 1963, 1965; Miller and Rice, 1967). Briefly, he means by this term that task which an organization or institution must perform in order to survive. The organization may, and usually does, also perform secondary tasks. An important question then becomes, how do the members of the group relate to the primary task as represented by the leader? Do they accomplish the parts of it that, when put together, complete the total task? Do they fight to destroy it, betray it, sabotage it, work toward redefining or changing it? Do they compete for the position of leader? How do they conceive of authority in the group? Looking at these and other attitudes toward leader, leadership, and authority are ways of understanding the functioning of the group as a whole.

The second major change that has taken place under Rice's directorship is a shift in emphasis away from the small group to the institution as a whole. The total conference is conceived as an interplay of the various groups of which it is constituted. Further, the institution as a whole includes the relationship with groups outside, such as the college in which the conference is located, the institutions that provide staff, members, and sponsorship; and the national and international environment that impinges upon the life of the conference. This means, of course, that the conferences deal with a much larger order of complexity than was the case in 1957. Anyone who has worked with a small group knows of the enormous number of factors operating in it and feels the need both to organize these factors into some kind of pattern and/or to exclude some of the data impinging upon his nervous system in order to make any kind of meaningful statement about the group. If one is focusing upon an institution of 50 to 70 members, its constituent parts, and its relationship to institutions outside itself, the situation is obviously even more difficult. In order to manage it at all, it is necessary, first, to have some experience and practice in taking this overall view, and, second, to have some concepts and guidelines that help to make sense out of the overwhelming mass of data. Thus, the sharp focus upon a particular aim, such as the study of the nature of authority and leadership is the other side of the coin which necessarily accompanies the wider view of the institution as a whole, including its external relation.

It is quite possible, of course, to design a conference with another primary task than that of the study of leadership and the nature of authority. It is one essential characteristic of these conferences that they attempt to state their aim clearly and to focus upon it, whatever that aim may be. The staff of each conference at the present time tries to make a clear statement about its own purpose and position and to adhere to this purpose and position no matter how difficult it may become. At the same time the staff invites and encourages questioning of its task, purpose and position, on the part of the members, and is constantly engaged in self-questioning of its own activities. A major value to which the leadership is committed is ruthless honesty in thinking about oneself and one's group without any assumption that such honesty will necessarily lead to resolution of conflict. Thought, intellect, and rationality are highly valued, as are clear and firm decisions made in the service of a stated goal.

There is recognition on the part of the leadership of the conferences that human beings readily — all too readily — form groups, that they form mobs that lynch, groups that glorify fanatical leaders, groups that easily slip into orgiastic experiences or into the warm glow of togetherness. On the other hand, the formation of a human group seriously or consistently dedicated to a serious task, without fanaticism or illusion, is an extremely difficult process and a relatively rare occurrence. Human beings have the potentiality for this kind of group formation, however, and when it occurs, even briefly and imperfectly, it is one of the most valuable human phenomena, as well as one of the most individually satisfying experiences. Without some element of this, groups, both large and small, tend to remain childishly dependent upon a leader or a set of slogans, to seek an enemy against whom to unite, or to disintegrate in one way or another.

One of the major aims of the conferences is to contribute to people's ability to form serious work groups committed to the performance of clearly defined tasks. Whether or not members of such groups feel friendliness, warmth, closeness, competitiveness, or hostility to each other is of secondary importance. It is assumed that these and other feelings will occur from time to time, but this is not the issue. This issue is the common goal to which each individual makes his own differentiated contribution. A second major aim, closely related to the first, is the development of more responsible leadership and followership in group life.

2.
Selections from:
EXPERIENCES IN GROUPS
Wilfred R. Bion

Using his psychoanalytic experience Freud (1913, 1921) attempted to illuminate some of the obscurities revealed by Le Bon, McDougall, and others in their studies of the human group. I propose to discuss the bearing of modern developments of psychoanalysis, in particular those associated with the work of Melanie Klein, on the same problems. Her work shows that at the start of life itself the individual is in contact with the breast and, by rapid extension of primitive awareness, with the family group; furthermore she has shown that the nature of this contact displays qualities peculiar to itself, which are of profound significance both in the development of the individual and for a fuller understanding of the mechanisms already demonstrated by the intuitive genius of Freud.

I hope to show that in his contact with the complexities of life in a group the adult resorts, in what may be a massive regression, to mechanisms described by Melanie Klein (1931, 1946) as typical of the earliest phases of mental life. The adult must establish contact with the emotional life of the group in which he lives, this task would appear to be as formidable to the adult as the relationship with the breast appears to be to the infant, and the failure to meet the demands of this task is revealed in his regression. The belief that a group exists, as distinct from an aggregate of individuals, is an essential part of this regression, as are also the characteristics with which the supposed group is endowed by the individual. Substance is given to the phantasy that the group exists by the fact that the regression involves the individual in a loss of his 'individual distinctiveness' (Freud, 1921, p. 9), indistinguishable from depersonalization, and therefore obscures observation that the aggregation is of individuals. It follows that if the observer judges a group to be in existence, the individuals composing it must have experienced this regression. Conversely, should the individuals composing a 'group' (using that word to mean an aggregation of individuals all in the same state of regression) for some reason or other become threatened by awareness of their individual distinctiveness, then the group is in the emotional state known as panic. This does not mean that the group is disintegrating, and it will be seen later that I do not agree that in panic the group has lost its cohesiveness.

In this paper I shall summarize certain theories at which I have arrived by applying in groups the intuitions developed by present-day psychoanalytic training. These theories differ from many others, in merits and defects alike, in being educed in the situations of emotional stress that they are intended to describe. I introduce some concepts new to psychoanalysis, partly because I deal with different subject matter, partly because I wanted to see if a start disencumbered by previous theories might lead to a point at which my views of the group and psychoanalytic views of the individual could be compared, and thereby judged to be either complementary or divergent.

There are times when I think that the group has an attitude to me, and I can state in words what the attitude is; there are times when another individual acts as if he also thought the group had an attitude to him, and I believe I can deduce what his belief is; there are times when I think that the group has an attitude to an individual, and that I can say what it is. These occasions provide the raw material on which interpretations are based, but the interpretation itself is an attempt to translate into precise speech what I suppose to be the attitude of the group to me or to some other individual, and of the individual to the group. Only some of these occasions are used by me; I judge the occasion to be ripe for an interpretation when the interpretation would seem to be both obvious and unobserved.

The groups in which I have attempted to fill this role pass through a series of complex emotional episodes that permit the deduction of theories of group dynamics that I have found useful both in the illumination of what is taking place and in the exposure of nuclei of further developments. What follows is a summary of these theories.

THE WORK GROUP

In any group there may be discerned trends of mental activity. Every group, however casual, meets to 'do' something; in this activity, according to the capacities of the individuals, they cooperate. This cooperation is voluntary and depends on some degree of sophisticated skill in the individual. Participation in this activity is possible only to individuals with years of training and a capacity for experience that has permitted them to develop mentally. Since this activity is geared to a task, it is related to reality, its methods are rational, and, therefore, in however embryonic a form, scientific. Its characteristics are similar to those attributed by Freud (1911) to the ego. This facet of mental activity in a group I have called the Work Group. The term embraces only mental activity of a particular kind, not the people who indulge in it.

When patients meet for a group-therapy session it can always be seen that some mental activity is directed to the solution of the problems for which the individuals seek help. Here is an example of a passing phase in such a group:

Six patients and I are seated round a small room. Miss A suggests that it would be a good idea if members agreed to call each other by their Christian names[1] There is some relief that a topic has been broached, glances are exchanged, and a flicker of synthetic animation is momentarily visible. Mr. B ventures that it is a good idea, and Mr. C says it would 'make things more friendly'. Miss A is encouraged to divulge her name but is forestalled by Miss D who says she does not like her Christian name and would rather it were not known. Mr. E suggests pseudonyms; Miss F examines her fingernails. Within a few minutes of Miss A's suggestion, the discussion has languished, and its place has been taken by furtive glances, an increasing number of which are directed towards me. Mr. B rouses himself to say that we must call each other something. The mood is now a compound of anxiety and increasing frustration. Long before I am mentioned it is clear that my name has become a preoccupation of the group. Left to its own devices the group promises to pass into apathy and silence.

For my present purposes I shall display such aspects of the episode as illustrate my use of the term work group. In the group itself I might well do the same, but that would depend on my assignment of the significance of the episode in the context of the group mental life, as far as it had then emerged. First, it is clear that if seven people are to talk together it would help the discussion if names were available. In so far as the discussion has arisen through awareness of that fact it is a product of work group activity. But the group has gone further than to propose a step that would be helpful in any group no matter what its task might be. The proposal has been made that Christian names should be used because that would make for friendliness. In the group of which I am speaking it would have been accurate to say that the production of friendliness was regarded as strictly relevant to therapeutic need. At the point in its history from which the example is taken, it would also be true to say that both Miss D's objection and Mr. E's proposed solution would be regarded as dictated by therapeutic need; and in fact I pointed out that the suggestions fitted in with a theory, not yet explicitly stated, that our diseases would be cured if the group could be conducted in such a way that only pleasant emotions were experienced. It will be seen that the demonstration of work-group function must include: the development of thought designed for translation into action; the theory, in this instance the need for friendliness, on which it is based; the belief in environmental change as in itself sufficient for cure without any corresponding change in the individual; and finally a demonstration of the kind of fact that is believed to be 'real'.

It so happened, in the instance I have given, that I was subsequently able to demonstrate that work-group function, though I did not call it that, based on the idea that cure could be

1 See also the discussion of taboo on names in *Totem and Taboo* (Freud, 1913, p. 54).

13

obtained from a group in which pleasant feelings only were experienced, did not appear to have produced the hoped-for cure; indeed was being obstructed by some sort of difficulty in achieving a limited translation into the apparently simple act of assigning names. Before passing to the discussion of the nature of the obstructions to work-group activity, I would mention here a difficulty, which must already be evident, in the exposition of my theories. For me to describe a group episode, such as the one I have been discussing, and then to attempt the deduction of theories from it, is only to say that I have a theory that such-and-such took place and that I can say it again only in different language. The only way in which the reader can deliver himself from the dilemma is to recall to himself the memory of some committee or other gathering in which he has participated and consider to what extent he can recall evidence that could point to the existence of what I call work-group function, not forgetting the actual administrative structure, chairman and so forth, as material to be included in his review.

THE BASIC ASSUMPTIONS

The interpretations in terms of work-group activity leave much unsaid; is the suggested use of pseudonyms motivated only with a view to meeting the demands of reality? The furtive glances, the preoccupation with the correct mode for addressing the analyst, which became quite overt subsequently, cannot profitably be interpreted as related to work-group function.

Work-group activity is obstructed, diverted, and on occasion assisted, by certain other mental activities that have in common the attribute of powerful emotional drive. These activities, at first sight chaotic, are given a certain cohesion if it is assumed that they spring from basic assumptions common to all the group. In the example I have given it was easy to recognize that one assumption common to all the group was that they were met together to receive some form of treatment from me. But exploration of this idea as part of work-group function showed that ideas existed invested with reality by force of the emotion attached to them, that were not in conformity even with the somewhat naive expectation consciously entertained by the less sophisticated members. Furthermore, even sophisticated individuals, one member for example being a graduate in science, showed by their behavior that they shared these ideas.

The first assumption is that the group has met in order to be sustained by a leader on whom it depends for nourishment, material and spiritual, and protection. Stated thus, my first basic assumption might be regarded as a repetition of my remark, above, that the group assumed that 'they were met together to receive some form of treatment from me', only differing from it in being couched in metaphorical terms. But the essential point is that the basic assumption can only be understood if the words in which I have stated it are taken as literal and not metaphorical.

Here is a description of a therapeutic group in which the dependent assumption, as I shall call it, is active.

Three women and two men were present. The group had on a previous occasion shown signs of work-group function directed towards curing the disability of its members; on this occasion they might be supposed to have reacted from this with despair, placing all their reliance on me to sort out their difficulties while they contented themselves with individually posing questions to which I was to provide the answers. One woman had brought some chocolate, which she diffidently invited her right-hand neighbor, another woman, to share. One man was eating a sandwich. A graduate in philosophy, who had in earlier sessions told the group he had no belief in God, and no religion, sat silent, as indeed he often did, until one of the women with a touch of acerbity in her tone, remarked that he had asked no questions. He replied, 'I do not need to talk because I know that I only have to come here long enough and all my questions will be answered without my having to do anything'.

I then said that I had become a kind of group deity; that the questions were directed to me as one who knew the answers without need to resort to work, that the eating was part of a manipulation of the group to give substance to a belief they wished to preserve about me, and that the philosopher's reply indicated a disbelief in the efficacy of prayer but seemed otherwise to belie earlier statements he had made about his disbelief in God. When I began my interpretation I was not only convinced of its truth but felt no doubt that I could convince the others by confrontation with the mass of material — only some of which I can convey in this printed account. By the time I had finished speaking I felt I had committed some kind of gaffe; I was surrounded by blank looks; the evidence had disappeared. After a time, the man, who had finished his sandwich and placed the carefully folded paper in his pocket, looked around the room, eyebrows slightly raised, interrogation in his glance. A woman looked tensely at me, another with hands folded gazed meditatively at the floor. In me a conviction began to harden that I had been guilty of blasphemy in a group of true believers. The second man, with elbow draped over the back of his chair, played with his fingers. The woman who was eating, hurriedly swallowed the last of her chocolate. I now interpreted that I had become a very bad person, casting doubts on the group deity, but that this had been followed by an increase of anxiety and guilt as the group had failed to dissociate itself from the impiety.

In this account I have dwelt on my own reactions in the group for a reason which I hope may become more apparent later. It can be justly argued that interpretations for which the strongest evidence lies, not in the observed facts in the group but in the subjective reactions of the analyst, are more likely to find their explanation in the psychopathology of the analyst than in the dynamics of the group. It is a just criticism, and one which will have to be met by years of careful work by more than one analyst, but for that very reason I shall leave it on one side and pass on to state now a contention that I shall support throughout this paper. It is that in group treatment many interpretations, and amongst them the most important, have to be made on the strength of the analyst's own emotional reactions. It is my belief that these reactions are dependent on the fact that the analyst in the group is at the receiving end of what Melanie Klein (1946) has called projective identification, and that this mechanism plays a very important role in groups. Now the experience of counter-transference appears to me to have quite a distinct quality that should enable the analyst to differentiate the occasion when he is the object of a projective identification from the occasion when he is not. The analyst feels he is being manipulated so as to be playing a part, no matter how difficult to recognize, in somebody else's phantasy—or he would do if it were not for what in recollection I can only call a temporary loss of insight, a sense of experiencing strong feelings and at the same time a belief that their existence is quite adequately justified by the objective situation without recourse to recondite explanation of their causation. From the analyst's point of view, the experience consists of two closely related phases: in the first there is a feeling that whatever else one has done, one has certainly not given a correct interpretation; in the second there is a sense of being a particular kind of person in a particular emotional situation. I believe ability to shake oneself out of the numbing feeling of reality that is a concomitant of this state is the prime requisite of the analyst in the group: if he can do this he is in a position to give what I believe is the correct interpretation, and thereby to see its connection with the previous interpretation, the validity of which he has been caused to doubt.

I must return to consider the second basic assumption. Like the first, this also concerns the purpose for which the group has met. My attention was first aroused by a session in which the conversation was monopolized by a man and woman who appeared more or less to ignore the rest of the group. The occasional exchange of glances amongst the others seemed to suggest the view, not very seriously entertained, that the relationship was amatory, although one would hardly say that the overt content of the conversation was very different from other interchanges in the group. I was, however, impressed with the fact that individuals, who were usually sensitive to any exclusion from supposedly therapeutic activity, which at that time had come to mean talking and obtaining an 'interpretation' from me or some other member of the group, seemed not to mind leaving the stage entirely to this pair. Later it became clear that the sex of the pair was of no particular consequence to the assumption that pairing was taking place. There was a peculiar air of hopefulness and expectation about these sessions which made them rather different from the usual run of hours of boredom and frustration. It must not be supposed that the elements to which I would draw attention, under the title of pairing group, are exclusively or even predominantly in evidence. In fact there is plenty of evidence of states of mind of the kind we are familiar with in psychoanalysis; it would indeed be extraordinary, to take one example, if one did not see in individuals evidence of reaction to a group situation that could approximate to an acting out of the primal scene. But, in my opinion, to allow one's attention to be absorbed by these reactions is to make difficult any observation of what is peculiar to the group; furthermore I think such concentration at worst can lead to a debased psychoanalysis rather than an exploration of the therapeutic possibilities of the group. The reader must, then, assume that in this, as in other situations, there will always be a plethora of material familiar in a psychoanalysis, but still awaiting its evaluation in the situation of the group; this material I propose for the present to ignore, and I shall now turn to a consideration of the air of hopeful expectation that I have mentioned as a characteristic of the pairing group. It usually finds expression verbally in ideas that marriage would put an end to neurotic disabilities; that group therapy would revolutionize society when it had spread sufficiently; that the coming season, spring, summer, autumn, or winter, as the case may be, will be more agreeable; that some new kind of community — an improved group — should be developed, and so on. These expressions tend to divert attention to some supposedly future event, but for the analyst the crux is not a future event but the immediate present — the feeling of hope itself. This feeling is characteristic of the pairing group and must be taken by itself as evidence that the pairing group is in existence, even when other evidence appears to be lacking. It is itself both a precursor of sexuality and a part of it. The optimistic ideas that are verbally expressed are rationalizations intended to effect a displacement in time and a compromise with feelings of guilt—the enjoyment of the feeling is justified by appeal to an outcome supposedly morally unexceptionable. The feelings thus associated in the pairing group are at the opposite pole to feelings of hatred, destructiveness, and despair. For the feelings of hope to be sustained it is essential that the 'leader' of the group, unlike the leader of the dependent group and of the fight-flight group, should be unborn. It is a person or idea that will save the group—in fact from feelings of hatred, destructiveness, and despair, of its own or another group—but in order to do this, obviously the Messianic hope must never be fulfilled. Only by remaining a hope does hope persist. The difficulty is that, thanks to the rationalization of the dawning sexuality of the group, the premonition of sex which obtrudes as hope, there is a tendency for the work group to be influenced in the direction of producing a Messiah, be it person, idea or Utopia. In so far as it succeeds, hope is weakened; for obviously nothing is then to hope for, and, since destructiveness, hatred, and despair have in no way been radically influenced, their existence again makes itself felt. This turn accelerates a further weakening of hope. If, for purposes of discussion, we accept the idea that the group should be manipulated in order to encompass hopefulness in the group, then it is necessary that those who concern themselves with such a task, either in their capacity as members of a specialized work group such as I shall describe shortly, or as individuals, should see to it that Messianic hopes do not materialize. The danger, of course, is that such specialized work groups will either suffer through excess of zeal and thereby interfere with innocent, creative work-group function or alternatively allow themselves to be forestalled and so put to the troublesome necessity of liquidating the Messiah and then recreating the Messianic hope. In the therapeutic group the problem is to enable the group to be consciously aware of the feelings of hope, and its affiliations, and at the same time tolerant of them. That it is tolerant of them in the pairing group is a function of the basic assumption and cannot be regarded as a sign of individual development.

The third basic assumption is that the group has met to fight something or to run away from it. It is prepared to do either indifferently. I call this state of mind the fight-flight group; the accepted leader of a group in this state is one whose demands on the group are felt to afford opportunity for flight or aggression and if he makes demands that do not do so, he is ignored. In a therapeutic group the analyst is the work-group leader. The emotional backing that he can command is subject to fluctuation according to the active basic assumption and the extent to which his activities are felt to fit in with what is required of a leader in these differing states of mind. In the fight-flight group the analyst finds that attempts to illuminate what is taking place are obstructed by the ease with which emotional support is obtained for such proposals as express either hatred of all psychological difficulty or alternatively the means by which it can be evaded. In this context I would remark that the proposal to use Christian names, in the first example I gave, might well have been interpreted as an expression of the desire for flight in a fight-flight group though, in fact, for reasons connected with the stage of development that the group had reached, I interpreted it in terms of work-group function.

CHARACTERISTICS COMMON TO ALL BASIC-ASSUMPTION GROUPS

Participation in basic-assumption activity requires no training, experience, or mental development. It is instantaneous, inevitable, and instinctive: I have not felt the need to postulate the existence of a herd instinct to account for such phenomena as I have witnessed in the group.[2] In contrast with work-group function basic-assumption activity makes no demands on the individual for a capacity to cooperate but depends on the individual's possession of what I call valency—a term I borrow from the physicists to express a capacity for instantaneous involuntary combination of one individual with another for sharing and acting on a basic assumption. Work-group function is always in evidence with one, and only one, basic assumption. Though the work - group function may remain unaltered, the contemporary basic assumption that pervades its activities can be changing frequently; there may be two or three changes in an hour or the same basic assumption may be dominant for months on end. To account for th   ate of the inactive basic assumptions I have postulated the existence of a proto-mental system in which physical and mental activity is undifferentiated, and which lies outside the field ordinarily considered profitable for psychological investigations. It must be borne in mind that the question whether a field is suitable for psychological investigation depends on other factors besides the nature of the field to be investigated, one being the potency of the investigating psychological technique. The recognition of a field of psychosomatic medicine illustrates the difficulty that attends any attempt at determination of the line that separates psychological from physical phenomena. I propose therefore to leave indeterminate the limits that separate the active basic assumption from those I have relegated to the hypothetical proto-mental system.

Many techniques are in daily use for the investigation of work-group function. For the investigation of basic-assumption phenomena, I consider psychoanalysis, or some extension of technique derived directly from it, to be essential. But since work group functions are always pervaded by basic-assumption phenomena it is clear that techniques that ignore the latter will give misleading impressions of the former.

Emotions associated with basic assumptions may be described by the usual terms, anxiety, fear, hate, love, and the like. But the emotions common to any basic assumption are subtly affected by each other as if they were held in combination peculiar to the active basic assumption. That is to say, anxiety in the dependent group has a different quality from anxiety evident in the pairing group, and so on with other feelings.

All basic assumptions include the existence of a leader, although in the pairing group, as I have said, the leader is 'non-existent', i.e. unborn. This leader need not be identified with any individual in the group; it need not be a person at all but may be identified with an idea or an inanimate object. In the dependent group the place of leader may be filled by the history

2 In contrast with W. Trotter (1916) but in agreement with Freud (1921, p. 3)

of the group. A group, complaining of an inability to remember what took place on a previous occasion, sets about making a record of its meetings. This record then becomes a 'bible' to which appeal is made, if, for example, the individual whom the group has invested with leadership proves to be refractory material for moulding into the likeness proper to the dependent leader. The group resorts to bible-making when threatened with an idea the acceptance of which would entail development on the part of individuals comprising the group. Such ideas derive emotional force, and excite emotional opposition, from their association with characteristics appropriate to the pairing-group leader. When the dependent group or the fight-flight group is active, a struggle takes place to suppress the new idea because it is felt that the emergence of the new idea threatens the *status quo*. In war, the new idea — be it a tank or a new method for selecting officers — is felt to be 'new-fangled', i.e. opposed to the military bible. In the dependent group it is felt to threaten the dependent leader, be that leader 'bible' or person. But the same is true of the pairing-group, for here the new idea or person, being equated with the unborn genius or Messiah, must, as I have said before, remain unborn if it, or he, is to fulfill the pairing-group function.

3.
THE WORK OF WILFRED BION ON GROUPS

Margaret J. Rioch

Since 1965 the Washington School of Psychiatry has sponsored a series of residential Group Relations Conferences in the tradition developed in England by the Centre for Applied Social Research of the Tavistock Institute of Human Relations. The focus of these conferences is the group, as a whole dynamic field in relationship to other fields. Their uniqueness lies in the highly disciplined concentration on the part of the staff upon this focus. The individual's personal life, his individual characteristics, and his dyadic relationships are not the subject of the study. A grasp of the work in this area by the British psychoanalyst Wilfred Bion can be helpful not only to participants in these conferences but to anyone who is occupied with groups. Since his work on first reading often seems obscure, a brief explication of his major ideas may facilitate understanding.

The shift in perspective from the individual to the group is difficult to make in actual practice although it is often given lip service. It is like a shift to a higher order of magnitude, which is not easy when the lower order is in itself very complex and by no means thoroughly understood. But the shift is necessary in order to grasp social phenomena. From this perspective it is often possible to see the problems of the individual or the pair in a new light. This is well known to family therapists, who find an individual child or a marital relationship more comprehensible when seen in the framework of the entire family.

The Washington School of Psychiatry-Tavistock Conferences provide opportunities for members to study behavior in large groups of 50 - 60, in small groups of 10 - 12, and in intergroup situations. No particular theoretical framework is prescribed, and staff members come with various theoretical points of view and from various professional orientations, including sociology, psychology, psychoanalysis, and business administration. But Bion's concepts have been especially useful to the staff since they formulate group psychological processes in integrative terms. A. K. Rice, who has directed most of the British and American conferences since 1962, was strongly influenced by his membership in a training group conducted by Bion in 1947-48, as well as by Bion's theories.

Much of the material on which Bion based his theories and many of the examples which he gives come from the small groups which he conducted at the Tavistock Clinic. He does not deal exclusively with these, however, but also discusses large social institutions such as the army and the church. His interest in group processes was stimulated when, as an officer in the British Army during World War II, he was engaged in the selection of men for leadership roles and in charge of a rehabilitation unit of psychiatric patients. He began at that time to think of treatment of the whole society of the hospital not as a makeshift to save psychiatric manpower, but as the best way to get at the malady as he perceived it, namely the inability on the part of the patients to function adequately as members of society or, in other words, as group members. He saw this inability with reference both to the hospital community and to society at large.

Because Bion's name is so much associated with groups and because he emphasized the phenomena of total fields rather than of individuals he is sometimes thought of as having talked about the group as a mythical entity instead of talking about human behavior. This is not the case. He defines a group as a function or set of functions of an aggregate of individuals. It is not a function of any one part separately, nor is it an aggregate without a function.

For example, if a dozen strangers are lying by chance in the sun on the same beach they do not constitute a group according to his definition. But if someone in the water cries for help and the twelve individuals respond by trying to save the swimmer from drowning in some kind of concerted action, however rudimentary the concertedness may be, they have become a group in that they now have a function. This may last for only a few minutes or it may turn into an organization of life savers which goes on for years.

Although Bion thinks and speaks of instincts, he does not postulate a herd instinct or a group mind. He thinks that ideas of this kind are often developed by people in groups, but that when they occur they are symptomatic of regression. In his opinion groups bring into prominence phenomena which can best be understood if one has some experience of psychotic phenomena as well as of normal and neurotic behavior. The belief that a group or group mind exists, as something other than a function of a number of individuals, appears to Bion to be a distorted figment of the imagination which emerges when people are threatened with a loss of their individual distinctiveness.

He emphasizes that people do not have to come together in the same room to form a group. In his view a hermit in a desert is inevitably a member of a group and cannot be understood unless one knows what the group is from which he has separated himself geographically. People have to come together in a room in order that group phenomena may be demonstrated and elucidated but not in order that they should exist. This is similar to the situation in psychoanalysis in which the patient has to enter into a therapeutic relationship with the analyst in order that the analyst may demonstrate and analyze the transference, but not in order that transference phenomena should exist.

Bion's central thought is that in every group two groups are present: the "work group" and the "basic assumption group". This may all sound less mysterious if one says that in every group there are two aspects, or that there are two different ways of behaving. Bion's terminology is a short cut which may lead to the belief that he thinks of each group of ten people as consisting of twenty invisible people sitting in two separate circles and talking, now in normal rational voices and now in another voice as in O'Neill's *Strange Interlude*. And in fact he does think in this kind of metaphor. At the same time he is quite clearly aware that it is a metaphor, which some of his less poetic readers tend to forget. He does not mean that there are two groups of people in the room, but that the group behaves as if that were the case, and he considers that this is the unconscious fantasy of the people in the group.

His concept of the work group will be described first and then that of the basic assumption group. The work group is that aspect of group functioning which has to do with the real task of the group. This exists in a committee which has come together to plan a program, or a staff of an organization which proposes to review the activities of the past year, or a small group met to study its own behavior. The work group takes cognizance of its purpose and can define its task. The structure of the group is there to further the attainment of the task. For example, if a group needed to collect dues it would appoint a treasurer. But it would not appoint a finance committee unless there were real matters of policy to be taken care of by such a committee. The number of vice presidents would be limited by the functions which vice presidents had to perform. The number of meetings would be dictated by the amount of business which had to be conducted. The leader of the work group is not the only one who has skills, and he leads only so long as his leadership serves the task of the group. The members of the work group cooperate as separate and discrete individuals. Each member of the group belongs to it because it is his will and his choice to see that the purpose of the group is fulfilled. He is therefore at one with the task of the group and his own interest is identified with its interest. The work group constantly tests its conclusions in a scientific spirit. It seeks for knowledge, learns from experience, and constantly questions how it may best achieve its goal. It is clearly conscious of the passage of time and of the processes of learning and development. It has a parallel in the individual with the ego in Freud's sense, in the rational and mature person.

Groups which act consistently like the one just described are very rare and perhaps even non-existent in pure culture. A large part of Bion's theory has to do with why groups do not behave in the sensible way just described as characteristic of the work group. Man seems to be a herd animal who is often in trouble with his herd. Ineffective and self-contradictory behavior seems at times to be very common in groups — even though highly effective functioning is common at other times. The work group is only one aspect of the functioning of the group. The other aspect is the one which Bion calls the basic assumption group.

Bion is probably best known popularly for the names which he coined for the three kinds of basic assumption groups — namely, the dependency, the fight-flight, and the pairing groups. It should be emphasized that he himself used the word "adumbrated"—that is, vaguely outlined—to characterize his classification of these groups, and it may well be that the classification should be made differently or that other categories should be added. This is not the main point.

It is important to understand what the term *basic assumption* means, for otherwise one may get lost in the more important point, which is the commonality of all three. Basic assumption means exactly what it says — namely, the assumption which is basic to the behavior. It is an "as if" term. One behaves as if such and such were the case. In pre-Columbian days seafaring men operated on the basic assumption that the world was flat and that they might fall off its edge. Therefore they did not venture very far from the coast. So on many different levels, by observing the behavior of individuals and of groups, one can tease out the basic assumptions on which they operate. Bion uses the term to refer to the *tacit* assumptions that are prevalent in groups, not to those which are usually outside of awareness. Nevertheless, they are the basis for behavior. They are deductible from the emotional state of the group. The statement of the basic assumption gives meaning to and elucidates the behavior of the group to the extent that it is not operating as a work group.

According to Bion there are three distinct emotional states of groups from which one can deduce three basic assumptions. The first of these is the dependency basic assumption.

The essential aim of the basic assumption dependency group is to attain security through and have its members protected by one individual. It assumes that this is why the group has met. The members act as if they know nothing, as if they are inadequate and immature creatures. Their behavior implies that the leader, by contrast, is omnipotent and omniscient. A group of sick, miserable psychiatric patients, for example, and a powerful, wise, loving, giving therapist easily fit this picture. The power, the wisdom, and lovingness of the therapist are, of course, not tested. The patients are often united in the belief that if they sit long enough, the wise leader will come forth with the magic cure. They do not even need to give him adequate information about their difficulties for he knows everything and plans everything for the good of the members. In this emotional state the group insists that all explanations be extremely simple; no one can understand any complexity; no one can do anything that is difficult; but the leader can solve all difficulties, if he only will.

He is idealized and made into a kind of god who will take care of his children. The leader is often tempted to fall into this role and to go along with the basic assumption of the group.

But since no one really can fill this role and since anyone who is doing his job will refuse to fill it, he can never succeed in meeting the group's expectations. In failing to be omniscient and omnipotent leader of these people who are presenting themselves as inadequate weaklings, he inevitably arouses their disappointment and hostility. The members will try for a long time to blind themselves to this and will try not to hear what he says in interpreting their dependency to them. They often try quite desperate maneuvers to wring his heart and to force him to take proper care of them. One of the most frequent maneuvers is to put forth one member as especially sick and requiring the special care of the leader. Such a member may actually be pushed by the others into a degree of distress which he had not really felt at all, but the group needs someone who will wring the leader's heart or else show him up to be an unfeeling demon. The interesting thing is that whereas the group seems to be concerned about this poor person and his trouble, it is actually more concerned about the group aim to get the leader to take care of it and to relieve its feelings of inadequacy and insecurity. A person who falls into this role can very easily be carried away by it until he oversteps the bounds, and then he may find himself abandoned by the group.

When the leader of such a group fails to meet expectations, as he is bound to do, the group searches for alternative leaders. These are often eager to accept the role, and to prove that they can do what the original leader could not do. This is a temptation which the group offers to its more ambitious members. When they fall for it, they are usually in for the same fate as the original leader.

One of the frequent concerns in the dependency group has to do with greed. This is understandable enough since in manifesting the kind of childlike dependency characteristic of this basic assumption, the group members are perpetuating a state appropriate to an earlier stage of development and each one is demanding more than his share of parental care. There is often conflict in this group between the dependent tendencies and the needs of the individuals as adults. Resentment at being in a dependent state is present as well as a desire to persist in it. Although anger and jealousy are expressed, they do not usually arouse a tremendous amount of fear because of the basic assumption that a super-being exists in the form of the leader, who will see to it that the irresponsibilities of the members will not go too far and will not have dire consequences. There is often conflict between the desire to express feelings irresponsibly and the desire to be mature and consider consequences. The basic assumption dependency group in pure culture does not exist any more than the work group in pure culture. But the more it tends to be dominant over the work group, the more the relationship of the members to the leader takes on the characteristics of a religious cult. The work function will often then be felt as a challenge to a religion. Some of the same phenomena will occur which have occurred in the world in the conflict between science and religion, as if the claims of science were challenging the claims of religion. The words or writings of the leader become a kind of Bible and the group engages in exegesis of his works. This tends to happen particularly if the leader has already demonstrated his human inability to satisfy the demands of the group for a deity. His written words or remembered words may then be taken in place of his person.

The outside world often looks cold and unfriendly to the basic assumption dependency group. Sometimes when the members feel deserted by their leader, they forget their internal squabbles, close ranks, and snuggle up to each other like little birds in a nest. A warm groupness develops which gives a temporary sense of comfort and security. To challenge this is heresy and is persecuted as such.

The second basic assumption group is that of fight-flight. Bion joins these together as two sides of the same coin. The assumption is that the group has met to preserve itself and that this can be done only by fighting someone or something or by running away from someone or something. Action is essential whether for fight or for flight. The individual is of secondary importance to the preservation of the group. Both in battle and in flight the individual may be abandoned for the sake of the survival of the group. Whereas in the basic assumption dependency group the sick person may be valued for his ability to engage the leader as a person who will take care of others, in the fight-flight group there is no tolerance for sickness. Casualties are to be expected.

A leader is even more important than in other basic assumption groups because the call for action requires a leader. The leader who is felt to be appropriate to this kind of group is one who can mobilize the group for attack or lead it in flight. He is expected to recognize danger and enemies. He should represent and spur on to courage and self-sacrifice. He should have a bit of a paranoid element in his makeup if he wishes to be successful, for this will ensure that if no enemy is obvious, the leader will surely find one. He is expected to feel hate toward the enemy and to be concerned not for the individual in the group but for the preservation of the group itself. An accepted leader of a fight-flight group who goes along with the basic assumption is one who affords opportunity in the group for flight or aggression. If he does not do this, he is ignored.

This basic assumption group is anti-intellectual and inimical to the idea of self-study; self-knowledge may be called introspective nonsense. In a group whose avowed purpose or work task is self-study, the leader will find when the group is operating in basic assumption fight-flight that his attempts will be obstructed either by expressions of hatred against all things psychological and introspective, or by various other methods of avoidance. The group may chitchat, tell stories, come late, be absent, or engage in innumerable activities to circumvent the task.

In groups engaged in more overt action, it is possible to observe the close connection of panic and the fight-flight group. Bion contends that panic, flight and uncontrolled attack are really all the same. He says that panic does not arise in any situation unless it is one that might as easily have given rise to rage. When the rage or fear are offered no readily available outlet, frustration arises which in a basic assumption group cannot be tolerated. Flight offers an immediately available opportunity for expression of the emotion in the fight-flight group and meets the demands that all basic assumption groups have for instantaneous satisfaction. Attack offers a similarly immediate outlet. Bion thinks that if the leader of such a group conforms to the requirement of the fight-flight leader he will have no difficulty in turning a group from headlong flight to attack or from headlong attack to panic.

The third basic assumption group is that of pairing. Here the assumption is that the group has met for purposes of reproduction, to bring forth the Messiah, the Savior. Two people get together on behalf of the group to carry out the task of pairing and creation. The sex of the two people is immaterial. They are by no means necessarily a man and a woman. But whoever they are, the basic assumption is that when two people get together it is for sexual purposes. When this basic assumption is operative, the other group members are not bored. They listen eagerly and attentively to what is being said. An atmosphere of hopefulness pervades the group. No actual leader is or needs to be present, but the group, through the pair, is living in the hope of the creation of a new leader, or a new thought, or something which will bring about a new life, will solve the old problems and bring Utopia or heaven, or something of the sort. As in the history of the world, if a new leader or Messiah is actually produced, he will of course shortly be rejected. In order to maintain hope, he must be unborn. Bion emphasizes the air of hopeful expectation which pervades the group. He says it is often expressed in cliches' — such as, "Things will be better when spring comes" — or in simple-minded statements that some cure-all like marriage or group therapy would solve all neurotic problems. Although the group thus focuses on the future, Bion calls attention to the present, namely the feeling of hope itself, which he thinks is evidence that the pairing group is in existence even when other evidence is not clear. The group enjoys its optimism, justifying it by an appeal to an outcome which is morally unexceptionable. The feelings associated with this group are soft and agreeable. The unborn leader of this group, according to the basic

27

assumption, will save it from feelings of hatred, destructiveness, and despair — both its own feelings and those of others. If a person or an idea should be produced by such a group hope will again be weakened, for there will be nothing to hope for. The destructiveness and hatred have not really been reduced and will again be felt.

These then are the three basic assumption groups which Bion describes. It is clear enough how different they all are from the work group. Although each one has its own characteristics, the basic assumption groups also have some characteristics in common. Basic assumption life is not oriented outward toward reality, but inward toward fantasy, which is then impulsively and uncritically acted out. There is little pausing to consider or to test consequences, little patience with an inquiring attitude, and great insistence upon feeling. Basic assumption members often are confused, have poor memories, are disoriented about time. They do not really learn and adapt through experience but actually resist change, although they may shift very readily from one basic assumption to another. Often there are reminiscences about the good old days. The language of such groups is full of cliches, or repetitive phrases, and of vague and loose generalizations. Another important aspect of the basic assumptions is that they are anonymous. They are not formulated by any one member in the group and cannot be attributed to any one member. No one wants to own them. There is a kind of conspiracy of anonymity, which is facilitated by the fact that identities and names get mixed up; statements are attributed falsely or vaguely. The basic assumptions seem to be the disowned part of the individuals, and individuals seem to fear the basic assumptions as if they might take over and leave nothing of the mature, rational persons in the group. Since the basic assumptions are anonymous, they can function quite ruthlessly, which is another reason why they are feared. There is much vicarious living in a basic assumption group, particularly through roles, so that often a person becomes fixed in a role which the group needs for its own purposes and then cannot get out of it. Basic assumption groups also constantly attempt to seduce their leaders away from their work function.

Neither the work group nor the basic assumption group exists in pure culture for very long. What one sees in reality is a work group which is suffused by, intruded into, and supported by the basic assumption groups. One can make an analogy to the functions of the conscious ego, which are suffused by, invaded by, and supported by the irrational and unconscious aspects of the personality. So it seems that the basic assumptions represent an interference with the work task, just as naughty, primitive impulses may interfere with the sensible work of a mature person. And this is one important side of the picture. There is another, more positive side to the basic assumptions, however, which Bion emphasizes just as much as the negative aspects, and that is the sophisticated use of the proper basic assumption by the work group. For example, a work group such as a hospital can and should mobilize the basic assumption dependency in the service of its task of taking care of sick patients. Bion identifies the church as that major institution in society which mobilizes and uses in a sophisticated way the basic assumption dependency; the army as that one which mobilizes basic assumption fight-flight; and the aristocracy as that one which is most interested in breeding and therefore mobilizes pairing. Whether or not the aristocracy can still be considered to exist, even in England, as an important institution is an open question, along with what takes its place if it does not. Bion himself does not think that the aristocracy can be considered to be a real work group which uses its basic assumption in a sophisticated way, for if the work group characteristics were dominant in the aristocracy then the interest in breeding would be manifest in some such way as a subsidy of scientific genetics research. But this is obviously not the case. If we consider the army, for example, it is clear that the relevant basic assumptions badly interfere with its function if they get out of hand. Fight-flight when engaged in simply as irrational basic assumptions lead to panic or ill-conceived attack. However, when mobilized in a sophisticated way, fight-flight represents the motive force for battle and for organized withdrawal. As indicated earlier, both the work group and the basic assumption group are abstractions; they are concepts which are useful in thinking about ways of functioning which occur in groups. Bion's idea is that both are occurring simultaneously, but to varying degrees, in all groups.

It is necessary now to introduce another one of Bion's concepts, namely that of valency. This is a term which is used to refer to the individual's readiness to enter into combination with the group in making and acting on the basic assumptions. A person may have a high or low valency depending on his capacity for this kind of combination, but in Bion's view it is impossible to be a human being without having some degree of valency. The thing that Bion is trying to do with all his concepts and constructions is to produce useful ways of thinking about man in his function as a social animal. In his concept of valency he is saying that everyone has the tendency to enter into group life, in particular into the irrational and unconscious aspects of group life, and that people vary in the amount of tendency they have in this direction. Bion thinks of this tendency as something which is manifested on a psychological plane to be sure, but which is so basic to the human organism that it should not be thought of as purely psychological. He thinks of it as biological and speaks of it as analogous to tropism in plants rather than as analogous to more purposive behavior. By borrowing a word from physics rather than from psychology or sociology he emphasizes the instantaneous and involuntary aspects of the kind of behavior he is talking about, which he calls instinctive. Valency in the basic assumption group corresponds to cooperation in the work group. But whereas cooperation requires thought, training, maturity, and some degree of organization in a group, valency requires none of these. It simply occurs spontaneously as a function of the gregarious quality in man.

Individuals vary not only in the degree of valency which they manifest but in the kind to which they have the strongest tendency. With some it is toward basic assumption dependency; some toward fight-flight; some toward pairing. Every human being has the capacity for all three, but usually one or another valency predominates. This has nothing to do with whether a person has been psychoanalyzed or not. It is not possible to analyze valency out of a human being as one is supposed to be able to analyze neurosis. For effective functioning in groups, however, and especially for leadership functioning, it is desirable to know oneself well enough to know to which valency one tends. An effective society uses the valencies of its members to serve its various purposes. For example, the educator can find a good outlet for his valency toward basic assumption dependency. The combat commander can use appropriately his valency toward basic assumption fight-flight. The valency toward basic assumption pairing finds a useful expression in individual interviewing and, of course, family life. There are various types of chairmen and directors of organizations. One type will be solicitous for the welfare of his members and will take a special interest in the weaker ones or in anyone who is sick or disabled. Another will see his main function as fighting for the interests of his organization against any outside or inside attack. Another will find that he does his job best by going around after hours to each one of his members separately, convincing each one of what he wants done. When the meeting takes place everyone is already in agreement and the decisions have all been made. Any and all of these ways can be effective, though each one may be more appropriate at one time than at another.

In the naive or unconscious fantasy, the leader of the dependency group has to be omnipotent; the fight leader has to be unbeatable and the flight leader uncatchable; the leader of the pairing group must be marvelous but still unborn. But in the mature work group, which is making a sophisticated use of the appropriate basic assumptions, the leader of the dependency group is dependable; the leader of the fight-flight group is courageous; and the leader of the pairing group is creative.[1]

For effective functioning the basic assumptions must be subservient to and used in the service of the work task. They make good servants and poor masters. The various tales about fantastic machines, demons, genii, and so forth, who perform miraculous tasks for their masters until one fine day they take over and go on a binge of destruction, are mythical

1 For these formulations the author is indebted to a personal communication from A K Rice, who wrote approximately these words in *Learning for Leadership*. p. 72

representations of the capacity of human beings for harnessing tremendous energy effectively and at the same time of the danger of such energy when it is not harnessed. *The Lord of the Flies* provides another illustration of what happens when the work group is weak and the irresponsible basic assumption group takes over.

The work task is like a serious parent who has his eye on intelligent planning. The basic assumptions are like the fun-loving or frightened children who want immediate satisfaction of their desires. What Bion emphasizes is that both exist and that both are necessary. The basic assumption group, however, exists without effort. The work group requires all the concentration, skill, and organization of creative forces that can be mustered to bring it into full flower. The writers who derogate groups as tending to reduce the intellectual abilities of the individuals in the group are, according to Bion, talking about the basic assumption functions, not work group funcions. Bion holds to a very consistent middle way between the glorification and the derogation of the group. The latter is to be found in Jung's statement, "When a hundred clever heads join in a group, one big nincompoop is the result, because every individual is trammelled by the otherness of the others."[2] Bion holds that a group, like an individual, may be stupid and cruel or intelligent and concerned. He does not hold that great achievements are always those of the individual working in solitude. He says that in the study groups he has been in he has made interpretations of behavior just because he believes that the group can hear them and use them, and experience has borne him out. In his own words, he attributes "great force and influence to the work group, which through its concern with reality is compelled to employ the methods of science in no matter how rudimentary a form" (p. 135).

Individuals seem to fear being overwhelmed by their valency for group life; or one might put it that they fear being overwhelmed by the basic assumptions. It is not uncommon in self-study or therapy groups to hear phrases like "the fear of being sucked in by quicksands," or "the fear of being homogenized," which express the fear of being immersed in the group and thus losing one's individuality. Bion thinks that there is not actually so much danger as people think there is of being overwhelmed by the basic assumptions. He has a healthy respect for people's capacities to function on a work level. He thinks that in groups met to study their own behavior, consistent interpretation of the basic assumption tendencies will gradually bring them into consciousness and cause them to lose their threatening quality. The parallel here to the psychoanalysis of unconscious impulses is clear. Presumably, the more the basic assumption life of the group becomes conscious, the more the

2 Quoted from a letter from C. G. Jung (Illing, p. 80)

work task can emerge into effective functioning.

But the individual in a group is not always convinced of this. Bion thinks that the task of the adult in establishing adequate contact with the life of the group or groups in which he lives is truly a formidable one. His first, second, and often third attempts are likely to be failures and to result in regression. When individuals in a group feel that they have lost or are about to lose their individual distinctiveness, they are threatened by panic. This does not mean at all that the group disintegrates, for it may continue as a fight-flight group; but it does mean that the individual feels threatened and very likely has regressed.

Bion says clearly that he thinks of the value of a group experience as the conscious experiencing of the possibilities of the work group. This must be differentiated from the coziness and so-called closeness of feeling in the basic assumption group. The work group which Bion is talking about does not depend upon great amounts of love or warm feelings or an oceanic oneness of the group members. It does depend upon the increasing and developing ability of each individual to use his skills responsibly in the service of the common task. It is not anything like the "togetherness" which is a function of the fear of being alone or on one's own. In the work group, each individual is very much on his own and may have to accomplish his own part of the task in a very lonely way, as for example someone who is sent upon a secret mission or someone who has to make the ultimate policy decision where the buck stops. The reluctance to take the final responsibility for decisions and actions can be seen as a basic assumption dependency phenomenon and is not characteristic of the work group member, especially not of the work group leader.

The anxiety which one tends to feel in groups and the difficulties with which group membership faces one stem from the double danger of either being isolated like a sore thumb of the total body which may be amputated, or being swallowed up by the total body and losing oneself. When the basic assumption group is strong, the individual tends to feel either in danger of being victimized and extruded, or swallowed up in the anonymous unanimity of group feeling. The usual case, even when work elements are present, is that the individual is wavering somewhere in between the two dangers, with an uneasy sense that he is in a dilemma out of which no right way can be found.

When anxiety becomes severe the group may, as Bion says, resemble the mysterious, frightening, and destructive Sphinx. The Sphinx was made up of disparate members. She had the seductive face of a woman and a body composed of parts of powerful and dangerous animals—the lion, the eagle, and the serpent. To those who wished to pass by her she posed the riddle: "What walks on four legs in the morning, two at noon, and three in the evening?" Those who could not answer she flung to their deaths over the cliff, and that included everyone until Oedipus came by and told her that it was man.

Oedipus had been to Delphi to try to find out who really were his parents; and later too, to his sorrow, he searched for the murderer of the king. He sought after knowledge even when it meant his own undoing. Not by chance was it this man who, as the legend has it, grasped immediately the concepts of time, change, and development implicit in the riddle of the Sphinx. So long as we think in static terms that there *is* an entity which walks on four legs or which *is* the personality or which *is* the group, we can never grasp the complex and apparently disparate phenomena of the world, in time, in which we live. When Oedipus grasped the complexity in an intuitive vision of the whole, the fearful Sphinx threw herself off the rock. But unfortunately she constantly climbs back up again and waits with a new riddle for a new Oedipus to come by.

When the Sphinx lies in wait with her dreadful question, representing the frightening complexity and uncertain behavior of the world, especially the world of groups, one feels terrified at what John Fowles calls "the eternal source of all fear, all horror, all real evil, man himself" (Fowles, 1967, p. 448). But the same man or the same group which has filled the world with horror at its capacity for evil can also amaze by its capacity for good. If the Sphinx were to ask, "What is it that on Monday is wrangling, cruel, and greedy; on Tuesday in indifferent and lazy; on Wednesday is effectively and intelligently collaborative?", one could easily answer, "That is man and it is also ten men in a group." If she asked, "What made the difference?", a few partial answers could be given. One of them is that on Wednesday the group had a clear goal to which all of its members wanted to devote themselves. Another is that the roles of the members were clearly defined and accepted. Still another has to do with the boundaries between this and other groups. But if the Sphinx were to go on and press about what to do in order that the Wednesday behavior should become more constant and the Monday and Tuesday behavior less frequent, we *might* find ourselves with no satisfactory answer hurtling over the cliff.

4.
GROUP CONSCIOUSNESS AS A DEVELOPMENTAL PHASE

Arthur D. Colman

A core concept of Bion's theory of group behavior is the explanatory utility, under conditions common to many forms of group life, of a "group mentality" or "group consciousness." The distinction between the work group and the basic assumption group is critical to his formulation. Individuals meeting together in an agreed upon work task find themselves caught up in "emotional drives of obscure origins" which "sometimes hinder, occasionally further" the progress of this work task. Bion found that "a certain cohesion is given to these anomalous mental activities if it is assumed that emotionally the group acts as if it had certain basic assumptions about its aims." (Bion, 1952). The basic assumptions (which he formulated as dependency, pairing, and fight-flight) are unconsciously shared by the group in a shifting pattern contingent on a variety of factors which include the difficulty of the overt task, the quality of leadership and followership, and the psychological valences of the members. These shared assumptions are seen by Bion as regressive, defensive operations used by the individual to cope with psychotic anxieties brought on by the fragmenting, boundary dissolving effects of the group process. "In this contact with the complexities of life in a group, the adult resorts in what may be a massive regression to mechanisms described by Melanie Klein as typical of the earliest phases of mental life" (Bion, 1952). Klein's formulations of the primitive defensive positions (paranoid-schizoid and depressive) used in earliest infancy and including mechanisms such as splitting and projective identification, describe for Bion the regressive states which are defended against by individuals through the basic assumptions, thereby creating the common group mentality (Klein, 1948).

Other theorists have elaborated the notion of a shared group consciousness — often referred to erroneously as group-as-a-whole model — without such heavy reliance on Kleinian mechanisms. Bion's notion that the group can be unconsciously perceived by its members as a maternal entity has been referred to by others in terms of a preoedipal mother, "The perception of the group as an ever waiting, potentially symbiotic mother " (Gibbard, et al, 1974). From a slightly different perspective, the

---

1 A portion of this paper is based on a more general analysis of the origins of ecstatic consciousness in *Love and Ecstasy* by Arthur and Libby Colman

group may be perceived as a transitional object of the kind Winnicott describes, with its psychological mechanism then corresponding to that stage of regression (Winnicott, 1953). Most provocative to this paper are occasional references in the literature to the possibility that the group experience evokes a psychological state on a developmental continuum prior to individuation and individual identity (Gibbard, et al, 1974).

The concept that an individual may in part lose his or her individual identity to a group intersects with two other developments current in psychology that are germane to this paper. The first is the recent explorations of merger states — research into areas of human activity previously reserved for religious inquiry — in which specific techniques, both modern and traditional, are used to facilitate loss of personal identity, loss of the ''I,'' in order to produce an altered state of consciousness (Tart, 1969). Group interactions, natural and artificial, are often used to evoke, support, and amplify these experiences (Eliade, 1959). Bion's theory is both useful to and could be enriched by studying these phenomena. (This paper itself grew out of consideration of consciousness states which focused on some of the differences between solitary, dyadic, and group merger experiences.)

The second relevant development in psychology is the recent work of Margaret Mahler on early stages in infant consciousness. (Mahler, 1972). This work has yet had little impact on depth group theory despite its obvious relevance to notions such as group consciousness and regressive experience. Like Klein, Mahler is concerned with the earliest stages of infant development, both from an individual and a dyadic frame of reference. Through this dual perspective she attempts to trace the process by which the infant develops a sense of individuality as it first appears in the three year old toddler.

The purpose of this paper is not only to explore the relevance of Mahler's theory to the phenomena of group consciousness but also to suggest that the state of group consciousness itself may be an important developmental link in the origins of individuality.[2]

MAHLER'S THEORY OF SEPARATION - INDIVIDUATION

Mahler believes that ''the biological birth of the human infant and the psychological birth of the individual are not coincidental in time. The former is a dramatic and readily observable, well circumscribed event; the latter, slowly unfolding intrapsychic

---

2 The terminology in this paper generally follows Mahler's lead, with some additions. ''I'' is taken to indicate that which is experienced inside one's personal boundary, the core, continuous identity that provides an awareness of separateness from others. Group consciousness or dyadic consciousness are subjective states in which ones ''I'' is weakened or lost through merger with others. In these states we do no experience a separate identity, but rather feel fused with others and in touch with elements of identity which go beyond the ''I''. ''Self'' is used to name the aspect of consciousness that lies beyond the ''I''.

process'' (Mahler, 1972). For Mahler, psychological birth is the process through which individual subjectivity is achieved. She calls this process *separation-individuation* and suggests that it is the dominant psychological task in the first two year: of life, if not over the entire life cycle.

According to Mahler, the infant begins life without the ɔncept of another person. He is in a state of *normal autism*; that is. he is not oriented toward the external environment, but rather perceives everything in an omnipotent mode which Mahler describes as a ''primitive hallucinatory disorientation.'' For the infant there are no boundaries, no inside and no outside. There is only a universe of experience that *is*. The mother is the total world even though she is not yet perceived as a person apart from the rest of matter that surrounds him. The child is totally fused with her caring, nurturant system which envelopes his experience and his consciousness. For the infant, it is not the person of the mother that matters, but rather her functions. The mother's acute sensitivity to the infant's needs helps her perform this role. Her breasts, skin, arms, and comforting noises are marvelous providers for the first few months. However, the infant does not perceive the total person beyond these encompassing parts and functions. The individual is interchangeable with any other total system that would continue to provide the same comforting services, whether it is father, nanny, grandmother, or other surrogate.

Some time after the third month, the infant begins to display behavior suggesting perception of the world outside as separate. He is moving from the stage of *normal autism* to what Mahler calls the *symbiotic* stage. He begins to perceive boundaries of self but these are vast and diffuse, specifically including mother in the self rather than in the outside. Infant and mother are now a true, merged dyad or, in Mahler's terms, part of the mother/infant symbiotic common orbit. The self boundary has diminished from all-inclusive to encompassing only the mother/infant unit and excluding the rest of the outside world. The infant's experience of merger has begun to shift from totality to a special person. This person is yet to be recognized as separate but the first steps toward individuation have been taken.

The security of this dyadic matrix allows the infant to move toward his own separation and individuation. The realization that there are boundaries *within* the dyad comes very gradually, beginning with the sixth or seventh month of life. The infant begins to perceive his own body and its functions as distinct from mother, a process which is accelerated by the increasing verbal and motor repertoire at his command. His perception of the non-self world also becomes more complicated, for in it are differentiated neutral objects and intimate objects, all different from the one special mother object who is the other half of the original dyad.

Mahler labels the developmental period during which the infant separates from the infant/mother orbit as the phase of *separation-individuation*. It lasts from approximately six months, the end of the symbiotic phase, through the third year of life. She divides this phase into at least three subphases: differentiation, practicing, and rapprochement, which trace the vicissitudes of the mother/infant relationship from the "hatching" of the symbiotic egg, through the "growth and functioning of the autonomous ego apparatus in close proximity to the mother," to the final sharing of the new autonomy with a mother in a more acute recognition of separateness. The differentiation of individuality is described as occurring entirely in reference to the mothering figure; in terms of the developmental process, dyadic consciousness is transformed to individual consciousness.

Mahler's restriction of her theory to the enfolding relationship between mother and child makes it only partially useful in understanding the development of individuality for a child growing up in more complex groups containing siblings, fathers, relatives, and friends. Even casual observations in such a human environment suggests that the infant and young child is enveloped in intense relationships outside of the orbit of his mother. More critical still is the observation that the pretoddler child's behavior *varies depending on the composition of the group of which he is a part.* He acts very differently when in the presence of his mother alone, with his father, with his mother and father, with his siblings but without his parents, with his entire family, and so on. This suggests the phenomena of role behavior and raises the possibility that group merger experience may be part of the developmental process bridging the dyadic merger with mother and the separation-individuation outcome.

GROUP CONSCIOUSNESS AS A DEVELOPMENTAL PHASE

Once the infant shows a definite preference for his mother, he is signalling an awareness of the two distinct parts of the dyad, the experience of total merger is behind him and even the dyadic union is diluted. He is now likely to recognize friends, enemies, and neutrals. He not only knows more about what is happening inside the dyad, he is beginning to react more to people outside the dyad. He begins to alternate between kinds of relating. He can relate to himself, to the outside world, or to his mother. Motor development potentiates this change. When he can crawl, he can choose to leave his mother. He can explore other objects and people. He can develop special relationships with additional members of the family. He may seek out his brother, or give a special smile to his father. He starts to incorporate other family members into his sense of self. Thus by six or seven months, the infant's symbiotic boundary is being stretched to include significant others outside of the mother/infant dyad. Faces and gestures of individuals are observed and touched as if to find out who qualifies for entrance into his self group. These new persons in the infant's life are checked against the face and gestures of the mother, sometimes in wonderment and other times in despair. As selection criteria are broadened to include familiar faces and gestures belonging to others besides the mother/child dyad, the concept of outside also becomes more specific. The "stranger-reaction," an apprehensive, anxious startle response in the child when confronted with an unfamiliar face, develops sometime after six months and before one year. It signals an entirely new complex level of perception. By this point, *the symbiotic dyad has been replaced by an "inside," bounded self containing a mosaic of familiar persons.* The outside non-self contains individuals and objects recognized as "not belonging."

It is difficult to imagine the subjective experience that corresponds to these developmental changes. The infant is no longer as totally filled up with the merged world of mother/infant. Other people have become part of that consciousness. The child's new sense of inside is probably closer to a blend of gestures and faces, some of which are more linked to his sense of self than others. The primacy of the mother/child union in the child's world of self slowly gives way to a union with multiple others within the family environment. *Dyadic consciousness crystallized out of the earlier stage of merger with totality; it now gives way to group consciousness.*

The kind of primitive group consciousness sensed by the infant at this stage can be considered to be the forerunner to the adult's experience of total involvement in the basic assumption life of the group; that consciousness state when immersion in the group identity transcends individuality, when behavior is dictated almost entirely by role, when thinking is exercised as part of the group mentality. To be caught up in group situations which emphasize basic assumption life such as mass political or religious rallies, athletic contests, and even Group Relations Conferences is to be so submerged that non-group is experienced as outside, alien, and hostile; individuality within the group is rarely more than a fleeting, insignificant sensation. The individual is literally lost in union with others.

For the adult, the loss of individuality that is part of profound group experiences is tempered by an awareness of pressure by the group to conform and the loss of the self's ability to respond beyond the limits of the role dictated by the group. There may be conflict between whether to "go with the crowd" and allow further submergence of the "I" into the group consciousness, or whether to emerge from the mass-self as an individual. The obscurity that a group provides may be comfortably irresponsible. That same obscurity may also be a potent stimulus to search for an identity that will establish the "I" above and beyond the group. This is the force which creates charismatic leaders or dictators out of individuals who are particularly sensitive to prolonged loss of self. Their ''I'' becomes the group; they need the group to feel whole.

The child of six to nine months old cannot yet experience this conflict between merging with the group and maintaining the ''I''. There is not yet a true individual identity. He is just beginning to develop a self boundary which encompasses more than the symbiotic dyad. This stage of primitive group consciousness, in which the self is experienced as a mosaic of the selves around him, furthers the separation from the original pair and heightens the embryonic individual identity. As the child experiences part of his own potential in each new piece of his mosaic self, he begins to discover an ''I'' that is constant in all these situations.

For the child, this enlargement of self beyond the dyad increases the scope of his actions and makes him dependent on many other social configurations than the maternal relationship. Like any other role player, he explores the potentials of each new group situation. He may begin to play with other children, showing independence with them in ways that would be impossible if he were alone with mother. A unique set of behaviors develops when he is alone with father or other parenting figures who were more distant in earlier infancy, but who become increasingly important now. He behaves one way alone with father, another when mother is still in the room. He may ''merge'' in the family constellation, become ''one of the kids'', finding times and ways that he can be acknowledged, finding his special place in the family society.

Out of the matrix of shifting group consciousness, the child gradually crystallizes a perception of uniqueness and separateness: he develops a consciousness of ''I''. This individuation process undoubtedly takes place in parallel with a similar crystallization from the weakening dyadic symbiosis which Mahler categorizes in her subphases of separation-individuation. It is likely that for most infants the dyadic merger is more intense and resistive a bond than the group merger, much as the adult's experience of group merger is often felt to be plastic and superficial in comparison to the dyadic relationship in which merger experience is prominent, such as lover relationships. This distinction between the dynamics of dyadic and group merger adds to the importance of recognizing group consciousness as part of the developmental process out of which individual identity is forged. It provides for a continuum of consciousness between the dominating mother/child linkage of earliest life, to the later, looser connections of family and social groupings, through to the final precipitation of a unique person who is capable of recognizing his separateness and difference apart from either mother or the variety of family constellations which supported his development.

COMMENTS

This paper suggests that group consciousness is a psychological stage in early childhood predating and contributing to the development of individual consciousness and the later group relationships. It stands in the same relation to group development in latency as the slightly earlier mother/child symbiotic state does to the oedipal relationships. The early mother/child merger must be differentiated before the face to face encounter of the oedipal period is possible. Yet all dyadic interaction is nourished by its roots. Similarly the stage of group consciousness provides the experiential framework for later group behaviors such as evolve in school age children and continue through adulthood. What is newly learned in latency are extrafamilial group interactional skills. The unconscious anlage of group experience, what Bion calls the basic assumption of group life, are already part of the child's developmental past.

There are a number of implications to this developmental theory beyond its specific relatedness to Bion's work and developmental group psychology which will only be briefly noted in this paper. One is its potential for understanding the differential dynamic importance of group and dyadic relationships for a given individual. Those persons raised in situations in which group and family life were early, powerful influences may have very different attractions to group life as adults than those persons for whom the mother/child orbit was predominant. Obviously there can be no simple, one to one causality here. A child for whom mother was the critical link between merger and individuality may grow to adulthood frightened by the intensity of two person relationships and find freedom in a life style emphasizing multiple group situations. Similarly, a child raised in a large family with a primary linkage to group experience as a prelude to individuality may later yearn for the uninterrupted bliss of closeness with one other. Nevertheless, increased understanding of the relationship between dyadic and group merger states in early childhood should provide a firmer basis for making the developmental links between child and adult experience. Beyond the elucidation of individual development is the relationship of these ideas to cultural differences; for example the relative importance given in a community or nation to group and extended family ties compared to one-to-one ties in early childhood. The variations in the developmental sequence suggested here could provide a framework for examining cultures along a continuum of "we-ness" and "I-ness".

Finally, it may be important to relate the theory presented in this paper to Group Relations Conferences, group therapy, and other learning experiences which emphasize group process. For example, many of us have found that Group Relations Conferences provide powerful personal growth experiences as part of the task of learning about group process and authority relationships. The form of these personal experiences is remarkably similar; the individual, after gradually becoming immersed in the group and feeling himself powerfully wedded to the group corpus, suddenly breaks free from this group consciousness with an accompanying acute, exhilarating sense of his own uniqueness and originality. Such experiences often have mystical or spiritual overtones; the individual is discovering and creating himself for the first time. These remarkable rebirths are adult experiences in their own right and can lead to major changes in personal values and goals. Yet they are also recapitulations of the initial experiences of individuation out of the group matrix, the first magical creation of what has been called the "ideal state of self" (Joffee and Sandler, 1965). Such personal experiences, spawned by the group process, may be treated as important but outside the group task, as done in the conferences, as the product to be manipulated, as is the case for some evangelistic religious movements, or as opportunities to support attitudinal change and growth, as in the treatment situation. However they are used, it may be important to more clearly recognize their origins and their importance in the developmental process.

5.
Selections from:
SYSTEMS OF ORGANIZATION

E. J. Miller and A. K. Rice

A CONCEPTUAL FRAMEWORK

Any enterprise may be seen as an open system which has characteristics in common with a biological organism. An open system exists, and can only exist, by exchanging materials with its environment. It imports materials, transforms them by means of conversion processes, consumes some of the products of conversion for internal maintenance; and exports the rest. Directly or indirectly, it exchanges its outputs for further intakes, including further resources to maintain itself. These import-conversion-export processes are the work the enterprise has to do if it is to live.

One intake of a biological organism is food; the corresponding conversion process is the transformation of food into energy and waste matter. Some of the energy is used up in procuring further supplies of food, some in fighting, or in securing shelter from, hostile forces in the environment, some in the functioning and growth of the system itself, and some in reproductive activities. In the same way, a joint stock company imports capital through the sale of shares or the raising of loans, converts the capital into income by the investment in commercial and industrial enterprises, uses some of the results to maintain itself and to grow, and exports the remainder in the form of dividends and taxes. A manufacturing enterprise imports raw materials, converts them into products, and sells the products. From its returns on the sale it acquires more raw materials, maintains and develops the enterprise, and satisfies the investors who provided the resources to set it up.

Other kinds of enterprise have different intakes and different conversion processes, and the returns they obtain from the environment in exchange for their outputs take different forms. An educational enterprise, for example, imports students, teaches them and provides them with opportunities to learn; it exports ex-students who have either acquired some qualification or failed. The proportion that qualifies and the standard the individuals are perceived to have attained determine the extent to which the environment provides students and resources to maintain the enterprise. In a learned society the primary pay-off may not be expressible in monetary terms or in terms of securing further material or human intakes but rather in prestige and self-esteem. Such pay-offs, however, are important for educational enterprises and may not be unimportant for profit-making enterprises as well.

Just as the study of living organisms requires the integration of many different theories, so the study of enterprises requires scientific theories corresponding to the anatomical, physiological, and ecological disciplines of the biologists. Organizational anatomy is concerned with the nature and structure of the resources through which the enterprise carries out its tasks; organizational physiology with the processes of task perform-ance, including the interrelations of different internal processes; and organizational ecology with the place of the enterprise in its physical, social, cultural, and economic environment.

But we are concerned not merely with developing theories that will help us to understand the structure and functioning of enterprises; we have also to bear in mind that enterprises and human beings, unlike other living organisms, need theories to apply to the solution of their own practical problems of organizations.

Accordingly, in presenting our theoretical framework we start with an examination of the systems of activity through which the enterprise carries out its import-conversion-export processes. We attempt to use concepts at a level of abstraction that makes them applicable to the functioning of all types of enterprise.

SYSTEMS OF ACTIVITY AND THEIR BOUNDARIES

We shall first consider the enterprise in terms of the systems of activity through which the import-conversion-export processes are carried out. We shall distinguish between operating activities and maintenance and regulatory activities, and we shall then discuss the definition of the boundaries of systems of activity and the control of transactions across them.

THE PROCESSES AND ACTIVITIES OF AN ENTERPRISE

A process is a transformation or a series of transformations brought about in the throughput of a system, as a result of which the throughput is changed in position, shape, size, function, or some other respect.

An activity is a unit of work. The transformations that contribute to a process are brought about through interaction of the inherent characteristics of the throughput and operating activites, which are carried out on the throughput. Activities may be carried out by people or by mechanical or other means. We call the producers of activities resources.

An enterprise relates to its environment through a variety of import-conversion-export processes, which require a correspond-ing variety of activities. A manufacturing company, as we have said, imports raw materials, converts them into products, and acquires a pay-off from selling the products. But it also recruits employees, trains them, assigns them to jobs, and sooner or later exports them by resignation, retirement, or dismissal. It imports and consumes stores and power. It also collects intelligence about its market and its competitors, analyses this information, makes decisions about design, quantity, quality, and price of products, and issues communications of different kinds as a result of the decisions taken.

In the analysis of a enterprise, or of a unit within an enterprise, we reserve the term *operating activites* for those activities that directly contribute to the import, conversion, and export processes which define the mature of the enterprise or unit and differentiate it from other enterprises or units. Thus in a shoe-manufacturing company the operating activites are those that procure the leather and other raw materials, convert these materials into shoes, and sell and dispatch the shoes to customers. Similarly, in an airline the operating activities are those that directly contribute to the process of transforming potential travellers into ticketed passengers and of transporting these passengers from a departure point to a destination. If the unit of analysis is an accounts department, then the operating acitivities will be those through which the relevant data are acquired, processed, and exported in the forms of invoices, cheques, cost reports, payrolls, and accounts of various kinds.

Besides operating activities, two other types of activity may be identified: maintenance and regulation.

Maintenance activities procure and replenish the resources that produce operating activities. Thus not only the purchase, maintenance, and overhaul of machinery, but also the recruitment, induction, training, and motivation of employees come under this heading.

Regulatory activities relate operating activities to each other, maintenance activities to operating activities, and all internal activities of the enterprise (or unit) to its environment.

Maintenance and regulatory activities can themselves be analysed in import-conversion-export terms. In regulatory activities, for example, the intake is information about the process being regulated, the conversion process is the comparison of the data against objectives or standards of performance, and the output the decision to stop or to modify (or not to stop or modify) the process, or the decision to accept or to reject the product. Similarly, to take the selection procedure for new employees as an example of a maintenance process, import activities procure an applicant, conversion activities apply the procedure through which comes the decision to select or to reject, and export activities place the new employee or dispose of the rejected applicant.

SYSTEMS OF ACTIVITY

A system of activities *is that complex of activities which is required to complete the process of transforming an intake into an output.*

A task system is a system of activities plus the human and physical resources required to perform the activities. The term 'system', as we use it here, implies that each component activity of the system is interdependent in respect of at least some of the other activities of the same system, and that the system as a whole is identifiable as being in certain, if limited, respects independent of related systems.

Thus a system has a boundary which separates it from its environment. Intakes cross this boundary and are subjected to conversion processes within it. The work done by the system is therefore, at least potentially, measurable by the difference between its intakes and its outputs.

But a measurable difference between output and intake does not of itself imply that the boundary so identified is the boundary of a system of activities. For example, in an automatic transfer line a component passes through a succession of machines, each of which performs a distinct operation, the output/input ratio of which can be measured; yet the machines are so interconnected that all either operate together or stop together. Even if variable-feed devices are introduced between the machines, the output/input ratio that is significant is that of the whole line. A system boundary implies a discontinuity. We make the hypothesis that the discontinuity at the boundary constitutes a differentiation of technology, territory, or time, or of some combination of these (Miller, 1959).

In a simple system there are no internal system boundaries either between one operating activity and another or between operating activities on the one hand and maintenance and regulatory activities on the other. A complex system contains such internal boundaries. In a large complex system there may be several orders of differentiation: major operating systems themselves being differentiated into bounded sub-systems, which in their turn may also be differentiated, and so on until simple undifferentiated systems are reached.

Most enterprises have the characteristics of complex systems: they include a number of identifiable sub-systems of activities through which the various processes of the enterprise are carried out. These constituent systems, like the enterprise as a whole, are open systems which acquire intakes from the environment, transform them, and export the results. Thus one department in a manufacturing process may have as its intakes part-processed products which are the outputs of departments preceding it in the process. In its turn, it exports to succeeding departments the same products at a later stage in manufacture. The total enterprise is therefore a significant part of the environment for its component systems of activity.

When maintenance activities are carried out in differentiated component systems of an enterprise they too can be treated as systems of activity with their own operating activities and related maintenance and regulatory activities.

MONITORING AND BOUNDARY CONTROL ACTIVITIES

What distinguishes a system from an aggregate of activities and preserves its boundary is the existence of regulation. Regulation relates activities to throughput, ordering them in such a way as to ensure that the process is accomplished and that the different import-conversion-export processes of the system as a whole are related to the environment.

Most processes are in some measure 'self-regulating' in the sense that the nature or structure of the process imposes disciplines and constraints on the associated system of activities. Thus a given operation that is part of a series of operations is 'regulated' by preceding and succeeding operations. Similarly, in parts of the chemical industry, once chemicals have been mixed, and heating, flow, and other processes started, technology takes over and for the most part determines quantity, quality, and speed of output. Important though these inherent constraints and disciplines are, they are not regulatory *activities* as such.

In the analysis of systems of activities two types of regulatory activity can be identified: monitoring and boundary control.

Whenever an operating activity is stopped, for however short a time, to check that it is achieving its purpose, a regulatory activity is introduced: operating activity/check/resumption of operating activity. Thus when a carpenter, sawing a piece of wood, pauses to make sure that his cut is in the right direction, he is changing his activity from operation to regulation. An example of a less perceptible change of activity occurs in the task of a salesman. In his transactions with a potential customer the salesman is carrying out a regulatory activity whenever he monitors what he has said already, assesses what effect this has had on the customer, and on this basis decides whether to continue the same approach or to adopt a different mode of attack. We use the term *monitoring* to refer to such intrasystem regulatory activities, which are different in kind from, and not directly related to, the controls activated at the boundaries of the system.

Regulatory activities that relate a system of activities to its environment occur at the boundary of the system and the environment and control the import and export transactions across it. Boundary regulation is therefore external to the operating activities of the system. The important implication is that the boundary round a system of activities is not simply a line but a region with two boundaries, one between the internal activities of the system and the region of regulation, and a second between the region of regulation and the environment. For this form of regulation we use the term *boundary control function*.

BOUNDARY CONTROL FUNCTION

The relation of a boundary control function to the import-conversion-export process is shown in *Figure 1*. *Figure 2* depicts the system of activities in topological form and shows the relation of the boundary control function to the operating activities.

FIGURE 1 Regulation at the boundaries of a process

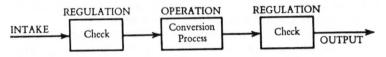

FIGURE 2 The boundary control function of a system of activities

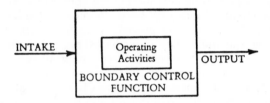

The boundary of a system of activities therefore implies both a discontinuity and the interpolation of a region of control. We shall see that difficulties arise if an organizational boundary is imposed at a point in a process which does not satisfy these two criteria of the boundary of an activity system. Unless there is a discontinuity, there can be no boundary region and thus no sense in which activities carried out within the supposed system are insulated from other activities 'outside'.

We have pointed out that regulation can itself be analysed as an import-conversion-export process: import activities are the collection of data from measurement or other observation; conversion activities, the comparison of these data with objectives or standards of performance; and export activities the decisions to stop or to modify the process or to pass the product. Simple examples are the inspection functions of manufacturing enterprises, by which raw materials are tested before being accepted and products inspected before dispatch. In most large factories inspection functions are also interposed between departments. Provided the inspections occur at boundaries between the enterprise and its environment or between differentiated constituent systems of the total enterprise, there are few problems of boundary confusion. The problems increase when we consider the organizational effects of the introduction of continuous automatic controls, particularly those that incorporate feedback and self-correcting devices, and hence eliminate the need for the pause for checking between one system of operating activities and the next.

MONITORING ACTIVITIES

A simple form of automatic regulation can be illustrated by contrasting the sawing of a piece of wood by a carpenter, who pauses to check the direction of his cut, with the same operation performed on a mechanical saw, when the direction of the cut is determined by a pre-set jig. In the mechanical operation the saw-minder regulates the quantity, and probably the quality, of the intake, but the conversion activity is controlled automatically. The saw-minder's task is to monitor; the actual sawing is carried out by the machine.

The next step is the introduction of mechanical devices to link the sawing operation with the preceding and succeeding operations. By these devices raw materials are acquired, checked, sawn, and transferred without pause to the next operation. The devices make and implement decisions about adjustments to these operations without halting the process.

The consequences of introducing a continuous monitoring function are illustrated in *Figures 3* and *4*. *Figure 3a* shows the simple interposition of checks between three consecutive processes, and this is contrasted in *Figure 3b* with a continuous monitoring function. When there are pauses for regulation, each part of the conversion process is potentially, at least, carried out through a differentiated system of activity, each with its own boundary control function. But when there are no pauses for checks the boundaries between the operating systems are removed and the different operating activities are carried out in a single operating system. *Figures 3a* and *3b* are shown in topological form in *Figures 4a* and *4b*. The boundary control function shown in *Figure 4b* both regulates the transactions of the three operating activities with the environment and monitors the intra-system transfers between the operating activities.

The general point to be made at this stage is that it is possible to construct a scale or hierarchy of regulatory activities as decisions are required at progressively higher levels of abstraction, or as new variables have to be taken into account in the decision-making process. The simplest regulation is that carried out by an operator who halts an activity to check that it is fulfilling its purpose — the carpenter who pauses in his sawing; at the next level an operator monitors a single activity or a simple series of activities — saw-machine operator; at the next, the data used for regulation are abstractions read from dials and gauges — as by the process operator in a chemical works; at the next, the data are read and processed automatically, and the decisions themselves are implemented as self-correcting devices — computer-controlled production from an automatic plant. A new level in the hierarchy of regulation is introduced whenever the data required for control purposes are beyond the data-processing capacity of the available regulatory resources.

However sophisticated the technology, there nevertheless

FIGURE 3A Checks between consecutive processes

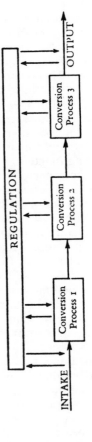

FIGURE 3B Continuous monitoring function

FIGURE 4A Three consecutive activities: independent regulation

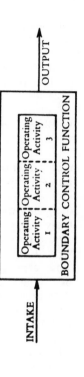

FIGURE 4B Three consecutive activities: integrated regulation

comes a point at which regulation cannot be mechanized and automated, and at which there has to be a pause to check the output of the system against the requirements of the environment. At this point a boundary region is introduced and an organization discontinuity occurs.

INDIVIDUALS, GROUPS, AND THEIR BOUNDARIES

Every enterprise requires resources to produce the 'units of work'— the activities — through which its processes are carried out. And besides the resources that actually produce activities, there are those that provide an environment within which the activities can take place. Thus the physical resources of a manufacturing company will include factories and the relevant machinery and equipment, all of which represent a major capital investment. If the enterprise is a partnership of general practitioners, the investment in physical resources will be more modest: surgeries and their equipment, waiting rooms, and receptionists' offices. Both in extent and in kind, the physical resources employed vary between one type of enterprise and another and between the different parts of any one complex enterprise.

Common to all enterprises, however, is the deployment of human resources. Regardless of the extent of automation, there are always some activities in an enterprise that must be carried out by human beings. Moreover, human beings do not exist simply as individuals; they are joined together in groups, small and large, and they interact in these groups both as individuals and as groups. Further, individuals can belong to many small groups in any large group and to many large groups in any environment. Indeed, an individual cannot exist in isolation, but only in relation to other individuals and groups. Even when he is alone, what he is and what he does are in large part a product of past relationships and of anticipated relationships in the future. Any theory of organization requires, therefore, not only a theory of systems of activities and their boundaries, but also a theory of human behaviour.

The theories of human behavior and of activity systems are in many respects analogous. Like a system of activities, an individual or a group may be seen as an open system, which exists and can exist only through processes of exchange with the environment. Individuals and groups, however, have the capacity to mobilize themselves at different times into many different kinds of activity system; and only some activities are relevant to the performance of the tasks of the various enterprises to which they belong.

Within our conceptual framework, the individual, the small group, and the larger group are seen as progressively more complex manifestations of a basic structural principle. Each can be described in terms of an internal world, and external environment, and a boundary function which controls transactions between what is inside and what is outside.

THE INDIVIDUAL

The personality of the individual is made up of his biological inheritance and the experiences through which he passes, particularly those of early infancy and childhood. In a modern industrial society ordinary men and women have three overlapping areas of conduct — family, work, and social activities — through which they can work out their own development. Through these areas of conduct they satisfy their physiological and psychological needs and defend themselves against the stresses and strains of having to come to terms with the relationships they make in them. A baby is dependent on one person —his mother. He gradually assimilates into his pattern of relationships his father and any brothers and sisters. As he grows into childhood he includes other members of the extended family and of the family network. The first break with this family pattern is usually made when the child goes to school and encounters for the first time an institution to which he has to contribute as a member of a wider society. It is his preliminary experience of what, in later years, will be a working environment.

The hopes and fears that govern the individual's expectations of how he will be treated by others and the beliefs and attitudes on which he bases his code of conduct derive from these relationships and are built into the pattern that becomes his personality. They form his internal world. This contains his primitive inborn impulses, and the primitive controls over them that derive from his earliest relationships with authority, usually represented by his parents. His internal world embodies the part of himself that longs to do what was forbidden or made impossible, and the part that is composed of the images of those who both excited the impulses and forbade them.

A useful contribution to our understanding of the development of personality is made by object-relations theory. According to this theory, the baby can make no distinction between what is inside himself and what is outside. He has no 'ego' that can differentiate his feelings and their causes. What he feels about an object that is outside becomes an attribute of the object itself. He 'projects' his feeling onto it. So far as it excites him and gratifies him, it is a 'good object' which he loves and on which he lavishes his care; so far as it frustrates or hurts him, it is a 'bad object' which he hates and on which he vents his rage. In his struggle to deal with these contradictory attributes he splits objects into good and bad, which represent their satisfying and frustrating aspects. But he has to learn that in reality it is the

THEORY: Miller/Rice

same object that sometimes satisfies and sometimes frustrates, that is sometimes good and sometimes bad. Both what later appears as protective love and what appears as destructive hate may originate in one confused and violent feeling that is inherently unstable because, in his very need to take in what is good, the individual also takes in what is bad, and hence threatens to destroy what he wants most to preserve. From this violent confusion of feelings for the same object come the later tendencies, on the one hand to idealize those who are felt to be protective and loving, and on the other to execrate those who are felt to be antagonistic and obstructive.[1]

In the mature individual, the ego — the concept of the self as a unique individual — mediates the relationships between the internal world of good and bad objects and the external world of reality, and thus takes, in relation to the personality, a 'leadership' role. The mature ego is one that can differentiate between what is real in the outside world and what it projected onto it from inside, what should be accepted and incorporated into experience and what should be rejected. In short, the mature ego is one that can define the boundary between what is inside and what is outside, and can control the transactions between the one and the other.

Diagrammatically, the individual may be represented on the pattern of a system of activity: see *Figure 5*. The ego is the equivalent of the boundary control region that mediates between the inner world and the environment.

The tendency for most human beings to split the good from the bad in themselves and to project their resultant feelings onto others is one of the major barriers to the understanding and control of the relationships between human resources and the tasks to which they contribute. And the difficulties of accepting that love and hatred can be felt for the same person are intensified in the relations between managers and the members of the enterprise they manage. The members of an enterprise depend on their managers to identify their tasks and to provide the resources for task performance. A manager who fails, or even falters, as inevitably he sometimes must, deprives his subordinates of satisfaction and thereby earns their hatred. But the leadership role of management is a lonely role and leaders must have followers; any hanging back or turning away is a threat to their own fulfillment. This inevitable, and mutual, dependence increases the need of both leaders and followers to defend themselves against the destructive power of their potential hostility to each other.

1 For a fuller account of this theory see Klein (1959).

FIGURE 5 Individual personality

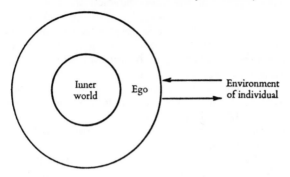

THE GROUP

We have described the internal world of the individual as made up of objects and part-objects derived from the relationships he has made. An individual has, therefore, no meaning except in relationships with others with whom he interacts. He uses them and they him. to express views, take action, and play roles. The individual is a creature of a group, the group of the individual. Each, according to his capacity and his experience, carries within him the groups of which he has been and is a member. His experiences as infant, child, and adolescent within his family, at school, and at work, and the cultural setting in which he has been brought up, will thus affect, by the way in which they are moulded into his personality, the working relationships he makes with superiors, colleagues, and subordinates.

Every group, however casual, meets to do something. In this activity the members of a group cooperate with each other; and their cooperation calls upon their knowledge, experience, and skill. Because the task for which they have met is real, they have to relate themselves to reality to perform it. For task performance they have to behave as rational human beings. As such, they have to have methods of communication between themselves and with the external environment about their task. In so far as they develop attitudes towards and beliefs about each other and about the group that transcend the purpose for which they have met, they are making assumptions about themselves as individuals and about the group as a group.[2] These assumptions, together with their attitudes towards their purpose, provide the emotional climate in which they meet.

The internal world of a group is made up, then, first of the

2 Cf. Bion (1961). Bion identifies three 'basic' assumptions. dependence, pairing. and fight-flight. Thus groups, whatever their overt task, behave, according to Bion, as if they had met to depend on one person to provide all physical or spiritual nourishment; to reproduce themselves, or to fight somebody or something or to run away from somebody or something

contributions of its members to its purpose and, second, of the feelings and attitudes the members develop about each other and about the group, both internally and in relation to its environment. At the level of task performance, members take part as rational mature human beings; at the level of assumptions they make about each other and the group, they go into collusion with each other to support or to hinder what they have met to do. The resulting pattern is one of cooperation and conflict between the members as individuals and between them and the group culture they produce.

The external environment of the group includes other individuals, groups, and institutions with which group members interact as individuals and as members of the group.

The two levels of the internal world of the group are depicted schematically in *Figure 6*. As members of a work group, individuals contribute overtly and consciously to the task of the group; simultaneously, they project into and out of the group, in ways of which they are unaware, their assumptions about themselves, about one another, and about their environment. Thus the group, behaving as if it had made assumptions about itself (the 'assumption' group), invades the boundaries of individuals; and, similarly, the external affiliations of individual members breach the boundary of the group.

A group, by definition, must consist of more than one individual; but groups of different sizes have different characteristic patterns of behavior. Thus pairs and trios obviously have different properties as groups; and, so far as we can tell at present, there are characteristic changes with each additional member up to five, six or even seven. Thereafter, as the group grows from seven to between eleven and sixteen members, though changes take place, the essential characteristics are those of the small face-to-face group. In such a group there are not so many members that they cannot sustain close and continuous personal relationships; but neither are there so few that the defection of one member can jeopardize the group's security. The small face-to-face group provides a boundary within which the member can be known and can feel secure; within which, as an individual, he can seek reinforcement and help; in return, however, he has to conform to the patterns of behavior imposed by the group, and contribute to the different assumptions that make up the group culture.

Larger groups may or may not be internally differentiated. Undifferentiated large groups are usually short-lived. Lacking the controls imposed by structured relationships at the work group level, they are correspondingly more prone to be dominated by irrational assumptions. Thus the members of a demogogue's audience or of a rioting mob shed their individual boundaries and are submerged in the group.

Beyond a membership of twelve or thereabouts, groups tend to split into subgroups. Since many enterprises require more

FIGURE 6 The two levels of the internal world of the group

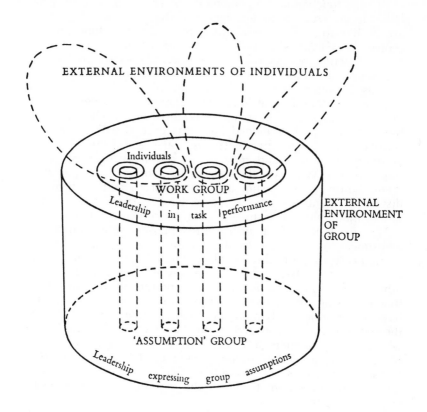

human resources than can be provided by a small face-to-face group, they have to take into account the phenomena not only of small groups but of large groups as well.

The large group is composed of individuals and of the small groups to which they belong. The small groups may be 'formal', in that their membership and purpose are consistent with the requirements of the enterprise; or they may be 'informal', directed towards other ends. The individual may be related to the large group through membership of more than one small group. The internal life of the large group consists, therefore, of the relationships between individuals and of the relationships within and between the groups to which they belong. Individuals have their own overt needs and unconscious strivings, and small groups their tasks and assumptions which identify them and hold them together. Moreover, individuals and groups interact at conscious and unconscious levels and at work and assumption levels simultaneously.

Whether a group is large or small, leadership, the equivalent of the ego function of the personality, is required to relate what is inside the group to its environment; that is, leadership of the group, like that of the individual, is a boundary function that controls transactions between inside and outside. Leadership is not a function necessarily or even usually exercised by one individual; at different times and in different circumstances various members may act on behalf of the group. In our terminology, therefore, it is activites that define leadership, not the verbal designation of someone as 'the leader'. 'The leader' of the work group may indeed have to contend with behavioral reality that leadership activities are a function of the 'assumption' group and may be in conflict with work-group requirements. Wherever they are located and whoever performs them, however, leadership activities express and confirm the distinctive identity of the group as against other groups, and differentiate between membership and non-membership.

The existence of a group presupposes some emotional investment by its members in the identity of the group and hence in the preservation of the boundary round it. Groups vary in the extent to which they invest emotionally in their boundaries; in other words, some groups are more important to their members than others are, or to use a different terminology, some groups have more *sentience* than others. Such variations are manifested through the transaction across the boundary — the control of which is the function of leadership. Whether this function is filled by one individual or by a member, the extent to which transactions across the boundary display consistency is one measure of the extent to which the members are emotionally committed to their group.

But, as we have said, individuals belong simultaneously to many different groups of different sizes. This is illustrated in *Figure 7*, which shows that C, a member of Small Group I, is also a member of Small Group III, and that G is simultaneously a member of Small Groups II and IV, and F of Small Groups II and III. (This diagram does not show external affiliations; nor does it depict the two levels of the internal world of the group: cf. *Figure 6*). Thus, for C, one of these small groups may have more sentience than the other; and the boundary of the large group may have more, or less, sentience for him than has either of the small groups.

Although our diagrams suggest similarities between the leadership of groups and the boundary control functions of systems of activity, it would be a mistake to press the comparison too far and to regard individuals and groups as simple activity systems. As we have said, individuals and groups can mobilize themselves at different times and even simultaneously in many different activity systems; and individuals can belong simultaneously to many different groups of different sizes. Indeed, in any hierarchical structure, every member of the

FIGURE 7 The large group

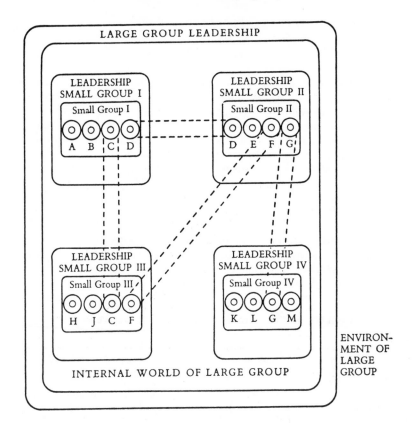

enterprise except those at the very top or at the very bottom must belong to at least two groups simultaneously - that of his subordinates, and that of his colleagues and superior (Likert, 1961).

INTERGROUP TRANSACTIONS

Any form of intergroup relations involves transactions of some kind across group boundaries. But for transaction across group boundaries, a group has to have some means of speaking as a group. It has to have a 'voice', and for the 'voice' to be coherent and understandable, not only outside the group but inside as well, some mechanism, some 'political' machinery, has to be devised. In other words, the group either has to speak in unison or has to be 'represented'. In the simplest case, in which Group A communicates with Group B through a representative (a), a new boundary and four new dimensions of relationships are automatically involved (as shown in *Figure 8*):

    (i) between Group A and its representative (a);
    (ii) between representative (a) and Group B;
    (iii) within Group B with the addition of (a);
    (iv) within Group A with the loss of (a).

The initiating group has to come to terms with what is being said or done on its behalf; and the representative has to reconcile his own views with the group policy he has to communicate. The receiving group's boundary is also crossed and the group has to come to terms with the intrusion from the environment and with the addition, however temporary, to its number.

When representatives from several groups meet together to establish intergroup relations between all their groups, still another boundary is added and another set of relationships: between the representatives as a group and the groups from which they come. This shown in *Figure 9*. It is not uncommon for representatives to be disowned by the groups they represent because they have transferred, or are suspected of having transferred, their allegiances to the groups they visit or to the 'group' of representatives.

FIGURE 8 The boundaries of representative activity

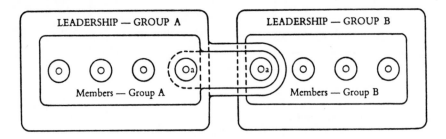

The sending out of any member to represent a group also reduces the power of a group as a group. If, while the representative is absent, the group is inactive, this means that all group activity is vested in the representative; and the group as a group is rendered impotent. Its leadership is being exercised by the absent member. If, on the other hand, the group remains effectively active while the representative is away and as a result of its activity grows and develops, then this means that the representative represents only the past, and his 'leadership' as expressed in relation to the environment is diminished. He no longer represents the group as it is, but only as it was.

In general, the setting up of any intergroup relationships

involves the drawing, temporarily at least, of new boundaries. And the drawing of new boundaries contains the possibility that the new boundaries will prove stronger than the old — that the new boundaries will enjoy greater sentience than the old.

Potentially, therefore, the setting up of any intergroup transactions has destructive characteristics since the relationship involved may destroy, or at least weaken, familiar boundaries. But any open system, in order to live, has to engage in intergroup transactions. The members of any group are thus inevitably in a dilemma: on the one hand, safety lies in the preservation of its own boundary at all costs and the avoidance of transactions across it; on the other hand, survival depends upon the conduct of transactions with the environment and the risk of destruction.

In practice, any enterprise has multiple transactions with its environment, and thus has to defend itself by the conditions it imposes on the nature, variety, and consistency or inconsistency of its transactions. Clearly, the more numerous the members

FIGURE 9 The formation of the representatives' group

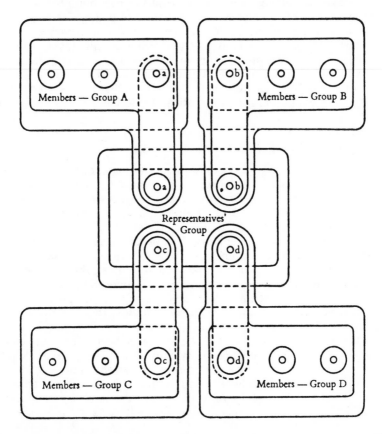

who 'represent' an enterprise to its environment, the greater the chance of inconsistency; and hence, as we have postulated, of reducing investment in the enterprise boundary.

TASK PRIORITIES AND CONSTRAINTS

Having outlined concepts of activity systems and their boundaries, and of human behavior, we shall now concern ourselves with task priorities: that is, with the priorities of the activities through which an enterprise is related to its environment and the parts of an enterprise are related to each other and to the whole. The concept of the primary task allows us to explore the purposeful nature of these relationships.

We have said that any enterprise may be considered as an open system, that exists, and only can exist, by exchanging materials with its environment. It imports materials, converts them, and exports some of the results. Its outputs enable it to acquire more intakes, and the import-conversion-export process is the work the enterprise has to do to live. The task of any enterprise can be defined in the most general way, therefore, as to secure pay-off by converting intakes into outputs — the minimum pay-off being the postponement of death.

But even simple enterprises, as we have shown, have multiple intakes and outputs and hence perform multiple tasks. They correspond to the operating, maintenance, and regulatory activities we have identified. We postulate that at any given time an enterprise has a *primary task* — *the task that it must perform if it is to survive* (Hutton, 1962; Rice, 1958, 1963).

THE CONCEPT OF THE PRIMARY TASK

The primary task is essentially a heuristic concept, which allows us to explore the ordering of multiple activities (and of constituent systems of activity where these exist). It makes it possible to construct and compare different organizational models of an enterprise based on different definitions of its primary task; and to compare the organizations of different enterprises with the same or different primary tasks. The definition of the primary task determines the dominant import-conversion-export system, and the operating, as distinct from the maintenance and regulatory, activites. It specifies the resources required and hence determines the priorities of constituent systems.

One implication of this is that there may be conflict between the way in which a constituent system defines its primary task and the way in which the superordinate system defines it. For example, the internally defined primary task of a factory department might be to maximize the output of a particular product; from the perspective of the enterprise, however, a greater pay-off might be secured by limiting the output of this department and increasing that of another, or even by requiring from it a different kind of output and modifying its resources accordingly. On a larger scale, the definition of the primary task of medical services as to save life can, in developing and overcrowded countries, lead to tragic consequences when what is required to sustain the inevitably increased population — food, housing, and other resources — is not also made available.

Similarly, environmental definitions of the primary task of an enterprise may differ from and impose constraints on its own definition. A community, for example, may define the primary task of the largest company in the district as that of providing essential employment for the local population. Such a definition may contradict the policy of the company, which, to improve performance of the primary task as defined by its own management — to carry out a profitable manufacturing operation — may require a more mechanized production process and a correspondingly reduced labor force.

In most industries, however, the general 'public' definition of the identity and purpose of an institution assigns long-term priority to a particular task and hence to a particular import-conversion-export system. Thus an educational enterprise must export some trained students and a manufacturing enterprise must produce some goods; and unless they secure such a return from their outputs that they are able to procure fresh intakes — of students and of raw materials, respectively — they cannot survive.

But tasks that are in the long-term ancillary to the primary task may temporarily become primary. For example, in a factory, the production system that converts raw materials into finished products has long-term priority, and the primary task is the conversion of raw materials into products. But if the machinery breaks down the primary task of the conversion system shifts from producing goods to repairing machines. The maintenance system of activities (which 'imports' malfunctioning machinery and spare parts and 'exports' repaired machinery) has priority. Similarly, an educational institution's primary task is jeopardized if it cannot procure staff, so that at certain times the primary task may shift from education to recruitment.

Such a temporary shift of the primary task may, however, lead to a permanent redefinition of the primary task of the enterprise and hence of priorities among the multiple tasks performed. To attract staff, it may be necessary for an educational institution to expand its research activities, in which staff can participate and from which they can earn academic prestige. As the ratio of research activities to teaching activities increases, so the definition of the institution's primary task may become, whether explicitly or not, progressively modified. The behavior of the enterprise may then indicate that its primary task is no longer the production of trained students but the production of research publications.

In some enterprises there is no settled order of priority. A teaching hospital provides a classic example. To survive, it must import medical students, train them, and export an acceptable proportion of them as qualified doctors; and it must also import patients, treat them, and export an acceptable proportion of them as convalescents. At any one time, one task or the other has priority, and in the operating theater the primary task may shift from moment to moment according to the progress of the operation. The prison service of the United Kingdom has three tasks: to punish the wrongdoer on behalf of society; to confine the socially dangerous; and to rehabilitate the delinquent member of the community. Given our present knowledge and resources, rehabilitation, which requires an open prison, and confinement, which by definition requires a closed prison, are not easily reconciled within the same system.

In the analysis of organization, the primary task often has to be inferred from the behavior of the various systems of activity, and from the criteria by which their performance is regulated. One may then be able to make such statements as: 'This enterprise is behaving as if the primary task were...'; or: 'This part of the enterprise is behaving as if the primary task of the whole were...'. Such formulations may be compared with explicit statements by the leaders of the enterprise and of its parts about their definitions of the primary task.

The primary task is not a normative concept. We do not say that every enterprise *must* have a primary task or even that it must define its primary task; we put forward the proposition that every enterprise, or part of it, *has*, at any given moment, one task which is primary. What we also say, however, is that, if, through inadequate appraisal of internal resources and external forces, the leaders of an enterprise define the primary task in an inappropriate way, or the members —leaders and followers alike — do not agree on their definition, then the survival of the enterprise will be jeopardized. Moreover, if organization is regarded primarily as an instrument for task performance, we can add that, without adequate task definition, disorganization must occur.

RESOURCES AND CONSTRAINTS

Resources provide, or facilitate, the activities through which intakes are converted into outputs. The resources required for any task performance are human and physical. In some enterprises, such as highly automated factories, the majority of activities are carried out by machines; in others, such as educational institutions or the selling departments of manufacturing companies, they are carried out by people. Yet, even in completely automated factories, the design of the process, and its maintenance and regulation, depend on people, with their scientific and technological knowledge, their skill and their experience. The extent to which resources exist or do not exist constitutes the major internal constraint on task definition and performance. The social, political, economic, and legal conditions of the environment constitute the major environmental constraints.

Thus, while the general definition of the primary task of any industrial or commercial enterprise is 'to make a profit', how it may be made, how much, and what can be done with it, are constrained by law, by custom, and by taxation. In addition, in most cases the human resources available for an enterprise come from the society in which it is located. The members of the society create its culture and hence bring to the enterprise in which they work the cultural constraints of their society. Environmental constraints are therefore inevitably built into enterprises and thus become a part of their internal culture. When an enterprise is itself valued both by its employees and by its society, the constraints on task definition and performance attract value as well, and become for this reason difficult to change. Both definition and performance are therefore constrained by the external environment and by the internal culture, and the interaction of the enterprise and its environment strengthens and confirms the constraints. Consequently, new knowledge, fresh experience — in general, new resources — are frequently difficult to introduce.

Constraints arising either from the environment or within the enterprise itself need, therefore, to be kept under constant review to determine whether they are in fact inviolable. Less than perfect task performance always has to be accepted because of known constraints; this performance is, of necessity, standard performance. A relaxation of constraints — a new invention, the development of a new skill — could lead to new tasks, or the better performance of old ones; but if there is no corresponding re-examination of task definition and of criteria for the judgement of performance, what was standard can become substandard.

In enterprises with more than one task and no adequate determination of priority, the performance of one task acts as a constraint on the performance of another. The teaching hospital has already been mentioned: given existing levels of knowledge and skill, patients may be necessary for the training of doctors; but this does not always mean that those patients who are attended by apprentice doctors get the best treatment. Large enterprises are differentiated into constituent systems, each of which has its own discrete primary task. In this sense, any large enterprise carries out multiple tasks. Further, the environment of any constituent system is comprised of other constituent systems and the whole, and the constraints on definition and performance in constituent systems include, therefore, those imposed by other constituent systems. The greater the differentiation of a large, complex enterprise, the more numerous the constraints imposed on each constituent system by the others and the whole; and the more subsidiary the constituent system, the greater the force of constraint on task definition and methods of performance.

THE CONSTRAINTS IMPOSED BY THE EMPLOYMENT OF HUMAN RESOURCES

More generally, once the primary task has been defined, and the definition accepted, other activities, however necessary and important, are subsidiary and can become constraints on primary task performance. Except in very primitive communities in which work, play, and family life are all integrated community activities, the members of an enterprise carry within themselves memberships of many different groups with many different activity systems. However positively they accept the definition and the methods of performance of an enterprise's primary task, it is unlikely that value derived from all their other different memberships will always be in harmony with those attached to work.

Therefore, a major constraint on the efficiency of any activity system is that technology has not eliminated, and never will entirely eliminate, the need to mobilize human resources, which bring with them into the enterprise more than the activities they are required to contribute. In the assignment of activities to roles and of roles to task groups, human needs may modify task requirements. On the scales of task-system efficiency are superimposed scales of human satisfaction and deprivation.

An individual may therefore be seen as experiencing satisfaction or deprivation in his work arising from:

(i) the interpersonal and group relationships directly involved in the activity system;
(ii) the harmonies or disharmonies of these relationships with other group memberhips.

To these we must add a third: the satisfaction or deprivation experienced in the activities themselves. The satisfaction obtained by a craftsman is frequently contrasted with the deprivation experienced by an assemblyline worker on repetitive work. Some tasks, by their nature, offer greater possibilities for intrinsic satisfaction than others; though not all individuals would agree about what was satisfying and what depriving. Moreover, some tasks offer not only greater possiblities for intrinsic satisfaction, but at the same time greater possibilities for deprivation. Menzies, in her study of hospital nursing services, says:

'Nurses are confronted with the threat and reality of suffering and death as few lay people are. The work situation involves carrying out tasks which, by ordinary standards, are distasteful, disgusting, and frightening. The work situation arouses very strong feelings in the nurse: pity, compassion, and love; guilt and anxiety; hatred and resentment of the patients who have aroused these strong feelings; envy of the care given the patient' (1960, p.98).

She showed that, given such a task, nurses had to have defenses against the stresses and strains they had to endure. She showed also, however, that the usual defenses, provided through the hospital organization, led to ineffective task performance:

'There is nothing more painful, more productive of anxiety, depression, and despair, than not being able to succeed in a task which has deep psychological significance for oneself' (1961).

In short, the nature of the task and of the activities involved in its performance can provide the individual with overt satisfactions — reward, prestige, accomplishment — or with overt deprivations — low reward, disrepute, boredom; it can also provide satisfaction and deprivation by reciprocation with his inner world of unconscious drives and needs for defense against anxiety.

Satisfaction and deprivation derived from the nature of the task, from relationships directly involved in the activity system, and from the harmonies and disharmonies with other group memberships, appear to be conceptually distinct, though in specific cases they merge: for example, satisfaction and deprivation derived from the nature of the task and from relationships directly involved in the activity system may be virtually indistinguishable in the saleman's job. For some tasks it is sometimes possible to construct organizations in such a way that not only do work-group boundaries coincide with task boundaries, but membership of the resulting work group provides considerable satisfaction for its members. Experimental changes in work organization in an Indian textile mill, for example, have shown that, where a task can be assigned to a small group, internally led, so that group leadership is coterminous with regulation of the system of activities, both system efficiency and human satisfaction are likely to be higher (Rice, 1958). Studies of British coal-mining have produced similar findings (Trist et al ., 1963).

These findings are important in demonstrating that work organization is not uniquely determined by the technical system and that alternative organizational models are often available. Even so, the organizations in which it is possible to match sentient groups to tasks — and so make task and sentient boundaries coincide — are the exception rather than the rule. What is more, a group that shares its sentient boundary with that of an activity system is all too likely to become committed to that particular system so that, although both efficiency and satisfaction may be greater in the short run, in the long run such an organization is likely to inhibit technical change. Unconsciously, the group may come to redefine its primary task, and behave as if this had become the defence of an obsolescent system. The group then resists, irrationally and vehemently, any changes in the activities of the task system that might disturb established roles and relationships.

As we attempt to separate the concepts of task group (the human resources required for an activity system) and of sentient group so that we may explore their interrelationships in a variety of organizational settings, it should become possible to see more clearly the consequences of different compromises made in different enterprises, and perhaps to foreshadow novel forms of organization that may be required in the future.

part two
METHOD

The conference educational method was developed by A. Kenneth Rice as a temporary institution designed to teach individuals about the covert aspects of group and organization life. In doing so he expanded Bion's notion of a "study group", to provide learning opportunities in Small Group/Large Group, Intergroup and Organizational process as a whole. His own and Dr. Rioch's description of the various conference events provide an intellectual analog of what is basically an experiential event. As with all experiential phenomena it is extremely difficult to convey an appreciation of what happens to the uninitiated. These articles are therefore best used in understanding the formal aspects of the model or in retrospective evaluations of a conference experience.

There have been several minor alterations in the method since Rice's initial descriptions. Many of them relate to redesigning a conference to fit into a smaller time and nonresidential formats' frame (the archetypal conference lasted for two weeks in a residential setting) or to focus on a particular issue such as male-female work relations in groups. Some of these newer innovations, including the use of this educational method in university courses, are described in the *Application* setting.

A.D.C.

6.

Selections from:
LEARNING FOR LEADERSHIP

A.K. Rice

THE BASIS OF CONFERENCE DESIGN

LEARNING FROM EXPERIENCE

In the *Social Problems of an Industrial Civilization*, Mayo (1945) pointed to the difference between skill and knowledge. He emphasized that a science starts with the acquisition of a technical skill, and grows with skilled workers' attempts to make explicit the assumptions that are implicit in the skill itself: '...scientific abstractions are not drawn from this air of uncontrolled reflection: they are from the beginning rooted deeply in a pre-existent skill'. He refers to the important distinction made by William James between 'knowing about', the product of reflective and abstract thinking, and 'knowledge-of-acquaintance', which comes from the direct experience of fact and situation. He quotes a letter from Alan Gregg: 'Knowledge derived from experience is hard to transmit, except by example, imitation and trial and error, whereas erudition (knowledge about) is easily put into symbols — words, graphs, maps. Now this means that skills, though transmissible to other persons, are only slowly so and never articulate.'

Two heroes die hard in our culture: the gifted amateur and the born leader. The hero of our education systems plays games well with little or no training, and gets first-class honors on the minimum of study. The great leader is independent of his environment or his followers. Scientific and technological advance has done something to destroy these myths. In recent years, in the West at least, introspection, the attempt to understand human motives, and even getting professional help to understand them, have become more acceptable, even fashionable. But it is doubtful if the pain and suffering associated with the experience of learning about oneself and about one's relations with others are yet generally accepted or acceptable. At least, most training for management or administration still tends to concentrate on techniques and to ignore the equally, if not more, important field of interpersonal and intergroup behavior. And for learning about this, 'knowledge-of-acquaintance' is essential.

There is even some danger that the very fashionableness of 'human relations training' will itself lead to the attempt to develop such painless techniques that learning itself will be jeopardized. The mitigation of pain, however desirable, may, unless we are careful, become self-defeating because real learning will not occur, and the skill will not be acquired. Let me emphasize that I do not believe that the inevitable pain of learning about oneself or about one's relations with others has any value for its own sake. Nor do I believe that 'trainers' have any God - given right to impose suffering on their students. Rather I believe that the capacity of a 'trainer' is limited. In the field of human relations he can provide opportunities for learning; he can teach little or nothing. Those who come as students must have the chance of learning or not learning, as they wish, or at least of learning at their own pace. The process of learning is a process of 'internalization', of incorporating felt experience into the inner world of fantasy and reason. The individual has the right to determine how quickly this process should go. He will resist learning if the process makes him anxious or frightened or if the rewards are insufficient. But successful learning and resistance are cumulative, and learning can be a part of a readiness for change that is inherent in any growing and maturing organism.

In the conferences described here, the basic method of providing opportunities to learn is to construct situations in which the task given to the members is to study their own behavior as it happens. In each situation so constructed one or more staff members apply themselves, so far as they are able, to facilitate that task to the exclusion of all others. Only staff roles and staff relationships are defined. No rules are laid down for members. They are free to make their own. The staff design the program and set a pattern of behavior, and by the program and their own behavior create an institution that gives protection to the members to experiment. In effect, four main 'boundary controls' are imposed: the total conference institution — visitors are admitted only under very special conditions, and no reports are ever made on individual members; the events — the primary task of each is defined, and one event is not allowed to overlap any other; staff roles — staff stay 'in role' and do not carry one into another; and time - events start and stop on time so that members know for how long the study of behavior will last, and for how long staff will maintain particular roles.

But the definition of the task of the conference as the study of its own behavior, and the absence of structure save for that of the staff, force members either to set up an 'organization' for themselves or to abandon the task. It is in the attempt to set up 'organizations' and in the taking of roles in them that members have the opportunity to experience for themselves the forces that are brought to bear on them when they take roles requiring leadership, and the forces they bring to bear on others who demand their following.

In the structured groups of everyday life, the specific roles and role relationships, the procedures, the recognized standards of behavior, provide defenses against the recognition of underlying processes. For conference members in their relationships with each other these defenses have been removed. In short, the basic conference method is to construct situations in which the conventional defense against recognizing or acting on interpersonal and intergroup hostilities and rivalries are either removed or at least reduced. This permits examination of the forces at work. The method consists therefore of lowering the barriers to the expression of feeling, both friendly and hostile; of providing opportunities for a continuous check on one's own feelings, and for comparing them with those of others, about given situations. Or, to put it another way, it is to check fantasy against reality. It means that the anxiety of learning is enhanced, and that therefore the ways in which anxiety is generated and controlled become part of the learning opportunity.

How the conference is designed, how it is managed, how competently the staff carry out their tasks are all parts of the situation in which learning can take place. Everything that happens in the conference, therefore, whether by design or accident, is material for study.

THE BASIC STAFF ROLE

A member of the staff, acting as consultant in any conference event, has his own conceptual frameworks within which he observes the behavior in front of him, including his own. He also has his 'knowledge-of-acquaintance' from his own 'learning by experience'. But when he is at work as a consultant he is a person who, in Rickman's words, 'at the moment of his most creative endeavors, lets these disciplines sink into the background of his consciousness and senses the direction of a process or the degree of freedom in the organization of persons seeking his advice' (Rickman, 1951; quoted by Sofer, 1961). In other words, he uses his own feelings to sense what is happening. He cannot observe with a detached objectivity that relieves him of the responsibility of taking account of what he is feeling himself. If he finds himself becoming embarrassed, anxious, angry, hurt, or pleased, he can ask himself why he is feeling what he is feeling, and can attempt to sort out what comes from within himself and what is being projected onto him by conference members. So far as he is sure that some of the feeling is being projected onto him and is not the result of some idiosyncrasy of his own personality, he can use himself as a measuring instrument—however rough and ready—to give him information about the meaning of behavior, both consciously and unconsciously motivated. If he can then find an explanation of the projection in terms of the specific task set for that event, he can make an 'interpretation' about the behavior of those present, including himself. The interpretation may be accepted, rejected, or ignored — but which ever it is, consultant and members are then faced by another piece of behavior related to his intervention.

So far as he is able, the consultant is concerned only with what is happening 'here and now'. Anything that has happened anywhere else or even 'here' a short time ago is relevant only in so far as it is evidence of the situation at the moment at which he intervenes. In practice, no interpretation is ever quite 'here and now', in the sense that speaking about it not only involves some delay, but changes the situation that gave rise to it. What the consultant is feeling, as he is feeling it, is what is relevant. If expressing the feeling changes it, then it is the changed feeling that becomes relevant. The skill of the consultant lies in his capacity to analyze — on a barely conscious intellectual framework — his feelings, and to express them in ways that will help the members of the group to understand their own feelings as they are experiencing them. But this does not mean that either the feelings, or the understanding of them, are necessarily conscious. Much of the communication and hence much of the learning take place at the unconscious and experiential level. Learning also takes place in post-conference reflection, and in the intuitive recognition of similar experiences in other situations at other times.

Hence the consultant's behavior is as important for learning as what he says; perhaps more so, since the words he uses to describe his feelings are symbols, of greater or less abstraction, of the behavior they represent.

In addition, in the conference the staff represent authority. Apart from the other roles they take as consultants and lecturers, collectively they represent conference management. The members inevitably project upon them their fantasies, fears, and doubts about authority and its power, and the analysis of this projection requires the analysis of the relationships among the staff themselves to distinguish what is intrinsic to the staff group and what is projected onto them by the members. Hence the authority relationships within the staff, and the way staff members conduct themselves individually and collectively, provide further 'here and now' learning opportunities.

CONFERENCE STRUCTURE

The conference institution is made up of two major sub-systems: pre-conference recruitment — the import system which produces the members; and the conference program — the conversion-export system through which those members who arrive pass on their way to becoming ex-members. Where the conversion process ends and the export process starts varies for different members. There is no clearly defined boundary between them and they cannot therefore be differentiated organizationally into discrete sub-systems.

PRE-CONFERENCE RECRUITMENT: THE IMPORT SYSTEM

The primary task of the import system is the production of conference members. In the framework of any one conference it is a discrete operating system in that, by the time the conference starts, its task has been accomplished. In the framework of successive conferences it is a continuing system, since inquiries are often carried over from conference to conference, and what happens at any one conference has effects on recruitment for subsequent ones. But with recruitment for a single conference as a frame of reference, imports are inquirers; conversion is the turning of inquirers either into members or into those who decide not to attend; and exports are therefore the members and non-members that result.

Task performance involves the publication and circulation of brochures and other forms of advertising, dealing with applications for places and with registration, sending out pre-conference information to those who become members, and interviewing prospective members. By these means inquirers become potential members and potential members become members. Recruitment of members entails booking accommodation, deciding at what stage to introduce waiting lists, and so on. The overt manifestations of these processes are the rules about dates of registration and of payment, and the issuing of joining instructions.

The major unsolved problem is how to communicate to inquirers what the conference can achieve, and how to prepare them for what will happen to them if they become members. The better the solution to this problem, the greater the freedom of choice inquirers will have.

Over the past seven years we have tried different methods of communication: seeing each potential member individually, arranging meetings of groups of inquirers to discuss the conference, and writing about it. If what members say during the conference can be taken as a reliable guide, none of these methods has been very successful. While this failure can be construed as confirmation of the hypothesis that learning can be achieved only through experience, I hope to provide a little more evidence on which to base judgments about participation.

THE PROGRAM: THE CONVERSION EXPORT PROCESSES

A conference program consists of several different kinds of events, each organized in a series. The major series are study group, large group, inter-group exercise, application group, and

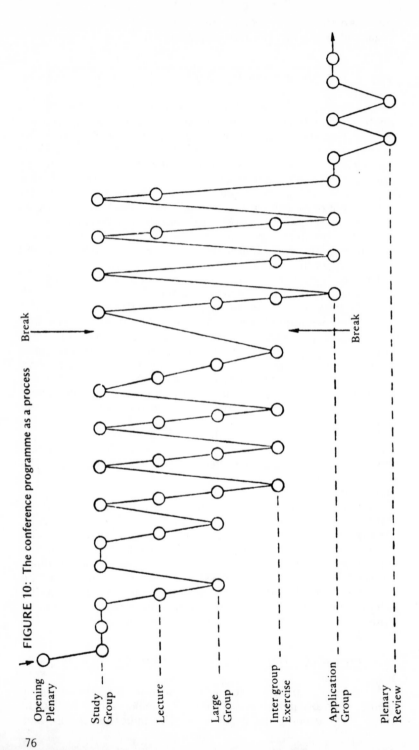

FIGURE 10: The conference programme as a process

Opening Plenary

Study Group

Lecture

Large Group

Inter group Exercise

Application Group

Plenary Review

Break

Break

FIGURE 11: Conference programme

July 1964

Times	Wed. 15th	Thurs. 16th	Fri. 17th	Sat. 18th	Sun. 19th	Mon. 20th	Tues. 21st	Wed. 22nd	Thurs. 23rd	Fri. 24th	Sat. 25th	Sun. 26th	Mon. 27th	Tues. 28th
8:15 Breakfast														
9:00—10:30		SG	SG	SG	SG	SG	SG	–	–	SG	SG	SG	AG	AG
10:30 Coffee														
11:00—12:15		Lect.	Lect.	Lect.	Lect.	Lect.	Lect.	–	SG	IGE	Lect.	Lect.	CR	AG
12:45 Lunch														
2:15—3:45	CO (3:15)	–	–	–	–	–	LG	–	LG	–	–	–	–	
3:45 Tea														
4:15—5:45	SG	LG	LG	LG	LG	LG	IGE	–	IGE	AG	IGR	AG	AG	
6:30 Dinner				IGE	IGE	IGE								
7:30—9:00	SG	SG	–				–	–	AG	–	AG	–	CR	

AG = Application Group; CR = Conference Review; IGR = Intergroup Review; Lg = Large Group; CO = Conference Opening; IGE = Intergroup Exercise; IGE = Intergroup Exercise; Lect. = Lecture; SG = Study Group.

lecture. In addition there is a plenary opening at the beginning of the conference, and plenary reviews towards the end. Residential conferences have usually lasted two weeks, though shorter ones of four and six days have been organized recently. The shorter conferences have had both fewer series and fewer events in each series. Non-residential courses have lasted for five or six months, two events taking place in a three-hour period once a week, with weekends for the intergroup exercise. Their program has been essentially similar to that of the two-week conferences.

The progress of a member through the various series of events at the most recent conferences is shown in *Figure 1*. The corresponding program is shown in *Figure 2* in which it will be seen that some compromises have had to be made to accommodate meal-times and times for rest, recuperation, and social activities.

With the conference program as the frame of reference, imports are members who actually arrive and, after the opening, are more or less committed to try to put the program into effect; the conversion process takes place in the events through which members move; the exports are the members who withdraw either temporarily or permanently before the end of the conference, and finally those who become ex-members at the end. Withdrawals before the end can be due to internal, personal, or group pressures; they can also be due to the intrusion of external reality.

THE CONFERENCE EVENTS

Conference events are discussed more fully later. Here I want only to place them in the context of the conference design and to discuss some of the reasons for their sequence and timing.

Members who arrive at a conference that is concerned with the interpersonal and intergroup relations involved in leadership are aware that this will involve their learning not only about others, but about themselves as well. They come to study their own and others' behavior in a setting in which they know, or at least suspect, that many of the conventional defenses against the expression and examination of feelings will be removed. They are therefore likely to be anxious. Verbal reassurance appears to be of little use in such a situation, and the conference is therefore designed to take members as quickly as possible into that series of events that experience has shown creates greatest anxiety. This is the series of study groups.

Study Groups

The task of the *study group* is to provide opportunities to learn about interpersonal relationships in small face-to-face groups. The primary task is therefore defined as the study of group behavior in the 'here and now'. The object is what is happening at any given time; the aim is to match current feeling with contemporary experience. All assumptions about behavior and beliefs on which behavior is based are open for investigation. For this reason each study group is made up of individuals drawn from working and personal backgrounds that are as heterogeneous as the membership of the conference allows, so as to avoid, as far as possible, the importation into the group of conventions of behavior from other common experiences. A study group consists of from eight to twelve members. That is, it is both large enough to enable individuals to relax from time to time without feeling that success in task performance depends on continuous effort, or that they are never out of the spotlight, and small enough to permit each member to maintain close personal relationships with all the other members.

A staff member acts as consultant to the study group. His task is to help the group to understand its own behavior. He has no other authority. Members may attend the group or not as they wish, as indeed they may for a conference event; they may discuss and do what they like; the consultant alone is prescribed. He is there to try, so far as he is able, to interpret the group's behavior to the group, and that of course includes his own contribution to it.

Because problems of interpersonal behavior are examined and worked at in study groups, and because any form of group or intergroup activity impinges on interpersonal behavior, the series of study groups has more events than any other in the conference and there is more overspill from it into other conference events. But because the study group is specially constructed to examine the underlying processes of small-group behavior and has therefore no parallel in normal everyday life, the series stops before the end of the conference. In this sense the later meetings of the study groups can be said to prepare the way for the end of the conference, and hence to be a part of the export process.

The Large Group

The task of the *large group* is also to provide opportunities to learn about interpersonal relations as they happen, but in a setting in which the number of members is larger than can form a face-to-face group. The definition of its task is therefore the same as that of the study group: the difference lies in the constraints on task performance. In the large group, the individual not only faces all the other individuals, but he may also face major subgroups, in the form of study groups or other spontaneously created subgroups. He may himself seek anonymity in the subgroup or as a member of the whole.

The large group consists of the total conference membership, and two staff members act as consultants to it. As in the smaller study group, the consultants have no formal authority other than that of consultants. Whatever the group discusses or does, they must endeavor, so far as they can, to help the group to get on with the task as defined, and they should avoid, if they are able, going into collusion with the group to do anything else.

The series of large groups starts after some work has been done in study groups, since, in other situations than conferences, identification with the smaller working group usually precedes identification with the larger whole. The series stops before the end of the conference because, being composed of the total membership, it can have no continuing existence when the conference is over; it stops before the series of study groups to give opportunity in the study groups to deal with some of the interpersonal problems that the conflicting loyalties of the large group may have given rise to. In this sense the end of the large-group series marks the beginning of the conference export process.

The Intergroup Exercise

The task of the *intergroup exercise* is to study relationships between groups as they develop. Experience shows that as individual identification with a group grows, so conflict and rivalry between groups tend to intensify. At the same time there is increasing curiosity about members of other groups and about what other groups are doing. For these reasons, the intergroup exercise starts after some work has been done both in study groups and in the large group. As soon as an individual identifies himself as a member of any group he takes on a new kind of loyalty. And this raises questions about his previous loyalties. If he likes his new group, he may find he is beginning to dislike other groups; if he becomes worried about what his new group is doing or believes in, he begins to wish he could change to some other group.

By the time the intergroup exercise starts, members have already experienced, in study groups and in the large group, some of the difficulties of communication; for communication between groups a new complexity is added — representation. In other words, for a group to communicate with another group as a group rather than individuals, some way has to be found whereby its views can be represented. Some kind of political machinery has to be devised.

Among the members of a conference there are, of course, many possible groupings, depending on the criteria for membership and on the study groups that have already met. But within the conference institution there are two clearly definable groups — that of the members and that of the staff. The staff group already has its ''political'' and administrative machinery, the members have none. In the intergroup exercise they are invited to divide up into groups in any way they wish, rooms are provided for meetings, and a given number of specified staff members are made available to those groups who ask for consultant help. If the members split into more groups, and if there are more requests for help, than there are staff available, some groups go without; if there are fewer groups, some staff members remain unemployed. The rest of the staff stay together in a room or space of their own and thus form a group for the exercise. They represent conference and exercise management.

Since the intergroup exercise involves the whole membership and the whole staff, it ends with a review at which all are present.

Lectures

A series of *lectures*, one of which is given on most days, is designed to give intellectual content to the learning taking place in other events of the conference. The lectures are intended to provide a framework for the articulation of the experience of the conference.

The lecture series has, however, an important secondary task: to provide a traditional form of teaching within a learning situation that is using unfamiliar methods. The hope is that the interpolation of a traditional method will have two effects: first, to provide some relief from the intense emotional experiences of other events—a working break; and second, to demonstrate a link between traditional teaching and the other methods used in the conference. Leadership does not consist only in understanding group processes; it requires as well an intellectual grasp of the problems of management, administration, and control. Learning about leadership has therefore to encompass all the techniques of learning.

The lecture series is in two parts. The first deals with theories of individual, small-group, and organized large-group behavior; the second, which is shorter, with problems of learning and with examples of the application of the theories discussed earlier to practical work situations. Which particular examples are chosen depends upon the lecturers. They speak from their own experience.

Application Groups

The task of the *application group* is to consider the relevance of conference learning to normal work situations. For this reason members are divided into groups that are as homogeneous as possible so far as jobs are concerned. Groupings of prison governors, of general, sales, and production managers, of parish priests, personnel officers, training officers, heads of schools, training college staff, psychiatrists in private and institutional practice, psychologists and other kinds of specialist, are among the many that have occurred. The materials of discussion in the application group are 'cases' provided by the members. In contrast to the other events, excepting lectures, the learning is not about behavior of the members in the 'here and now'; it is about past experience in other places, in the light of newly acquired experience and knowledge. All learning and teaching techniques are permissible: case conference, seminar, role-playing, led discussion, or any other method that is appropriate.

A member of the staff is attached to each application group. His duty is to help the group with its task. He is concerned with the 'here and now' of the application group in so far as what is currently happening in the group interferes with its task. Even then, he uses his recognition of group process not necessarily to make comments on group behavior, but to help him to help the group to overcome the obstacles to its progress.

Application groups are started late in the program so that members will have had some conference experience before coming to them and hence, it is hoped, will have some conference learning to apply. The conference ends with the application group because it is the series that is closest to everyday life, one that deals with the practical problems of members. In this sense the series of application groups is the real export process of the conference. In terms of the conference experience, members are by this time concerned with what they can take back with them. They have what they have, and have to accept it.

In addition to the events described above, two others are essential: the opening plenary and the closing reviews. And for conferences lasting two weeks we have always introduced a break of at least twenty-four hours midway through the period.

The Conference Opening

The *opening plenary* takes place as soon as the members have arrived. Its task is to provide a ritual, but meaningful, beginning. It is not expected that much can be said at this stage that will add to the literature that members have received before they arrive, at least not much that they can readily absorb. But they have by this time joined the conference and some event has to symbolize this implicit commitment to the conference aim. The staff are introduced at the opening plenary so that, as the members enter the events of the conference, they will be able to identify their consultants and other staff. Additional administrative arrangements not already notified are announced, and there is a statement of the program and some explanation of the design on which it is based.

This opening session, as can be seen from *Figure 11,* is short. The reason is that, though no bar is put on members' raising questions, experience has shown that very few are asked spontaneously. To stimulate a discussion at this stage of the conference would convey to members the message that the staff expected immediate participation. The purpose of the conference is to allow members to learn what they will, when they will, from the opportunities provided, and such a message would contravene this intention.

On past occasions, when more time was allowed, discussion after the director's opening seemed false and forced. Since we have redefined the task of the opening plenary, we have found that the few questions raised — never more than one or two at any opening — have been 'test-outs'. They have invariably implied doubts about administrative and management competence on the one hand, and about the reality of flexibility within a defined structure on the other. On every occasion, a direct answer has appeared to satisfy the members and there has been no supplementary. At that stage of the conference the test-out has been successfully handled and there have been no further questions.

Conference Reviews

The conference reviews have two purposes: one, the primary task, to allow members to discuss together, and with the staff if they wish, the experiences that have impressed them—favorably or unfavorably—with a view to crystallizing some of the learning that has taken place; the other, the secondary task, to provide an opportunity to learn about ending. The sessions, usually two, are both normal conference sessions, and hence longer than the opening.

The conference reviews, which take place in plenary sessions, also allow for a final manifestation of the conference as a whole. They are not, however, the final events of the conference. Application groups continue. The intention is to encourage both members and staff to work at trying to understand what has been happening and to concentrate on ending the conference without however applying closure to the learning process. The practice at the more familiar kinds of conference is to close with votes of thanks from members to staff for organizing the conference (whatever their quality). The staff, in their turn, usually thank the members for attending and tell them what a good audience they have been. Convention decrees that whatever members may think of the staff, or staff of members for that matter, the closing ritual shall consist of an exchange of compliments. Since the purpose of the conferences described here has been throughout to examine the roots of behavior and thus to question the attitudes and feelings that may lie behind such an exchange, it seems important that what happens at the plenary reviews should be consistent with that purpose. A conventional ritual, for convention's sake, would suggest a failure in conference learning.

Nevertheless, since the conference is a special kind of institution in which the normal social conventions of interpersonal and intergroup behavior of everyday life are either removed or controlled, it seems essential that in the process of transition back to ordinary life some of the conventions should be re-established: the review sessions provide one such convention.

The Mid-conference Break

Members use the break in various ways: some stay in the conference center; others visit in the neighborhood; others return home; and some, when the break occurs on a weekday, return to their normal jobs.

The break is short so that the contrast between life in the conference and out of it is not unduly prolonged. But it is long enough to renew experience the external world, as a counterbalance to the sense of unreality that might begin to creep into the conference itself. The break, in effect, is a rehearsal for the end. It has the advantage, shared by all rehearsals, that it is not a final performance. It also gives members the opportunity to absent themselves from the remainder of the conference if they so wish. In addition, of course, the break provides a welcome rest from the intensive work of the conference itself.

Follow-up

There is at present no follow-up event as such. Previous conferences included this event as a definite post-conference phase. It has been dropped until we can both be sure of our definition of its task and feel that we have a reasonable technique for performing it. Four possible purposes could be fulfilled by a follow-up: a meeting of an alumni association, a reassurance that something had been accomplished, 'closure', and further learning. The major constraints on any of these are time and hence cost. It has never been found possible to devote more than a weekend to the follow-up event.

A meeting of alumni could be — and indeed has been — a pleasant renewal of the relationships made at the conference. But since the task of the conference is learning for leadership and it is only a transitional institution, its primary task is not the making of permanent relationships. A meeting of alumni could not, therefore, rank as a primary task of a follow-up event. Nor does it seem appropriate to meet merely for reassurance that we have together accomplished something in our two weeks of hard work. Who needs to be reassured — and about what? It is not certain. 'Closure' is equally unsatisfactory. There can never be any end to learning about human relations; any closure achieved could only be false and could be construed as a defense against further learning.

Hence, the only appropriate primary task that we can find for a follow-up event is further learning. In other words, the follow-up event would have to become an extension of the conference. Short of designing a different kind of conference with long intervals between various events, or series of events, a brief follow-up to what has been a fortnight's intensive work does not give adequate time for much further learning. Technically, we have no answer. This is not to say that conferences could not, or should not, be designed to take place in two or more parts with intervals between. Unless, however, such conferences formed part of a longer training program they would present difficult organizational and administrative, as well as financial, problems. So far none has been attempted.

The only kind of follow-up has been the creation of an advanced training group at subsequent conferences. Membership of the advanced training group is, however, by special invitation for special purposes.

CONFERENCE MANAGEMENT ORGANIZATION

Some conference management — control, coordination, and service — is essential if the conference is to take place at all. The problem is to ensure, so far as is possible, that the methods of management and the behavior of 'managers' are consistent with the conference task. And since the primary task of the conference is to provide opportunities for learning about leadership, or, in management terms, about interpersonal and intergroup relations in situations in which authority and responsibility are the subjects of study, it is inevitable that conference management becomes one subject of study. This means that management roles have to be described and their boundaries of responsibility and authority defined, in such ways as to encourage, or at least not actively discourage, examination.

Conference management has three tasks: first, to design and plan the conference; second, to implement the plan in the pre-conference phase; and third, to run the conference. Each of these managerial tasks is different. The first is the responsibility of the professional staff to whom it is delegated by the institution(s) responsible for organizing the conference. They bring to bear knowledge about learning and teaching as well as experience of previous conferences. 'Management' in this task consists of convening the necessary meetings and running them in such a way that decisions about design and staffing get taken. The model for this kind of activity is that of a group of colleagues with a chairman appointed by themselves.

The second task — getting out the brochures; receiving and dealing with inquiries, booking, and registration; organizing accommodation and sending out essential information — demands efficient administration. The model is that of a manager with the necessary subordinate staff.

If, in the design and planning phase, the staff could predict the course of every conference event, as well as the whole; and if, in pre-conference administration, they could lay down procedures for every administrative contingency, the management required at the conference itself would be minimal. The professional staff members would carry out the various events for which they were responsible, administration in the sense of coordination and control would be a 'service' function, and the staff group would be on the model of a group of colleagues with a chairman, as in the design and planning phase. But because the conference is about what it is about, prediction is impossible and contingencies or even emergencies always arise. The staff cannot always, as a group, act with either the speed or the decisiveness that the emergency demands. They become deeply involved in the events, and in the groups for which they are responsible, and cannot but lose some perspective on the conference as a whole, and hence on the indirect, as distinct from the direct, causes of the emergency. For this reason we have instituted the office of director.

In contrast to the earlier conferences in which the 'officers' of management included a chairman, a program director, and joint conference secretaries, we have now defined only two 'officer' roles: director and secretary, both of whom are appointed by the institution(s) responsible for the conference, and explicitly accepted by the professional staff taking part in the conference. In the design and planning phase the director takes the role of chairman of the staff group; the secretary is secretary to the meeting. In the pre-conference phase the director acts as conference general manager, the staff group becomes advisory to be called on   only if required, and the secretary acts as manager of the import system, taking responsibility for the actual operations involved. In the conference itself the director combines the roles of executive chairman and director; he is vested with authority, and carries the responsibility to act in what he believes to be the best interests of the members irrespective of previous decisions and roles. The secretary takes charge of all administrative arrangements, is in liaison with the staff who are providing accommodation for the conference, 'looks after' the members in a practical way. The consequences of these changes of role, and hence of the pattern of management, will be discussed later. The resulting management organization is shown in *Figure 12*.

CONFERENCE CULTURE

If learning about the real feelings underlying one's behavior towards others and their behavior to oneself can be painful and even distressing, then a conference that provides opportunities for such learning must provide some measure of security both for its members and for its staff. The basis of this protection is the way the conference is institutionalized. The structure of the conference institution — its design, formal organization, and management — has been described above. I shall now attempt to

FIGURE 12: Conference management organization in recruitment and programme phase

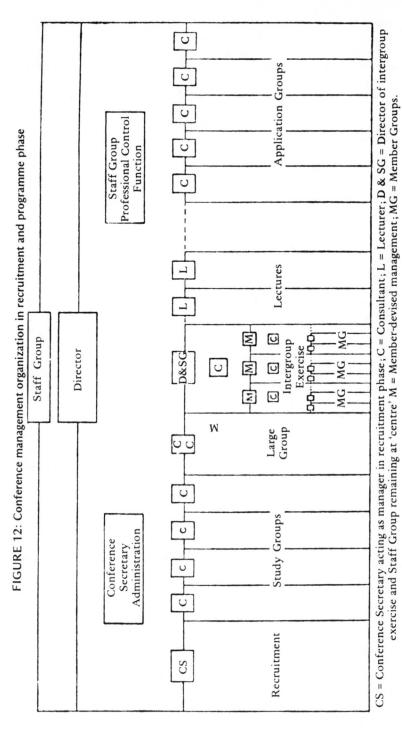

CS = Conference Secretary acting as manager in recruitment phase; C = Consultant; L = Lecturer; D & SG = Director of intergroup exercise and Staff Group remaining at 'centre' M = Member-devised management; MG = Member Groups.

87

describe the kind of culture that we try to build up. The culture, together with the structure, forms the texture of the institution, gives it its 'life' within which individuals can exist and know something about where they are; can move and know something about whence they come and where they go. The culture of the conference is its customary and traditional ways of thinking and doing things, which, eventually, is shared to a greater or lesser degree by staff and members alike. It covers a wide range of behavior — methods of work, skills and knowledge, attitudes towards authority and discipline, and the less conscious 'cultural congruence', the extent to which the culture fits' the task of the institution, is as important for effective task performance as structural fit.

Because of the nature of the conference, the culture has to be one in which aggressive behavior, expressions of hostility between individuals and groups, can be studied and their effect on decision-making examined and learnt about, without their becoming destructive — either of the individual or of the conference. And since the task of the conference is to provide opportunities for learning about leadership, the pattern of authority and responsibility in the conference has to be sufficiently explicit to be capable of examination, and sufficiently stable to be able to tolerate critical and even hostile scrutiny. A culture that did not actively encourage such scrutiny would be incongruent, as would be one in which any particular conventional attitude towards human relationships became established.

The task of the conference is to provide opportunities to learn. How far members take the opportunities is their responsibility. Thus neither they nor the staff can predetermine how much part they will play in the life of the conference and hence in the building of its culture. At the beginning of the conference, therefore, it is conference management, conference setting, and staff behavior that have to provide the means by which the basis of conference culture is established.

One other important protection for members is a conference setting that provides some degree of isolation from their normal working environment. It is for this reason that no reports of any kind — written or verbal — are ever made about members who attend conferences, no tests are given, no diplomas or other certificates awarded. In other words, so far as the staff are concerned, nothing that could be ascribed to any individual is ever disclosed outside the conference. Such protection, of course, can be no more than partial, since the staff cannot guarantee members' respect for confidentiality about each other. They can only set standards for themselves that they hope will be followed by members.

LEARNING ABOUT THE ANXIETY
OF MAKING DECISIONS

Decision-making, the constant occupation of leadership, can frequently cause anxiety — anxiety about the amount and quality of information available on which the decision has to be based, anxiety about the capacity to make the decision, and anxiety after it has been made while waiting for its consequences. It is unlikely that much can be learned about anxiety without the learners themselves becoming anxious. The problem of the conference institution is not, therefore, to avoid anxiety, but to provide opportunities to examine its effect on behavior and to learn ways of dealing with it, so that its outcome is constructive. The technical problem is to provide situations which, though they may provoke anxiety about behavior and decision-making, yet still allow members to learn as much as they want to learn and at the rate at which they want to learn it. If a situation is actually worrying, then there is reality in worrying about it. The difficulty is to equate the nature and extent of the worry with the reality. Worrying about dangers that do not exist, or not worrying about dangers that do, are alike problems of testing reality against fantasy for the recognition and solution of which the conference exists.

But because the capacity to tolerate anxiety differs between individuals at different times and in different situations, it is inappropriate for one group at the conference, the staff, to try to teach another, the members, what to worry about, or to suggest that members should worry when they are not worrying or stop worrying when they are. The task is to provide members with the opportunities to learn, not to insist on their learning; but when they do want to take the opportunity provided, to help them to realize its potential.

Since one cannot learn about anxiety without becoming anxious, members of staff who are not made anxious at some points in a conference are unlikely to be in close enough touch with what is happening in it to fill their own roles adequately. What is important is that the staff demonstrate that they can contain and understand their own anxieties and use them to further conference experience for the members; that is, that they can learn themselves from their own anxiety and through this provide opportunities for others to learn as well.

Furthermore, the staff must be able to cope with the kinds of situation they help to create. Even though they provide only opportunities for learning, and members must take their own responsibility for how much they learn, the provision of the opportunity itself implies that it is safe for members to take it. Moreover, members are not offered learning situations created by the staff alone; they are also subjected to situations created by other members, out of opportunities presented by the conference institution and the way it is run. The staff, therefore, cannot absolve themselves from responsibility for anything that occurs in the conference, whether inside or outside actual conference events. The capacity of the staff to take this responsibility lies not only in their individual abilities but in their collective skills organized in a conference institution to which, for a time at least, they have committed themselves.

It can be assumed that when members arrive at such a conference they are at least going to wonder what they have let themselves in for. They bring to the conference their own culture, with its expectations of 'structured' situations, of 'civilized' interpersonal and intergroup behavior, of how leaders should behave under different conditions, of rules and procedures for regulating antisocial or deviant behavior. They know from what they have read or heard, or from previous experience, that the techniques of conference learning include the removal of some of the common and expected social defenses, the lowering of barriers to the expression of feeling, and an examination of the values that are placed on externally accepted modes of behavior. Though they come willingly, it is unlikely that they will be sure altogether that they have acted wisely. In that state, while most of them are strangers to each other, and before they have had an opportunity to experience just what a conference is like, they can only turn to the conference staff for help.

It is not the director's or the staff's job to reassure them, to tell them that there is nothing to worry about — there may be. Rather it is the staff's job to demonstrate that they know what they are doing and what they are not doing, to be prepared to tell members what they can do and what they cannot do, and to show that they can be depended upon to do what they say they are going to do. This, in Bion's terms, is a sophisticated use of the dependent basic assumption. At that stage, knowing nothing or very little about the actual experience they will encounter, members are, in reality, dependent: they depend on the staff for leadership. But if members are to accept staff leadership in this situation and to commit themselves to learn in such a conference institution then the staff must be demonstrably dependable. Knowledge of the job to be done, and a demonstration of competence, do not however mean omniscience and omnipotence, and the reality of staff dependability and the contrast between the knowledge and competence ascribed to them by members and how much they really know and how competent they really are will be tested during the course of the conference.

In short, the culture that we try to build is one in which, within a given framework, members will feel able to examine their own and others' behavior in a series of settings that, while being specially constructed for the conference, throw light on the underlying processes of behavior in common and familiar external situations.

CONFERENCE MANAGEMENT CULTURE

At the beginning of a conference different members accept or reject staff leadership in their own way. In varying degrees they accept the mores and customs of the institution they have entered, and in so doing add their own contribution to the conference culture. In this sense every conference is unique, but each is built on a type of management and a code of staff behavior that are intended to provide an institution of sufficient stability to afford security, and of sufficient flexibility to permit members to experiment with different ways of tackling problems of leadership and followership.

For the members, the institutional framework is the program of events, the roles taken by the staff, and the conference setting. No rules are laid down for them: they may attend events or not as they wish, and within the constraints laid down by the place in which the conference is held, do as they wish.

So far as the staff are concerned, the program is adhered to. Events start and stop at the published times. Members can arrive late or leave early; the staff stick to the plan laid down. This does not mean that the program is inviolate. If something occurs that makes it desirable to vary the timing of the event, it can be changed. But it is important that the reasons for changing be adequate and real; that management is not led into making change for change's sake, to prove its own flexibility or its subscription to democratic principles. Because the discipline of time is imposed only on the staff, no bells are rung or other signals given to mark the beginnings of sessions; nobody shepherds the members into events.

In practice, the timekeeping at conferences has so far been remarkable. The usual pattern is for the members to be waiting for the staff. When no other conventional rituals are available, time can itself be used as a boundary control. Members accept timekeeping as a means of establishing their own discipline, of determining what is inside and what outside the boundary of an event. Inside, behavior is under scrutiny and conventional defenses are questioned; outside, normal social practice holds. As will be seen, timekeeping in the sense of staying until the programmed end of a session can also be used inside the boundary as a defense against further work. 'Sitting-it-out' can itself become a ritual.

As much factual information as possible is given to members before they arrive: the names of other members; their allocation to study and application groups; a plan of the buildings; where they will sleep, eat, and work; a list of amenities; and where possible the actual allocation of accommodation and workrooms. When they arrive their names are on the doors of the rooms they will occupy, and a conference office is open to deal with practical queries.

Name labels are not issued. The individual member is helped

to get to know his surroundings by the information sent to him, and in the opening plenary he can identify the members of the staff with whom he will work. But he is not given artificial help to get to know other members, since the study of this process is a part of the conference content. Labels that identify name and organization—even when they can be read—are a conventional means of introduction at conferences. But the convention does not ensure personal contact; indeed, a label can be a defense against finding out what lies behind it. This defense is removed.

If the conference organization fits its task, the role designed for a member of the staff in any event is consistent with the task of the event. Events and roles then fit into a coherent whole. In consequence, the staff do not allow themselves, without good reason, to go into collusion with members to make un-thought-out or arbitrary variations in role or event. Of course, the fit is never as good as it should be; the authorities and responsibilities never match perfectly. The urge to make changes can therefore be very strong. And the more able and sophisticated the members, the more they can cloak their temptations as reasonable requests and thus inveigle staff out of role and away from the task. For, after all, the attempt to destroy authority and to make leadership impotent is one of the aspects of relationships between leaders and followers that the conference is called upon to study.

The more appropriate the conference organization is to its task of providing opportunities to learn about interpersonal and intergroup problems of leadership, the surer are those who operate the organization of their roles in it. The better they can stay in role, however many and various the roles they have to take, the greater the security members feel in an anxiety-provoking situation. Indeed, the demonstration that such aspects of human behavior can be examined and discussed provides a framework in which members too can release for discussion data about themselves that they might otherwise be unwilling to release.

So far as is possible the conference structure defines the events, and the roles, responsibilities, and authorities of the staff in the various events in which they are engaged. The serious attempt to match the delegation of authority and responsibility, and to define the boundaries of events, puts severe constraints upon the staff. But there are compensations. Thus, though there may well be differences in technique and language among the staff who act as consultants to the study groups, the groups in the intergroup exercise, or the application groups, once they have been assigned their tasks, what they do and how they do it is up to them. Theoretically at least, staff are not assigned to conference roles unless they subscribe to the overall concept that has been worked out, but once they are appointed, they have not only the responsibility to implement that policy but the authority to do it in their own way.

The ability of the staff to take roles and to stick to them, to recognize the extent and the limits of the responsibility their roles carry, and to exercise authority within those limits are manifestations of their capacity to run the kind of conference they are running. This capacity, it is hoped, will encourage members to experiment themselves with different kinds of role-taking and with organizations of their own. They can then experience the kinds of responsibility they feel they can carry in different circumstances, and the amount of authority they can exercise.

STAFF BEHAVIOR

Essentially, staff behavior has to be 'professional'. By that I mean that members of the staff have to accept full responsibility for what they say and for how they behave. They have to know, usually without thinking about it, what is confidential and what is not, and to respect confidence without being secretive; they have to be able to differentiate between person and role, between task and personal needs, and to recognize when their personal feelings are affecting their role performance. They have also to be able to accept that they will never be paragons, and will inevitably be proved fallible; that making mistakes, as they will, is less important than the ability to recover from them. This means, in effect, that they strive always to remain in role, and that their behavior, so far as they can control it, is appropriate to it.

In events they do what the event defines they should do; on social occasions they behave socially. They do not, if they can help it, merge the one with the other. This does not mean that at meals, in the bar, or on other social occasions they refuse to discuss the conference or its events if that is what interests those with whom they are talking—such behavior would be antisocial. But it does mean that, outside conference events, their contributions to such discussions pay adequate regard to the confidential nature of the information at their disposal, and they avoid getting involved in additional 'extramural' events.

In 'public' events in which some members of the staff have no working role, as for example in a lecture, rules for staff behavior are explicit. The primary task of a lecture is communication between the lecturer and the members. The 'platform' at such a session is therefore occupied by the lecturer or lecturers, and the body of the hall by those for whom the communication is intended—the members. Any staff who attend such a session, but are not on the platform, have therefore to regard themselves as being privileged visitors. They can participate in the discussion following the lecture only when they are certain that their contribution will help both 'platform' and 'hall'. It is inappropriate that they should intervene on either side to defend or to attack the lecturer. If staff not on the platform disagree with the lecturer, as can happen, the disagreement has to be dealt with privately, unless their comments would help lecturer as well as members. In other words, once the task of giving a lecture has been delegated to a lecturer, he has to be trusted to do it.

By contrast, in public events such as the conference opening, the plenary sessions of the intergroup exercise, and the conference reviews, those who are on the platform have not only the right but the obligation to do their best to help the members; and if this means shooting down the speaker in the interests of the members, then he has to be shot down. That is to say, open disagreement among the staff in front of members is appropriate if the disagreement furthers task performance. The judgement about task performance is not easy, and in practice public disagreement seldom occurs—the point is made to emphasize the insistence, in conference events, on the staff staying in role as far as they possibly can.

CONFERENCE SETTING

Conferences are usually held in colleges or the halls of residence of universities, occasionally in hotels. My own, and my colleagues', preference is for a university setting, which, though not necessarily as comfortable as a hotel, provides a working educational institution as a background. It is also cheaper. So far as the buildings used for conferences allow, all members have a room of their own, and three common rooms, apart from workrooms, are provided: one for members, one for staff, and the third (usually the bar) for both.

In a conference where the existence of different feelings for the same person—love and hate, like and dislike, trust and distrust—is accepted and where the hostility inherent in any human relationship is acknowledged, members need somewhere where they can let off steam privately and where they can collectively say exactly what they think about the staff. They need to be able to compare and contrast the behavior and competence of different staff members, and to rehearse all the protests they want to make about conference organization, methods, and management. For this reason, their common room is inviolate to the staff. Once in their own common room, members can be assured that no member of the staff will be present by accident or design to overhear anything they may say.

In the same way, however, the staff too in their worry about the conference and about themselves want to be able to have not only technical discussions about what is happening and what they should do next, but also the opportunity to deal, in private, with their own anxieties, their own interpersonal conflicts, and their own feelings of inadequacy in the situations they have created. They also want to talk about the members. For this reason, they too have their own common room, which not only serves them as a workroom, but is also a place where they can relax, where their behavior is on view only to one another and not to the members.

Given this segregation, it is easier for members and staff to meet in the bar over drinks, to mix in the dining room, and to talk about the conference or about anything else.

Not all places where conferences are held provide enough accommodation for workrooms, lecture rooms, and common rooms, and complete geographical separation is not always possible. In these settings, we have to make the separations by time. If an exclusive common room has to be used by staff and members for work, then for that time only is it declared not to be a common room. At all other times it is a common room to which common-room regulations apply.

In the same way, in conference events, the arrangement of the furniture represents, within the constraints of what is available, the structure of the event. Thus at the opening plenary and in the plenary reviews the total staff responsible for the conference are on the platform facing the members. At the plenary sessions of the intergroup exercise the different staff roles are represented by the grouping on the platform. In the large-group event there is no platform, the chairs being arranged in two, three, or more rings depending on the number present and the shape of the particular room. In the small-group events the arrangement of the chairs, the presence or absence of a table, are left to each individual consultant — and, of course, often become matters for discussion with the group.

In short, given the tasks of the total conference and of the events within it, as defined, we do the best we can to see that the roles and structures are appropriate to, and the culture congruent with, the task performance. The test we apply to any suggested change in design or arrangement is to what extent it fits task definition and what effect it might have on task performance.

CONFERENCE EVENTS

DISCUSSION IN THE STUDY GROUP

In spite of all that has been written and said about study groups, most members appear surprised and even embarrassed when, at the beginning of the first session of the group, they find that the consultant does not behave like a traditional discussion group leader. In the opening plenary the consultant has been introduced by name to the conference; the task of the group and his role has been defined, and both have been described in the literature sent out in advance. Members nevertheless appear to expect some kind of introduction from him, even if it is only an announcement that the session should start.

Though there are, of course, individual variations, most consultants start as they intend to continue. That is, they study

95

the behavior of the group, which includes their own contribution to it, and intervene only when they think that their intervention will illuminate what they believe to be happening. They therefore seldom speak until they have some evidence of behavior on which to base what they have to say. At the beginning of a series of study groups, they can have little or no evidence about the behavior of the specific group. Hence, they remain silent.

At the first session of one study-group series the group, most of whose members had heard or read about consultant behavior in study groups, arrived, more or less together, a few minutes before the session was due to begin. I arrived as the last members were going in, and went straight to one of the armchairs that I had previously arranged in a circle. There were two or three low tables in the circle on which ashtrays had been placed. There was a lively chatter as the members sat down, moved the tables to more convenient places, asking each other if they smoked, moved again to allow two friends to sit next to each other (it was not completely heterogeneous). Gradually, the chatter died down, until at the time the session was due to start there was complete silence. It was as though everyone had not only been looking at his watch (I did not observe anybody doing so), but had previously synchronized it with every other one. The members turned to me. I remained silent. After a few seconds, the member sitting on my right suggested that everybody should introduce himself. He announced his name and the organization from which he came. He was followed by the member on his right, and so on round the group until the introductions finished with the member on my left. Before I could work out—and still less have time to say — what this meant in terms of group behavior, in such a way that any comment I made could help the group to understand why it had ignored my non-participation in this way, two members started to discuss a particularly brutal murder that had taken place two days before, and was still front-page news in the daily press. Gradually, other members joined in, and the discussion, which was very serious, ranged over other similar crimes and on to capital punishment.

After fifteen minutes the discussion started to falter, contributions appeared to become forced, various attempts to revive the discussion by introducing new aspects of the incident and its implications were not taken up. Embarrassment grew, members found it difficult to look at each other, and started to look at me again. After about twenty minutes there was silence and I made my first comment. I said that I felt that so far as the group was concerned I was the one who had been 'murdered', in that I had been prevented from getting on with my task. I pointed out that the group had been discussing an external event and had paid little attention to what was happening 'here and now', but that by their serious discussion they had made it difficult for me to intervene. I added that I felt that the faltering and embarrassment arose because members were feeling guilty about what they had done to me; but that they had done it to escape from the task they had met to perform. This comment was greeted with scorn and derision:

'We certainly haven't murdered you — what a way to talk!'

'I've never heard such nonsense. I'd just forgotten you were there.'

'You were perfectly free to join in the discussion.'

But I was not free to join in the discussion, except in so far as I believed that my contribution would be pertinent to the study of group behavior. In Bion's terms, the prevailing assumption at the beginning was dependent; when I failed to take the role of leader of the dependent group, the member on my right stepped in; when that failed, a pair of members took over and the assumption was 'pairing', but the lead they gave produced 'flight'. My comment turned this into 'fight', with myself as the object of the hostility.

On another occasion at the start of a series of study groups the same lead was given—that is 'let us introduce ourselves'—but at the end of the introductions there was another awkward and embarrassed silence. And while I was wondering what to say:

'Well, we didn't learn much from that—in fact I've forgotten most of the names already. I seldom do pick them up the first time.'

So the members went round the group again, but not so systematically, asking each other questions: how to spell names, what each other's organizations did. This conversation died as the other had done, in embarrassed silence. Slapping his hands on the table (on this occasion we were in upright chairs round a table) a member said loudly:

'Well, that's cleared the decks!'

I commented that they had perhaps been cleared for a fight and that the fight was going to be against me for not doing what was expected of me—for not giving the kind of leadership they expected. I pointed to their hostility, shown by lack of support, to others who had tried to take a lead. The members individually and collectively denied they had any such feelings:

'I don't feel hostile, but I do feel afraid of what is going to happen. If only we had a clear purpose.' .

'We need to establish formalities to enable us to discuss.'

'We're trying to find a common denominator. This is an unnatural situation. The trouble is that nothing is happening. There is nothing to study. We're not competing for a job or anything...(a pause, in which tension in the group could be felt to mount). We all look at Mr. Rice...(then another pause). For God's sake somebody else talk!'

And the tension was broken by laughter.

Even though members have been told what their task is, they find the absence of the traditional leader, who will instruct them in how to tackle it—a task that is in reality difficult—worrying and even frightening. They feel as though they are being threatened by their lack of progress. Most groups struggle with this situation, and in the struggle seem able only to unite in hostility towards the consultant because he does little to relieve their distress. The assumption seems to be that he could help, if he would, and that it is only perversity on his part—or a trick, or manipulation — that stops him. He does not care enough for them, but when he suggests that they hate him for this:

'I don't understand what all this talk of hatred is about, I don't feel hatred for anybody here, not even for the consultant.'

'It's nonsense, I don't hate him, but I think he should speak more often. After all he's paid to do that and we've paid to listen to him.'

Later these expressions modify:

I don't understand all this talk of hatred and hostility, but I certainly get irritated with the way he keeps on harping on the subject. I'd forgotten he was here. I was interested in the topic.'

'He said he's not here to teach. I think he's here to enrich the Tavvy's experience.'

'Hell, I didn't pay for that!'

These exchanges lead usually to more overt discussion of 'leadership' and the qualities required of a leader. Invariably, the discussions become more abstract and intellectual:

'The leader has to personalize himself.'

'A leader has to be a man of integrity; he has to create an organization.'

'He has to see that the group gets on with its job, and provide the necessary equipment and knowledge to do it. If the group hasn't got it, it's his job to see that it is obtained.'

If the consultant intervenes, as he does, to suggest that it is his leadership that is found wanting, he is, in the early stages, either ignored or reassured. He is told that they are trying hard, but just have not got the knowledge. He is accused of holding back, or he is asked to elucidate some difficult point. Although it is not often said directly, he gets the impression that if only he would relent and give just a short dissertation on leadership, all would be well. Members show distress more openly, and when this happens others look at him with a 'There, see what you have done.' If he points out that the group is behaving as if it only had to produce a sufficiently moving case to make him try to do what he knows to be impossible, the group either gets angry with him or displays still more distress.

At some stage, particularly when he has prefaced some intervention with 'I feel that...', he is brusquely told that his feelings are his own concern and that the group is not interested in them. As the sessions follow each other, there is occasionally an attempt, usually short-lived, to create a more familiar type of organization. Somebody suggests that a chairman and a secretary should be appointed, agenda and minutes prepared. Only one group that I have worked with has ever got to the point of electing members to these roles, and on that occasion only one said that he would accept office, but even he changed his mind before taking it:

'Don't we need a chairman to organize our discussions? He could bring out people and keep order.'

'He could fertilize our discussion and direct it so that it doesn't wander.'

'I was scared stiff when you suggested me for chairman. I knew just what you'd do to me if I accepted.'

'How do you mean "what we would do to you"?'

'You'd treat me as you've — I mean we've — treated Mr. Rice, or anybody else who has tried to get us to work at our job.'

With the failure of the members to sustain intellectual discussions either of group problems in general or of leadership problems in particular, and with their inability to arrive at any acceptable form of organization, there frequently follows a period of depression and hopelessness. There is nothing to be learnt from this exercise: 'It is a waste of time' and 'It was a mistake to come' are common remarks. Members often deal with the depression by making jokes and by maintaining a strenuous belief that silences are no longer disturbing:

'I visited the shrine of Cardinal Wolsey this afternoon.'

'Well, we're not interested.'

'Do psychiatrists put the price up when there is silence?'

'Would it be useful if I suggested...'

A chorus of 'No!'

'It's strange, but I don't find it nearly so difficult to tolerate silence as I did at the beginning. I feel more at home with you all.'

And when one member who had been silent for an unusually long time was asked why:

'I'm practicing to be a consultant!'

Gradually, this kind of joking behavior, interspersed with long and often discursive discussions about group process, about leadership in other situations, well-known leaders, religious conversions, the bringing up of children, usually leads to a more hopeful discussion about what has been learned: the toleration of silence, the relief at being able to express feelings more openly, the reassurance that their expression need not be destructive, that there is meaning in the study group:

'Let's list some of the things we've got from this group. For example, we know what we mean when we say a group fights or runs away; that it is dependent on its leader; that we let pairs try to find solutions for us; the group splits in different ways about different things, and different people take the lead, not necessarily those who should do. These very things happen back home in our boardrooms, departments, schools, and committees. If we have these things pointed out when we're experiencing them, they really mean something, they really come home.'

At this stage I am accepted, even praised, as the 'leader' who has brought this about. But this phase invariably takes place long before the end of the series. My refusal to go into collusion with the group in assessing how well it has done, and my interpretation of the 'stock-taking' as an attempt to escape the end of the group before the end has been reached, frequently lead, after denials, to a discussion of the techniques of running groups. If I go on to point out that the group appears to be assuming that, because we know that 'projection' takes place, we shall avoid it in future, the group tends to turn to an examination of my 'skill' in taking groups. If I then take this up as an attempt to make me once more into the 'good' leader, who will not let them go away empty-handed, there is either more joking or a further period of depression:

'What were we talking about that we were so keen to get on with?'

(Silence)

'We were talking about why we attacked and ran away, and why we didn't seem able to control it.'

(Silence)

'Something about groups and individuals who make them up.'

(Silence)

And even irritation and anger seem useless. The depression comes from the realization that there is no escape from work if group behavior is to be understood. A renewed attack on me or on the conference as a whole is normal, but by now the attacks are more sophisticated, and the inquiry into their origin and form is more deliberate and penetrating. Members who take a lead are not 'destroyed' so briskly and the reasons for dissatisfaction with their leadership are examined more closely. In one group a member said:

'I feel everything I thought I'd learnt has been useless; even what I thought I knew when I came seems of little value now,'

— and she burst into tears. But when other members of the group tried to comfort her and to reassure her that she was good at her job:

'Don't be such fools. I can at least cry here and look at why I'm crying.'

Not only is the group preoccupied with its ending, but feelings about it are the more intense because the group will finish before the end of the conference. By this time it is always difficult for members to accept the special nature of the study group and hence the reality of the need to finish it early; to acknowledge that it has only a limited value within the context of the conference. In this dilemma it is not unusual for members to say that the experience has been useless and has no value outside the conference setting, and that therefore the group can be disbanded without compunction or regret. But they find it difficult to accept that it can have been entirely useless when they have spent so much time in it. If, by contrast, they believe it to have been a wonderful experience, then it should not end before it has to, that is, at the end of the conference. Hence, its ending is either a major act of hostility on the part of the staff of which the consultant is a member, or the members have been misled by the staff into thinking the group would be more productive than it has been — and this too has been the consultant's fault for not making it better. Study groups usually end with members having feelings both of relief at the end of a trying experience and of regret and mourning for something valuable that has been lost. But if, mixed with these feelings, there can be some work at what ending means, then perhaps the study group has achieved its aim.

CONSULTANT TO A STUDY GROUP

Most members of study groups attend them to learn about what happens in groups. They know that this means the study of their own as well as of others' behavior. They know that their own behavior will be exposed to the scrutiny of the consultant and of their fellow members. They suspect that, though the consultant will not comment on them as individuals, what he says will refer to them and may imply cirticism of their past behavior.

In the group the consultant has only his own observations and feelings to guide him. He can feel worried, rejected, angry, confused, and embarrassed; or he can feel calm, wanted, happy, and relaxed. He can ask himself why he is feeling as he is feeling, and judge what arises from within himself as part of his own personality make-up and what comes from the group, what the group is projecting upon him. He can ask himself what these expressions of feeling mean it terms of group behavior, and why the group is treating him in this way. If he can explain his feelings, and why they have arisen, he may then be able to help the group to understand its own behavior.

Inherently, the members of any study group must at times feel hostile to their consultant. By becoming members of a study group and by accepting his role, they are consciously or unconsciously accepting that they need to understand more about their own behavior towards others and about others' behavior towards them. Inevitably they must hope that their learning will be largely about others, and that any change they may feel they have to make in their own behavior will not reflect on themselves, but only suggest ways of accommodating to the foibles of others. But whatever the rationalization, unconsciously they have to accept that they might have failed in the past. This acceptance in itself, as it is realized, can be felt as an affront to their self-respect. They are not likely to let it go without challenge. The consultant's job is to confront the group, without affronting its members; to draw attention to group behavior and not to individual behavior; to point out how the group uses individuals to express its own emotions, how it exploits some members so that others can absolve themselves from the responsibility for such expression.

As a group fails to get its consultant to occupy the more traditional roles of teacher, seminar leader, or therapist, it will redouble its efforts until in desperation it will disown him and seek other leaders. When they too fail, they too will be disowned, often brutally. The group will then use its own brutality to get the consultant to change his task by eliciting his sympathy and care for those it has handled so roughly. If this maneuver fails, and it never completely fails, the group will tend to throw up other leaders to express its concern for its members and project its brutality onto the consultant. As rival leaders emerge it is the job of the consultant, so far as he is able, to identify what the group is trying to do and to explain it. His leadership is in task performance, and the task is to understand what the group is doing 'now' and to explain why it is doing it. Drawing attention to interesting phenomena without explanation is seldom useful.

THE STUDY GROUP IN THE CONFERENCE

The only overt constraints placed on the study group are the definition of its task and the consultant's persistent attempt to refuse to do anything else. Members can do what they like. They frequently ask:

'Why don't we go and watch a football match, or talk about racing?'

'Why don't we take a walk in the country?'

'Why do we even bother to sit in this room?'

Nothing but group pressures and their own conscience is stopping them from doing anything they wish. No sanctions can be imposed. The only discipline is imposed on the consultant, who will not, if he is able to avoid it, go into collusion with the group to do anything other than study the behavior of the group, and that only for the time laid down in the program. He 'controls the boundary' of the group, and thus provides security for the members in three ways: he stays in role; he starts and stops on time; and he maintains confidentiality.

In practice, members of study groups discuss almost anything from leadership as an abstract concept to the kind of leadership they are getting in their own group; from external events that have nothing whatever to do with their task to their own feelings for each other. Gradually, during the course of the conference, they learn that it is possible, in the study group, to express their feelings more openly and frankly than is usual in other groups; to question assumptions about value systems that it is difficult, if not impossible to question in more conventional settings; and to build up a feeling of intimacy and security that here, in this group, they can be themselves without fear of the consequences. This is what usually gives rise to the euphoric feeling, part way through, of having learnt so much.

The first crack in this euphoria comes with the realization that the group will end, that death and coming to terms with it by adequate mourning are an essential part of any living experience. Members realize that after the end of the conference some of them may meet each other again, but that the group, as a group, will not survive the conference. If it is so valuable then some means should be found of making it live on. The reality that it will not calls into question the process by which such intimacy and such reassurance have been achieved:

'I'd never had believed this kind of feeling was possible—but what is it? I feel I know you all well, and you me, but to what end? Haven't we really been fooled all along?'

'I'll be glad when this session is over. The first time I've really felt like this.'

'I think the (coffin) lid is down and screwed home, but are we right about the identity of the corpse?'

'It's going to be a difficult grave to arrange. Whoever lies next to...will have an uncomfortable time. He's bound to turn.'

'This feeling is as hard as a wall. Nobody dares to make a serious remark.'

'There's not much time. Why do we stay here to the bitter end? There's good clean air outside.'

In the study group members are face to face with a leadership that is neither destroyed by hatred nor rendered impotent by love. The consultant accepts a task responsibility and an authority that imposes no discipline on the members. He cannot impose any sanctions for failure to cooperate in task performance, nor, perhaps more importantly, can he reward good performance. Learning is its own reward; lack of learning its own punishment. It is for many members a new task, a new kind of authority, and a new kind of leadership, whose strength they can experience for themselves. They can defend it or attack it, imitate it or denounce it; they can learn from it.

The whole experience is within their grasp; nothing that happens outside the group is relevant to the task they have to perform. As a group they have no external environment to contend with; as individuals they have only each other and themselves. It is the most simple, and at the same time the most primitive and direct, experience of the forces that impinge on them when they lead and that they bring to bear on those who lead them.

In most conferences there are between twelve and fifteen study-group sessions, two or three of which take place before any other event is started. Thereafter members have to contend with an increasing number of different events. By contrast with experience of other events, study groups, when they are not in session, are frequently said to be warm and secure:

'You know where you are in a study group. You are intimate with everybody in it. It's safe to express your feelings there.'

Thus, in spite of its impact, it is one of the conference events that provide protection for experiment in other situations. It is for this reason that, though study groups finish before the end of the conference, they continue beyond the ending of other 'here and now' experiences. Ending them before the end of the whole is an attempt to ensure that if they have gained a false value—as comforting and secure—the test of the reality, the 'let down', is taken in the conference itself, while members are still there, and have the staff and each other to help them to cope.

THE LARGE-GROUP EVENT

Many devices have been used to increase the participation of members in the events of conferences and training programs. They have been developed in the hope and belief that participation, by reducing passive attendance, makes communication more effective. Small groups have always been used for training and learning. Since the Second World War many institutional conferences have adopted a pattern whereby speakers address the whole conference, and then discussion of the lectures takes place in small groups, which subsequently reassemble in plenary session to report back to the total membership. In 1947, at a conference run jointly by the Tavistock Institute and the Industrial Welfare Society, this technique was modified in that there were few speakers, and they only set themes, leaving the members to decide the content of the conference. Many variations are now common: in some, the small groups are given a specific question to discuss, either all the same question, or different ones for different groups; in others, usually the larger conferences, sections have their own speakers. 'Buzz' sessions (in which members form small units of from two to six persons without moving out of the conference room), role-playing, sociodrama, brains trusts, panel discussions, and debates are among techniques that have been used with success. Other conferences that have been concerned with understanding problems of human relationship and leadership have introduced forms of 'joint consultation' — committees composed of members and staff—in an attempt to reproduce, in the conference, the kind of relationship and leadership the conference has been advocating. All are attempts to establish organizational mechanisms that will allow an individual member to make his views heard without exposing him to the difficulty of addressing a large group.

Even in the small group it is not easy to expose one's feelings or to put forward ideas that have not been fully formulated, but at least the attempt can be made in an atmosphere of intimacy. In the small group as compared with the large group the individual is more likely to have a chance to explain himself without being made to feel guilty about taking more than a fair share of the available time, and to speak without feeling that he will be irrevocably committed to a point of view and have little or no opportunity of correcting himself. The large group provides a more public occasion, and the greater the number present, the greater the exposure. The large group therefore poses special problems for its members and its leaders. It demands different qualities of its leaders and different kinds of communication between its members if task peformance is to be effective.

In the conferences I am describing the large-group event consists of a series of meetings of all members, together with two or more consultants from the staff. A large group, for conference purposes, is defined simply as one that is too large for face-to-face relationships. It is taken, literally, to be a group that cannot conveniently sit in one circle of a size that would allow members any hope of being able to make intimate reltionships with the members opposite to them. In the large group, because of its size, some members have to sit behind others; hence a speaker can neither see nor be seen by everyone in the group.

There are, so far as we yet know, no specific limits on the numbers that should comprise a 'large group', though the characteristics displayed by groups of certain sizes will obviously preclude them from being studied in the way we have devised for use in conferences. My own experience, not only in conferences, but in industry, commerce, government service, and education, makes me feel that with up to six members a group changes in its characteristics with each additional member; that thereafter there is a different kind of change that differéntiates a group of seven or more from one of less than seven. As the group grows from seven to eleven or twelve, other changes take place but without changing the essential characteristics of a small group. With over twelve members there is a tendency to split into subgroups; and the next 'total' group change does not take place until there are more than twenty-four or twenty-five members. Once there are more than can conveniently hear a member speak without his having to raise his voice to oratorical level or use some mechanical aid, a new dimension will certainly be added.

The smallest number we have so far used for the 'large group' is twenty, the largest fifty. My experience of acting as consultant to a large group is that, with only twenty members, even though they were sitting in two rows, I found it difficult to distinguish sufficiently between behavior that was due to the largeness of the group and behavior that I would expect in a smaller study group. Group behavior was different and more difficult to understand, but I was more aware of the difficulty than of the differences, and, in consequence, felt my interventions to be less effective than they should have been. My experience did, however, lead me to propose that for the next large-group event there should be more than one consultant, if only to avoid my being too selective in what I took up. This account is taken from the experience of Pierre Turquet and myself as joint consultants to large-group events. Even with two of us we found the task difficult, but when we did observe behavior we were more certain that what we were observing was characteristic of the large group, and was not just extrapolation from small-group experience.

THE ORIGIN OF THE EVENT

My colleagues and I had felt for some time that in our attempts to provide opportunities for members to learn about problems of leadership, we had devised for the most part only small-group situations. The exceptions were the lectures and the opening and closing plenaries. In accordance with the definition of their task and organization the former were 'led' by the lecturers, and the latter by the director and staff. The members had no opportunities to experiment for themselves in large-group situations.

Moreover, for some time we had been unhappy about our conduct of plenary sessions. No matter how well prepared the opening plenary, very little that was said appeared to communicate to members at the manifest level. We were also doubtful, and still are, about appropriate techniques for the plenaries held towards the end of the conference. Indeed, we had had some trouble in defining their primary task—they have been called by various titles: 'evaluations', 'closing plenaries', 'reviews'—and it had even been suggested that they should be dropped entirely. Earlier, we had tried having no formal presentation by a staff member but running the meetings as free-for-all discussions; so far as we could tell, little work had been done in those sessions. We had also tried having various members of the staff give their impressions of what had happened in the conference, as a stimulant to discussion, with little better result.

In the first two conferences after I became director, I reviewed the conference as seen from my role. I gave a lecture which was intended to set a framework for subsequent discussion. Towards the end of the conference that immediately preceded the one in which the large-group event was introduced, I closed my lecture in the following way:

'...work groups can behave with sophistication and maturity, and we can use the basic assumptions to assist task peformance; the emotions associated with one basic assumption are then used to control and suppress the emotions associated with others. Mature work groups expect their leaders to mobilize the appropriate assumption for task performance. If the appropriate assumption is dependent, the leader has to be dependable but realistic; if pairing, potent, but with due regard to the limitations of his potency; if fight, constructively aggressive, brave but not foolhardy; if flight, able to extricate the group from a difficult situation, but no coward; nor must he expect to be able to solve all the group's problems in the process of extrication.

This conference ends the day after tomorrow. The task before us and the kind of leadership I have to give seem clear.'

At the time that I gave that review, I had a feeling—shared by most members of the staff—that some of the anger that members felt towards the staff had not come out during the conference, and that we were in danger of finishing without having exposed a major problem of leadership. I had therefore set out to give as good an account as I could of what I thought the conference had been up to. I had tried to give a demonstration of dependable leadership. I hoped that if this could be experienced, then there was a chance that in the remainder of the present session and in the whole of the second session we could mobilize the fight-flight basic assumption, to get into the open some of the anger that had not been expressed, and subsequently mobilize 'flight' as a sophisticated way to end the conference.

I spoke in all for forty-five minutes, making use of many diagrams (based on those prepared for my theoretical lecture on organization [Rice, 1963]) to illustrate my theme. I had stated that I was putting forward one framework as a possible basis for the consideration of conference events, and invited others to make alternative suggestions. As soon as I had finished speaking members started to ask questions. At the time I felt strongly that the questions were not asked to clarify what I had said but rather to prolong the lecturer/audience relationship:

'How does this conference compare with others you have held?'

'How do you judge whether a conference has been successful?'

I felt that the members were behaving in this way to avoid the work involved in reviewing the conference experience—though I was less clear than I should have been about what 'review' meant. My evidence was that I was being asked to go on feeding information; but nobody appeared to have taken much notice of the information I had already given. None of the questions seemed to bear any relation to what I had said. I had, of course, to wonder whether what I had said had been so superficial or inaccurate as to be inadequate as a review. I had some evidence that this was not so: while I had been speaking, members had been leaning forward in their chairs, had seemed very attentive, had responded to my mood—laughing at the humor and showing feeling at the more serious passages—and were now paying great deference to me in the way they asked their questions.

With all these feelings inside me I did not answer the questions I had been asked, but I did comment on what I thought the conference was trying to do to me and why. I said I thought that the members were refusing to accept that I had told them what I could, that they still believed that I had all the answers, if only I would, like them, believe in my own omniscience. I explained that if I did this, however, I would fail, and thus give them a justification for ignoring me and what at the moment I symbolized--the conference experience. I pointed out that the questions I had been asked were unrealistic: this conference was not yet finished and so could not be compared with earlier ones; and I wondered how I could measure success, when success was to be judged by what the members had learned, not by what I had learned or though they had.

Members became obviously angry; there were intakes of breath, mutters of 'nonsense', the last questioner looked very aggrieved. Some members subsequently described the incident as 'shocking'. But—and this is where something went wrong— the anger did not really come into the open until after the session. I learned subsequently that groups of members — mainly from study groups—had collected together in the bar and in the common room and had expressed great indignation about the way they had been treated. There was talk of organized protest and much writing of manifestos.

The second session, on the following morning, opened silently. After some desultory discussion one member read out notes that he said resulted from a private members' meeting held on the previous night. He summarized what members had felt about the unfairness of my behavior, and he acknowledged his own anger, and his frustration at not being able to express it at the time. There was a long silence when he had finished. He then burst out:

'What has happened to all those of you who were expressing so much indignation last night? Why aren't you doing it again now? We have been asked to do it if we want to, but nobody seems to be accepting the invitation.'

Subsequently, members did work at reviewing the conference, but seemed more preoccupied with the problems of review in so large a group than with the conference itself. It was clear that they felt they had had too little experience in working in large groups, at least in the conference setting, to be effective. By not answering questions unless I felt sure that they were genuine inquiries related to the review — a lead followed by other members of the staff who were on the platform—I had destroyed a traditional form of platform/audience organization and had thrown the members back on their own resources.

During the second session members talked to each other, answered each other's questions, argued with each other as well as with the staff, and at one time set up what appeared as a debate with proposer and seconder on one side of the room and opposer and seconder on the other. At that stage I was presumably cast in the role of independent chairman. There was, however, insufficient time or sanction, within the context of a plenary session called to review the conference, to explore all the kinds of organizational machinery that were available and to use them. Some of the anger came out: I had 'blinded them with science', 'put up diagrams of structure to avoid describing the culture', and so on; but there was little time to work out the reasons for these feelings, either real or fantasy.

It is worth noting, in parenthesis, that whatever I did to the members, I certainly mobilized a fight in the staff group, but against myself, and, as with the members, delayed in its manifestation. My colleagues gave me a very rough time in the staff common room after the first plenary session. They expressed considerable dislike of the way I had handled the session, and dismay at the content of my review: it was too complete; did not leave the members anything to say; too facile; too theoretical; they did not know what I had been getting at; could not follow my reasoning and doubted my interpretations of members' behavior; but they had not felt sure enough of themselves to take me to task in public.

THE PRIMARY TASK OF THE LARGE GROUP

The experience of this review and consideration of previous attempts to get work done in plenary reviews suggested that we had set two tasks for plenaries: first, to review the conference, and second, to examine behavior in a large-group setting. In the review we presumably meant to help members to articulate at least some of their experience, to try to catalogue something of what they had learned, and to see how they could report when they went back to the organizations that had sent them. We had pre-supposed some experience of working in large groups but had not provided any opportunities in the conference for such learning other than at lectures and in the intergroup exercise. The task of the intergroup exercise is to examine what is happening in a specific event; it will be discussed in the next chapter. Lectures are traditional, and exchanges between lecturer and audience after the lecture are customary. By delivering a lecture as an opening to the conference review, I had raised legitimate expectations about my subsequent behavior. By behaving as I did I had affronted the members, and they were right to be angry with me and to complain of 'shock'. Certainly I carried over experience of study groups into the large group and sought to make interpretations of behavior for which I had no sanction, and which, on reflection, would have been more appropriate to a study group than to a large group.

We have now therefore introduced the large-group event into the conference program. Its primary task is to study the phenomena of large-group behavior as they happen. The consultants' role is to help with this task. Their technique is, as in the study group, to use their observations and feelings to enable them to discern what is happening. But now they are faced by more complex phenomena than in the small group. The possible interpersonal relationships and subgroupings are more numerous, anonymity is easier to maintain, and boundaries are more difficult to draw.

THE CONTENT OF THE LARGE GROUP

The same kinds of phenomenon, of course, occur in the large group as in the small face-to-face group. The whole group can act on the same assumption, and often appears to seek to do so,, but more frequently the assumption is not unanimous — there is more room for opposition, and more rivals for leadership emerge.

The member of the study group has the problem of relating himself to a few other members. He learns, without structure or directions, to find his way about the various relationships he makes; to say what he feels about others and to accept their feelings about him. When he joins the large group, he has at least two other kinds of relationship available to him: his membership of the study group, with which he has already learned to identify himself; and his relationships with other members of the conference, some of whom he may know in a different way and more closely outside the conference setting, at home or at work. But other members of the large group, whether previously known to him or not, may themselves be members of other study groups, about whose behavior and progress he is likely to have become curious. He has probably already discovered at meals and on other social occasions, with some surprise, that, irrespective of different memberships and of different consultants, all study groups are struggling with much the same kinds of problem. In that sense, he can identify with these others as members of the conference going through the same kind of experience. In his own study group, however, he has become identified with his fellow members as individuals; and members of other groups, even though known to him, tend to be seen mainly as outsiders.

In the large group, therefore, in addition to the difficulty of trying to understand his own and others' behavior, the member of the study group faces many of the others as members of other study groups. He has to face his fantasies about their relationships with each other. He can hardly but project onto them feelings about his own group. He soon finds, however, that when he speaks he speaks as an individual and cannot speak for his group. He has then no group of his own but confronts other groups. He attributes cohesiveness and congruence to other groups that in the large group he cannot feel for his own.

'Why is it that I feel so at home with my study group, but as soon as I come into this room— and (*with a gesture*) there you all are—I no longer feel as though I am at one with you? As soon as I speak, I suddenly feel left on my own.'

'It's bad enough in a small group to feel isolated, but in this room, with this number of people here, and some sitting behind, it's even worse.'

'I'm looking for my friends—those I came here with—but they're in other study groups, they've got different consultants. It's not the same.'

At the opening of one large-group event the furniture available in the room consisted of twelve comfortable armchairs and a large number of hard wooden chairs. For the first session Dr. Turquet and I had arranged the comfortable chairs in as small a circle as they would form, with one row, and for parts of the circle two rows, of hard chairs outside of them. We occupied two of the comfortable chairs, but sat apart with two chairs between us so that we could not exchange signals or looks without making a movement that would be open for all to see. When the first members came in, they took hard chairs outside the inner circle, some fetching spare chairs that had been pushed out of the way and making a fourth row. Gradually, the inner circle of armchairs filled up, but the members who moved to them did so self-consciously and defiantly. The last two to arrive took the two comfortable chairs between us. All the time there was a lively chatter going on between members, though all were watching the way the room filled up.

That was the first session; thereafter for the next three sessions a kind of game was played with the seating. When Dr. Turquet and I arrived for the second session only two chairs in the inner circle were vacant and they, next to each other. I took one of them, but he spontaneously moved to one on the outer ring. At the beginning of the third, all the comfortable chairs were filled when we arrived. Dr. Turquet took one in the second row and I one in the third. In discussion some references were made to the seating: the comfort-discomfort, and the need to arrive early to get a comfortable seat; the feeling that the armchairs provided an inner caucus — but the game with the seating was a mild form of test of us. Would we behave differently if we sat in different places? Would we too compete for comfort?

In the first session of one large-group event the lively conversation that had been going on as the members collected died down a few minutes after the official time of starting; there was a brief silence and then a member suggested that they should begin by comparing notes about study groups, a suggestion that was accepted but followed up only in a desultory and general manner; nobody gave any specific details that could be discussed and compared. Members had to keep saying that they were speaking only as individuals and not on behalf of their groups. The problem, it seemed to us — as indeed we commented — was that of establishing the boundaries of the large group. But apparently this could be done only by examining the boundaries that existed within the large group. The study groups, however, existed to study their own behavior and no member had any sanction to discuss what went on in his study group outside the group. This led to a long discussion about the appropriateness of the large group to study its own behavior.

'This is not the size of group we would ever use for educational purposes — it is too large. Everybody knows that groups of forty are impossible.'

'The fifty people in this room don't form a group. There's nothing to get hold of.'

Even apart from the difficulty that many members appeared to have with counting, one would have thought from their comments that groups of a similar size never happened outside the conference. The interesting point is perhaps that, at this stage of the large-group event, it does not seem to matter how many actually constitute the group; it is never the appropriate size, and it is always one that does not exist in real life. There is usually little need for the consultants to point out the obvious error — in the large group some member will not only draw attention to it, but will also give an explanation for the denial:

'I seem to be the only person in this room who regularly has to deal with groups of this size! I don't believe it and I think we're all avoiding our job here now.'

At this point it is not unusual for some member to confess that, although he cannot rely on the support of his study group for anything he says, he has spent the first few minutes looking round to make sure that all his fellow members are present:

'Well, my study group is all here, I've counted, and somehow, this is comforting.'

But others, quick to note any sense of complacency, ask if that is because he thinks his group is better than any other, and the discussion about study-group and large-group boundaries tends to be resumed. The same discussion occurs at intervals during the event, and, at times, one cannot avoid the impression that, by contrast with the large group, the study group appears as a warm, cosy, intimate group with a well-defined task and a serious sense of purpose—an impression that is quite contrary to the reality of any study group of which I have been a member or to which I have been a consultant. In the later sessions it is possible to draw attention to the small groups as the keepers of the large-group morality; to demonstrate that, though in the large group they may appear to dissolve, yet, symbolically, they are points of reference that determine the way in which individuals should be treated, even if in the large group they are treated quite differently.

By the second or third session, periods of which have been frankly dull and boring, the attempts to use study groups or other groupings that arise outside the large group as alternatives to the large group are acknowledged to have yielded little result, and attention is turned to the large group itself. Attempts to define the boundaries in terms of the task invariably fail. There are always too many members ready to say that they feel nothing; that they have no sense of loyalty to the group as a group; they talk either of hoping to learn something, or of doubting that they will come again or even stay for the particular session:

'I don't feel anything here, nothing happens. Nobody has any constructive suggestions to make. But we could all do one thing —we could leave, and not meet tomorrow.'

In one group, this question gave rise to an alternative proposal, which was to split into smaller groups to discuss the problem and then report back to the whole:

'If we split here (*making a gesture that separated Dr. Turquet and myself*), we might have more chance of coming to some conclusion.'

This suggestion led to a lively discussion, in which two parties were formed — split and the anti-split. The discussion became acrimonious, the anti-split party arguing that to split would defeat the object of the exercise; the split party demanding some kind of 'experiment', even if the experiment jeopardized the continuation of the large group. During these exchanges—which went on intermittently for several sessions— Dr. Turquet and I tried to clarify what we thought to be happening. We pointed to the apparent need to find some abstract concept outside the group to which we could subscribe; to the need to have something — an ideal, a faith, or an enemy — which would define the group's boundaries and allow a leader to arise to embody the group purpose. A rational task was not enough. The alternative appeared to be to find the in- and the out-groups within the large group itself — each with its own recognized leaders. We made the hypothesis that what was feared was the undirected, unstructured power of the group, the fear of its potential violence. We took as our evidence the comfort and liveliness of the acrimonious debate that had developed, the reassurance that was felt as soon as an anti-group had been found to oppose the power of the group, the attempt to split us by enlisting us into opposing camps. If the group could neither find something outside itself to give it definition, nor guarantee acceptable and conflicting parties within, the only possibility appeared to be complete impotence, or discussion that dealt only in trivialities:

'It seems we can be united only if we are split; we can become one only if we are more than one.'

This theme, with more sophisticated variations, and with discussions of its parallels in real life — party politics and the concept of parliament, management and trade unions — is a constant preoccupation of the large group. How to control the potential destructiveness of the large group, and the fear that, in spite of individual choice, it could get out of hand in a crisis. At times one of us has been awarded a halo and the other horns; there have been attempts — part realistic and part fanciful — to analyse the differences between us as role-takers and, far less directly, as persons. Escape into laughter is easy, but the impression is of passing time rather than of working.

Time and time-keeping become important. It is as though time itself can provide a boundary; that the large group exists only for the time of the session and what happens in between starting and stopping the session is irrelevant. But the testing of this boundary soon proves that it is fragile. In one session of a large-group event nearly all the members were sitting in the room some five or more minutes early. Everyone appeared to be in lively conversation with his nearby neighbors. At the time the session was due to start there was a sudden silence — and nobody apparently had anything to say. After some minutes a fitful discussion started about the difficulty of talking in the large group, and when the contrast between immediately before and immediately after the starting time was pointed out, some members said that the earlier talking had been between individuals and that there had been no group "present". At the following session, though members were obviously aware of the time, as shown by the numerous glances at watches, there was no sharp dividing line, and the boundary of time had been broken.

At other sessions there have been suggestions to leave early, or to move out and move in again; and members have tried experiments, sometimes singly, sometimes in small groups. But none of the experiments has aroused much feeling in the group as a whole. Those who have left one session early have been accepted at the following session without question or with only casual non-caring questions about how they felt. Those who have announced that they were going out

'for ten minutes, and will then return to test whether what one of the consultants said yesterday about our being afraid to go out because we might not be allowed in again is true or not,'

have themselves, on their return, not been sure whether they have proved anything.

But leaving that is due not to deliberate experiment but to group and personal pressures has given ample evidence of the fear of the potential indiscriminate destructiveness of the large unstructured group. At one conference, the fourth session of a seven-session large-group event coincided with a first division football match in the city. About six members chose the football match instead of the session. They just did not turn up. On the same day another member had to be away at a function in his own job and he had announced this in advance. In spite of his friends' protestations that he had apologized in advance and even that a condition of his being released to attend the conference had been his fulfilling this particular engagement, there was far more discussion of his absence and of his motives for it than of the absence and motives of those who had gone to the football match.

Later in the session the group referred to the empty chairs that had been left in the second row by the absentees and asked the three who were in the third row — of whom I was one — to move. After some discussion about my sitting where I was, and an invitation to move, which I did not accept, the group turned to the two others. One announced that he liked it where he was and was staying there; the other commented that he felt more a part of the group than he had ever felt before:

'...probably because I feel that it is the first time that anybody has paid any attention to me. It appears you have to get outside this group to get anybody in it to take any notice of you.'

There was some discussion of leading from outside and of nihilism inside, and the member then got up, saying:

'Since you want to complete the circle I will now join you,'

but as he moved to an empty chair in the second row:

"How do you know we want you now?"

and he was left, embarrassed, being invited by some to sit down and being asked by others if he felt welcome. He sat down, but within seconds he got up saying:

'It seems I'm not wanted, so I'll go,'

and left the room. As he went, the discussion returned immediately to those who were sitting outside the circle: why they did it and what effect it had on the group. After some minutes one member burst out:

'I believe we have just committed an act of violence,'

to be followed by an outbreak of statements about why the particular member had just left. He had not wanted to come; he had said at the beginning that if the session was as futile as the last one, he would leave before the end; it has always been his intention to go — statements that were belied by his obvious embarrassment and discomfort, and his hesitation both on his way to the door and when he got there. Both Dr. Turquet and I drew attention to the way we were all shedding responsibility for what had happened, blaming it all on the individual. This led to a long and acrimonious discussion about who had said what and why, and there were moves to stop the session at once. Those who, up to this time, had been silent then started to express their concern, their feeling of helplessness:

'I can't understand how we could be so heartless, I'm shocked by our cruelty to — and we still sit here doing nothing. I feel terrible about it and I'm doing nothing. I can't avoid the responsibility, but I can't carry it either.'

In subsequent sessions when this member had returned, and so had those who had been to the football match, it was acknowledged that the person they had wanted to get at was me, but they had picked somebody else sitting 'outside' the group instead; and that even getting at me was a displacement of their anger at those who had attended the football match, and thus expressed their contempt for the group and its activities. My own responsibility as director in having so arranged the program that the session coincided with the football match was not taken up until two sessions later, and by that time the mood of the group was one in which the conference in general and the large group in particular were being idealized as a learning situation, and there were too many ready to leap to my defense for the hostility to be very manifest.

The need for some form of structure, however rudimentary, is often shown by the ease with which the attention of the group can be focused. At the beginning of a session, closing the door, somebody moving his chair, even coughing, seems enough to bring the meeting to order. Subsequently, just standing up to make a statement stops all discussion at once, or, if anybody does go on talking, he or she is told in no uncertain terms to shut up. But such rudimentary structures are accepted for the relief they bring — somebody is going to do something, anything, so long as it avoids examination of what lies behind behavior here and now. Any attempt to look seriously at an incident such as that described above can lead to anarchy, in which any constructive suggestion is either destroyed at once or, equally effective from the point of view of avoiding real work at studying behavior, blown up to preposterous proportions. On one occasion the suggestion that we should look at what had just happened had become, before the end of the session, a proposal to appoint a secretary to write the history of the large group and of the other events of the conference that impinged on the large group. The session ended with a spurious voting procedure which, like so many voting procedures, was quite inconclusive, and by which nobody felt, or perhaps even had the slightest intention of feeling, bound.

As the group grows more experienced in dealing with an unfamilar situation there is some recognition that the group and those who lead it can be used by individual members for the projection of many of their more primitive impulses. Unlike the small group, for which as a member the individual accepts some responsibility, the large group, being so difficult to control, so anonymous, can be an easier receptacle of feelings and urges that most of us would disown.

'Yes, this ties up with what I learnt last night. When I accused people of being childish and then I had a discussion with one of the people I had so accused, I recognized that what made me so angry was the childish part of myself which I had put into them.'

'I divide people into three kinds: there are those I think agree with me; there are those who don't but I think I can work with them and discuss it; and there are those I don't even want to talk to, and they are the bastards in here.'

'Now I've been sitting here all this time and nobody has done anything to me. I've wanted to know how people have been feeling, but I haven't dared to ask — but I've learnt I can't absolve myself from responsibility for what this group, of which I am a member, has been doing to other people, even though I've been sitting back doing nothing. People all round the room have at various times in these sessions shown that they need help, but all we do is just sit back.'

'The painful thing I have learned about myself is my willingness to sacrifice others.'

This use of the large group also means that if an individual feels he has something good to contribute — and members made many insightful comments — then the very contribution arouses all his own paranoid fantasies. He fears in advance that it will be destroyed and that the group will do it. But because it is also a part of himself that will contribute to the destruction he hesitates, and does not express his real feelings until he has found out if he is going to get support.

'Why didn't you put it more clearly and make it a proper proposition?'

'Well, I wanted an echo before I could do anything definite. I was just talking, waiting, but if there's an echo and I have support, yes, I will propose...'

'I see bits of myself in everybody here, and some of them I don't like.'

The recognition that many of the organizations we invent, the controls we accept in our everyday life, are not so much constructive attempts to solve our problems as defenses against our own lightly buried primitive impulses can be painful. So also can be the recognition that what we find so difficult to tolerate, and will go to considerable lengths to deny, is uncertainty about our decisions and inability to understand our human problems.

CONSULTANTS TO THE LARGE GROUP

I do not know how many consultants there should be to how large a group. I have so far worked on my own and with one other colleague. On my own I found myself bewildered by much that was happening; I would no sooner work out something to my satisfaction than I would realize that a change had taken place. I was always trying to catch up with my own thinking and feeling. I found myself at the end of sessions unable to recall what had happened or what had been said, and quite empty of ideas. When I have worked with Pierre Turquet I have felt reassured by his presence. I might not know what is happening, but he might. And if he has not known either, then at least a colleague whose insight I respect and trust is in equal difficulty and I can comfort myself that it may not be entirely my own stupidity or insensitivity that is leading me astray.

More positively, I believe we have complemented each other in the events we have taken together, seeing sometimes the same evidence but from different points of view, and sometimes different pieces of evidence that have been mutually illuminating. We have each had, in the other, a point of reference, and in analysing our feelings for each other we have, I am sure, been able to see more clearly what the group has been doing to us. In our discussions after the sessions we have at least both been talking about the same events and have been able to compare our reactions to them and to each other's interventions. In particular, in both sessions and subsequent discussions we have been able to study the roles in which we have been cast by the group and which we have accepted or rejected, and our reasons for acceptance and rejection. And when we have both been bewildered, we have, in some measure, been able to ask each other why; and when, as has sometimes happened, we have found different reasons for our bewilderment, the very differences have enabled us to understand what the group was projecting onto us to cause it.

I think that so far we have both found it more difficult to maintain austere professional roles in large groups than in study groups. By that I mean that we have both entered more into the mood of the group, laughing at the jokes, worrying about individuals, feeling helpless to stop somebody's being hurt and guilty about our own inaction. But that, maybe, is because neither of us is yet sufficiently skillful.

The phenomena with which we deal in the large group are more primitive, more complex, and more diffuse than in the small group; intervention has to be more direct and forceful. The most important characteristic of the large group is that it is large. Without an abstract ideal or an external enemy its boundaries are difficult to define; without boundaries, and hence without even an elemental structure, action is impulsive and hence potentially dangerous; the group's very freedom to experiment can become anarchy. The study of the large group as a group is thus made the more difficult because the object of study is itself so tenuous. In this emotional climate the members turn to the consultants for reassurance that they, at least, can control the violence; the fear, and it is shared by the consultants, is that they too will be unable to act quickly or wisely enough to avert disaster.

Again because of its size, and the amount of 'noise' — in engineering terms — it can create, the large group is able to ignore its task and its consultants for a long time. Denial of difficulty, refusal to look at what is happening, are easier. Distractions are many, and as consultants we frequently found ourselves distracted, but without being aware of it, without being so certain, as in a study group, that what we were observing was intended to distract. We both found ourselves fed with so much information that we frequently floundered in our attempts to extract what was relevant to the task of the group, to distinguish when it was working at its task and when it was playing. As individuals, we have to be aware of , and accept, a close scrutiny of our behavior, as distinct from what we say. Members concentrate less on us as individuals than on the similarities and differences between us, denying the difference when they want us to be united to hold the group together, emphasizing them when they want to split the group and to play one of us off against the other. We have to use our own awareness of our support for each other and of our conflicts to test the reality of their feelings against their projections upon us.

Sometimes we answer questions directly, but attempt so far as we can to answer them in the light of the task we have set ourselves. As on one occasion, when Pierre Turquet was asked if he would express his real feelings now, he replied:

'Bewildered.'

And that faced the group with the problem of his fallibility, at a time when they had been trying to believe him omniscient. In the large group, even more than in the small group, the consultant is very tempted to take a traditional leadership role; the need for a leader and for structure is so manifest and the fear of violence is so great. It is easier in the large group to forget that groups can also be constructive, and so allow oneself to be seduced into trying to be its saviour.

THE LARGE GROUP IN THE CONFERENCE

Members of earlier conferences in which there was no large-group event, who have attended recent ones for more advanced training, have told us that the large group appears to be dealing with what, at previous conferences, had to be dealt with by the members in their own informal meetings. At first there appeared to be some danger that the large group would become a mopping-up operation, and would thus put all small groups together — study groups, intergroup exercise, and application groups — and avoid the contrasts of experience that these different events were intended to afford. We now believe that it is an experience in its own right, and that it adds a new dimension to the learning situations provided, offering an opportunity that some members of previous conferences used to make for themselves. When that happened, however, the results could not then manifest themselves until the plenary review sessions, and then, because the end of the conference was so near, they could not be adequately worked out in the remaining time.

The large group is the one event, apart from the more formal plenaries, in which members can experience the forces that a large group brings to bear on its leaders, in a setting where the prescribed task is to study those forces. Because the large group does contain the total membership, it is the first event to end, and thus offers an appropriate preparation for ending. It provides the first experience of the need for mourning.

It is the event in which the individual finds again that he has to take personal responsibility for his actions. If he is to behave in a mature and adult manner, he cannot just dissolve into the group, but has to accept the responsibility for stopping something of which he disapproves, or the guilt for not doing so. But to get to this realization he has to be prepared to examine many of the myths and value systems he has previously accepted with few questions: that the 'goodness' or 'badness' of groups depends entirely on the 'goodness' or 'badness' of the individuals who make them up; that on matters of principle majorities and minorities have very much relevance; that structure and leadership are always positive and not, as they are found to be, defenses against anxiety. He has to be prepared to question many of the beliefs and attitudes that in a complex modern society support most of its social, political, and working institutions. He has to face the difficulty of tolerating uncertainty about outcomes and the inability always to understand human affairs. He also has to learn to recognize that, in the chaotic complexity in which so much of human life is lived, simple solutions provided by dogmatic leaders work only if the reality of the complexity is denied.

THE INTERGROUP EXERCISE

In the first intergroup exercise in the 1959 conference, the members were asked to split into groups in any way they wished and, by negotiations between the groups, to decide on the content of four sessions in the conference program. They were provided with a summary of information gathered from registration forms that they had filled in before coming to the conference. These forms included a section on 'special interests' not covered by the formal conference program. Members were also given information about the staff's competence to deal with some of the topics listed. The members succeeded in filling the sessions allocated to them, albeit with some difficulty. The staff tasks were seen as responding to requests for expert help with particular topics and, at the same time, helping members to learn about intergroup processes.

In subsequent conferences the same task, that of filling sessions, was given to the members, but the task of the staff was seen as concentrating on the relations between the groups that were formed for this pupose. At the 1959 conference, members were invited to choose their own method of dividing into groups;

in later conferences they were allocated by the staff, as for study and application groups.

Among the staff there has always been discussion about the different tasks of the intergroup exercise and about the desirability of defining one of them as the 'primary task'. Was it to fill spare sessions of the conference, to deal with members' interests that were not otherwise catered for, or to learn about intergroup relations? The staff group itself did not seem clear, and there was evidence that the confusion extended to the members. Preparation for the sessions that were filled as a result of the exercise always involved members in considerable spare-time activity, and the sessions themselves did not appear to give much satisfaction to either members or staff. When the exercise, as an exercise, was reviewed before the planned sessions had taken place, the review was affected by doubts about the plans and, when the plans had been implemented, there was dissatisfaction with performance. More particularly, in the review members often commented that consultants to member groups interfered with the task of filling sessions by drawing attention to what was going on in the 'here and now'. I have always found it difficult to accept that an 'interpretation' of behavior that hinders rather than helps task peformance can ever be justified. But where there are two or even three tasks, help with one of them can clearly interfere with performance of the others. I recognize, of course, that the comments of members might not be anything more than projections of their own sense of futility at the results of their efforts and that the consultants might be acting as scapegoats for members' own dissatisfaction with what they have accomplished. Equally, I have always felt that while confusion between the different tasks existed, so would the role of consultants be confused and hence their ability to help diminished. Members' opportunities for learning about intergroup processes would therefore also be limited.

THE PRIMARY TASK OF THE INTERGROUP EXERCISE

The more precise formulation of the task of the total conference helped us to simplify that of the intergroup exercise. Special interests that fell outside the total conference task became irrelevant and were therefore dropped. Members are now asked, before they come to a conference, in what way the conference task has particular relevance for their work. This simplicification, however, still left two tasks to the intergroup exercise. If we were to define a primary task, we had two possibilities. The first would be to drop the task of learning about intergroup relations to minor status. The primary task of the exercise would be to fill a number of sessions. Staff might be able to help with this task, and in so doing might make comments about intragroup and intergroup processes, but such comments would be appropriate only if they helped with the primary task. To direct attention to the study of intragroup or intergroup relations for their own sake would be inappropriate. For the most part, staff would try to observe how the intrusion of problems of intergroup relations helped or hindered task performance. If they believed them to be helping, they would do nothing; if hindering, try to remove the hindrance. In the review session, staff would then have to take a teaching role and disclose the results of their observations.

This is a valid way of learning about intergroup processes but it has to be recognized that it is a by-product of primary task performance.

The second possibility was to define the primary task as the study of intergroup relationships. The filling of sessions or any other subsidiary task would then become a vehicle for this purpose. Experience of earlier conferences suggested that the study of intergroup relations was difficult, and the danger of providing a vehicle other than the subject of study was that the vehicle became more important than the journey. It therefore seemed to those of us who are now running the conferences about which I write that we should attempt one task only and that it should be the study of intergroup relations. In the choice of method we had no doubt that, in order to be consistent with the purpose of the conference as a whole, we should try to provide experience rather than theory, and this meant that we should study intergroup relations as they happen.

Various experiments have been tried since that decision was taken. I should emphasize that the account given here is my version of the intergroup exercise and of its place in a residential conference. Many of my colleagues feel that I have sometimes used my authority as conference director to impose my design on the exercise and that I confuse directorship of the exercise with that of the conference. I do not at present believe that in a residential conference these two roles can be adequately differentiated by the members (let alone myself), and I think that it is better to accept the confusion and try to learn from it than attempt to set up artificial structures to avoid it.

What follows is an account of where my thinking about intergroup exercises in residential conferences has reached. For illustration I shall, however, use some incidents from exercises held on non-residential courses. My colleagues are already experimenting with different methods in non-residential settings, and will give their own accounts of them. In the course of time it should be possible to carry out controlled experiments to enable us to assess what is learned from the various approaches.

For a group to communicate as a group, it has to have a 'voice.' For the 'voice' to be coherent and understandable, not only outside the group, but inside as well, some mechanism, some 'political' machinery has to be devised. This enables a group to agree on what its 'voice' is to say. It also has to agree on a mechanism for the reception of communications from other groups, and on a framework of beliefs and attitudes within which it can interpret these communications.

Representation involves at least four kinds of relationship:

1. Between a representative and the group he represents or is supposed to represent:the group has to come to terms with what it believes is being, or has been, said on its behalf; and the representative has to come to terms with the often confused policy and message he has to communicate.

2. Between a representative of one group and the group he is visiting on behalf of his own group: he has to be sure of the role he is taking, and of the role he is being put into by the group he is visiting. The group has to interpret his message and his role and come to terms with discrepancies between them.

3. Between representatives from different groups: this is affected by the extent to which each representative is believed to be loyal to his own group, by the credibility of the point of view he expresses, and by the growth of in-group feeling among representatives—the extent to which the representatives form a group of their own in conflict with the groups they represent.

4. Among those who are represented but left behind when the representative has gone to represent them. The remaining members of the group have to deal with doubts and fears and about how they are being represented, and with the effect this has on them and on their attitude to what they have done or not done.

There are also, of course, the relationships between members of various groups when they hear, through other channels of communication outside the exercise, what impressions their representatives are making on other groups, and what other groups are thereby inferring about themselves.

This list could be continued. Each relationship can affect all the others, and difficulty in any one area can destroy the constructive intentions that groups may have about their relations with other groups. Most of the problems of negotiation, and their concomitant difficulties about leadership, loyalty, and confidentiality, are involved.

Broadly speaking, three kinds of representation can be differentiated. It matters less what titles are used to distinguish the different types of representative than that the differences in their functions should be clearly understood:

(a) Observer: a representative dispatched to find out what is happening elsewhere, to try to obtain information from other groups, but without any sanction to express views or to take action on behalf of his own group. His job is to observe, but not to give information.

(b) Delegate: a representative sent out to deliver a message, express a given point of view, or take a given action on behalf of his group. He represents, but has no sanction to vary the message, the view he is expressing, or the action he is taking in the light of what he finds outside. If a delegate finds that he cannot get an answer to his message, that the point of view he is expressing is not acceptable, that the action proposed is not feasible, he has to refer back to his group before making any changes on its behalf.

(c) Plenipotentiary: a representative sent out with flexible terms of reference. He is to do the best he can in the light of the known views or known policies of his own group. He may be given limits beyond which he cannot go but within these terms of reference he can commit his group to a view or to a course of action.

Clearly, there are many variations in the precise power that a representative may exercise, and he may combine the functions of more than one kind of representative, depending on the constraints put upon him in the light of a prediction of the circumstances he is going to meet. The definitions of observer, delegate, and plenipotentiary are three points on a continuum. There can be more than one observer, delegate, or plenipotentiary; communications and negotiations between groups can be public or private; groups can send out a mixed team of plenipotentiaries, observers, delegates, and other variations. The problems for the group and its representative lie in the precision with which responsibility and authority can be defined and in the certainty with which the group can predict the behavior of other groups in the environment in relation to itself.

THE STRUCTURE OF THE INTERGROUP EXERCISE

I have said earlier that when members first arrive at the conference the event that appears to cause them most anxiety is the study group, and for this reason the study group is put into the conference at an early stage. Once the study groups have become established, the large-group exercise is introduced to give members a chance of experiencing the different problems that arise and the difficulties of leading and following in such a setting. In particular, they learn how they feel when all the study groups are brought together. The study of intergroup relations is put in after the large group has met at least twice. The sequence of the events is geared to the increasing complexity in the variables involved in leadership. Starting with a small face-to-face group, members move into the large group and then to the intergroup event. I believe that the intergroup exercise would perhaps be more effective if the large group could meet more often before the exercise starts, but the time available for conferences places constraints on program flexibility.

I have also discussed in earlier chapters the many possible identifications and differences among the members. They are drawn from different backgrounds; but some are more closely identified with each other outside the conference than within it; many have professional links through the kind of work they are doing, and may or may not be members of the same organization; others know each other socially. Within the conference itself they are already members of study groups, and are to become members of application groups. The staff also come from different institutions or different parts of the same institution, and have usually been trained in different disciplines. In a recent conference the staff came from the Universities of Leicester and Bristol, the Prison Department of the Home Office, the Tavistock Institute, and the Tavistock Clinic. Members of the staff also appear in different roles in the various events in the conference.

In general, then, possible intergroup relations within the conference are numerous and complex. However, within the setting of the conference itself, and in particular at the beginning of the intergroup exercise, the dominant intergroup relationship present in the room as the exercise starts is that between the staff, who are running the exercise, and the members, who are to take part in it.

At this stage there are four major differences between members and staff:

1. There are more members than staff. The members form a large group; the staff, a small face-to-face working group.

2. The job of the staff is to help members to learn about intergroup relations, not to study them for their own sake. That is not to say that the staff do not also learn by taking part in the event. Indeed, one of the difficulties of writing this account is that I feel I learn so much in each exercise that what I write will be out of date before it can be published. But staff learning is secondary to their main job. Members, on the other hand, may or may not take the opportunities provided; they have no particular obligation, beyond being present, to take part in the event at all.

3. The staff know more about the running of an intergroup exercise than do the members. Though it did not feel as if this was so the first time that such an exercise was held, the justification for staff membership is that they know enough to help members to learn. Whether by the end of the exercise the members would accept this particular difference, the staff at least have been through it before, and have some idea of the kind of experience to expect.

4. Perhaps most important, the staff already have a 'political' organization. By contrast, the members have not as a rule achieved, or needed to achieve, any kind of organization among themselves. They have no mechanism by which they can communicate as a body of members to the staff, even if they

have anything to communicate. I hold office by virtue of the authority vested in me by the other members of the staff. I am, in that sense 'elected', but in terms of the total conference the franchise is small and powerful. How good the organization of the staff is may, of course, be one of the objects of study in the intergroup exercise. How far I can 'direct' the exercise may be called into question. How far what the staff have delegated to me and what I, in turn, have delegated to them, represent what the original delegation meant, and how far as the 'representative' of the staff I represent the staff point of view may also be tested.

THE RULES OF THE EXERCISE

Because there are more members than can form a face-to-face group, a number of rooms are made available for members' meetings. The number is limited, but is sufficient to allow members to split into face-to-face groups. They may split into more and smaller groups if they wish, but, so far as the staff are concerned, the territorial boundaries of members' groups are fixed by the rooms allocated for this purpose. A space is also designated for the staff group. Whenever the building allows it, this space is in a hall or on a landing. The idea behind this location is that as a part of the provision of learning opportunities the staff relationships will be conducted in public. The lecture room in which plenary sessions take place is designated as common to all groups for intergroup meetings.

In addition to these arrangements concerning space for meetings, a number of staff members are made available to help member groups in their study of the problems of intergroup relations. If the members split into more groups than the number of staff available, then there are no staff to help some of them. If they split into a smaller number of groups than there are staff available, or if they do not call on staff help, then some staff are left unemployed as group consultants. Members are given the right to call or not to call on help from staff members. Another member of staff is designated as consultant to the staff group and to meetings between representatives or between whole groups. In the definitions of representatives used earlier, the staff who are called on for help are plenipotentiaries: the policy within which they operate is laid down in advance — to help members to learn about intergroup relations; within that policy, they do the best they can in the circumstances in which they find themselves.

We have frequently discussed the problem of whether the staff should be assigned to rooms and go there irrespective of whether the members use those rooms. So far, at any rate, I have always held the view that to assign staff members to rooms, whether groups of members meet in them or not, is begging the question of whether members can learn more or less by being given the right to accept or to reject help. If staff consultants are allocated to rooms, members going into a room within the bounds of the exercise automatically get the services of the staff member there, and the problem of not getting help is complicated for them by their having to find another room and put themselves outside the territorial boundaries of the exercise in order to avoid it.

We have also considered whether groups of members should have the right to ask for specific staff members, and hence raise for members the problem of competition for different staff members, and for staff the problem of why some are preferred to others. This particular variation, with the problems it will give rise to, should, I think be tried. So far however, in order to simplify the exercise for members and staff we have named the staff who are to act as consultants to groups of members, and have laid down the order in which they will be made available (usually alphabetically on the first demand and thereafter in rotation).

Members of staff who are not available as consultants to groups or to intergroup meetings, or who, if available, are not called on, form the staff group, and as such represent the management of the exercise. Consultants in groups are there to help members but they are also representatives of the staff group. Hence anything that is said or done in their presence can be communicated to the staff group. But it is emphasized that the staff will not act as representatives of member groups; that is, they will not communicate from member group to member group via the staff group.

The last session of the exercise, whatever state has been reached, consists of a review held in plenary session.

By the rules the only identifiable group that remains constant throughout the exercise is the staff group. The members may split or not as they wish, they may have staff help or not as they wish; they may or may not set up a system for intergroup communication. The only disciplines imposed are on the staff members: the roles they will take, and the territory and time within which they will take cognizance of what is happening. No rules are laid down for members' behavior or even for their participation. Just as members will discuss what is happening in the exercise outside the event, so, of course, will the staff discuss it among themselves as well, but in the exercise they are concerned only with what is happening in front of them and then only in so far as it relates to intergroup relations.

THE BEGINNING OF THE EXERCISE

So far all the intergroup exercises have been opened in plenary session, by the director's stating briefly the concepts behind its design and announcing the rules that have been described above.[1] When I have done this I have been accompanied on the

1 On one occasion, before we had invented the role of 'consultant to the staff group and to intergroup meetings', Pierre Turquet acted as director of the exercise and I as consultant to a group.

platform by the staff members taking part, seated in groups according to their roles in the exercise. At the end of my statement I have passed the exercise over to the members. Before we had differentiated between the roles of 'director' and 'consultant to intergroup meetings', the whole staff stayed in the room at this stage. In recent exercises I have finished my statement by asking if there are any questions and, when these have been dealt with, I have then led the staff from the room to the staff 'territory'.

At the conference where this type of exercise was first tried, and the staff stayed when I had finished my statement, the room was emptied within twenty-five seconds. On that occasion I had stood to make my statement. As I sat down, and indeed before I had resumed my seat, members were on the move out of the room. As they went, they called on the various staff members who had been named as consultants to go with them. At the time it was tempting to think of an organized plot, but such evidence as was available suggested that this could not be so. Members looked far too puzzled about what they were doing. Odd remarks were picked up as they went, such as:

'What does he expect *us* to do now?'

'Well, I'm going to find a group that at least has some women in it this time!' (*This was from a member of a study group composed entirely of men.*)

It may be that some members had a conscious plan, though nobody ever admitted to it, and put this plan into effect. The move having started, others followed. It seemed quite clear, however, that though there may not have been any conscious plan, there was an unconscious agreement, and that, at the simplest level, was to get out of the room as quickly as possible. Members were running away from somebody or something. But the question that had to be answered was from whom or from what? They were not running away from the staff as staff, since those who had been designated as consultants to member groups were asked to go with them; nor, at the time, did they appear to be avoiding the problem of splitting into groups, since they took that problem with them, as was evidenced by the amount of tramping about and banging of doors in the various rooms allocated for members' meetings. The only conclusion I could come to was that they wanted to get away from me. I could not believe from what had been happening in the rest of the conference that I was so hated that members could not bear to be in the same room with me. I could only conclude that for some reason they did not want to tackle the task of building their own 'political' machinery in front me. I now believe that I only symbolized the problem, and, as I shall show, the same phenomenon has occurred even when all the staff have left the room. Experience of the large group suggests that the flight is from fear of the potential violence of unstructured groups. It is not rational but impulsive. I still think that the interpretation that the flight was from me in my role of director was not entirely incorrect, but that I greatly exaggerated the importance of the authority symbol I represented. The only way I could have stopped the flight was by exercising authority structurally, that is by telling the members how to split or, at least, by asking them to discuss a particular way of splitting.

The second time an exercise of this kind was held (on a non-residential course in London), some members who had taken part in the residential exercise were members of the course and therefore present. They knew what had happened on the residential course. In addition, many other members of the course had heard stories about the exercise. Nevertheless, no sooner had I finished the opening statement than some members started to move out of the room. Those who had previous experience of the problems that such flight could cause immediately tried to stop the stampede. They said that members should stay in the room to decide how they could most profitably split up to learn about intergroup relations. These voices, however, had no effect and all the members had left, including those who had tried to stop the move, within a minute and a half.

On the third occasion I was not director of the exercise, and Dr. Turquet took this role. He introduced some variations into the procedure, one of which was to send the consultant staff off to the rooms that they were going to occupy before he finished his statement. Even so, the room cleared in just over one minute after he had finished. On the fourth occasion, after asking if there were any questions and receiving none, I led the staff from the room. The last staff to leave were almost pushed out of the way by the members following them. Had we not had our previous experience, I do not see how we could have avoided the interpretation that I had led the flight myself.

Only once so far, on a non-residential course in London, have we repeated the exercise with the same members. The first exercise had, like others, concluded with a review in the course of which the reasons for the rapid emptying of the room had been discussed. On the whole, the interpretation, similar to the one given above, had been accepted. At the repeat, members said that they were determined to discuss the problem of splitting, not just to split as they had done the first time. But most of the discussion turned into members asking questions of the staff about the previous review, about the rules of the exercise, about what I had said and done:

'It's two months since we did it, we've forgotten the rules you laid down.'

'Well, we've not exactly forgotten them, but we've distorted them.'

'Why don't you just repeat them?'

When I replied that I was sure that everybody knew perfectly well what the rules were since they were so simple and so few, and that I believed I was being asked to repeat them as a means of avoiding or at least postponing examination of member-staff relations in general and of my leadership in particular, there followed a long discussion that started from the difficulty of considering staff-member relationships. However, this soon turned again into a discussion of the previous exercise and members admitted that once the stampede had happened they had all been flabbergasted by it. After some time, there seemed to be a consensus of opinion that because of the flight from the problem of splitting into groups the last intergroup exercise had been a complete disaster. But nobody wanted to query in what sense of the word 'disaster' was being used. If, as everyone agreed, the members' failure to set up any political machinery was a 'disaster', then the assumption must have been that the primary task of the exercise was to learn how to set up political machinery. Yet almost any member of that course, given the task of devising and creating joint consultative machinery or a committee to discuss ways and means, could have done so in a very short time. The important question that could not be answered was whether they had learnt anything about the relations between themselves as members of groups involved in intergroup relations. The solid attendance at the second exercise implied that, if the last had been a disaster, they were prepared to face another.

Eventually, an hour after the opening, a number of members said that they were getting nowhere and would get nowhere while they stayed as a total group. Five people got up and started to move out of the room; three others followed them immediately. The rest then split themselves into two groups by some process of selection that was not disclosed and moved into the other rooms available for the exercise.

THE CONTENT OF A GROUP MEETING

Immediately after the split, groups express concern about themselves as groups; why the particular members who have assembled in any one room have been there is hardly questioned. So far, in most of the conferences that have been held, an examination of the group composition after the split has shown that the exercise groups consist either of the existing study groups, when the number of rooms available has equalled the number of study groups — a situation we try to avoid if we can — or of an equal number of members from each study group. The possibility that these compositions could have happened so often by chance is so small as to make it virtually certain that study-group membership has for the time being overwhelmed any other kind of group membership inside, or outside, the conference. So far as members have been concerned with intergroup relations, they have been more concerned at first with those between study groups than those between themselves as members and the staff. In effect, they have chosen the easier boundaries to work with.

When the split has been into study groups, members have sought to continue study-group experience, but in a setting in which what is happening 'outside' becomes a legitimate subject for study; that is, a study group in which the group cannot be accused of 'flight' when it discusses something 'out there' instead of 'in here'. In another sense members have also expressed hostility to management for being asked to perform some other task and have proposed to continue an experience that has become familiar.

When members have split into groups that comprise an equal number from each study group, they have usually tried to conduct the intergroup exercise within the groups so formed. They have started to discuss the similarities and differences between study groups. It is as though they do what they have been told to do — namely, study intergroup relations — but in such a way that they can avoid having to come to terms with problems either of representation or of their relations with authority. This involves denying that the staff consultants are members of a staff group and that the relations established with a consultant are relations with another group. It is also, of course, an attempt to split the staff acting as consultants from the staff group, and hence from conference management. If consultants can be beguiled into acting as study-group leaders, then they can be set up as leaders in breaking the rules laid down for the exercise, and hence management authority can be destroyed.

The initial preoccupation of most groups, in other words, is their own identity. At first, they avoid the nature of the split, the panic that they feel, thus:

'I went out of the room, and just looked over the banisters to see who was following me.'

'We two walked away together and found four others going into the same room. That started it.'

'I couldn't understand what was happening. I was flabbergasted, everybody else seemed to be going somewhere, so I went too.'

'I didn't want to be left behind. I wanted to know what the others were doing.'

Only when study groups have met for the exercise has there been any manifest attempt to account for the composition of other groups. Even then, the comment was:

'Well, it's the same for all of us, we've got used to each other already. We thought it would be easier.'

At one conference in which the number of rooms assigned to the exercise was one less than the number of study groups, those study groups whose rooms were still within bounds immediately occupied them, leaving the deprived study group to sort out its own problems. Though its members were absorbed quite quickly, the difficulties that had been created were smoothed over rather than solved. Later on, in most exercises, when some of the facts of composition have been pointed out, usually by the consultants, there have been attempts to reassemble the total group in plenary session so that the problem of splitting can be studied and, if necessary, a new start made; but these attempts have never, so far, succeeded.

It seems that, having come together, by whatever processes, conscious and unconscious, the groups become so concerned about what might happen in their own groups and what might be going on in other groups that they have to establish some kind of defense forthwith; they have to find a structure. In effect, they accept the members that they have, and proceed immediately to try to establish some kind of organization. They cannot tolerate an examination that would show whether those who have met are those best qualified for the task they have to perform. Any individual who suggests that the composition of the group be subject to scrutiny is always rejected. Since scrutiny of selection inevitably implies looking at criteria for rejection, belief in some magical identification process is necessary in the first anxious minutes. Members are, in reality, faced with the very difficult problem of selecting groups to perform a familiar task — the conduct of intergroup relations — in very unfamiliar circumstances. They have no structure to control the strong feelings that might arise. In this situation they have to act, to take action, for action's sake. Usually they act impulsively, clinging to the only structures they have been given — the management 'rules' on the one hand and the existing conference grouping on the other.

At this time groups tend to regard with suspicion any visitors — they may be rejections from other groups, seeking a new group to join. At one conference a member who proposed that the group should study how its members had come together and was ignored until he suggested finding out about other groups. He was then sent out, but without any instructions or, indeed, any invitation to return. He wandered from group to group asking the members if they had settled anything, each time expressing the hope that, if they had, he would be allowed to join them.

At the same time visitors, and suspicions about them, may be welcomed as a means of providing distractions from internal problems. The need for some kind of structure is so great that apart from a quick attempt to appoint a chairman and a secretary, little is done other than to discuss machinery for communication. There is usually more talk about sending out representatives to 'communicate' than about internal organization and administration, or even what the communication is to be about. It is not unusual at this stage for the 'elected' officers to find themselves powerless to bring any order into the meeting, and to resign or otherwise cause confusion. If visitors from other groups arrive during this phase they can act as a reproach to the group: other groups have apparently organized themselves. It is usually round about this time that a significant appointment is made, that of ''doorkeeper'. His job is to establish the group boundary and to ensure that some order is introduced into the transactions across it. He greets visitors, inquires their business, and finds out if they can be received. He introduces the 'pause' for thinking in an attempt to reduce the confusion.

In the groups that do take quick initiative one or two voices may be raised to suggest the election of a chairman and a secretary, but leadership is vested in those who want to do something about making contact with other groups. On one occasion — and it is typical — almost as soon as the group assembled a member suggested the sending out of representatives:

'I vote we send out representatives to find out what other groups are doing. Let's see if they know as little as we do.'

He was promptly asked why he didn't go himself. He stood up and moved to the door. As he went he was encouraged to go ahead by most of the group, though it seemed to me, who was consultant on that occasion, that their expressions as they encouraged him were more of relief that somebody was doing something than of positive support for what he was doing. As he reached the door, he paused and asked what he was going as. There was a chorus of 'plenipotentiary'. I commented that that meant he was to do the best he could within the known policy of the group. I wondered if he knew what that was. I added that I had not become aware of any policy and therefore I could only infer that the 'power' given to the plenipotentiary was illusory and that he was being given no sanction at all except to see if other groups knew more than this one. But this one had not even tried to find out what it knew, and hence even the mission was illusory. The representative was halfway through the door. He stopped in his tracks. There was a silence—it seemed long, but was probably about half a minute:

'If I stop while that is discussed, I'll never get out.'

And with that he went, leaving his group shocked at the way in which it had been led into a course of action without thought or even discussion.

This representative was away for a long time. At first there was an attempt among the remaining members to discuss why they had let him go as they had. This discussion was unproductive and it was not difficult to point out that he had in fact led the group in flight from its task and that, whatever he might say, the real message that he would convey to other groups was precisely this. The group felt a sense of futility; now the representative had gone, there was nothing to do until he got back, but he could not be fetched back because that would weaken his authority, which was, however, still undefined. When he did return he reported on the composition of the three other groups that had been formed, and on the very different receptions he had had from each of them. It soon became clear that some at least of the differences in the way he had been received had been due to his own attitude to the other groups and that, as he became less defensive, because he realized that they were just as confused as his own group, so his reception became more friendly. Nevertheless, the first 'failed act' in adequate communication bedevilled for the rest of the exercise the group's attempts to set up adequate machinery either for its own management or for the management of its relations with other groups.

After the first shock, a major problem that besets most groups is what to communicate about:

'If we knew what to communicate about, we could easily design the machinery for it. The trouble is the task has not been defined. We don't know what we have to do.'

But that they might communicate about their attitudes and feelings for other groups, that they might check their fantasies against such reality as is available to them, takes a long time to be accepted. For to communicate these matters to others they have to acknowledge them to themselves; and that would invite others to comment on them. The early activity—hyper-activity is perhaps a better description— is thus a denial of the task that has been set. Moreover, it can be seen that preoccupation with setting up machinery for communication and with sending out representatives to follow undefined or ill-defined policies is, in reality, a means of dealing with the group's own internal problems. It is an attempt to project confusion and doubts about potency onto others. The selection, or self-selection of representatives in the early sessions is also, of course, a means of removing those who are not easily integrated into an active, though probably thoughtful, group.

While uncertainty about internal problems, projected upon the staff as inadequate task definition or inadequately stated rules, makes policy about communication difficult to formulate, it becomes noticeable that those visitors from other groups who come with a specific purpose have little difficulty in taking over the missing group leadership. No amount of protest about 'courtesy to a visitor' can obscure the willingness with which the visitor is allowed to dominate the meeting.

Many groups only gradually come to accept this view of their behavior, but as they do, they begin to develop some kind of organization that is at least sufficiently secure to permit them to lower their barriers to ideas from other groups, and even to think of changes in membership; or at least of the formation of new groups made up of some members from groups previously formed. So far, however, agreement to do something as a total membership has seldom been more than verbal. Whenever representatives of all groups in a meeting of representatives have proposed definite action, however mild, there have been objections from the groups left behind. Even when agreement was reached by representatives, and confirmed by their own groups, that the representatives should meet with the staff at the center to exchange views about each other's behavior, and presumably about the staff's behavior as well, action was somehow delayed—by questions about procedure, by mistakes about time—until there was no time left in the exercise to implement it.

On one occasion, when the members split into two groups, their representatives finally agreed that they all wanted to reconstitute a plenary session and take the staff to task, not only for the conduct of the exercise, but for the timing of events in the conference and for the quality of the lectures that had been given to them. They were just about to achieve this—one group had actually reached the center—when it was discovered that a splinter group had been formed, which wanted and achieved a reopening of the negotiations. These lasted until the end of the exercise.

In general, agreed plans seldom lead to any action. The important lessons concern the difficulty of taking any action while divergent views exist; the virtual impossibility of getting unanimity on anything except rejection of what is not in the group; and the ease with which one person, provided he is from outside, knows what he wants, and is determined to get it, can take over the leadership of a group. The only unanimity is in the unconscious collusion to get on with internal affairs and to resist by all possible means—and there are many—intrusion of the external environment.

THE ROLE OF CONSULTANT TO A GROUP

On only one occasion has any consultant been left unemployed for the whole exercise. There were a number of possible explanations for this isolated occurrence. The consultant concerned was the only one, on that occasion, who was also a consultant to a study group. The members' behavior could have been an act of hostility to her as a study-group consultant, a symbolic rejection of study groups, or an attempt to avoid putting her in another role and thus endangering her 'goodness' as a study-group leader. There was no evidence in the exercise to suggest which it was, or, rather, there was so much evidence for each of these possibilities that they were probably all true in varying degrees.

Except for this instance, all the staff members made available as consultants have been called on, though there have been delays, and in two exercises one group has met for most of the time without consultant help. At all times consultants have had to be aware of the reality of the demand for their help. When they have been unsure that the decision to call them in has been a real one, they have questioned the sanction for their presence, and sometimes have left while the group has made up its mind.

An important dynamic that is introduced into the exercise by the fact that some, but not all, of the staff are available as consultants to groups, is a built-in incentive to members to split the staff group. At the same time, however, they are facing themselves with the possibility that the consultant may not be helpful to them but may consciously or unconsciously sabotage their efforts to unite in opposition to the staff. The consultant has always to be aware of the ambivalence with which he or she is regarded, and of the temptation to secede from the staff group that will be offered. He will also be aware, however, that if he succumbs to this temptation, his usefulness to the group will thereby be limited. Capture, however attractive to the group and to the consultant, inevitably negates his capacity to provide opportunities to learn about intergroup relations, since this involves his being at least sufficiently detached from group affairs to be able to explain some of the frustrating phenomena that occur. More importantly, perhaps, capture of a consultant by any group calls into question the effectiveness of the whole staff group, and hence the stability and dependability of the conference management. Its stability and dependability may indeed be questionable, but to question them safely a group needs support from the other groups as well, and that involves making appropriate relations with other groups.

Consultants have greater difficulty in dealing with the group's desire to treat the exercise as an extension of the study-group experience. If a group has to come to terms with its own identity and with its own internal relations and organization as a prerequisite of effective communication with other groups, then there is reality, in the need to sort out internal problems. To study interaction there has to be some interaction, and to achieve coherent interaction there has to be some kind of internal structure. In this sense the consultant should help with the sorting out of internal relations and the setting up of the necessary organization. But whereas in the study group he is concerned only with the internal life of the group, in the intergroup exercise he is concerned with it in relation to the external environment, and hence his interventions are bound to be different. The difference is that in the study group the consultant is concerned only with what is happening 'here and now'; in the exercise he is concerned with the 'here and now' in relation to the 'there and then'. Because unless there is a member of another group actually present, information about other groups, whose relations with his own group are his concern, must always be based partially on reports of what has happened somewhere else.

One consequence is that it is difficult for the consultant to avoid standing on one side, making comments on the effectivenes or ineffectiveness of the behavior of the group. He can thus appear even more omniscient, and unhelpful, than a study-group consultant. He is not as personally exposed as other members of the group, and certainly not as personally exposed as he is in the study group. Whenever I have been consultant to a group—and I believe this feeling is shared to some extent by my colleagues—the ease with which, as an outsider, I can point to ineffectiveness and ineptitude, without being exposed to the same sort of test myself, tends to inhibit my attempts to help members to understand the problems with which they are faced. They can, and do of course, attack the staff group and my interpretation of the staff role, but I have an external referent that is politically well organized to fall back on, and it is not just my personal competence that is under close scrutiny.

Nevertheless, a member of the staff who is designated as a consultant to a group, and yet remains a member of the staff group responsible for the exercise, is put in a difficult position. The staff group frequently tries to find a more simple solution. It is not unusual, for example, for the staff to suggest that those who are consultants should cease to be a part of the management. But it seems improbable that that kind of separation would work; members would not believe that the consultant was not part of the staff group, and the staff group would be in collusion with the members to split itself right down the middle. The dilemma does not seem unlike that of any board of directors or other group with collective responsibility for an institution, whose members also take managerial or professional roles within it. As members of the group they carry a joint responsibility for leadership of the whole; as individuals they are responsible for their own management or professional function. The two roles are often in conflict, and compromise or resignation may be the only possible outcomes.

THE STAFF GROUP

What is left of the staff group stays in its own 'territory'. It too has its own consultant (one of its own number) whose job is to help the staff group to learn about its own intergroup relations. The staff group makes members available as consultants, who, when they are in other groups, are plenipotentiaries in that they are vested with full powers to do what they can, within the rules laid down for the exercise, in the circumstances in which they find themselves. So far, the staff group has never recalled those it has so sent out. It has sent out delegates with instructions to inform other groups about management's views, and observers to find out what is happening. But for the most part, having made consultants available, those left behind have remained passive, waiting for groups or representatives of groups to visit them. When that has happened the consultant to the staff group acts as consultant to the intergroup meeting.

The first visits, apart from those to request the help of a consultant, are usually for clarification, to ask questions about the rules of the exercise. Though some groups are confused about what they have been told at the opening, and their questions have some reality, there is invariably behind the questions some test-out of staff intentions and integrity. In the early stages the staff are usually put in the position of saying 'no' to requests—to negotiate about a party, to extend the number of available rooms, and so on. Saying 'no' can itself be reassuring, because it implies that complete anarchy will not prevail—at least one group knows what it will not do. It also makes it easier for members to say 'no' to the staff and thus to test, in a valid way, what will happen if they defy authority.

An implication that frequently becomes stronger as the exercise goes on is that the staff have 'fixed' the whole exercise and can therefore predict what will happen. Though I have given here of necessity a generalized account of the intergroup exercise, the staff never know in advance what will happen, or when, on any given occasion. But the implication is that the staff are all engaged in a conspiracy to produce a predetermined result. Within this reasoning the director does not need to be told anything: he knows, and what is more, he knows in advance. Yet members also know that if the director behaved as if he knew what was going to happen and when, then he could be out-maneuvered by clever members and hence could be destroyed. His destruction would then prove that the exercise, and the conference, were based on false theories and false hypotheses and need not be taken seriously.

Perhaps one of the odd things about the exercise is how seriously it is taken. Members frequently express amazement at this themselves. The exercise is a charade, a game, yet as they play it members seriously question the staff's qualifications and right to expose them not only to the exercise, but to the conference as a whole. By such questioning they can deny, or attempt to deny, that work, hard and painful work, is required if the problems of leading and following are to be understood. Such questioning can also be used to obscure the anxieties that arise trom the inability to tolerate uncertainty about task performance. There are few work groups which are uninterested in success, and if criteria for measuring success are difficult to lay down — as in any exercise for learning by experience they must be — toleration of uncertainty is bound to be severely tested. The danger is that intolerance can lead to a change of task definition in an attempt to find more measurable criteria.

In an intergroup exercise the staff are in constant danger of imagining that they are managing an exercise for its own sake; that is, that they are managing a communication system, but not necessarily a learning process. The staff feel impotent when nothing appears to be happening and rapidly get to the stage at which they want to take action, if only to relieve their own anxiety. Part of the way through one exercise the staff could not see that anything was being achieved; they became so anxious that they even started to take decisions about the strategy of future exercise. They found themselves discussing what they would do or would not do the next time. In their fear that they had made a mess of the current exercise—before it was over— they comforted themselves with anticipation of success in the next. But this behavior of course denied their task of helping members to learn from the current exercise, and had they persisted they might easily have taken unwarranted decisions about the future.

Typically, in practice the amount of information reaching the staff group is sparse, and what little is reported is usually trivial. Representatives of groups, on their way to visit other groups, sometimes call on the staff group to tell the director to which group they are going; occasionally they tell him why; and, still more rarely, on their way back they say what the result has been. It appears to be assumed that though the director need not be told anything important, he should be told all that is unimportant. He needs, in other words, to be treated with respect and consideration, and a way of doing this is to propitiate him with token gifts. Behind the respect and consideration, however, is the hope that providing him with useless information may keep him from finding out anything useful; and hence make it easier to discredit him. The major communications to management are inferential; they have to be deducted not from what is said, but largely from what is not said.

Perhaps the most important inferential communication has been mentioned above: that what members want to use the exercise for is to examine whether it does provide opportunities to learn about leadership. Inevitably, they become preoccupied with conference and exercise leadership. The intergroup exercise is the one event in which the primary task invites them to examine, in detail, their relations with the staff as a whole and the internal relations of the staff group—the leadership elite of the conference. In the large group members are faced by consultants, and even if one of these is the conference director they do not meet management as management. They may discuss conference leadership and management, but that is not the task of the event. The only other events in which they meet the staff, and hence management, as a group, are the opening and ending plenaries. The former is too early and the latter too late for real work on member-staff relations. In the exercise however, they find that for some reason it is difficult to attack exercise leadership directly, as a total group, even with assistance from staff as consultants. They can only attack indirectly by cutting leadership off from evidence of what is going on.

It is never easy to analyse adequately the reasons for the fear of direct attack. At one level it can be suggested that there is no agreement among members that an attack is desirable. There are real but varied opinions about the effectiveness of both exercise and conference. At another level, the hurry to get out of the room at the beginning could suggest that as a potential enemy the staff are felt to be too powerful. The acceptance of some staff as consultants to groups shows that this feeling does not apply to individuals on the staff because the same phenomena occur whoever are nominated as director or consultants. It is the roles and not the persons who are feared.

In one exercise, I arrived at the place that the staff group was to occupy about a minute before a session was due to start. I found it occupied by a group of members. As I entered there was a laugh and, turning to me, one member said.:

'Well, we've taken over your territory, what are you going to do about that?'

I glanced at the clock and replied:

'Nothing now, because the session hasn't started. But in about half a minute, when it does, I shall try at least to understand what is happening and I expect I'll make an interpretation about it.'

But by the time the session started there was nobody left to make an interpretation to.

Outside the exercise the members often succed in much they have been trying to do within it. They certainly succeed in splitting the staff, in particular in setting consultants against their own headquarters. As director I am frequently taken noisily to task by my colleagues for the 'impossible' position into which I have put them, either by my words or manner in the opening, or by my replies to representatives who have visted me. Dr. Turquet, when he directed an exercise, complained that everybody out in the groups appeared to know just what was happening, whereas he was not told anything by the groups, and even his colleagues only confused him. At the time I was acting as consultant to a group and had been feeling that he was getting much more information than my colleagues ever gave me when I was director!

Nevertheless, a consultant on his return to the staff group is faced by two problems. The first is the real difficulty of giving a brief appreciation of a confused situation, and the second is his need to get his confusion out of himself. A catalogue of events, an account of who said what and when—the gossip—is often fascinating, but it leaves the recipient to make his own appreciation of the situation before he can make sound decisions; and if the decisions have to be made quickly the need to listen to so much content—however interesting—can be exasperating. On the other hand, consultants who have been bewildered by what has been happening in the group in which they have been working, and who are, in consequence, uncertain about their own performance, need to have somebody to whom they can unburden themselves. The incompatibility of these two needs— of the director for an appreciation, and of the consultant to 'externalize' his confusion — can add to the staff-group difficulties in making decisions about what action is best to further members' learning opportunities.

Certainly as director of the exercise I often feel that I do not need to be told about members' behavior. I have only to observe staff behavior. That epitomizes what is happening in the exercise. The technical problem, as yet unsolved, is that these observations, which are so informative, are often made outside the time and territory of the exercise and not within it. Perhaps this is inevitable since the whole conference is, in one sense, one large intergroup exercise mediated through a series of events. In other words, though the primary tasks of the different events are different, each event, apart from the intergroup exercise, has as its secondary task the examination of the model of leadership and management as demonstrated by the staff group.

THE ENDING OF THE EXERCISE

The intergroup exercise ends with a plenary session. This session is opened by the director giving a review of what he has observed in his role, and reporting the inferences he has drawn from his observations. His statement is followed by discussion among staff and members. The exercise, unlike other 'here and now' events, is concluded by a review because its nature splits members into different groups and hence no one person can have an overall view of what has happened. Learning takes place in all member groups and in the staff group, and not just in a member's own group.

The director's review gives a chronological account of the main events of the exercise, and a commentary on the interpretations that were made at the time. It concludes with a brief overall interpretation of the reasons for these events. The purpose is to try to present the data coherently and in a pattern which relates cause and effect. The overall interpretation is given as an example of some of the learning that might be articulated. So far as I am able I discuss the pattern of staff relationships and the changes that have occurred as a result of members' impact on them:

'...By this time, more than an hour had passed. The staff began to feel paranoid. There had been no requests for help. Clearly the consultants who had been offered were not wanted. We began to consider whether we should take some action. We were responsible for the exercise and it was unpalatable to think that we were not wanted and that we could not do anything. In the event what we did was to quarrel about our social behavior. Some of us by this time had got ourselves drinks from the bar, and some members of the staff questioned our ethics in drinking during the working session. Though voices were raised and the quarrel became acrimonious, there did not feel to be very much reality in it, and directing attention to what it symbolized, that is, the attempt to split the staff group, dealt with it for the time being, albeit somewhat uneasily.'

'...By this time only the secretary and myself were left at the staff headquarters. I had nothing left to do but take her out for a drink — which I did. The serious point was the extent to which, by having delegated all jobs to other members of the staff, I had rendered myself impotent by abdication. On reflection I felt that I had not so much abdicated as given myself the problem of how long I would leave them without trying to find out what they were doing. I felt as though I had eight parts of myself scattered round the building and had constantly to reassure myself that they were all doing what I would have done had I been there.'

I hope that such disclosures, like the overall interpretation, will encourage members to examine the behavior of their own groups in a similar way, and hence help them to become aware of similar experiences in other groups and meetings outside the conference.

APPLICATION GROUPS

The purpose of application groups is to explore the potential relevance of conference learning to normal working situations. Members choose the material to be studied. A consultant attached to each application group tries to help members to look at the case material produced in the light of conference experience. Application groups are therefore composed of those doing the same or similar jobs in their ordinary work. In contrast to study groups, application groups are as homogeneous as possible.

We have found the application group to be among the more difficult events to conduct. Technically, it should be the easiest.

143

Members of staff who have a clinical background are familiar with the case-conference method of teaching, and those with an educational background are accustomed to tutorial groups and to seminar-type events. Some of the difficulty arises from the problem of articulating conference learning, and hence of finding ways in which it can be applied. Some arises from the conference institution in which the application group occurs. Even when members of the staff have attempted to use more than conference learning by adding special knowledge or experience of their own about the problems being discussed, there has seldom been the spontaneity that would be expected in more traditional educational institutions.

EARLIER FORMS OF APPLICATION GROUPS

In the 1957 conference (Trist and Sofer, 1959), each application group was given a project, outside the conference, as a part of its case material. Thus an application group composed of members with an educational background visited the Leicester Education Authority to discuss the Leicestershire experiment in the transfer from primary to secondary education, an innovation of national importance in view of the controversy over the eleven-plus tests; a group concerned with penal institutions and delinquency visted the Leicester Police to examine and discuss the selection and promotion scheme that had recently been instituted; one industrial group visited a company that had been running a successful experiment in industrial co-partnership for some years; and another visited the government training and rehabilitation center.

In subsequent conferences external projects were dropped. The visits were not easy to arrange. They involved much administrative work, agreeing times and dates of meetings, arranging for return visits of personnel from the various bodies or companies concerned in the projects, and preparing the material that was to be used in the conference. In addition, the introduction of a large number of the conference members into external organizations and of representatives from external organizations into the conference further complicated interpersonal and intergroup relationships already sufficiently complicated. But, most importantly, we felt that neither the staff nor the members could do adequate justice to the host institutions in the midst of all the other things that were going on in a short conference. We did not feel that our hosts were adequately repaid for the time they spent and the trouble they took to display their problems and their attempted solutions. It seemed that, faced with the need to make some contribution, neither staff nor members could do other than applaud indiscriminately or appear destructively critical. There was too little time to make the constructively critical study that might have both helped conference learning and repaid the host institution for its exposure and hospitality.

In practice, the projects were intrusions into the conference process, though members of some application groups were impressed and moved by what they had seen and heard (Trist and Sofer, 1959). In those groups the project dominated subsequent application-group sessions to the exclusion of what was happening elsewhere in the conference. In others, in which the project did not 'take', it was experienced as a distraction. The idea behind the projects was sound: to provide members of application groups with case material that was the same for all of them, and was relevant to their jobs. But such projects need far more time than could be given in the conference or by the host institutions. It may be possible to reintroduce them when conference methods are extended and introduced into longer training programs.

At subsequent conferences attempts were made to get application groups to follow a predetermined routine: to take a problem census; to search for a theme; to identify problems within the theme; to survey available cases to determine their appropriateness to the explication of identified problems; and then to make formal presentation of the case material prior to discussion. While this technique did, to some extent, make it easier to put into words what had been discussed and what had been learned during application-group sessions, neither technique or learning was intrinsically consistent with, or even relevant to, the rest of the conference. The sessions were too often additions to, and outside, conference experience. Not only members but staff as well felt too constrained by the technique.

At various conferences the place of application groups in the program has been changed. At one conference we tried putting application groups as the first working event, immediately following the opening session. It was hoped that, since members came to the conference from their own jobs, application groups would provide a familiar connection between job and conference. It was also hoped that the homogeneity of application groups would help members to feel more at home than if they were put into the heterogeneous study groups straight away. It soon became clear, however, that on arrival at the conference members were far more concerned about study groups than they were about application groups. In these conferences the early application-group sessions were largely wasted; members were impatient to get into study groups. It was as though, having dealt with their anxiety sufficiently to apply for membership and subsequently to arrive, they wanted to get on with what they felt to be the most significant conference experience. Application groups now start late in the program, and the program ends with them.

THE PRIMARY TASK OF APPLICATION GROUPS

The primary task of application groups is to consider the application of conference learning to members' normal work. Performance of this task must of necessity relate what has happened and is happening in the conference to the external environment. It involves therefore two other sub-tasks: some assessment of conference learning and a preparation for return to the real world outside. Application groups are thus a major part of the conference 'export' process.

The problem of fitting application groups into the total conference pattern is as yet not fully solved. Most members find application groups both a relief from the intensive and unusual methods of the rest of the conference and, at the same time, a disappointment and a let-down after other experience. Those members who want to continue with study-group, large-group, and intergroup experience inevitably seek to turn the application groups into one or the other and try to trap their consultant into going into collusion with them. Consultants to application groups have sometimes been accused by members of leaning over backwards to avoid turning them into study groups to such an extent that they have diminished their value even as application groups. As against this, those consultants who have unwittingly colluded with members to change the task of their application groups have found that, though at first both they and the members have felt a greater satisfaction with their meetings, they have faced an almost insoluble problem when bringing the group to an end. They have had no means of getting out of the situation other than by an exchange of compliments and thanks, an exchange that both know to be a denial of reality.

In the plenary reviews there have been members who have protested strongly against the flatness of the application groups as compared with the other small-group activity, the study group. There have equally been those who have welcomed the flatness as a means of giving them time to prepare themselves for returning to the more ordinary world of work. Holders of both views experience the application groups as unexciting when compared with other conference events. Application groups, as part of the export process, have to provide an opportunity to deal with the mixture of depression, elation, and anxiety that accompanies the loss of what have become valued human experiences. They are intended to deal with the let-down within the conference rather than leave it all until after the conference is over, when members have neither each other nor the staff to help them. It may well be that without the experience of flatness application groups could not accomplish this part of their task, and that this inevitably begets a sense of frustration in the attempt to articulate and apply conference learning.

The staff share both the depression and the frustration, but in the application groups have not readily to hand, as in the study groups, the techniques for dealing with them as group phenomena, and the problem of maximizing the learning opportunity of the mixed feelings remains.

Perhaps it is even more important that the work of application groups conveys unmistakably that what has been learned, if anything, does not automatically solve all the problems raised; that, however intensive the experience of conference learning, however firm the conviction that much has been learned, only new ways of looking at problems, not solutions, have been offered. Any lingering belief that earlier conference experience would magically provide solutions to problems previously thought intractable is, in the application groups, dispelled. What has to be learned is that, even with new approaches, most human problems, and particularly those of leading and managing, still require hard work; and even then some of them will be insoluble, or it will not be possible to implement the solution.

My own view is that we should try a different order of priority in the tasks of the application group, and that we should define the primary task as the accomplishment of the export process. Application groups would then be less concerned with case material produced by members, and the emphasis would be on conference ending. In our present program the large-group event is finished before the application-group event begins, the intergroup exercise is almost over, and the end of the study groups is in sight. Ending is the current preoccupation of members and staff alike. The application of conference learning to this process would have considerable value for its own sake. In this sense it could use case material produced by members from their own working backgrounds, but case material from the 'There and then' of the conference would also be relevant. The danger would be that the transfer of conference learning to other external situations would be largely by analogy. Staff acting as consultants to application groups might have to be prepared to produce more material themselves, and do more teaching from it. This would place a considerable burden on staff and I am not sure that it is one that can be adequately carried.

CONTENT OF APPLICATION-GROUP DISCUSSIONS

Even at the end of a conference, many members still appear to be in difficulties, and are sometimes distressed about getting an intellectual grasp of what the conference has been about. This is epitomized by the demand, that used to be made so frequently, that the staff should help members to prepare a report about the conference that they can take back to their own organizations.

'I've spent a lot of time here and my company has paid a lot of money for me to come. They're not going to be very pleased when all I can tell them is that I've had an interesting experience. They didn't give me the time and pay the money for that.

Now that a large number of conferences have been held and more members of the same organizations have attended, this demand is less insistent than it was at the beginning. Nevertheless, a number of those who come to conferences are expected, on their return, to make a report to their colleagues or superiors, and this they find difficult.

It is perhaps not surprising, therefore, that towards the end of a conference some members are concerned to get something practical and specific out of it that has immediate application in their own organization, even if it is only a kind of second-hand consultation on a current problem. In earlier conferences, 'special interest' sessions tried to satisfy this demand. On some occasions we have introduced special events such as role-playing, panel discussion, and other training techniques. Though such techniques are valid methods of training in their own right, and though material thrown up at the conference was used in the events given to them, we now feel that as events they were out of keeping with the rest of the conference. Their primary task was to demonstrate a technique of training for the sake of the technique and hence they did not fit into the pattern of a conference that was designed for a different purpose. This does not mean that such techniques cannot be and are not introduced into application groups whenever their use helps to illuminate the problem being discussed; but they are then introduced for the sake of the problem, not for the sake of the technique.

In the same way, the conference structure and culture can themselves serve as case material. The consistencies and inconsistencies in its structure, culture, and task can throw useful light on the problems the conference is called upon to study; not, again it should be emphasized, to try to teach conference design for its own sake, since that is not the purpose of the conference, but to illustrate the problems of fitting structure and culture to a task; similarly, staff behavior can illustrate some of the problems of taking different kinds of leadership roles.

An application group usually starts with a definition of its task by the consultant. This is followed by an invitation to the members to consider possible subjects for discussion. At this stage the consultant encourages members to look at a number of topics that may be relevant to the learning of the conference, and discourages the too premature production of a 'case'. This phase, which may last for two or more sessions, is intended to deal with some of the problems of the transition to a new way of working, and to give time for a general look at the similarities and differences in members' experience and background.

It is usual at this stage for members to ask to change their application group. They have been assigned to these groups as a result of information they have given on their registration forms. But it is sometimes difficult to be sure from the information given that members have sufficient in common to form a relatively homogeneous group; and furthermore, in practice, members may feel that they belong elsewhere. Though we recognize that some of the requests for a change may be due less to the unsuitability of the allocation than to the acting-out of other problems of relationship, arrangements for transfer can be made with the mutual consent of the groups concerned.

By the second, third, or fourth session some member of the group will present a detailed case history of a management, organizational, or professional problem from his own work, and this is then discussed until the group decides to change to some other case. The first cases produced are not infrequently stories of success, or, at most, of only minor difficulty. Members are wary of exposing their real problems to scrutiny. In this they are of course affected by the composition of the groups. With the best will in the world it is not possible to avoid building into some application groups external hostilities or rivalries of which staff are ignorant. Even when attention is drawn to them it is not always possible to make other arrangements. Industrial or commerical competition can usually, though not always, be avoided; but ill feeling between, for example, a teacher training college and a university institute of education may be not only unknown to the staff, but not even disclosed in the conference until an application group that contains members of both has been meeting for some time.

Material produced for discussion is also affected by the relative status of the members of a group. Job titles and necessarily brief descriptions of duties are notoriously ambiguous means of identification and unreliable guides to the responsibility carried and authority exercised. Too wide differences in status can introduce difficulties in relationship that may inhibit members' willingness to expose either themselves or their own organizations. Ideally, conference members would be recruited through their anticipated homogeneous application group membership—but, so far, in the particular conferences I am describing this has not proved possible; it is noticeable that in other conferences with which we have been concerned and in which membership has been limited to one main source— industry, education, or the church — application groups have been easier.

In some conferences particular application groups are faced with trying to help one of their members with a specific and urgent problem. In one, a member heard, halfway through the conference, that in his absence a major company reorganization had been announced. So far as he could tell the repercussions of this would drastically change his own job, cut down his responsibility, and destroy much of his authority. He decided not to return home at once but to ask his application group to help him with his return. The reasons for the reorganization were discussed, the new organization was studied, and two sessions were devoted to role-playing his anticipated meetings with his colleagues and chairman. In the role-playing he took each role in turn, including his own, and other members of the group took his role. Many months later he expressed considerable gratitude to the other members of the group for the help he had had in coping with a particularly difficult period in his work. Such incidents and opportunities are fortunately rare. The more usual case material is about the everyday problems of managerial and professional life.

THE ROLE OF CONSULTANT

The task of consultant to an application group is defined as assisting members to relate conference learning to their normal work. His job is to relate knowledge that has been available to members in the conference to the case material they produce; and hence to avoid, as far as possible, introducing other special knowledge or experience. In other words, we now feel that it is not appropriate for a consultant with special knowledge to contribute that knowledge — unless there have been opportunities in the conference for the members to acquire it also.

For these reasons consultants to application groups are chosen, not for their special knowledge of the field represented by the members of the application group, but for their ability to help the application group to which they are assigned. By this device we hope, first, that consultants will be, to some extent, protected from becoming 'experts' on content; and, second, that two-way communication will be improved. Application-group members have to teach consultants about their own field, about the skill required and the conditions in which it can be exercised. The consultant can then help to demonstrate how insights obtainable in the conference can be used to illuminate the problems raised. He brings to bear his experience of relationships to throw light on the relationship problems in the cases presented.

Such, at least, is the theory on which we are working at present, but it would be idle to pretend that we are very satisfied with the results. First, the insights that the consultant gets from a conference are different from those that the members get, because he observes from a different point of view; second, as consultants attend a number of conferences they inevitably become familiar with most of the fields of work represented by the members; and third, the familiarity they thus acquire is based only on second- or third-hand experience, and is not, therefore, necessarily helpful either to the consultant or to the members. The dilemma is not easy to resolve. On the one hand, if a consultant contributes his own special knowledge — for example, if a psychiatrist contributes psychiatric knowledge to a discussion about executive counselling in an application group composed of production managers — he is inevitably led into didactic teaching of a subject that is not part of the conference task; on the other hand, if a consultant has no experience of the work of the members, either they have to spend most of the time teaching him, or he will be tempted into making superficial and oversimplified general contributions.

One learning opportunity is provided by the behavior of the consultant in his leading of the application group. And an important aspect of this leadership is the demonstration of the use of insight into group processes to help the task of the group, without turning the application group into a study group. The application group is a 'there and then' learning event, not a 'here and now', and the consultant has to demonstrate how to use insight into the 'here and now' without exceeding his terms of reference or assuming a sanction to explore private feelings that he has not been given. A potentially dangerous implication of study- and large- group exprience is that whenever the performance of a committee or other working group is inhibited by the rivalries, envies, and hostilities inherent in the interpersonal and intergroup relationships of its members, these feelings should be exposed and 'worked through'. But in ordinary working groups there is seldom any sanction for the exposure of one's own, let alone other people's, feelings and attitudes. All that is permissible is the use of insight into the state of the group as a guide to one's own behavior.

THE PLENARY SESSIONS

The plenary sessions consist of the conference opening, the lectures, and what we have so far called the conference reviews, though we now doubt if that is the correct title for them.

The first conference in 1957 recognized the principle that conferences designed to provide members with opportunities to learn about the interpersonal and intergroup problems of leadership must provide for their full participation in the conference process. Even so, in retrospect, I now feel that the traditional expectation of regular plenaries, for work or social activties, led us to include more plenaries in the program than were required for conference task performance. One consequence was that in planning subsequent conferences there was confusion about both the task and the timing of plenary sessions and indeed about the need for members to meet at regular intervals. At times it has seemed that the primary task of some plenaries has been to allow members to meet for the sake of meeting, and that it has therefore been the staff's job to find them something to meet about.

The introduction of the large-group event for the study of large-group behavior has, to some extent, removed this need. We have been freed to give more attention to the purpose of various kinds of plenary session. At one stage we almost decided to experiment with a conference that had none. A number of the lessons that were learned in earlier conferences have now been clarified and, as in other events, some of them that were lost in subsequent experiments have been relearned.

The 1957 conference was opened by an address of welcome from the Vice Chancellor of the University of Leicester; this was followed by the conference chairman's explaining administrative and residential arrangements, and conducting a tour of the buildings. A second session was then given to a technical description of the conference by the program director. The first of these sessions lasted two hours, and the second, after tea, for an hour and a half. At the time no one had a clear idea of what could be communicated at this stage and how best to communicate it.

'The original plan had been to hold the first Study Group sessions at 4:30 p.m. This was found to allow too little time for introduction and they were postponed until after dinner. There was some evidence that this period of waiting, short though it was, increased the tension to some degree inevitable in anticipation of an unknown experience' (Trist and Sofer, 1959).

It was found subsequently that very little had been communicated by this form of opening. Since then many different kinds of opening have been tried, including the sending out of far more explanatory literature in advance of the actual opening session. If we judge from what members say during the conference, none has succeeded in communicating with any reality what the conference is about, and, as I have said, there have been suggestions of abandoning any attempt at a formal beginning.

THE CONFERENCE OPENING

Nevertheless, the first event of a conference does mark a change in status for both members and staff. Up to that moment, the conference has been a plan, a paper exercise. As soon as it starts, experience begins. Conference membership is the only characteristic that is common to all members and the only thing that unites them. They have left their normal jobs to come to the conference at the invitation of the conference sponsors; their only identification with the conference is through their membership; and the only way in which that can be given corporate realization is by a meeting of all. We have therefore kept the first session as a plenary. But since we do not expect to communicate much at this stage, we have reduced it to what is, in effect, a ritual.

Even as a ritual, however, it still has to have a meaning. In the first session, therefore, the director gives a formal welcome to the members, introduces the staff (who are with him on the platform), gives the conference secretary the opportunity to make any administrative announcements, and then makes a brief statement about what is to happen. This last is a slight amplification of the brochure that members have already received. Questions are then invited. Experience has shown that the questions, if any, are largely of the 'test-out' kind; that is to say, that it is not the questioners' intention only to elicit information, but also to find out if the staff are properly prepared. The questions are usually administrative:

'May we borrow books from the library?'

'Will lecturers provide papers or notes of their lectures or do we have to take our own?'

and so on. All these questions are treated factually and if possible answered. If we do not know the answer we say so, and set in motion means of finding out. No attempt is made to interpret the meaning of the questions or the reasons for their being asked.

When we first introduced this kind of opening session, we allowed a normal period of one and a half hours. There were so few questions, however, sometimes none at all, that short of stimulating discussion artificially or anticipating the large-group event there seemed nothing to do but close it early. We now allow only half an hour for the opening plenary and have found this adequate so far. We recognize, however, that announcing on the program that the session will be so short discourages questions, and the time allowance may have to be changed if a future director changes the kind of opening I have used. The important points to be achieved during the opening are that the conference secretary, whose job during the conference is to look after members, should make herself known, should let her voice be heard, and that members shortly to go into study groups should be able to identify their consultants.

No attempt is made to reassure members about the experiences they might be anticipating. What reassurance there is, if any, is in a demonstration that the staff, as represented by the director and the secretary, know what *they* are going to do. Nor is there any attempt to tell members what they ought to get from the conference. In Bion's terms: members arriving at a conference are inevitably dependent upon the organizers for organizing it; therefore the appropriate basic assumption to be mobilized for an opening event is dependence; and for this the leader has to show himself dependable. This is what I try to do as conference director; and by my conduct of the session I try to display the relationship between the various roles the staff will play and my own.

My colleagues and some members have sometimes felt that I make my statement almost too flat and impersonal; that there is a bit too much of a 'this is it — take it or leave it' attitude. When I look back on the various opening sessions I have conducted I am conscious that I have intended to provide members with a last opportunity for withdrawal before they become involved in the conference process, and the way I behave could suggest that I am advising anybody who has doubts about his attendance to leave at once. An implication of these accusations is that I do too little to help the members to settle down, that I leave them too anxious about what is to happen next. There may well be truth in these comments, but I am not sure that I know any other way of avoiding the greater dangers: on the one hand of going on too long in an attempt to communicate a full description of conference events, and hence of raising anxiety unbearably; or, on the other, of giving false reassurances that make it more difficult for members to accept the reality of the study-group experience that follows, and, more importantly, the integrity of staff intention.

Immediately after the opening, tea, or if the time is different, some other appropriate drink, is served, and then within half an hour the first study-group session takes place.

THE LECTURE SERIES

Lectures, as has been said, are primarily to give the theoretical framework on which the overall design and events of the conference are based. We are not concerned with conference design for its own sake, but with the articulation of the concepts of behavior that have contributed to the design. Lectures are offered on theories of individual and group behavior, and on organization. Other lectures give examples of the application of the theories to practical problems within the lecturers' own experience. As far as possible each lecture is timed to take place when members are preoccupied with its subject-matter. The intention is to offer the theoretical framework appropriate to the move through the conference process. The timing is decided in advance. Though it would be possible to adjust the order and to put in different lectures if we found the timing wrong in practice, we would then have to face the problems that would arise from a change in the program, on which members depend for some of their security. So far, we have adhered to the program.

The lectures, however, have a second purpose: to provide a familiar form of teaching in what is otherwise an unfamiliar, and for most people in the United Kingdom a strange, experience. By giving lectures we hope to demonstrate both that it is possible to use lectures in such a setting and, at the same time, that purely intellectual devices have limitations when it comes to learning about emotional experiences. Members find lectures reassuring, not only because they are familiar with the method but also because they have the opportunity to meet the staff in traditional academic roles; thus they have a kind of standard by which to judge the staff's performance in the less familiar roles in other events. The lectures, in other words, provide a familiar baseline for judgements about unfamiliar experiences.

The lectures are staged as academic events. There is no chairman to mediate between, or to control, lecturer and audience; the lecturer is on the platform on his own, and conducts his own discussion after he has finished speaking. This arrangement is possible because there are never outside lecturers, for whom symbolic institutional sanction in the form of a chairman would have to be given. Lecturers are members of the staff, who, in other events, take other roles. The choice of lecturers, and hence of subjects, is thus limited and there are variations in the lecture series from conference to conference. Our experience of visiting lecturers, however competent as lecturers, has been that they find it difficult to attune themselves to the mood of their audience. Members' experience in other parts of the conference makes them demand much of their lecturers, particularly in the discussion that follows the lecture. As a minimum they expect familiarity with the life of the conference.

From experience of lecturing at these conferences the audience could be described as critical but attentive. In the 1957 conference we did not expect the lectures to be particularly well attended. We thought they would be treated like university lectures, attendance depending both on the subject and on the reputation of the lecturer. But at that conference the attendance was virtually complete; and at all subsequent conferences the same thing has happened. To be a lecturer is in my experience always worrying, but I have found, and other lecturers have found that the other events in the conference, being so vivid in the minds of the members, have supplied such apt illustrations of what the lecture is about that understanding between audience and lecturer has been easy to achieve.

THE PLENARY REVIEWS

Because, at the end of the conference, members return to their ordinary jobs, and application groups are closest in texture to normal working, application groups provide the most fitting ending to the conference. At the same time, by the end of the conference, members have had experience of many kinds of relationships with each other, and with the staff in various roles. Most members have to some extent developed feelings and attitudes, both for and against, the conference as a whole and the events in it. By that time the conference has meaning for them as an institution. Plenary reviews are intended to provide an opportunity for the realization and recognition of these feelings and attitudes. Because they belong to the whole conference, the appropriate setting is a plenary session. But because they are looking backwards and inwards to the conference, they are put near, but not at, the end. They are not intended to provide closure, but only to prepare for ending.

Any attempt to suggest that conferences of this kind can be summed up in a few words would be a denial of the experience that members have been through. The task of the plenary reviews is to try to help members to end the conference but not to stop learning. In the process they might be able to crystallize some aspects of the totality of their experience.

A number of ways of staging and conducting plenary reviews have been tried. The initiative has been left to members, with the chairman or program director acting as seminar leader; or one or more members of the staff have taken the initiative by giving a review. Members and staff have been mixed together in the audience; or some staff have been on the platform, with others grouped at the back of the room or to one side.

To leave the initiative entirely with members implies a number of unproven assumptions: that member-staff relations have reached such a point of resolution that members can and will express their views publicly; that members have learned sufficient to be able to articulate their views coherently; that they have had enough time to prepare for the sessions to make them effective; and that the staff have no further contribution to make except in general discussion. I prefer staff initiative — at least to the extent of setting the scene. This assumes that the staff still have some contribution to make to the learning process. For the same reason, I also prefer to stage the reviews with the total staff on the platform. On occasions when hostility towards the staff has not been fully worked out, this can be and has been interpreted as aggressive and threatening; but I think it is preferable to mixing staff and members, or to having staff at the side or back of the room. At least with staff on the platform members know at whom they are shooting and whence the staff fire will come. Putting the whole staff on the platform also gives a visual demonstration of their collective responsibility for the conference. No arrangement of seating can stop those in the front rows from feeling that they are being shot in the back by other members sitting behind them; but this phenomenon has at least been explored in the large-group sessions.

There are two review sessions. Until recent conferences, into which we have introduced the large-group event, I had started the first session by giving an account of what I had observed of the conference in my role as conference director. I had tried to state what my experience had been, and what I believed I had learned from it. I did not try to tell members what I thought they should have learned, but, by talking about what I thought I had learned, I tried to set a framework for a discussion in which others, members and staff, could give their versions of their experience. My hope was that, by making the statement personal, I would encourage others to make a personal assessment as well. This behavior has seemed to me to be consistent with my role as director. The point of view was unique, and was the only one that was consistently concerned with the total conference.

It was the experience of unsatisfactory reviews that led to the introduction of the large-group event. Once that event had been introduced we had to rethink our methods of dealing with the review. One conclusion about previous reviews was that, by doing as elaborate a job as I had done, I had made it difficult for the staff, let alone the members, to introduce different frameworks or even to put forward constructive alternative explanations within the framework I had given. I had thus made it difficult for other individual contributions to be much more than destructive criticism. By exercising my authority I had also given a demonstration of power that made it impossible at that stage of the conference for the members to combine effectively to oppose me. I had reasserted my leadership and thus, far from preparing to end the conference, I had gone back to the beginning and restarted it. The complaints that I had 'blinded the members with science' had much reality, and they were right to be resentful when, having raised expectations of a lecturer-audience relationship by my opening, I had subsequently answered questions with interpretations of their behavior.

As a result of thinking about the changes required, we have now modified the presentation of the opening. In it I define the task of the review as a continuation of the conference process, as a further opportunity to learn about interpersonal and intergroup relations and particularly to learn about their ending. I draw attention to any particularly significant events and then leave it to members to take up what they wish. I do not think we have yet got this event right, probably because we are too aware of the pitfalls involved. On the one hand there is little we can teach; on the other we must not concentrate so much on our own problems that we either ignore those of the members or, worse, claim their sympathy for our difficulties.

This opening, which takes only five to ten minutes, is usually followed by questions about conference design and about the differences between training and therapy, all of which the members of the staff try to answer as fully as they can. At one conference there was criticism in the first review session of the timing and the content of some events, but the staff came away feeling that it had been a profitable session. The second session, later on the same day, was very different. It opened by a member's saying that he dreaded it, but he did not explain why. There were long periods of silence, and the silences were tense. I was told that I had evaded every question I had been asked in the first session, but little evidence was produced to support this view. It is true that to a large number of the questions that had been asked we had not given satisfactory answers; and what members found difficult to tolerate was that we really had no satisfactory answers to give. And the discussion veered onto the topic of how you became better at our job.

'How do you become a big cheese in this field?'

'Big cheeses take a long time to mature.'

Nobody added, and I regret I did not think of it myself at the time, that big, mature, cheeses can also smell.

Members discussed ending, and the inappropriateness of exchanging ritual compliments in such a conference. Between contributions there were longer and longer silences. After some time, I began to feel that a new ritual had been invented— sitting out time. There had been some comments on the remarkably good time-keeping at the conference, and as I thought about them I realized that a decision had been taken by the members: to sit out the session but to do no more work. Unfortunately, it took me a long time to work out that this was what was happening, and to review the data that supported my conclusion. Eventually, some minutes before the end of the session I became convinced that my observation was correct and so I made it to the members. I suggested that this ritual, like others, was being used to deny the need to work, but I added that it was now so late in the review that the work would have to be left for the application groups. I then closed the session ahead of time.

At other conferences I have not felt such an abandonment of the task and the session has ended like others, on time, but with no conclusions reached. Though it is difficult to relate cause and effect, it is noticeable that reviews conducted in this way, are invariably followed by very hard-working application groups. In this sense they may be achieving their purpose of ending the conference without applying closure to learning.

7.
"ALL WE LIKE SHEEP--"
[Isaiah 53:6]: Followers and Leaders

Margaret J. Rioch

The full verse in the King James version of the Bible from which the title of this paper is taken is: "All we like sheep have gone astray; we have turned everyone to his own way; and the Lord hath laid on him the iniquity of us all." The passage might be interpreted and enlarged upon in more contemporary idiom something like this: "All of us are baffled in these troubled times and we don't know which way to turn. Each one is doing his own thing; but that is not really as satisfying as being committed to a common goal or belonging to a stable community. Surely somewhere there is a good leader who knows the answer, but our actual leaders are bad and are responsible for all our ills and ailments."

The Biblical image of sheep which have gone astray instead of following their shepherd is not very complimentary to man. The sheep is not generally thought of as intelligent like the fox or wise like the owl or strong like the lion, but rather as a mindless animal, requiring someone to think for him and protect him. To the extent that "all we like sheep have gone astray," we do indeed long for a shepherd who will guide us into green and safe pastures. The trouble with this simile, when applied to human beings, is that the shepherd is another sheep. He may be dressed up in a long cloak and accompanied by a tall staff with a crook on the end of it or by other formidable symbols of high office. But underneath the cloak is one of the sheep, and not, alas, a member of a more intelligent and more far-seeing species. But the wish, and sometimes the need, for a leader is so strong that it is almost always possible for one of the sheep to play the role of shepherd of the flock.

"Leader" is a word which implies a relationship like father, son; mother, daughter, as opposed to words like "man" or "girl", which can stand more independently. Just as the word "son" does not have any sense without a parental word like "father" or "mother" implied in it, so the word "leader" does not have any sense without a word like "follower" implied in it. The interrelationships of followers and leaders are among the most significant of human relationships. In fact most

159

relationships can be looked at as variations on the theme of leadership-followership.

The relationship of teacher to student and of psychotherapist or counselor to patient or client are cases in point. The teacher-student relationship is at the heart of the educational process. It is worth noting that the word "educate" comes from the Latin *educere*, meaning to lead out, which suggests that this process has traditionally had something very important to do with leadership and followership. This paper will focus upon followership and leadership in the field of education.

In formal education most people learn some very practical things, namely reading, writing and arithmetic before they are 10. Aside from technical knowledge, people are likely to think of other important aspects of learning in school and college, if indeed there are any, in association with certain teachers to whom they looked as leaders. These teachers are frequently idealized in retrospect and also at the time. The student attends to something in them and in the relationship to them which is distinctly pleasurable, with an ad-mixture of respect, occasionally even adoration, and also something erotic.

In Plato's *Phaedrus* there is a poetic description of this when Socrates, talking about the recollection of heavenly beauty when reawakened by the sight of the soul's earthly namesake, says:

But he...who has been the spectator of many glories in the other world, is amazed when he sees any one having a godlike face or form, which is the expression of divine beauty; and at first a shudder runs through him, and again the old awe steals over him; then looking upon the face of his beloved as a god he reverences him, and if he were not afraid of being thought a downright madman, he would sacrifice to his beloved as to the image of god...During this process the whole soul is all in a state of ebullition and effervescence, which may be compared to the irritation and uneasiness in the gums at the time of cutting teeth. [pp.456-457]

Growing pains are apparently similar whether of the baby cutting teeth or of the adult soul growing wings, the wing being, according to Socrates, "the corporeal element which is most akin to the divine" (p.452).

In this description which Plato gives us of Socrates' discourse on Eros or the "winged one", he speaks of the *attribution* to the beloved of qualities which really belong to the god and of the tendency to *imitate* these qualities. He also refers to the process as one of *educating* into the manner and nature of the god.

Of course, Socrates has not given an explanation of this particular kind of follower-leader phenomenon. But a poetic description or a myth often brings together elements which the more prosaic ones leave separated. This dialogue illuminates the nature of the followership of a charismatic leader. It makes clear that the charisma is not *in* the leader but is in the follower-leader or lover-beloved relationship. How frequently it happens, in encountering someone whom we have loved or followed years earlier, that we wonder how we could have attributed such extraordinary qualities to him. And yet we did, and something in that person made the attribution possible, as well as something in our own need to attribute.

The passage in the *Phaedrus* is concerned with a relationship in which the beloved or leader awakens in the lover or follower recollections of the sight of the divine truth or absolute reality which, according to the myth, the soul glimpses in an instant occurring only once in a thousand or ten thousand years, when the gods stand for a moment on the outside of heaven as the revolution of the sphere carries them around. Obviously such a recollection can have potential only for good. The soul who thus catches a vision of the truth is preserved from harm and her wing can be nourished. But there are charismatic leaders who, instead of awakening in the soul a recollection of divine truth, unleash all the viciousness of hell. Hitler was a charismatic leader of that sort, and there are other lesser ones, no doubt, closer to us.

When, like sheep, we have gone astray, we may in our urgent need for a shepherd, follow the wrong one. How shall we know when we are following a good shepherd and when we are being misled? A discussion of the student teacher relationship may help to clarify some of the problems of the more general follower-leader relationship.

Not infrequently a teacher wields an important and subtle influence over his students, especially if he is capable of a dramatic classroom performance which put his students under a kind of spell. Occasionally, a teacher or a teacher-substitute may thoroughly destroy the preconceptions, assumptions and values formerly held by his students or followers. The vacuum thus created is abhorred by most young people. Something usually rushes in to fill it. As Pascal put it, "It is natural for the mind to believe, and for the will to love; so that, for want of true objects, they must attach themselves to false" (p.24, No. 81). The false object to which the mind and the will attach themselves is often the *person* of the charismatic leader.

Whereas in Plato's description in the *Phaedrus*, the lover is imitating heavenly *qualities*, such as truth, beauty, virtue, which he merely *attributes* to his beloved and which really belong to the god; in the murkier regions which have the smell of hell about them, the follower is not imitating divine attributes, but is giving over something of himself—to use Pascal's terminology, his mind or his will—to the leader.

The power and strength of the leader are based on the weakness and helplessness of the follower. To quote Pascal once more, "The power of kings is founded on the reason and on the folly of the people and especially on their folly. The greatest and most important thing in the world has weakness for its foundation, and this foundation is wonderfully sure; for there is nothing more sure than this, that the people will be weak" (p. 93, No. 330). It is by no means sure that students will be weak. But to the extent that their own strength and intelligence are burdensome to them, they will try to get rid of them and to give them over to the teacher or to whomever they find as a leader in the teacher's place. The teacher or teacher-substitute who consciously or unconsciously seeks and enjoys the exercise of power for its own sake (and who does *not', to some degree?*) places his person at the disposal of the student as a receptacle for the student's unwanted will, which may also be called his competence, strength or intelligence.

The person of the charismatic leader then becomes the object of the follower's devotion. If the follower is a student, his enthusiasm is not for the ideas, the methods, the principles, for which the teacher stands, or for the knowledge and understanding which can be gained through his teaching, but for the teacher as an individual. It may be something like this that Isaiah was referring to when he said that "we have turned everyone to his own way." The cult of personality and doing one's own thing have much in common. When, as the prophet put it, "we have turned everyone to his own way," we are easy game for any teacher or any leader who wants to take us over. For there seems to be a tendency in human beings, which becomes aggravated when they are isolated or faced with unfamiliar situations, to find the exercise of their own powers to mind and will extremely burdensome. Many people hotly deny this tendency in themselves, but it is much more widespread and much more insidious than even sophisticated observers of human nature usually imagine. In the extreme it is the phenomenon which we observe in hypnosis.

One of the best treatises on the subject is in the form of a short story by Thomas Mann called "Mario and The Magician." The story culminates in an account of the public performance of an extraordinarily skillful hypnotist which takes place in an Italian seaside resort and which is billed as entertainment for children as well as adults. The evening turns out to be far from entertaining in the conventional sense. It ends, in fact, in tragedy. As the hypnotist, Cipolla, proceeds to demonstrate more and more dramatically his extraordinary powers over his audience, the interplay between subjugation and freedom of the individuals concerned becomes more and more intricate and the difference between the two less and less clear. What begins as freedom turns into subjugation and vice versa. The audience's admiration for the hypnotist's performance evolves into uneasiness and finally into murderous hatred when Cipolla gives to a young waiter, named Mario, the suggestion that he, Cipolla, an ugly, repulsive hunchback, is the beautiful girl whom Mario loves unrequitedly, for the girl is interested in another. In rapture, believing that she has now at last turned her favor to him, Mario follows the hypnotist's commands and publicly kisses him. Awakening from his trance, he becomes aware of his humiliation, draws his pistol and shoots Cipolla on the stage as the final act of this very serious psychological melodrama.

The reader who is also fascinated with Cipolla's performance looks back at the end of the story with a shudder, not so much at the denouement, as at the framework in which this final event is set. The framework concerns not just the two characters in the last scene, the hypnotist and the hypnotized, but all of us. The story is told from the point of view of a nice German family, a couple with two young children, who are vacationing in the little Italian resort town. The time is obviously the period after Mussolini's accession to power and before Hitler had taken over the reins in Germany. Small unpleasantnesses occur to the Germans, such as a fine imposed by the police because their little girl took off her bathing suit on the beach. As events like this pile up, the narrator, who is the father of the family, comments with increasing frequency that they should have left the place the first time something like that happened. But they didn't. On the last evening of their stay they attend the performance of the hypnotist, who is announced as a magician, for the sake of the children who want to see the magic, and just for something to do.

At the performance the narrator comments similarly over and over that they should have gone home earlier. The evening drags on to a shockingly late hour for the young children, who, when they are not falling asleep, beg not to be taken home. The narrator is painfully aware that the excuses he gives himself, for not insisting that they leave, are weak and untenable. He himself draws the analogy between staying glued to their seats at the performance and staying in the resort town, even though the atmosphere was unhealthy and the treatment they were receiving from the authorities was very shabby.

Thomas Mann makes clear that this passive toleration of minor ill treatment and injustice is akin to the hypnotizability of the audience by the sadistic hypnotist, Cipolla. Mann does not point a moral, but he paints a picture, which leads the reader to see the clear line of a continuum running from the minor snubs suffered by the German family, through the humiliation of Mario at the hands of Cipolla, to the large political scene in which the population of Italy suffered its tyrant, if not gladly, then with the same uneasy combination of subjugation and freedom. It is not difficult, of course, to see the shadow looming ahead, of the even greater tragedy which befell when the Germans also sat glued to their chairs by the hypnotist Hitler, and neither threw him out nor left the audience.

Mann does not paint Cipolla as a likable character, but he does arouse in the reader a degree of reluctant sympathy and admiration for the tremendous, even though perverted, effort which was required for him to accomplish the work of imposing his will upon the audience. The so-called imposition of Cipolla's will is experienced by his subjects as freeing them from subjugation to their own wills. They can now do what they wanted to do all along.

Cipolla knows his trade well for along with the masterful commands, always underlined by swishing his riding whip, he also speaks seductively. "Dance," he says, urging a particularly reluctant gentleman to give in to his hypnotic command, "who wants to torture himself this way? Do you call that freedom; this kind of forced submission of yourself?...How good it will feel finally to let go of your will. There, you're dancing already. Now it's no longer a struggle; it's really a pleasure" (p.121).

The description in "Mario and the Magician" and the one in the *Phaedrus* exemplify extremes of a leader-followership relationship in which the leader is felt to be charismatic. In the former, the follower is responding to the person of the leader; in the latter the follower is responding to that for which the leader stands—his ideas, his vision, his values, or his work. Most of the time in actual life we encounter mixtures with a predominance of the former or the latter kind of relationship. It may be possible to distinguish which of the two kinds is dominant by asking whether the follower continues to follow and to develop further in the way the leader has shown even if the leader himself is no longer present. If the follower continues and develops further in the leader's path after the leader's death or disappearance from the scene, it means that the former has integrated the latter's ideas, has made them part of himself and now acts on the basis of a theory, a set of convictions, or values, even if they are very primitive, but not on the basis of personal attachment and loyalty. If we are essentially following a person rather than his ideas and his philosophy, we need not understand the ideas and the philosophy, even though we mouth them. Our followership consists of a kind of hypnosis, of giving over our will to the other and losing thereby that terrible burden which we carry so reluctantly: responsibility for our own acts.

The student, or any person, who is looking for a leader will be fortunate if he finds one closer to Plato's model than to Cipolla. And the educator who is responsible for leading his students into green pastures, not into barren ground or over a cliff, and who finds himself in a charismatic relationship with his students, will do well not to misuse his gift as Cipolla did in the case of Mario. Since psychotherapists, psychoanalysts, and counselors in the mental health field can be thought of as educators even when they are also doctors, the problem applies to them as well as to classroom teachers.

With or without charisma the teacher or teacher-substitute has a role to perform as a leader of his students. Traditionally he performs several functions: (1) He transmits facts and theories discovered or developed in the past. (2) He tells students what to do in order to develop skills such as penmanship, drawing, tennis, and the like. (3) He presents himself as a model for imitation—for example, in performing a surgical operation.

There is also another function, more important, more generally neglected. I wish to devote the main portion of this paper to a description of a particular teaching situation that exemplifies it. The function, whose nature will emerge in the course of the description, occupies a central position in the methods developed in the Centre for Applied Social Research of the Tavistock Institute of Human Relations of London. These methods were developed primarily by the late Dr. A. Kenneth Rice and institutionalized in the Group Relations Conferences held at the University of Leicester in England.

Kenneth Rice used to indicate his way of viewing a situation by a large gesture describing a semicircle. It was a gesture of inclusion, indicating that it would be well to lift up one's eyes from a particular problem or a particular individual and include a larger field. In this larger field he always sought to identify the critical factors, since it is obviously impossible to consider all factors operating even in a smaller field. The approach is particularly congenial to those of us who had come under Harry Stack Sullivan's influence. It is, of course, related to field theory and systems theory. Dr. Rice developed a set of concepts about organizations which facilitated the practice of this approach in education, in management, and in group life generally.

In 1965 the Washington School of Psychiatry and Yale University Department of Psychiatry began the process of transplanting Rice's educational methods to the United States. When the conferences first began, the emphasis was on the study of the small group of about 10 people. Over the years Kenneth Rice's gesture of inclusion grew larger. Some conferences have now been run without any exercise for the study of small groups at all. The emphasis has shifted to the study of larger groups of up to 60 and 70 people sitting together in the same room, and even more to intergroup studies. It was Rice's contention that all group processes are intergroup processes. He included in this statement whatever occurs within a single person since he conceived of the individual as made up of a number of different parts which one can call id, ego, etc., or the various roles or personae who at different times speak from the same mouth. Rice thought of the ego as performing a leadership function for the individual, as a shepherd performs a leadership function for the flock, deciding which way it shall go, how it shall and shall not behave, and what shall be allowed to come in and go out. Within the flock and within the individual there may be smoldering or open rebellion about these decisions, but somebody wins out and the flock turns either right or left as the individual performs or does not perform a particular act, either with internal harmony or in spite of internal conflict. As psychotherapists know, the study of such individual acts or non-acts is a complex matter. In a conference of around 50 members the study is obviously much more complex. No one claims to have mastered this field. The conferences simply offer an opportunity to study the phenomena of group and intergroup processes as they are going on.

In order to think about these processes some integrating concept or concepts are necessary. Rice's book about the conferences is called *Learning for Leadership*. More recently the primary task of the conferences has been described as the study of the nature of authority. The concepts of leadership and authority have been defined and differentiated elsewhere. It will suffice for the purposes of this paper if they are taken according to any dictionary definition. The essential point here is that they are integrating, unifying principles with the help of which it is possible to consider complex phenomena, just as the concept *forest* helps us to consider a large number of trees without getting lost in them. Without such integrating concepts, the study of group processes, while they are going on, returns, of necessity, to the study of particular individuals with the group as a background. This may, indeed, have merits. It may be exactly what is indicated in therapy groups, for example; but it is not the same thing as the study of groups as integrated systems.

The Group Relations Conferences, as they were developed in England and more recently in the United States, are for most people a period of stress and anxiety. The situation is strange; familiar landmarks and routines are obliterated. An opportunity is offered to learn new ways of relating to the world. It is not that new ways are delineated or prescribed, but the situation itself tends to be mutative. Metaphorically speaking, one is pushed swiftly to the edge of a chasm and carried by the forward impulse in a long leap across the abyss to new and undiscovered country on the other side—unless, of course, one falls back into the old country or into the depths. Clearly this process of letting go of old ways of behaving involves a risk. People who are already under stress or who are subject to a great deal of chronic anxiety should be discouraged from taking this kind of risk. They are, in fact, discouraged from attendance at these conferences. The statement is underlined that the conferences are not designed as therapeutic events, but are intended for mature adults capable of absorbing considerable stress.

The conferences vary in length: the longest so far is of two weeks duration; the shortest one which includes all the exercises, four days. The first ones held in this country were all residential. This has the advantage of creating a cultural island so that members can immerse themselves in the experience. However, nonresidential conferences have also taken place and have their value.

The conferences usually open with an introduction by the director who outlines the task, sets the tone of the conference, and makes clear the sources, the extent, and the limits of his authority as well as that of the other staff members. He also introduces the staff, who sit in a row in the front of the room facing the members.

The program or schedule is printed in the brochure announcing the conference and changes are made in it only if there are very urgent reasons. The design is carefully thought through by the director and his advisers and the sequence of events is decided upon, on the basis of experience and the best predictions that can be made about the way learning is most likely to take place. Each session is an hour and a half long.

There are four major exercises, or events, as they are now called. The first event following the introduction is traditionally the study of the small group, which continues for one or more sessions each day, but stops before the last day of the conference. The second event usually also begins on the first day. This is the study of the large group, which includes all conference members. On the second day the formal study of intergroup events begins.

Toward the end of the conference small discussion groups are scheduled for the purpose of applying conference learning to the work which members do at home. They also try to examine unresolved conference problems and assist people in making the transition from the "cultural island" of the conference to their situations outside. They are conducted in a familiar manner with the consultant taking a role like that of the traditional seminar instructor. This exercise is not concerned with the "here and now" but looks backward and forward in time.

In the "here and now" Small Group Event about 10 members with their consultant sit in a circle. The major characteristics which distinguish the Tavistock small groups from others, such as encounter groups and sensitivity training, are the nature of the task and the role of the consultant. The task is to study the processes going on in the group as a *whole* while they are going on, especially the covert processes, with a particular focus, which is at present upon the nature of authority and the problems encountered in its exercise. The role of the consultant is to provide opportunities for the study. The role requires of the consultant a high degree of self-discipline. He is to intervene only when he can facilitate the study of the ongoing processes and at no other time and in no other way. His role prescribes further that he will do this for the period set aside for the exercise in the space provided for it. Thus he begins and ends precisely on time and does not leave the assigned room except for an emergency. He rarely addresses one individual and he concerns himself with individuals only as they represent some aspect of the total group life. It often happens that questions are addressed to him which he does not answer if he thinks that a direct answer would not be in the interest of the self-study of the group. As in most new situations there is an initial uneasiness about who everyone is and what may take place.

People hope that their self-esteem will be enhanced, but they fear it may be damaged.

The consultant does nothing to try to make the group members feel more comfortable. Their uneasiness often increases when the consultant points out the maneuvers in which members engage to cover up or to get around their painful uncertainty, such as introducing themselves, making small talk, moving chairs, or attacking someone who sticks his neck out. The consultant does this, not for the sake of making people uncomfortable, but for the sake of the task of learning. He simply comments, to the best of his ability, on what he sees going on and tries to make sense of it. However, it is hard for members to believe this. They tend to think that the increased uneasiness which they feel was intended by the consultant as a part of a manipulative plan. This is the beginning of the paranoia which is a frequent phenomenon in the conferences. The assumption is that if something happens, someone must have planned it — if not for a good reason, then for a bad one. Since people are reluctant to blame their discomfort on God, the "management" must be responsible. The extent to which sane, "normal" people engage in paranoid thinking of this kind is astonishing to themselves when they become aware of it.

Even in today's outspoken culture there is usually a good deal of reluctance about confronting directly the authority personified by the consultant. Since all the conference members are adults who have presumably come voluntarily with the avowed purpose of studying the problems of authority in and among groups, they do attempt to fulfill the purpose and to join with the consultant in the common task of understanding the processes in the group as they are occurring. But as Wilfred Bion pointed out, there is present in every group, along with the intelligent, task-oriented activity, another side of group life, which he called the basic assumption aspects. The consultant in conference groups, as indeed the leader in any group, is always subject to pulls and tugs of enormous strength on the part of the members to give up his role and his task. The power of these pulls and tugs is, of course, not weaker because it is to a large extent outside awareness.

The accusation which is so often made of the consultant that he is grim, unsmiling, and severe, has more than a grain of truth in it. It is scarcely possible to enter into this activity lightheartedly. From past experience it can be assumed that there is going to be a struggle. This may be invigorating; it may in the end be satisfying and fulfilling. But it is grim because it reaches into the depths of human nature. One needs scarcely more than a glance at every morning's newspaper to see that our present human society resembles an old-fashioned madhouse more than Utopia where lion and lamb lie down together. It is therefore not surprising that phenomena familiar in society and in the old madhouse emerge in the microcosm of the conference. It often becomes clear that the elements in our society which produce crime, insanity, riots, wars, and the manifold injustices which we deplore, are present in the conference, in each group of nice, intelligent individuals who come full of the best intentions.

Some of the same things which occur in the Small Group also hold true in the Large Group Exercise, which has as its task the study of the processes in a Large Group as they occur, again with the focus on the problems of authority. All 50-60 members of the conference with consultants participate in this. The sessions are usually held one a day through most of the conference period.

Whereas in a small group each person can and often does become important to all others and distinguishable by all others, this is manifestly impossible in a large group, especially over a short period of time. It is, of course, *completely* impossible in groups larger than conference groups, such as the population of a city, or a government agency. This relative anonymity is very painful and exerts a pull upon the more aggressive members to make themselves known at whatever cost. The quieter ones tend to become still quieter and some never speak at all in the Large Group.

The concentration upon the group as a whole, whether large or small, with the focus on the concept of authority, is felt by the members to be impersonal and lacking in warmth. In an important sense it is just that. "Warmth" is usually experienced as something one individual feels for another or a very few others. It does, of course, happen in a Tavistock group that a consultant feels warmly toward an individual in his group. If he allows himself to remain in this happy feeling or to give voice to it without further reflection, he has obviously been caught off balance. His job is to see how this feeling of warmth for an individual arose in the group, how the seduction (not necessarily at all a conscious seduction) fitted into the life of the total group. It happens occasionally that the group is quite happy to see one member, particularly a female member in a group with a male consultant, occupy the consultant's attention and engage with him in a pairing relationship even though jealousy is present at the same time. This happy interlude seems to augur well for the release of positive feelings generally in the group. The consultant is then sorely tempted to rest in the enjoyment of the peace and warmth engendered in the pairing relationship which is being smiled upon, temporarily, by the others. But his job is not to rest and enjoy the situation, any more than it is to enjoy the situation of openly expressed anger and resentment. His job is to try to comprehend the meaning of this relationship in the context of the whole. The girl in question has probably thought of herself simply as an individual who is attracted by the good looking consultant. She is delighted that at least for the moment she can see that the attraction is reciprocated. Happy at having captured the consultant, she basks in her success. She is unaware and is usually quite resistant to becoming aware that she is one strand in the texture of the whole, that the others were willing, more than willing, to have her play this role; in fact, they needed her for it. Otherwise she could not have played it. She would have been drowned out by other concerns. The consultant's job is to understand her as a wave carried on the surface of the deep current of the group stream, and to help the group to perceive her and themselves in this same way. This view does not suppose a group mind operating in some mysterious way. It does suppose a system which is a set of interrelated events. A change in any part means a change in all the interrelationships in the system.

When a person in a group becomes aware of himself in this way, the awareness is often accompanied by a weird feeling of being no longer one's old familiar self. The sense of having a will of one's own, of being free to make one's own choice, disappears, and the individual experiences himself as a marionette pulled by the strings of the group or as being a channel through which the group pours its energy and expresses itself. On one occasion a woman, who happened to be the only woman in a particular small group, found herself crying without knowing why and even without feeling that she wanted to cry, but as if, so she said, the group were crying through her. She felt this as strange and uncanny.

People enter groups with certain tendencies developed through their past experiences and pressed upon them by tradition. Thus it is not surprising that it was the woman in the group who found herself "elected" to cry for the group. In the beginning phases of a group it is the readily recognizable, stereotyped tendencies of each member that are used to represent the various aspects of the group's life. There are one or two "aggressive guys" who do the fighting, a "funny man" who cracks the jokes, a "wise" person, a peacemaker, a motherly one, a sexy one, a shy quiet one, and so on. Later, especially if a group works well together, people can shift out of their stereotypes and find that they express richer and more many-sided aspects of themselves.

The converse of the marionette phenomenon also occurs, especially in large groups, when an individual experiences himself as able to do anything with the group that he likes, sometimes so much so that he believes he *is* the group. This is often accompanied by a pseudo-religious fervor which carries the individual away into a grandiose sense of power. And this too is uncanny. An individual in this state with relation to the group does wield an enormous influence. The members are fascinated with him and find themselves unable to put their attention on anything else.

These two experiences, the sense of being all-powerful and the feeling of being a marionette, although they appear to be opposite, are essentially two sides of the same coin. They feel uncanny because an aspect of our lives is revealed in them to which we are usually blind, namely the unity of the individual with the whole.

It is possible to argue interminably, as people have done, about whether the true power in a group lies with the leader or with the masses who permit the leader to lead; whether the true responsibility lies with the individual who commits an act, for example a criminal act, or with the society which brought the individual forth. Looking at these questions as "either-or" alternatives ignores the fundamental unity of the individual and the whole. Tolstoy in *War and Peace*, speaking of the Napoleonic invasion of Russia had this to say:

Had Napoleon not taken offense at the demand that he should withdraw beyond the Vistula, and not ordered his troops to advance, there would have been no war; but had all his sergeants objected to serving a second term then also there could have been no war. Nor could there have been a war had there been no English intrigues and no Duke of Oldenburg, and had Alexander not felt insulted, and had there not been an autocratic government in Russia, or a Revolution in France and a subsequent dictatorship and Empire, or all the things that produced the French Revolution, and so on. Without each of these causes nothing could have happened...In order that the will of Napoleon and Alexander [on whom the event seemed to depend] should be carried out, the concurrence of innumerable circumstances was needed without any one of which the event could not have taken place.

Man lives consciously for himself, but is an unconscious instrument in the attainment of the historic, universal aims of humanity....[pp. 669-670]

These comments of Tolstoy seem to me to illuminate the interplay between leader and followers, or to put it another way, between the individual and the group, which is always a subject of discussion in the conferences. The theoretical conclusion seems inescapable, that responsibility within a system, if it is anywhere, is everywhere. In practice, what occurs is that many people leave the conferences with an increased ability to behave in a thoughtful, reliable way in their own institutions, with increased ability to take reasonable action when they might formerly have sat helplessly, apathetically glued to their seats; and this in spite of a clear realization that their behavior is determined by the groups to which they belong and have belonged. The paradox was expressed poignantly by one member toward the end of a conference. "When I look for the group," he said, "I find myself. When I look for myself, I find the group."

The relationship of the individual to the group in which he finds himself continues to be studied in the third conference exercise, which focuses on intergroup relations. Concentration upon intergroup events highlights other aspects of the same problem and permits the relationship to the authority of the staff as a managing body to come into the foreground. This exercise has a number of different forms which are used separately or together in various conferences. The exercise usually starts in plenary session like the beginning of the conference, with members sitting in rows as at a lecture and the staff in the front of the room facing the members. The director introduces the exercise. In his introductory remarks he states the task of the exercise and indicates the space that is available, sometimes listing the rooms by numbers, and suggesting that the members can divide up in any way they wish. Consultants are available to facilitate the task of studying intergroup relations as they happen. In one form of the exercise, the staff group leaves the plenary room immediately following the introduction and takes up its position as a group within the exercise in a territory of its own.

At a typical recent conference, many people then got up and immediately left the room. Some had made plans prior to the conference, having heard from colleagues what these events are like. Some simply wanted to get out as fast as possible from a situation which was too much like the Large Group for comfort. Some interpreted the opening remarks as a directive to go somewhere. This last is a very frequent occurrence. The listing of available rooms and the withdrawal of the staff are taken as heaven-sent guide lines of what to do, and people accordingly scramble to get to a room before they can be left out.

One group formed on the basis of wanting to be independent of the staff and subsequently became known as the rebel group. One group wanted to be thought cooperative and tried to be free of organizational restraints. One group wanted to devise a different schedule and negotiate with the staff to put it into effect. Most of the groups which formed did not hold with any great persistence to the avowed purposes with which they formed. They found enormous difficulty in getting together to do anything, and in allowing anyone to assume authority for the group. The problem of representation which exists in all inter-group activity became clearly visible.

If a group is to take any action as a whole in negotiating with or relating to another group, it means that each member has to give up something of his own autonomy to the person designated as spokesman for his group. The spokesman himself is limited in his autonomy by the degree of authority which the group confers upon him. If he oversteps the limits or if his groups thinks he has not adhered to its policy, he may be disowned. Many a person has come back to his room in this exercise full of what he has accomplished with representatives of other groups only to find either that his group had disbanded and disintegrated, or that it had changed course so that his accomplishment was as nothing. It is not easy for a representative to remain in touch with his group, to remain loyal to them, and to retain their confidence while he is away from home base, as members of United Nations can no doubt testify. The difficulties which spring from group members' reluctance to give over some authority to a representative are matched only by those which spring from the opposite tendency: namely the abdication of responsibility on the part of group members when they allow themselves to be taken over by a dictatorial leader. When this happens, the self-appointed dictator can lead the group by the nose whenever he chooses, but he gets no real support from his followers, for they are simply allowing him to do their work for them. They have given up their responsibility along with their authority and have placed it all in one person. He is thus in the unenviable position of being in charge of a group of zombies. It sometimes happens that, carried away by his power, he commits his group in a way which really goes too far. Perhaps he forms an alliance with another group to make a revolution to depose the staff and run the conference. But when the cost of this proceeding becomes clear, when his followers realize that they have not bargained for the kind of fight *and* work that would be involved, they may revolt against him and *he* may be deposed. If a consultant gets an opportunity at a time like this, he tries to point out that the dictator's acts were made possible only by the apathy of the group, which had happily let him do all the work until it turned out that they were going to have to pay a price for their inaction.

The situation of a working group in which the leader really represents a policy, thought out, understood, supported, and collaboratively carried out by the whole group turns out to be an exceedingly hard thing to accomplish, and one which rarely obtains for long stretches of time. Groups, like individuals, do not consistently function at their best. Either everyone is so involved in wanting his own way that a common task can be developed only with difficulty, and once developed, is not supported; or everyone is so indifferent to the stated task that the group either falls apart or falls into the hands of a dictator. The former case is the one referred to by Isaiah: "We have turned everyone to his own way." The latter case brings us back to Mario and the hypnotist, Cipolla, when the audience allowed itself to be led wherever Cipolla wanted it to go until Mario took revenge for all of them in his act of murderous outrage. An effective working group requires a task or goal which seems accomplishable and about which there is some reasonable consensus on the part of the members. The task is not always clearly formulated and consciously spelled out, but the members' interest must be invested in it if the group is to function.

During the conference as a whole, and most clearly demonstrated in the intergroup exercise, members pull and tug at the consultants to tell them what to do, to be leaders in the traditional sense of shepherds who guide their flocks up hill or down dale wherever they will find the greenest grass. At the same time members fight angrily against the staff because they resent feeling like sheep or school children. One member reported after a recent conference that he responded to this feeling by "behaving in a helpless manner, becoming overly dependent on others to provide for basic needs, saying, in essence, 'Where do we sleep? Where do we eat? What's next on the schedule?' " He added that it was the same experience he had had in military service, where everything seemed "planned for you so you don't have to think for yourself. If you think for yourself you may get into trouble. I am told that travelers in foreign countries often react this way to their guided tours."

It is striking how easily, not to say distortedly, this attitude of helpless dependency with accompanying resentment is generated. The member quoted above speaks for many, many others. It is not hard to see how the associations to three situations of great dependency—school, the military, the guided tour—are called up. As far as school is concerned, the conferences are announced as education institutions. Whenever possible they are held in a college or school in order to underline the message that this is a *learning* situation. As far as the military is concerned, the strict discipline of the staff, their formal use of last names and titles, sitting in a row in front of the room, adherence to time boundaries, and clear lines of authority can well evoke military images. The guided tour in a foreign country is an excellent symbol for the unfamiliar situation in which practical matters are well provided so that no one has to give thought as to where he will sleep or what he will eat, but where one is bombarded by new and strange sights and sounds challenging to prejudices and preconceptions.

It is striking that the dependency associated with these three situations occurs routinely and immediately in the conferences in spite of the fact that the written and spoken words introducing the events refer again and again to the fact that the teaching will not be carried on in the traditional manner, that how members learn and what they do is up to them, that staff members do not know and have not planned what will occur, that members are free in every sense of the word to come or go, learn or not learn what and as they please.

Two conclusions can be drawn from this consistent occurrence of dependent reactions: first, that the content of the spoken and written word is not as powerful as the behavior which evokes the associations of school, the military, and the guided tour; and second, that there is a tremendous readiness on the part of mature, intelligent adults, not to mention children and adolescents, to fall into this pattern.

It is this readiness of which Cipolla took advantage. It is this readiness which permits the conception to arise that we attribute to Isaiah when he says that the Lord hath laid on *him* the iniquity of us all. How easily we give over our wills and our minds if someone will take our sins upon him and free us from the terrible burden of responsibility for the choices we make. This can be seen very clearly in the conference situation. Members behave strikingly like sheep, and sometimes like goats. With great docility they do what they believe the staff would like them to do; or with terrible locking of horns they refuse to do what they believe is required of them. In either case they place the authority for their behavior outside themselves and in the staff with predictable regularity. The staff, for its part, is over and over again outraged at the way in which members behave like dependent children, as if the staff and its behavior had nothing whatever to do with it. The tendency in all of us is to think the iniquity is out there; it is laid on *him* or on them. This, of course, makes it possible to believe that salvation will also come from out there, from *him* or them. The tenacity of this belief has been demonstrated, so far, in every conference.

The staff sweats and bleeds and works for members to give up the fallacious struggle in which they are engaged; fallacious because the staff does not wish to humiliate, put down, vanquish, or tell members what to do. The staff does wish to collaborate and assist in learning, but will not collaborate in the fiction that it should or does make decisions and choices for the members.

As a conference director I have frequently experienced a phenomenon toward the end which is like a kinesthetic perception inside my skin. It is as if the membership made a 180-degree turn in giving up the fallacious struggle. Not every person does this, but enough people do, so that it can fairly be called a group phenomenon. A metaphor from the work of the French philosopher Dr. Hubert Benoit expresses it most clearly. It is as if the members had been staring out of a small barred window, straining every nerve and muscle to stretch and see out of it as far as possible, trying to see the light according to the ouside authority, shaking violently at the bars which may bend but do not break. Behind them at the other end of the room is an open door. They have only to turn around to walk out of their prison. But before they can let go their cramped hold on the bars and be willing to turn away from the precious bit of light which they perceive through the small window, they have to comprehend clearly that they really are—and have been from the beginning—free. They have to comprehend that the power and authority which they had ascribed to the staff belong not to anyone outside themselves but to them, to each person who is his own authority.

In most of our schools, in spite of the influence of John Dewey and many other educators, students *take* courses *given* by instructors. The words take and give are significant. The model seems to be not even sheep with a shepherd, but a nest of little birds with their mouths open waiting to be fed. In recent years the food brought to the nest has become unpalatable and the little birds have become large birds with huge claws and sharp beaks who attack those who try to feed them. It seems to me that the model is inappropriate. It is true that a teacher sometimes needs to transmit facts and theories from the past, to tell students what to do in order to develop skills, and to present a model for imitation. But much more importantly his function is to insist that the students take unto themselves the authority which tends to be foisted on the teacher. This can be done if the teacher refuses steadfastly to accept the authority. He will probably find that the students, the rebellious ones as well as the docile ones, will try in a thousand ways to force him or seduce him to accept it.

There is a sense in which the authority in the Tavistock conferences and in educational institutions generally can not be taken over by each member or student for himself. This has to do with the authority to manage the institution, that is, the right to perform the function of setting up the necessary practical arrangements, of designing the exercises, acting as consultants, and doing whatever needs to be done to provide optimal learning opportunities. This responsibility lies with the whole staff and particularly with its leader. In the conferences it is derived from the sponsoring institution or institutions which confer upon the director and through him upon the staff the authority to perform these functions. By coming to the conference and paying the required fee, members implicitly confirm this authority and agree to allow the staff to perform its function. For the exercise of such authority some power is necessary. The power lies in large part in the competence of the staff. It can be used and also misused. It must be placed in the service of the task, for power not in the service of an honorable task becomes corrupt. Commenting on a concert she had just heard, Dr. Frieda Fromm-Reichmann once said: "It was not only great music, it was the perfect performance of a service." Competence and talent, whether in music or in interpersonal relations or in anything else are marvelous sources of gratification to the person who exercises them. The dissatisfaction which so many people feel in their working lives often stems from not finding a way to put their talents, large or small, in the service of a task.

The task of conducting the Tavistock-Washington School of Psychiatry conferences is felt by the staff to be very arduous work requiring great self-discipline, entailing a great amount of anxiety, and paying a small amount of money. Yet being on the staff is a coveted prize. Many would say it is the most important and gratifying work that they do. It is clear that this is not in spite of its being so arduous and requiring so much commitment of oneself, but exactly because of this. This is not to preach a moral but to state a fact. Human beings are never more fulfilled than when they are united to a whole. The mystics speak of this in terms of the cosmos. Perhaps it is a small inkling of this total union which makes the experience in a working group committed to a common task so fulfilling. It is not possible really to do this unless the phenomenon referred to as the 180-degree turn has taken place. The individual must know that he himself, on his own authority, has made the commitment to put his competence in the service of the common task.

To return to Isaiah, the passage seems to say that there can be no human society so long as each one turns to his own way. A group cannot function so long as each one insists upon his own autonomy. But paradoxically neither can a group function if each individual abdicates his autonomy. Resolution of this apparent contradiction requires two things. First, that the individual should perceive clearly his freedom to belong or not to belong. To be sure, the choice in extreme cases may mean death or imprisonment, but there remains an essential freedom which Socrates demonstrated when he chose to drink the hemlock rather than to emigrate. And second, that the individual should see the essential unity of himself and his group.

The leader of a group does, as Isaiah says, bear the iniquity and also the virtue of the group, since he, more than any other member represents the task of the whole group. This passage and many like it are commonly interpreted to mean that the leader *alone* carries the sins and the redemption of the group. This interpretation leads to the idea that if the leader does it, the others do not need to. But another way to interpret the passage is that since the leader does it, the others can do it too.

In the field of education, whether in psychotherapy or in the classroom, the teacher has as his function the training of future leaders. His students may become leaders only in their own families; or they may become leaders of nations. In either case the problem of putting one's power in the service of the group task remains essentially the same. There can scarcely be a more central problem for any teacher.

part three
APPLICATION

The group relations and organizational theories presented in this volume are based on a systems approach and are task-oriented, making applications possible on different levels in many fields. While the membership at conferences has always been drawn from a variety of organizations, the staff are predominantly mental health professionals. It is not surprising, therefore, that most applications have been in the field of mental health. As interest and demand have grown, regional affiliates of the A.K. Rice Institute have undertaken training programs and are beginning to provide qualified consultants with different professional backgrounds. As this progress continues, the number and variety of applications will grow as well.

At no time has the need for rationalizing decision making by including the effects of covert alliances and unconscious processes, been more important than it is now. Our technologies have tremendous power and our sciences can explore any number of areas, but the size of human populations, resource depletion and the potentially dangerous consequences of some of our discoveries are fast bringing us to the point where we cannot afford mistakes or false starts. We have to address the right problems and perform the tasks well in dealing with them.

For the purposes of this volume the papers are organized into three main areas in which most work has been done: clinical, educational, and organizational analysis and consultation. The section on education includes some experimental applications in professional training, because the introduction of this knowledge directly into the different professions will encourage practitioners and researchers in those fields to develop and use the model to meet specific needs. A fourth, more specialized category of application, in architecture and planning, is added to show some of the potential uses of the theory in a previously unexplored and seemingly unlikely area. In fact the field of environmental design and planning is extremely important because it affects many people and has ecological significance. These examples illustrating the way that irrational, unconscious processes can affect and even control methods thought to be rational and technical, provide some impetus for exploring and further developing group relations concepts in policy planning at different levels of our society.

W.H.B.

A
Clinical

8.
THE APPLICATION OF GROUP RELATIONS METHODS AND CONCEPTS

William Hausman

Although the "Tavistock" group relations concepts owe their origins to Bion's observations stemming, in part, from his studies of the group behavior of psychiatrically disordered war casualties during World War II, the application of these concepts to clinical psychiatry has received relatively little attention in the literature. The dearth of publications is all the more striking since a large proportion of those attending the many Group Relations Conferences held in the United States since 1965 have been identified with the mental health field. Yet this particular approach to the study of group and organizational behavior offers a rich field for the clearer understanding of social processes related to psychiatric treatment.

The data available to the clinical-investigator who seeks to study the relationship between theory and practice and between the Group Relations Conference as a learning exercise and day to day work in the clinic, emerges from a variety of sources. Few who have worked in any roles in Group Relations Conferences have failed to see repeated evidences of behavioral manifestations of members approximating common experiences in the clinic. On some occasions these events have been dramatic and blatantly "clinical" in nature but more often they are subtle, transient, but strongly reminiscent of similar events in the purely clinical setting. Nor are these events always suggestive of "psychopathology". Discussions with conference members following the termination of a conference have frequently evoked spontaneous descriptions of the experiencing of personal changes which, among those who have had prior experiences in psychotherapy, felt familiarly similar to therapeutic progress.

A second source of data that lends itself to the potential for clinical application has come from those conferences which have been specifically identified as related to mental health or general medical administration.

An example is the Group Relations in Hospitals Conference

which has been held annually since 1970. Other conferences have been more specifically designed for the staff members of a given clinical institution. These in-house conferences have been developed after consultation with the authorities of the local facility. They represent a rich opportunity to examine the dynamic characteristics of a psychiatric treatment center from the unique vantage point of the consultant who embodies the methods identified with the A.K. Rice Institute.

A third source of information about the relationship of these theories and learning techniques to the clinical setting emerges from the clinic itself. As noted above, a large number of individuals who have attended Group Relations Conferences actively work in and supervise work of others in a variety of psychiatric institutions around the country. Many have sought ways of introducing these concepts into the therapeutic, educational and administrative life of the institution. The author's observations about the application of these concepts come in no small part from carrying a leadership role in a clinical-academic department which encompasses educational, service and research tasks.

Finally, one learns about application from the work of others. This may well start with a re-reading of Bion's first chapter in *Experiences in Groups,* moving on to Isabel Menzies' Study of Nursing Services, and the papers of Lofgren, Astrachan and colleagues, and David Singer and his co-workers. Because the boundaries of the clinical system are often contained within a larger organizational system, the reader may want to review the paper of Roy W. Menninger and the author's statement on "Reorganization of a Department of Psychiatry" (Hausman, In Press).

Individuals who have attended Group Relations Conferences (either as members or consultants) have all experienced the situation where the consultant was confronted by a group that insisted that one of its members was clearly bizarre in his behavior, "obviously" needed immediate treatment. In such a situation, the maintenance of the consultant's role boundary and his interpretations of the group's behavior usually permits the group to release that person from his "sick" role and the group to move from a basic assumption dependency mode back into a a work mode. This is consistent with Bion's observation about the ways in which groups create casualties to serve their basic assumption needs. On a rare occasion, this behavior may move beyond the small group into the conference as a whole and may become an issue for all of the staff and members of the conference. During one conference the author, as director, was confronted with a member whose behavior, midway through a conference, became so bizarre that a number of highly qualified psychiatrists who were members of that conference came to him with their clear diagnostic impressions of a classic psychosis and offered specific "assistance" in suggesting the names of hospitals where this persons might be sent. After considering the gratuitously offered advice the decision was made to permit the member to continue in the conference with the understanding that he would participate in its exercises. This decision was ultimately substantiated by his gradual but dramatic "recovery" toward the last days of the conference as he "worked through" the conflicts that he symbolized for the conference institution. In doing so he offered rich material for the membership to work on while he, himself, worked to re-establish a less taxing membership role. By the end of the conference it was clear to the staff that the member was free of symptoms. It was gratifying to learn from a sophisticated observer several months after the conference that the member "had never been better". More generally important was the fact that this individual and the membership shared in a very powerful learning experience of a very unique nature. Such experiences have specific relationship to application in that they clearly and dramatically emphasize the propensity of groups, in certain ambiguous and highly intense situations, to produce casualties. While this in itself is important, what is even more important is the capacity of the group, sometimes with outside help, to contribute to the reconstitution of such a casualty when the conditions of the group are changed. Such experiences are hardly an unique artifact of the Group Relations Conference situation but rather have direct application to the work of mental health professionals at all levels within the clinical institution.

The special purpose conferences have offered the opportunity to examine psychiatric institutions, ranging from a single ward unit to much larger facilities, through a variety of educational designs and aimed at permitting the staffs of these hospitals to learn about the nature of authority within the context of their own institutional setting. These conferences have permitted the examination of intra-staff dynamics within the institution and the opportunity to learn something about staff work with patients by way of their contributions to application groups. While these do not represent a large, or even representative, cross-section of psychiatric institutions, they offer valuable leads toward understanding staff and staff-patient dynamics. Similar information has been shared by staff and members of other institutions at the Group Relations in Hospitals Conference and at other more general conferences. Some of the authority issues described in these events include the difficulty mental health workers have in establishing work boundaries on the treatment unit and between units, the use of professional credentials to mask individual competence among the members of the working staff, the phenomenon of staff "splitting" with consequent splitting of patient groups. At one extreme there is a great propensity toward "egalitarianism" in the staffs of psychiatric units without particular relevance to its appropriateness to their task. At the other extreme there are psychiatrict hospitals marked by an authoritarian model of leadership, maintained with collusion at all levels, with the resulting institutionalization of a dependent and often dysfunctional culture.

Turning to experiences on the clinical service, a number of application issues emerge that closely approximate the Group Relations Conference experience. One of the most interesting of these is that of staff-patient mirroring. Here the patient groups, as the most dependent parts of the treatment system, tend to take on the special characteristics of the staff, often in a caricatured way. Thus, in the situation where patients become non-communicative and sterile in their group discussions, and where content is superficial and impersonal, one has clues that the leadership of the unit has been distant, controlling, non-communicative and defensive.

Another related phenomenon is seen on the clinical unit where there have been episodes of suicide or serious attempts at suicide. Here examination of the staff dynamics may demonstrate organizational chaos, a clear lack of functional boundaries between patients and staff and among the various groups of staff, and evidence of scapegoat-seeking by patients and staff to help resolve conflicts over which the patients and staff of the unit feel they have little control. Such problems of boundary definition among the staff also establish other types of scapegoating, usually at the expense of one or more patients. In such situations, one frequently finds that the sentient needs of the staff take clear precedence over treatment task and performance and that the units lack the sort of clear leadership which can define, embody and carry forward the clinical tasks in an appropriate way. One can elaborate on each of these types of clinical applications of group relations work. For our purpose here, it will suffice to point out that these and other phenomenon point to the importance of futher exploring clinical applications of group relations work.

Most of the above observations are addressed at the level of understanding the behavior of psychiatric patients and staffs in conceptual terms. Another approach to application is in the direct use of Group Relations Conference techniques in specific clinical work with patients. This approach is exemplified by the work of Lofgren in San Francisco. His work illustrates the introduction of several techniques (as well as concepts) derived from the Group Relations Conferences directly into the clinical setting.

The ultimate test of any conceptual system is its effective translation into new behavior. The application of the theories of Bion and Rice, and the work of the Group Relations Conference, in the clinic offers an important field for testing the validity of this work. If successful such application will not only close a circle begun by Bion's observations in the clinic but may well make significant contributions to the evolving field of social psychiatry as well as to the more effective care of the psychiatric patient.

9.
ORGANIZATIONAL DESIGN AND THERAPEUTIC EFFECT

Lars B. Lofgren

Investigation of therapeutic efficiency suffers often from lack of criteria of adequate personality functioning. Thus it becomes difficult to know what exactly to treat, or how to evaluate the result of treatment. Freud's dictum that to love and to work well is a criterion for psychological health remains probably one of the most useful ones but in a specific situation it remains too vague to provide a guideline for action. This paper will first try to introduce a relatively simple concept against which to judge adequate functioning and then try to discuss certain problems of organizational design against this background.

The concept of boundaries has been discussed as far as personality organization goes by Federn (1952) in a contribution that has not influenced psychoanalysis to any great degree and in a more generalized way by Rice (1963) and Miller and Rice (1967). In the most general sense everything that can be defined as set apart from the background in time and space must be bounded in some way. In so far as we are dealing with an open system there must be an influx and outflux across this boundary, which must remain functionable under this stress. An amoeba must be able to take in substances and process them internally and still retain its cell membrane intact. If the cell membrane is destroyed during the process the organism will soon die and becomes indiscernible from the background. Reversible damage will cause reversible malfunctioning. What is a physical reality as a cell membrane can be used as a concept when it comes to the psychological apparatus. When the infant is already a separate bodily entity its personality system is not clearly bounded from the mother. Such a symbiosis is postulated as a necessary step in development (Mahler, 1963). Later on the child needs the support of the adult to handle certain processes (A. Freud 1937). The general movement in development is, however, to establish the personality system as a separate entity with a well functioning boundary across which intake and output is possible. Erikson's (1959) concept of ego identity fits well into this view, especially Erikson's consideration of the impossibility of intimacy before identity is firmly established. Personality boundaries are threatened in the intense interchange with another person that intimacy involves.

The concept of personality system boundaries is applicable to a great many points of view of psychology. So is reality testing, basically the ability to discern the outside from the inside, obviously closely related to this concept. Adequate perception and the ability to deal with incoming material by logical thinking requires a well-functioning boundary. When adequate perception becomes impossible, the personality boundary becomes disturbed and thinking becomes more animistic (when dusk falls tree stubs become menacing figures). For a fuller discussion of this see Potzl's experiment on central and peripheral perception (Fischer, 1960). Encountering a complex and perplexing situation probably involves a temptation to regression. From the point of view of personality boundaries, regression means a move in the direction of malfunctioning boundaries, and on the other hand progression means reestablishment and reinforcement of boundaries. This becomes especially apparent when regression leads to projection, maybe of a paranoid nature, or projective identification, that is an attempt to locate a personal quality in another person. A child confronted with a difficult situation may recourse to a temper tantrum, on the other hand by acquiring certain skills a person can retain boundaries even in difficult situations. Here the concept of personality boundaries touches on learning theory in general. Some of these processes are clearly demonstrated in the Tavistock groups as described by Bion (1959). In this unfamiliar situation there is a universal tendency among the members to regressive behavior. In the dependency group the members merge together before a leader that is going to take care of the difficulties. By projective identification all skills are located in him and members become progressively deskilled (Rice, 1965). By judicious interventions the consultants to the group may reverse the process. Projections are recovered, personality boundaries reestablished and learning takes place. Members emerge with increased abilities to function in small groups, and there might also be a carry over to other difficult situations, i.e. a general therapeutic effect.

The psychoanalytical situation may also be treated as one where boundaries fluctuate. The difficulty of perceiving the analyst, the reclining position and the use of non-directed free association enhance regression. During this the boundaries of the personality system of the analysand become partly inoperative. The analyst is included in the boundaries of the analysand and qualities belonging to the inner world of the analysand are ascribed to the analyst: transference. Through the use of genetical interpretation the analyst helps the analysand to reestablish his boundaries. This work forms a crucial part of a psychoanalysis together with similar work on intrapsychic boundaries between ego, id and superego. The analysand emerges from a successful psychoanalysis with a kind of mastery of the psychoanalytical situation: regressions are shorter in duration, only partial, and can be terminated by the analysand himself. However, the gains are much more than this. Due to the non-specificity of the analytical situation, the skills may be applied to a wide range of social situations. Where before regression, projection and other nonserviceable reaction had taken place, learning and mastery now appear instead. The boundary disturbance is temporary and skills to deal with the new situation develop rapidly. The lifespace of the individual increases markedly, choice replaces anxious non-coping mechanisms.

It is easy to see that confusions, psychotic decompensations and similar states may be defined in terms of nonfunctioning personality boundaries, and that recompensation means reestablishing some boundaries.

Generally speaking, it becomes increasingly clear that the concept of boundaries can be used in order to discuss mental health. In this context there is some definite limitation to the term. A quite undeveloped and a very well developed personality system may at a given time both have adequately functioning boundaries. Thus the concept has more to do with defining optimal functioning of a given personality. In addition, the better developed a certain system is, the better are probably the possibilities that boundaries will remain intact under stress. Thus maturity and the ability to retain personality system boundaries are related.

Up to this point we have mostly dealt with rather gross disturbance of boundaries that are easily discernible in an isolated personality system. Certain boundary difficulties appear only in interactional systems. There are families where the husband is responsible for all punishment, hostility and aggression, while the wife remains calm and tender. By projective identification she has gotten rid of a particular part of her personality and deposited it in her husband. Chances are that he has done the same and transferred many of his tender feelings on to her. In such a way a situation is created where the personality boundaries between man and wife are incomplete with a resulting impoverishment of both. The situation is often reversible. Suitable therapeutic measures may reestablish the boundaries. The husband will discover tender feelings that he was unaware of and the wife may be conscious of a new asperity.

This last example leads us to discuss therapy in general. I will define the general therapeutic task as reestablishing boundaries or creating conditions where they can remain functionable. If there was minimal intervention that could establish boundary between the personality systems of man and wife in the last example this would seem to be the therapy of choice. Maybe one could enter into the family life in their home at a given moment ready to interpret the malfunctioning and remain until the situation seems to have changed definitely. This would be the paradigm of home visiting used for crisis resolution.

The situation is not that simple however. Some people may say that the observed boundary disturbance is just a specific sign that something is generally wrong: merely the tip of the iceberg. According to this view both contrahents in the marriage should be studied very carefully and helped to remedy the situation with the greatest possible amount of free choice. This would be the paradigm of psychoanalysis, ideally of both parties, and maybe their children too.

Of these two therapies one may call the first one *highly socially specific* and the psychoanalysis *highly socially nonspecific*. The first one may provide the parties with adaptive skills sufficient to settle the business between them and nothing else. The psychoanalysis will enrich their personality and provide maximal opportunity for a free choice not tied to any particular social situation.

Between these extremes fall a whole range of possible interventions, group therapies, conjoint therapy, institutionalization and others that can be ranged on this scale from social specificity to nonspecificity. Each of them may at least theoretically be quite effective in remedying the breakdown in personality boundaries in the given example. How choose? The important thing may be to see that the indications for certain methods are not dependent on the situation they are supposed to deal with. The choice must be made because of other criteria: the wishes of the couple, the skills and tastes of the therapist, ethical or financial consideration. In this sense psychiatric indication for therapy is very different from the rest of medicine.

INSTITUTIONAL TREATMENT

The rest of this paper will be devoted to a discussion of therapeutic institutions, mainly of the in-patient psychiatric type. If institutional treatment were to be considered in the given example the most specific way would be to admit the whole family to the institution and there study their interaction and intervene appropriately. In this way one could improve functioning in the family but little else. A few additional strains might have to be dealt with because of the presence of other persons in the institution but apart from that the treatment would be highly specific. Certain institutions function in such a way. In general, however, institutions do not operate in such a way. Instead one person, the one designated sick, is removed from a certain social situation and admitted to the institution. Very often his plight is considered not to be the result of social interaction in his particular locus, but a result of some overwhelming internal process. From another point of view, hospitalization can often be better understood as a collusive acting out between the doctor and the environment with or without the active participation of the sick person. Be that as it may, it can be stated that in order for the sick person to agree to hospitalization his personality system boundaries must be quite shaky. In my opinion, only psychotics, ambulatory psychotics and borderline cases agree to become hospitalized.

The expectation is now that during the hospitalization something should happen to the patient. The sickness should be cured, he should be discharged, and he should be able to deal better with the reality to which he must return. Our task will now be to examine certain conditions that make this goal possible. In a certain sense most in-patients are the same. They feel sick, they are ready to be taken care of, they agree to relegate decision making, they have no commitment to change. Values clustering around *dependence* are highly cathected regardless of the psychiatric diagnosis that may be attached to the particular patient. Every person who agrees to psychiatric in-patient treatment is ready to delegate many important personality functions to the staff. In other words, his personality system boundary is largely non-functioning.

It is evident that an important task will be to deal with this boundary disturbance. Let us first consider some ways in which this should not or can not be done. One temptation is for the staff to go along with this request on the part of the patient. This endangers staff personality boundaries. A situation is created whereby everything sick is delegated to the patient and everything healthy to the staff. Old state hospitals functioned in this way. This is an essentially stable social situation, an excellent medium in which to grow chronic cases. Attempts on the part of patients to get well were very often greeted with intense anxiety on the part of the staff, and the patients were forced back into sickness. Anyone who has tried to deal with such symbiotic wards can bear witness to such processes.

Individual psychotherapy is also to little avail. As Freud (1919) has pointed out, the cure must take place in an atmosphere of frustration. When the patient's dependency needs are met and the therapist has a factual authority relation vis-a-vis the patient, individual psychotherapy becomes only an acting out of dependency needs on the part of the patient. A seeming exception to this takes place in certain institutions of unusually complex design. Due to the many complicated interrelations that face the patient, relevant psychotherapeutic material is produced. Since this material stems from the institutional situation the tendency is for the psychotherapeutic process to create perfect patients. This may sometimes be a condition for discharge as will be discussed later.

Once again the reason why psychotherapy usually does not work in an in-patient setting is because personality system boundaries are not intact. The doctor is *really* responsible for much of the patient's life in the institution and this is an ideal situation for projective identification. This is a parameter that cannot be analyzed away (cf Eissler 1953) because it is a reality factor operating during the entire stay in the institution.

Therefore it is my firm conviction that ordinary psychotherapy is of little avail in the in-patient setting. Once again, this is also perfectly compatible with psychoanalytic theory. The reason for its remaining popularity is probably a devotion that focuses mainly on the one-to-one contact, i.e. a *method* rather than on adequate theory.

The therapeutic work in the institution must instead be centered around work with the patient's non-functional personality boundaries, rather than as psychotherapy would do on intrapersonal boundaries. The staff must be trained to observe signs of personality boundary collapse such as the tendency to projective identification, whether it is directed against staff or other patients, and to intervene with explanatory comments. Staff must consistently behave in relation to the patient in such a way as to recathect remaining independency values. This means assuming an attitude that may be perceived at least superficially as uncaring. This goes against the grain of medical personnel in general and constant staff education is necessary until the necessity of such an attitude is deeply understood.

An old view of an in-patient ward is that it is a kind of container where the patient is kept until some therapeutic agent has exercised its effect. The design of the ward becomes important only in so far that it increases the patient's safety and comfort. It seems unlikely that the patient's encounters with environment and objects while he is in a highly regressed state should not be of crucial importance. Therefore great care must be given to the general design of a ward.

The encounter with the ward culture will further enhance dissolution of the personality boundaries and by projective identification assigning many personality functions to the WARD or the STAFF. In so far as the staff is conscious of these processes and deals with them constantly, the patient will be able to deal with, or adapt to the ward, without damage to his personality boundaries. This is another way of saying that it is learning certain adaptive skills appropriate to the ward situation. If these skills have no outside relevance the patient is so much the worse for the experience. The adaptive requirements in a classical prison are of this kind, i.e. the outside relevance is absent. The inmate is changed in such a way that he either becomes a recidivist or becomes a member of a criminal subculture extra muros.

In order to be productive the adaptive work required by the institution should be maximally directed to the outside and minimally to the inside. The adaptive skills should paradoxically have little relevance to remaining in the institution but instead further discharge. As indicated before, some institutions are able to further discharge in the face of adaptational requirements of high internal relevance. I worked for many years in such a small therapeutic institution devoted to psychoanalytically oriented psychotherapy. Not because of active design this institution had many similarities with a small college. It was, therefore, logical that the institution would do well with young college dropouts: once they had mastered the institution they could also return to college. It seemed at times as if the institution was doing less well the more removed from this paradigm the patient was. With this in mind it might be possible to design treatment institutions specifically designed for anxious bankers, sick poets, etc., but the practical problems would be considerable. The religious retreats may partly be effective in this way.

The average institution has, however, obligations to serve a population of more or less diverse nature. This becomes especially the case when the institution must serve a catchment area instead of selecting patients to its liking. The director of such an institution controls the boundary between the institution and the catchment area and has to decide which policies would best serve the incoming patients. There seems to be a growing conviction that the stay in the institution should be short. The reintegrated patient should also hopefully be in better shape to deal with his life situation either by himself, by continued therapy of some sort, or by at least knowing where to turn for help before the situation deteriorates completely. The director has to institute a design that reflects current values in the catchment area as a least common denominator. The greater the heterogeneity of the environment, the more generally applicable must be the values of the institution. Stressing an honest day's work would probably be adequate in an institution serving the Pennsylvania Dutch, but would make little sense in an area riddled with poverty, crime and drug abuse. Through study of the situation in a very heterogenous part slum, part ghetto, part drug and street-people area, I have formed a tentative conclusion that at least in our Western culture there are certain minimal skills necesary in order to continue to live in any social niche. They are: 1. A certain measure of independence, 2. Some ability to make decisions, and 3. Some ability for interpersonal exchange in simple situations. These skills must be reflected in the values of any institution that attempts to perform a reintegrative function for any community. They also serve the criterion established above of having high external relevance and little meaning for continued institutionalization. As stated berore, the patient culture values are derived from dependency. Staff, of course, centers around independence. Therefore, when the patient under pressure from the adaptational requirements of the institution recathects his own previous independence values he no longer fits into the patient culture. As a rule he cannot become a staff. Continued stay in the institution therefore, becomes impossible and he will move to discharge.

The Mount Zion Hospital Psychiatric In-Patient Unit in San Francisco, California has been designed according to these principles. The incoming patients are usually grossly psychotic, confused, suicidal, depressed or show some other signs of grave mental disturbance. All of them have opened their personality boundaries and are ready for an extensive projective identification, assigning such functions as responsibility, decision making, health and so-forth to the staff. Thus patients form a uniform culture centered around dependency values. Partly by indoctrination and partly by inclination, the staff culture is centered around independence and values derived from this concept. Thus, there is constant tension in the organization between two cultures and the main therapeutic task takes place along this axis. We feel it is important that the independence values are demonstrated in action, in efficient encounters between patients and staff. These encounters are of two kinds mainly cognitive, and mainly expressive-emotional. The cognitive encounters consist of small groups and a community meeting (cf Edelson, 1970A and 1970B). The small group has two consultants concentrating their work around personality boundaries, thus listening more to the quality of the interchange in the group than to content and they intervene accordingly. The community meeting also has two consultants dealing with process in general and members of the nursing and O.T. staff who serve as resource personnel and stay in role. Each patient also has an individual nursing consultant who consults with the patient around up-coming issues deriving from the stay on the ward and the return to their society. The use of the word "consultant" in this context indicates the delineation of this role as different from the classical psychotherapeutic one.

In spite of these anti-regressive measures, there is always a tendency for patients on the ward to revert to the simplest form of emotional expression: the temper tantrum. We have thus isolated the components in the temper tantrum and dealt with them in separate patient/staff encounters where once again staff is stressing independence values. The kicking in the temper tantrum is absorbed through movement and dance sessions; the screaming through music session, the possible smearing and weeping through art sessions and the general tendency to dramatic display in sociodrama. In addition, we try to channel the patients' creative potential through O.T. work of a more complex nature.

It is very difficult in an interwoven design like this to evaluate the efficiency of each particular part. However, together they form a highly efficient organization for reconstituting a psychotic patient. A grossly psychotic patient usually reconstitutes to pre-crisis functioning in 8-10 days. It is not yet possible to give exact figures for rehospitalization but comparison with other hospitals who receive a randomly assigned proportionate part of the same patient material shows that our rehospitalization frequency is about one-third that of a conventional unit.

The details of the structure and a fuller evaluation of the results will be published elsewhere.

10.
SYSTEMS APPROACH TO DAY HOSPITALIZATION

Boris M. Astrachan, Hulda R. Flynn
Jesse D. Geller, and Henry H. Harvey

An understanding of the interrelationship between the goals and structure of psychiatric facilities is of importance in the development of effective treatment units. Theoretical constructs derived from systems theory can be of value in planning and utilizing treatment settings (Rice, 1964; Buckley, 1968; Von Bertalanffy, 1968). In this communication some of these concepts will be presented (e.g., primary task, the organization as an open system, boundary control) and then applied to problems typically encountered in designing one of the most frequently misunderstood treatment institutions, the day hospital.

PRIMARY TASK

While organizations may perform several tasks simultaneously and these tasks may lack a settled order of priority that persists over time, every organization has one task, a *primary task*, that it *must* perform in order to survive (Rice, 1968). A university, e.g. must educate, at least some of its students, a hospital must effectively treat some of its patients, an investor-owned corporation must make a profit, etc.

Day hospitals for persons suffering from psychiatric disorders have been established to pursue any one of the following primary tasks (Farndale, 1961; Kramer, 1962). They may provide: (1) an alternative to 24-hour inpatient hospitalization; (2) a transitional care setting whose task is to facilitate the reentry into the community of previously hospitalized patients; (3) a treatment and rehabilitative facility for the chronically mentally disturbed; and (4) a structure which delivers those psychiatric services which a specified community defines as an overriding public need. Other primary tasks may be approached through the development of appropriate day-hospital models. For example, day hospitals have been described as providing a training setting for a variety of mental health professionals and nonprofessionals. (Almond and Astrachan, 1969). We will not explore the complex interrelationships between service and training tasks in this paper.

Ideally, the structure of an organization is designed to support the performance of the primary task. All too frequently, however, organizational structures emerge haphazardly as the organization develops and may be inappropriate to task performance or even act as a hindrance. Unless organizational policies and structures are related to the primary task, an organization must either eventually collapse, or alternatively, redefine its primary task. For example, a day hospital that was originally planned to act as an alternative to 24-hour hospitalization may find itself gradually and unwittingly becoming a service for hospital recidivists with long-term illness if sufficient attention is not paid to the referral and admission policies and the organizational structuring of entry and discharge. Given these circumstances the hospital is faced with the choice of either redefining its task or attending to the restructuring of the organization to permit achievement of the original task.

PSYCHIATRIC ORGANIZATION AS AN OPEN SYSTEM

No organization functions as a closed system, independent of its environment. Organizations must receive inputs, convert these inputs within their system, and export their converted products back into the environment. In the case of organizations that offer psychiatric "treatment" the input consists of people who define themselves or are defined by others as in need of some kind of assistance in dealing with "problems of living." The output, it is hoped, are people whose troublesome presenting symptoms are alleviated, whose self-satisfaction is increased, and whose ability to cope with interpersonal transactions and with the world of work and play have been enhanced by the treatment received.

The conversion system of the organization is thus directed at the primary task of helping the entrants to change. As "successful" outputs they must meet certain criteria of "improvement" which may be well-defined or ill-defined in a given organization. Evaluation of programs in the field of mental health is extremely difficult to accomplish. There are substantial methodological problems in assessing the outcome of treatment. An important contributing factor to the difficulty is the reluctance of clinicians and hospital administrators to define precisely program objectives (Dohrenwend and Dohrenwend, 1965; Guy et al, 1969). Such lack of precision has led to overgeneralization concerning the merits of day hospitalization either in the direction of optimism (" all types of mentally ill patients are easily and effectively treated in day hospitals") or pessimism ("day hospital ineffectiveness is demonstrated by low census and difficulty in attracting patients").

The detailed activities that take place in the conversion system will obviously depend on treatment philosophy and values, the skill and commitment of staff, and their organizational roles and interactions. In many modern psychiatric facilities, the conversion system is likely to include group and individual psychotherapy in a therapeutic milieu and, often, structured activities directed at improving the patient's functioning in his family system. The primary task is that of facilitating behavioral and interpersonal (often including intrapsychic) change.

FIGURE 13: The Psychiatric Hospital as an Open System.*

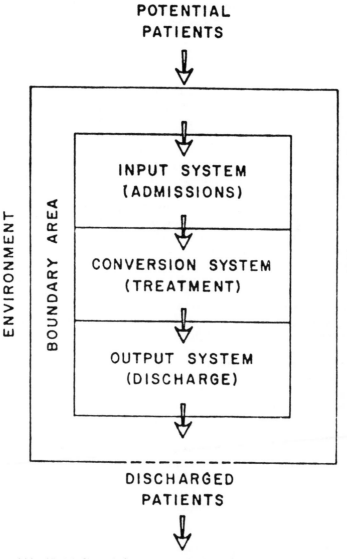

POTENTIAL PATIENTS

INPUT SYSTEM (ADMISSIONS)

CONVERSION SYSTEM (TREATMENT)

OUTPUT SYSTEM (DISCHARGE)

ENVIRONMENT

BOUNDARY AREA

DISCHARGED PATIENTS

* Mrs. Virginia Simon, Yale University School of Medicine, did the illustration.

This generalized description of any organization that purports to offer psychiatric treatment is, of course, oversimplified in order to emphasize the model of a psychiatric service as an open system that continually interacts with its environment. Figure 13 represents our conceptualization schematically.

Our conceptual framework draws heavily on the constructs of Rice (1964) and Miller and Rice (1967). This schematic model of the task system, adapted from their work, may or may not be related to formal or informal organizational structure. The diagram does not, for example, delineate leadership functions, (maintenance and control of boundaries, both between the system and its environment and between component parts of the system).

BOUNDARY CONTROL

The boundary area is that region separating the organization from its environment. It is the area where the organization transacts with its environment. The organization receives a multiplicity of inputs from its environment, some of which it accepts, and some of which are rejected. These inputs may be related to the organization's primary task (e.g., patients to be treated) or they may be inputs that are necessary to permit the organization to carry out that task (e.g. staff of various categories, food medication, supplies for occupational therapy, etc.). Again we omit here, for simplicity of exposition, the inputs that may be essential to the performance of other defined tasks of a psychiatric enterprise. For example, if the facility is a training institution, trainees, in our model, are inputs. Conversion of a trainee into a skilled professional requires an organization to develop a system of training activities. Since the trainee also usually provides service to patients, he occupies at least two statuses in the organization (those of student and staff member). The possibilities of personal conflict and organizational friction are legion.

Every organization must maintain some control of the boundary regions if it is to perform its task. Yet, psychiatric and service organizations have traditionally focused on their conversion subsystems and have been less concerned with questions that relate to the sources of input and the processes involved in the selection of patients. In addition, issues pertaining to the way in which patients are discharged from the system have received little attention. Although administrators are frequently aware of the need to have control over the flow of patients both into and out of their facilities the implications of the location of the organization's boundaries are generally considered only at times when the organization's conversion subsystem finds itself overwhelmed in some manner. This may occur when there is either a marked increase in the demand for entry into the organization (import system difficulties) or when the conversion subsystem becomes overloaded due to discharge (export) subsystem problems. For example, during the depression of the 1930s, large numbers of patients who could easily have maintained themselves in the community remained in hospitals because of their lack of jobs or economically viable families.

This tendency to behave as though the boundary around our treatment facilities bounded *only* our conversion system and its processes has characteristically led to difficulties in relating to the environment. Thus psychiatric facilities often encounter great difficulties in relating their efforts to those therapeutic activities which are undertaken outside their boundaries. The classical problem of relating successfully to rehabilitative agencies, social clubs, VNA, recreation agencies and family physicians still beset psychiatric facilities despite the increased attention that is being paid to the integration of services and attempts to provide comprehensive, continuous care for the mentally disordered. Day hospitals are, perhaps, more aware of these problems than are traditional facilities, since day-hospital patients and families often remain connected to other agencies in the community's service network. Therefore, the need for integration of services and transaction across boundaries is apparent to the staff.

This inability to accurately locate institutional boundaries both results from and further causes serious difficulties for psychiatric hospitals. Many psychiatric facilities have a very limited ability to control their boundaries. Often the facility's ability to exert control over the admission of new patients is limited by the statutory definition of the primary task of the hospital. Commitment procedures and political and community pressures further diminish the facility's control over the selection of its input. Lack of suitable dispositions for discharged patients (halfway houses, family care agencies) may lead to difficulties in discharging patients. To cope with this lack of boundary control, several solutions have evolved which often have deleterious implications for the total organization and for patients. First the relationship of the hospital to other care-taking agencies may be ignored. Next, such a hospital may tend to admit and discharge large numbers of patients in a "revolving door" fashion. Many of its patients consequently never enter into the conversion (treatment) subsystem. In order to protect its limited treatment capacities, the hospital may then erect a barrier around its conversion subsystem, ensuring the rejection of most treatment candidates. Other patients will be administratively controlled, numbered, categorized, and incorporated tightly within the hospital's boundaries. These patient's relationships to their own relevant systems, including family, school, work, and community are disputed.

Thus, the hospital with limited control of its own boundary and input system often finds it necessary to ignore the boundary between itself and its environment, allowing that area to be administratively controlled (commitment papers, community pressure, etc.). The hospital protects its treatment function by locating the boundary it can control around its conversion processes. Too often it transforms this boundary into a barrier in order to pursue its "treatment" with relatively limited interference from what is often perceived as an encroaching, manipulating environment. Thus those patients who are accepted for treatment are often tightly bound into the hospital's system.

As the hospital reerects its boundaries internally and places them about its "treatment" structure, it participates in further separating itself from its environment. The patient then often finds reentry into the community to be extremely difficult since effective programming for relating the hospital to its environment is generally neglected.

Indeed, many service organizations find that outside agencies (particularly governmental agencies) are in the position of being able to redefine the primary task of the service organization and thus to destroy the conversion system to which the agency may, in fact, be committed. As an illustration, state legislatures may define the hospital's task as treatment but appropriate only sufficient funds for the hospital to provide custodial care. The public may demand good "treatment" at the same time insisting upon the control of patients and their segregation from the "normal" community. In this type of situation the hospital is caught between its articulated goal and the externally defined primary task of protecting the community. Individual employees of the hospital may be enormously frustrated by their work in such a system because articulated objectives are impossible to achieve and they find themselves caught in a web of hypocrisy.

DAY HOSPITAL AS A TREATMENT SYSTEM

As stated earlier, day hospitals may be organized to perform a variety of different tasks. One day hospital's primary task may be only an incidental task of another. A day hospital may serve certain specified patient groups, ignoring others. The pursuit of specific primary tasks suggests the need for differing organizational structures, staffing patterns and management. The clear definition of task may enable us to design our treatment structures more appropriately. The design of a day hospital should be based upon a clear understanding of its primary task. For an organization to begin defining its primary task, it must come to grips with such questions as who sponsors it; what are the priorities of sponsoring groups (political structures, legislative groups, citizens' groups, patients at risk, other care-taking agencies, etc.); what are the skills and resources available to the facility; and what are the major perceived problems (e.g., needs of chronic patients, acute patients or such special patient populations as adolescents, addicts, etc.). It should also be remembered that a day hospital exists as a treatment setting only in relationship to a variety of other organizations. It is critical in understanding the functioning of any day hospital to understand its relationship to its environment. No single facility can meet all patient needs, and facilities need to begin to define relationships to one another in order to begin sharing resources. (The federal legislation establishing Community Mental Health Centers (PL 88-164, 1963) defined a number of "essential elements" of comprehensive mental health services. The problems of interdigitation of the facilities that provide these services so as to insure continuity of care are by no means solved. The potential exists, even under such federal legislation, for individual components to be essentially tightly bounded; for patients to fall between treatment systems, and for patients, even in community mental health centers, to be isolated from their communities.)

In the remainder of this paper we shall try to illustrate how systems concepts may be of assistance in understanding and designing day hospitals with different primary tasks. We shall focus on the manner in which a specific primary task has implications for organizational design, staffing patterns and management.

DAY HOSPITAL AS AN ALTERNATIVE TO FULL-TIME HOSPITALIZATION

A number of investigators (Guy et al, 1969; Zwerling et al, 1964; Wilder et al, 1966) have demonstrated that the day hospital provides a workable alternative to full-time hospitalization. Studies have indicated that up to two-thirds of the patients treated in partial hospitalization settings would have otherwise required full-time hospitalization if day hospitalization were not available. In addition, controlled studies have shown that when hospitalizable patients are randomly assigned to either day hospitals or full-time hospital programs, approximately two thirds of those assigned to the day hospitals have been able to remain in that setting for treatment without the necessity of transfer. It is thus quite clear that the use of day hospitalization as an alternative to 24-hour care is feasible.

In order to realize this promise, attention must first be paid to a number of critical issues. First, this conception of a day hospital is unfamiliar to many. As Hogarty et al (1968) have documented, there is a tendency for other agencies in the service network to see the day hospital as a day-care center, an extended care facility for less severely disturbed patients rather than as a treatment of choice for the hospital-bound patient. Consequently, referral sources need to be made aware that day hospitals can treat those patients who have routinely been sent to 24-hour facilties. This may be, and has been, difficult to accomplish and a number of day hospitals or their directors have even sought to assume control over input processes of much larger treatment systems to maintain full occupancy.

The model of entry into this type of day hospital is generally based upon an intensive evaluation of the patient's ability to be maintained within the community with only limited "hospital treatment." As part of this assessment, the hospital staff usually will explore whether there are adequate resources available for the patient within the home and community so as to enable him to continue functioning in relative safety during the large number of hours during evenings and weekends that he will be spending outside of the hospital. As such, it is often the family's willingness to participate in the treatment program rather than any specific patient characteristics which influences decisions regarding the patient's suitability for treatment.

The varieties and styles of treatment available within such day hospitals probably matches the diversity found within most modern inpatient "therapeutic communities". Such day hospital programs, however, often stress group and family therapy modalities. Group programs give the patient some sense of community while in the hospital and also stress the need to work on problems with the aid of others. By promoting peer group interaction, patient socialization is facilitated and withdrawal and dependency upon the staff and hospital structure are attenuated. Family therapy may have the goal of exploring family patterns of interaction in order to enhance the patient's ability to maintain himself outside of the hospital.

This type of day hospital is also likely to rely upon pharmacotherapy to modify patient behavior and to reassure patients, their families, and staff about the patient's ability to be maintained outside the hospital.

This type of day hospital has an obvious need for back-up treatment resources. Many programs have worked out relationships in inpatient units which provide boarding of facilities for patients in crisis for an occasional night or two. These day hospitals force the relationship of patients to their community throughout the period of crisis and illness. Such day hospitals can exert much less control over disruptive patient activity than full-time hospitals and the expectation is that patients, in spite of illness, will be able to behave responsibly. While such expectations on the part of staff and other patients powerfully affect what the patient does, there is the danger that the expectation can outstrip the patient's capacity. The limited control implies that staff, patient-staff, and patient-family decisions must continually and repeatedly be reexamined, because of the daily need to explore the patient's level of functioning, interaction with others, and of course, potential for self-destructive or other-directed destructive activities. This model obviously implies a high staff-patient ratio, and a clinically sophisticated staff that can tolerate a good deal of uncertainty.

Since this model is clearly rooted in the medical tradition, medical consultation is required and medical leadership is usually insisted upon. Community and referral sources generally look to medical leadership for the administration of health facilities, ignoring the limited correlation between technical-professional skills and administrative competence. Institutions also tend not to discriminate between areas of professional expertise and administrative areas. They often place medical staff with limited administrative competence in positions of great administrative responsibility. Too frequently medical administrators see their task as administration of professional activities, ignoring other areas, and without recognition, delegating the running of the facility to others who may be uninvolved with the organization's primary objectives. The management that is required in this type of day-hospital unit needs to know how to deal with acute patient problems. Thus, professional skills are of importance. It also needs to develop and motivate a staff team that can work well with it and with patients. Management must also develop ways to interact effectively with referral sources and agency or therapy resources for discharged patients. Thus, managerial, administrative skills are necessary.

The most important reason for the development of this alternative approach to 24-hour hospitalization was economic rather than theoretical or philosophical (Glascote et al, 1969). Such programs were slow to develop in the United States before the passage of the Community Mental Health Centers Act in 1963. This act proposed both new approaches to treating and financing the treatment of the mentally ill. Although the voluntary health insurance plans proliferated at an extraordinary pace prior to World Ware II, such plans did not cover mental illness (to some extent because carriers feared that inclusion of such benefit might lead to financial disaster). At approximately the same time the United Auto Workers developed a broad health insurance program which included provision for day treatment. The development of this and other programs has forced the large insurance underwriters to reevaluate their exclusions of coverage for partial hospitalization.

Although precise cost accounting methods for partial hospitalization have yet to be developed, (McCaffree, 1968) it is reasonable to assume that the cost of providing day treatment is a bit more than one half the cost of 24-hour care.

However, in spite of such cost effectiveness, there has been difficulty in maintaining day hospitalization as an alternative to full-time hospitalization. This may in some measure be due to the development of competing services, the tendency of referral sources to confuse day hospitals with day-care centers and the need for highly skilled and committed staff. (The proliferation of crisis-oriented, very brief-stay inpatient units may supplant the need for such day hospitals. These emergency units have many of the same goals and have greater potential control over disruptive behavior (Thomas et al, 1971; Langsley et al, 1968). However, they do not have available the structure to continue the treatment process beyond the crises situation).

201

REENTRY INTO THE COMMUNITY

The second type of day hospital has been utilized in several larger hospital settings to enable the rapid return of psychiatric inpatients to their relationships within family and community (Goshen, 1959; Babayan, 1965). The day hospital, so conceived, serves a boundary function between the medical-psychiatric setting and the community. As such it is caught in the obvious dilemma of any boundary organization, mediating between the needs of the two systems with which it is relating (e.g., the needs of the medical units as well as the needs of the community while trying to keep both systems satisfied with its services). Although the danger is obvious that the day hospital may be fragmented by the demands of the two systems with which it articulates, it also has the opportunity to develop innovative, exciting programs. It may serve as an important part of a larger hospital's outflow system bringing the whole hospital closer to the community that it serves.

This type of day-hospital service may either be provided by a 24-hour facility or may be offered by an autonomous unit. In the former case, day hospitalization is merely a "status" difference, comparable to obtaining increased privileges on the ward. When utilized this way it can provide a meaningful subgoal in the process of recovery. The availability of such a program may significantly shorten the length of inpatient hospitalization. On occasion, problems develop on such units because of intergroup rivalries. Day-hospital patients may identify themselves as different, "better," or even, at times, as deprived and no longer involved in "real" treatment. If separate staffs serve day patients and inpatients on the same unit, the potential for such conflict is great. Day-hospital staff may see a program that they are involved in (as, for example, a prevocational training group) as being more meaningful and valuable than total unit activities (e.g., a community meeting). When such a program is located on an inpatient facility, the need for careful integration of programs is apparent.

If this type of day-hospital program is relatively autonomous from inpatient units, the establishment of clear criteria for transfer is necessary, lest important treatment relationships be inadvertently disrupted with attendant interunit conflict.

Day hospitals which serve this function have focused upon resocialization activities and to some extent vocational rehabilitative activities as major features of their conversion systems. The involvement of families has been an important activity on these units. Because such units tend to focus upon patient health rather than patient illness, an insistence upon patient responsibility, openness, participation in decision making, and trust can be structured into these programs.

In these units medical staff serves to facilitate appropriate transfer of patients from the inpatient to day hospital unit.

Medical staff also continues to monitor those elements of patient care that are medical and psychiatric. However, since the focus of the unit is on the movement of patients back to the community, social workers, nursing personnel, occupational therapists, and rehabilitation workers have the opportunity to develop programs that help return patients to their homes and careers. For example, nursery programs help young mothers care for and learn more about their children and home visiting programs to provide direct assistance to patients moving out of the hospital facilitate the transition from hospital to the community. Unit management is concerned with developing relationships to hospital and community and this should be the primary task of unit leadership. Medical-professional skills can be provided on a consultative basis. A particularly vexing problem for leadership of such units exists relative to the development of innovative treatment programs when funding and sponsorship derive from governmental (state and federal) agencies. Established procedures and programs may define unit functioning without any consideration of the specific unit task. Leadership may be hamstrung in pursuing its task by procedures developed in other settings, relevant to other communities at other times.

REHABILITATIVE SETTING FOR THE CHRONICALLY ILL

This treatment model has some similarities to the one previously described, but is directed towards serving the needs of a more chronic patient population and thus pursues more limited goals. Because the patients who are treated with this model of day hospitalization cannot be expected to achieve a consistently high level of functioning, the criteria for evaluating successful task performance are less demanding. Increasing the range of activities of patients incapacitated with neurotic problems or maintenance of long-term psychotic patients outside the custodial long-term wards of a state-hospital system would, in the current climate of opinion, be a criterion of success.

This type of setting can be located either within psychiatric facilities or external to them. The program that this type of day hospital offers is rehabilitative and reeducative. It may be addressed to psychotic patient populations, neurotic populations, or both (Jones et al, 1963; Freeman, 1962). It may benefit from psychiatric consultation, but obviously does not need to be organized as a psychiatric facility. There is little need for medical leadership. The day-hospital program may be integrated with other rehabilitative programs involving socialization experiences, work training experiences, and sheltered environments (foster homes, halfway houses, and also at times, sheltered workshops). The organization of these activities has not usually been defined as within the area of expertise of mental-health professionals, but, too frequently, has not been included in any one else's special area of competence. Day hospitals organized in this manner need the service of staff with specific training in occupational therapy or vocational rehabilitation. Nurses have increasingly been trained to perform and organize such services (Robinson et al, 1966). Leadership staff should possess rehabilitative skills as well as abilities to develop effective relationships to community resources and referral sources.

In dealing with its environment, the boundary transactions of a day hospital thus conceived must constantly be directed at correct assessment of its primary task. It cannot afford to be viewed in terms of the first model we described, a facility for acutely disturbed patients. Nor can it permit the other rehabilitative agencies with which it must deal to expect too much of its output. Staff must be prepared constantly to help families and agencies with the problems that they face in dealing with long-term mentally disturbed relatives and clients in their systems. If this is not done, placements in workshops and halfway houses will become impossible to achieve and families will tend to look for a means of having the patient hospitalized.

DIRECT PSYCHIATRIC SERVICES TO A SPECIFIED DEFINED COMMUNITY

A day hospital that is organized to provide a specific service to a given community must, of necessity, begin to define its task in terms of the articulated needs of the community (e.g., day care for the geriatrically mentally ill or for drug-dependent adolescents). The unit is organized in such a manner as to allow the community to define the therapeutic task (e.g., the community obtains funds for the unit, establishes priorities, and hires a staff to carry out the program) or at least to participate as full partners in the therapeutic enterprise (e.g., community members participate in policy making decisions of the unit and help plan for programming).

In order to survive, the hospital unit must meet the perceived and articulated needs of a community group, rather than the "established" standards of a professional group. The unit is much less dependent upon professional good will (i.e., referrals, professional support, integration with other agencies) than community approbation. The day hospital must be prepared to modify policy and practices based on its interaction with the community. A community may, for example, express its need for service more in the area of treatment of alcoholics and addicts than in the treatment of the chronically depressed. It may wish rehabilitative resources for addicts rather than acute treatment for psychotics. If such a day hospital is to be viable, it must maintain its "credibility" with the community, that is, its values must be compatible with community values. It may even be necessary to have the ethnic and racial characteristics of such a day hospital's staff be similar to those of the community being served, if the hospital's primary task is to serve a specific community in a true partnership with it.

Within such a setting there is, of course, an enormous danger should the leadership of the day hospital fail to identify what its skills are and what they are not. Lack of clarity in defining its skills may lead to a day hospital's promising things which it cannot deliver and to overcommitting its resources. The organization of such a day hospital must be related both to the needs of the community and to staff expertise. In setting up the organization of such a day hospital, decisions about task and treatment program must be made *before* hiring staff, if possible, so that an appropriately skilled staff can be employed, or existing staff retrained.

Unit leadership will have to be prepared to deal with multiple, at times contradictory, community demands. These may be legitimate (e.g., relating to existing programs or insisting on new priorities within the unit's capabilities) or unrelated to the unit's area of expertise or the resources available. Leadership will need to avoid the trap of undertaking tasks it cannot accomplish, lest it dissipate resources, frustrate legitimate community aspirations for improved "more relevant" care, and demoralize staff members by continual redefinition and lack of success.

Boundary problems will obviously become apparent in this type of setting. Questions will arise as to whom the day hospital represents, the parent institution or the community? How does the day hospital articulate with these two systems? How does it identify accurately what *is* the community or who represents it? How does it maintain its integrity in a situation in which it perceives its boundaries may be continually subject to stress? It is possible that some such day hospitals are, in fact, utilized by parent organizations to localize the boundary disturbances *outside* of the parent institution and to allow the latter a degree of relative stability and autonomy.

CONCLUSIONS

A given day hospital may attend only to its primary task or to a variety of tasks. All secondary tasks will, of course, interfere with the performance of the primary task and inhibit the day hospital's ability to do its primary task most effectively. Therefore, pursuit of multiple tasks implies intrastaff conflict, since some staff will represent one area of interest vis-a-vis staff representing another area. It is probable that the tasks of facilitating patient reentry to the community and of rehabilitation can easily be combined since staff can probably work out approaches that will allow for the performance of both tasks in the same setting. It is possible that the tasks of providing acute treatment and of facilitating reentry to the community can be handled together (but probably with the need for an enlarged and enriched staff with some clear specialization around tasks).

It is, however, extremely difficult to see how *all* of the tasks we have listed can be accommodated within any single day-hospital structure and, of course, even more difficult to visualize how all of these tasks can be accommodated within a structure that also has as an important task the training of either professionals or paraprofessionals. Choice of task primacy and priorities must be made if the survival of organizations is at stake. Day hospitalization is too promising a mode of service to be allowed to wither from a want of systematic analysis of its role.

SUMMARY

Systems theory provides constructs which may enhance our understanding of the way in which the goals of psychiatric treatment and the structure developed to implement goals are interrelated. Several of these constructs (primary task, the psychiatric organization as an open system, boundary control) are defined and then utilized in analyzing the structure of four different types of day hospitals. We differentiate day hospitals that are primarily organized to: (1) provide an alternative to 24-hour inpatient hospitalization; (2) act as transitional. care settings which facilitate the reeentry into the community of previously hospitalized patients; (3) serve as treatment and rehabilitative units for the chronically mentally ill; and (4) deliver those psychiatric services that a specificed community defines as an overriding public need. Systems constructs point to the need for different organizational structures, staffing patterns, and leadership skills in these distinct day-hospital models.

11.
AN ALTERNATIVE TO TRADITIONAL MENTAL HEALTH SERVICES AND CONSULTATION IN SCHOOLS:
A Social Systems and Group Process Approach

David L. Singer, Mary Beth Whiton, Matthew L. Fried

This paper grew out of work we have done, either individually or collaboratively over the past four years, in school settings ranging from the rural South through suburbia to the inner city. It was motivated by the feelings of frustration, ineffectiveness, and lack of appreciation we have experienced as we tried to provide "mental health" services of one kind or another in schools. We suspect that we are not alone in these feelings. In this paper we shall present an analysis of the difficulty and an approach to psychology in school settings which we believe can lead to a more productive and satisfying relationship between psychologists and educators.

The basic difficulty as we see it is that psychologists and educators have been operating on the basis of different versions of their mutual contract. Psychologists have been functioning as diagnosticians, therapists, and consultants in schools on the assumption that their goal was to promote the mental health of those within the school systems. Educators, on the other hand, have been yearning for help with their job of helping children to learn. They have implicitly been judging the usefulness and success of psychologists by *educational criteria:* Have they helped the child to function better in the classroom? Is he learning better? In many schools, psychological services have come to be regarded as a useless and expensive, but accepted ritual.

Unfortunately, however, educators have continued to collude with psychologists in maintaining the ·myth of mental health services. Psychologists, even when they want to, often have difficulty in obtaining authorization to work on educational problems. For one thing, professional rivalries exist; for another, it is threatening for some teachers to accept help. Too often, psychologists and educators are locked into situations where the normative request is, "Just test the child." Despite good intentions by both parties, this contractual ambiguity has left everyone dissatified.

This situation arose because psychologists derived their original legitimacy in schools by doing the testing necessary for various types of student placement decisions. The clinically trained psychologists who provided these services brought with them a way of looking at children—and indeed, life—which focused on individual psychodynamics. This led to the development of the assumption, shared by psychologists and educators alike, that problems in educational process are traceable to individual psychopathology.

The fact is, however, that the mental health model has failed to provide the anticipated educational benefits. Psychotherapy, even when effective, takes a long time; the teacher has to deal with the child in the here-and-now. Diagnostic reports, even when accurate, are frequently of little use to a teacher. They are often written in language which is unintelligible to a non-psychologist, or they make impractical recommendations. Mental health consultation, an attempt to alleviate some of these difficulties, is more realistic in terms of supply and demand of professional time, and can often provide immediate, useful information and advice about a child and his needs (Sarason et al, 1966; Newman, 1967; Losen, 1964). This type of service is "psycho-educational" in its thrust and, for that reason, is frequently experienced as more relevant by the school. While decidedly a step in the right direction, to the extent that it focuses on individual psychopathology, this approach also falls short.

Our basic premise is that any psychological approach to education based only upon either psychopathology or a theory of individuals is inadequate. Psychopathology does not necessarily preclude educability; it may even facilitate it in some cases. Schizophrenics have obtained PhDs, and bright, psychologically normal youngsters with rebellious or independent tendencies have been educational casualties. Moreover, difficulties within schools seldom reside only in individual students or teachers. Closer examination usually reveals not only "problem children" or "problem teachers," but also a more general underlying conflict or difficulty within the class or group. Individuals with particular sensitivities tend to respond first and most strongly to issues and tensions which are common to the social system. Since schools are open social systems, a focus on the individual to the exclusion of the total context can prevent identification of salient issues.

OUR MODEL AND ITS THEORETICAL BASIS

Our model for psychology in schools has two basic elements: a definition of our primary task, and a definition of our role within the school. We believe that the primary task of the psychologist working in a school should be to *help the school carry out its educational mission.* Providing mental health services is a laudable task, but for the school it is subsidiary to its mission. However, while a mental health contract is not useful in schools, mental health personnel, with their understanding of interpersonal and group relations, can be.

Within our model, the role of the psychologist should be defined in an explicit contract with the school, under which services are provided by *mutual consent only.* No one can order him to provide a given service (e.g., testing a child), nor can he, on the other hand, order any one to accept any service or consultation. When consultation or services are provided, the psychologist takes full responsibility for their effectiveness. If, in the long run, his work proves useful, hopefully he is asked to stay; if not, the relationship should be terminated. The psychologist might be either an "inside employee" or an outside consultant. As an outside consultant, however, one is relatively less constrained by social pressures which can be applied if one works within an institution, so we prefer that type of arrangement. We see ourselves as co-professionals of the teachers and administrators, but with differing expertise to bring to bear on the educational process. What actually constitutes "education" is up to the educators.

Psychologists can aid the school with its task of education in two major areas. The first is by applying their knowledge to strengthen the *technical aspects* of education. For example, principles of learning and child development can be used to make curriculum and teaching skills more effective; research techniques can be applied to issues within the school.

More important, we believe, is the assistance psychologists can provide through their understanding of the dynamic aspects of education, the psychosocial phenomena which affect learning. The interests, goals, needs, and anxieties of individuals and groups within a school are constantly in dynamic interplay and are constraints on the success of education, all technical factors notwithstanding. These, rather than individual psychopathology, are the most significant hindrances to the work of education. Consider, for example, the students who are withdrawn and antagonistic because they feel, either with or without justification, that their teacher is "out to put them down." Consider also their teacher, who feels frustrated and unappreciated. Until this barrier to effective work is somehow overcome—either by compromise or resolution of the conflict— even the best curriculum, presented with sound principles of learning and using the best equipment, will have minimal effect.

Constraints on education occur at many levels: school, classroom, faculty, individual, etc. The school, for example, may be assigned covert tasks by the society at large or by its own school district. One such covert task is the perpetuation of cultural values, myths, and mores. The current furor over sex education in many communities has made clear the fact that, for many, the task of educating children is secondary to the task of value perpetuation. Or consider the ''model'' inner city school on whose fate a program and funds for the whole district hinge. Increased moral support, attention, and concern may enhance educational effectiveness; pressure and anxiety generated by the district office and constant politicking may make the teaching staff so uncomfortable that they lose some of their patience and effectiveness.

As an institution, the school has an organizatin, and this too is a source of constraints on work. *Authority relations*—the dynamics between persons in authority and those under them— pose problems on all levels: for the school as a social system, within grades or departments, and particularly within classrooms. Whether that authority is seen as legitimate is often an issue. *Peer relations*—the dynamics between ''equals'' in a group or social system—are similarly active at all levels. Membership in various groups, both formal and informal, generates loyalties, differences, rivalries, and anxiety, which at times can cloud judgment and lead to social misperceptions. Other constraints on the school's performance of its primary task come from the aspirations, fears, and fantasies of its members concerning competence, adequacy, achievement, and success.[1]

Conflict and anxiety are inevitable, existential givens which occur within each individual, group, and social system, though in differing ways and degrees. How they are handled is crucial in determining either constructive or maladaptive outcome for the individual or the educational process. Conflict and anxiety can be accepted, dealt with openly, and resolved if possible. If resolution is not possible, they can be lived with and integrated into the system. An opportunity to observe and participate in this process is an essential part of the educational process. The avoidance of anxiety can only limit, and therefore impair, the educational process.

How might these various dynamics manifest themselves in real life, and how might a psychologist use his understanding of them to facilitate education? Let us consider several situations. In each case, the problem solving approach is the same: (a) identifying a source of interference with the educational process, (b) understanding its dynamics, and (c) recommending and/or providing some sort of intervention.

Example 1: Situation: Defense against anxiety by flight. A drastic and unexpected rise in absenteeism is occurring among the entering seventh grade class in a large urban junior high school. The psychologist learns that a new program has

1 These phenomena were described by Bennis & Shepard (1956) and Slater (1961). A more theoretical presentation can be found in Rioch (1970). Although these principles and theories were largely developed through observation of self-study groups, in our experience the same processes are operant in classrooms, committee meetings, and other group settings, though perhaps in a more subtle form. For a somewhat more sociometric discussion of classroom social structure, see Glidewell, Kantor, Smith & Stringer (1966).

been instituted in which each child has an individually tailored program, based on his level of competence in each subject,which results in his having a unique class schedule. He knows that facing a new school and making the transition to a departmental system are both anxiety arousing. The new program, he believes, is depriving the children of a stable peer group which is a necessary source of emotional support; they are playing hookey to avoid this anxiety. He recommends that children be assigned programs in groups of five rather than on an individual basis.

Example 2: Authority relations in the first grade. A first grade teacher reports that her class has become increasingly disruptive, and suspects that several of the children are too disturbed to be in a regular class. The psychologist notes that the teacher is seven months pregnant and upon inquiry finds that she has not discussed this fact with her class. He suspects that the class is dealing with fears of abandonment by her and/or replacement in her affections by the new baby. Observation of the class confirms this guess and leads him to believe that the disruptive children are those for whom sibling rivalry is a particularly anxiety arousing issue. He recommends that the teacher discuss her pregnancy and her future plans with the children and help them to express their feelings and fantasies about the event. He offers to sit in and help the discussion along.

A work sample: "Children who could not learn"[2] One of the elementary schools in a surburban community requested psychological testing from the psychology service for an entire class: 13 fourth and fifth graders, 12 black and one white. All of the children had a history of conflict in previous classes and all were behind in academic work. The white child had been diagnosed previously as schizophrenic.

The purpose of the class was to provide intensive remedial education for the children so that they could be reintegrated into regular classes. However, the teacher, a reading specialist, felt frustrated in her attempts to get the children moving. She wanted psychological testing to tell her whether these children had the ability to benefit from her special class.

That the whole class had been referred for testing suggested that psychological testing was not going to be very useful. Most of the children had been tested before, and it seemed likely that the problem lay in the relationship between the class as a whole and the teacher. Nonetheless, it appeared that to gain any confidence from this teacher and therefore any authorization to work with her on redefining the problem, the children would first have to be tested. (We saw this as an essential compromise, and learned from it the value of explicit contractual agreements. Had the contract between the psychologists and the school been more explicit, and a consultative role for psychologists been

2 Similar work in a different type of institution and with older students is described in Klein & Gould (1970).

authorized, such testing probably would not have been necessary.) As we interpreted the tests, most of the children were functioning at the "low average" level of intelligence with no indications of brain damage. These findings were of little help to the teacher, but they eliminated the possibility that the children were not able to learn.

Observation of the dynamics within the classroom led to a different view of the problem. The children appeared to be actively engaged in a struggle to sabotage any attempts at learning and teaching. There was an unspoken agreement among them to present themselves as dumb and uncontrollable. Any individual attempt at or interest in learning was quickly sabotaged by the rest of the class. This problem was unwittingly compounded by the teacher, who heaped lavish praise on a child when he learned something, further alienating him from his peers.

We tentatively concluded that, as self defeating as this behavior appeared, it probably served to protect the class from a more central source of anxiety and threat. We therefore decided to work with the class as a group and to provide consultation for the teacher. We assumed that the class would re-enact with us the conflicts and expectations underlying its relationship with the school system which were interfering with learning. Within this context, we hoped to clarify with the class what we saw. Our focus was to be in terms of the group as a whole, rather than on individuals. We also hoped to provide for the children a model of forthright communication and a choice between continued sabotage of learning, or more effective problem solving around the underlying issues which could free them to learn.

Our goals with the teacher were to help her to understand what was going on between herself and this class, to understand particular dilemmas facing these children as a group, and to encourage her to try more straightforward ways of dealing with them. We shared our view of the situation with the teacher and presented our recommendations. She agreed, but with some understandable skepticism. Meetings with the class were set up for the last hour of the school day twice a week. The teacher was not present at these meetings; we met with her immediately afterwards. During the first meeting we introduced ourselves to the children as psychologists who were working with them because they "weren't making it in school." We further explained that they could choose the activities, and that we would try to help them to understand more clearly what went on in the classroom.

At the outset the class appeared chaotic, as if they were demonstrating the same pattern with us as with the teacher. They appeared to be implicitly asking us if we were going to play a punitive, authoritarian role, and testing to see if we could be induced into believing that they could not control themselves. We told them this was how we saw it, and refused to assume responsibility for control of the classroom. When, for example, fights among different children broke out in the first few sessions, the class pointed the fighting out to us and demanded that we intervene. We commented that the fights continued only because the other children sat by, and we wondered aloud why the rest of the class didn't stop them. At first the response of the class was to protest innocence and blame the fighters. Then they started to stop fights by themselves, and after the third week, fights were seldom seen.

In the following weeks the focus shifted from the unruliness of the class to the one white child who was constantly brought to our attention by the rest of the class for his "crazy" behavior. While this boy's behavior was bizarre at times, the class teased him unmercifully and took great glee in getting him to perform his routines. The message to us seemed to be that *he* was the focus of all the craziness in this class. This emphasis on the white boy's "craziness" led us to believe that these children had come to regard themselves as crazy and bad, and we discussed this with them, too.

The next issue which evolved was race. When the children liked us, they told us we were really black; when they were angry they called us racists. On one occasion they accused us of having murdered Martin Luther King.

The pieces of the puzzle were now beginning to fit together. It was clear to everyone that the school regarded these children as bad, unteachable, and a general nuisance. While five years ago these children would have been thrown out or punished, because of changing time they were now being provided with "compensatory education". Perhaps the placement of one psychotic white child with these black children, who were far from crazy, says something about the latent attitudes of the school and community. As we worked with the children, there was abundant evidence that they interpreted it as a statement that the white school and community regarded them as crazy. The children in this classroom appeared to mirror the feelings of their parents, the black minority in the community, many of whom worked as domestics for the white, middle class majority.

Although being regarded as crazy was frightening to the children, it also had its comforting aspects. They all had low self-esteem and a tremendous fear of failure and humiliation. As "crazy children" they could feel absolved of their responsibility to control their behavior and, more importantly, to take advantage of the available learning opportunity.

For the rest of the semester we continued working these issues and acknowledging the children's feelings. We pointed out continually that they were not making it better for themselves, but that they were, in fact, playing into their own worst fears. We confronted them with the choices they were constantly making. As time went on it became increasingly difficult for them to pose as irresponsible and incompetent to control themselves.

At the same time we were working with the teacher, discussing issues that were coming up in the group. We also discussed problems she had encountered and attempted to suggest possible ways of handling situations. When the black-white issue emerged, for example, we suggested that the posters in the room be replaced by real-life pictures including prominent Blacks. At times our comments seemed to fall on deaf ears. Yet, after a while they would quietly be accepted. Thus, despite protests that "pictures don't mean a thing to these children," posters with black faces were on the walls several weeks later.

Our work was not without difficulty. For one thing, there was ambivalence on the part of the principal and the teacher. The principal became very uncomfortable when the class seemed out of control and at times threatened to throw us out of the school. In retrospect it is clear that we did not adequately inform him about our ideas and technique. The teacher also became uncomfortable when too little or too much was happening. She and the school had taken a risk in allowing us to work in this experimental way. What if we succeeded and she didn't? How would it look if we failed? What would it mean to other teachers if she succeeded in teaching these children? What is the school's responsibility if children like these really can learn? What are the implications for the community? Clearly, we were not working in a vacuum. We also frequently felt confused and helpless, and outside consultation was needed to provide perspective.

By the end of the year, the class appeared to change their attitudes toward school and behavior in school. Absenteeism was down and achievement scores rose at least three grades for a majority of the children. For the most part they were no longer unruly and disruptive. These changes were not solely the result of our working with the class. They also reflected our successful collaboration with the teacher, who had changed many of her attitudes and ways of dealing with the children. She was much more open and straightforward. Near the end of the year, after a frank discussion of sex in our class meeting, the children wanted to test the teacher and revealed to her what we had been talking about. She came through with flying colors as she replied, "I'm older than the psychologists and probably know more about sex. Now, what is it you want to know?" And at the end of the school year she reversed an earlier decision and arranged to work once again with this type of class and requested a psychologist to do group work with them.

Our work with this class and teacher appears to have been a success. Yet, we must wonder how long-lasting these effects will be, and, in keeping with our social system perspective, about our impact upon the school as a whole. Any change within a sub-system will inevitably have repercussions for the entire system, either producing resistance and backlash or providing impetus for further positive change.

B
Education and Professional Training

12.
Selections from
THE ENVIRONMENT OF LEARNING

Elizabeth Richardson

HARNESSING THE EMOTIONAL FORCES IN THE GROUP

As the over-all leader in the work situation, a good teacher will have one main objective: to help his pupils to learn for themselves. For the one inescapable truth about the whole educational enterprise is that every child must, ultimately, accept responsibility for his own learning, whether he is an acknowledged leader in his form or its most retiring member. As individuals, the children in our classrooms want to learn. They want to acquire the skills of the adult world and to experience the excitement of discovery. Certainly, by the time they reach the higher forms of the secondary school, and probably by the time they enter the first form, they are aware that the kind of life that will be available to them as adults will depend on the use they can make of the opportunities the school gives them to do this growing and learning. Yet, as members of groups, their behavior is continually dominated at the primitive, unconscious level by emotional needs that may have little to do with growing or learning.

The relationship between the teacher and his own form is in essence a mutually dependent one, and a form teacher's role as the leader of a dependent group carries with it all the pains and anxieties as well as the pleasant characteristics of the dependent group culture. We must ask ourselves whether the teaching-learning situation, too, depends on the ability of teacher and class to use this dependent culture in a sophisticated manner, or whether another kind of relationship must be sought.

Certainly, if the teacher is not dependable, his pupils will not learn. Conversely, if he sees himself as omniscient, believing that all knowledge must emanate from him and merely be transmitted to his pupils, they will eventually become restless and frustrated. And here is the paradox. Children will submit for a long time to teachers who dictate notes to them or write notes up on the blackboard to be copied into notebooks; they will accept P.E. lessons that resemble army drill, demanding the same responses from everybody; they will allow a science teacher to organize their experimental work for them down to the last detail, and to impose on them set models for the writing up of the results; they will take for granted that they should all be given identical tasks for homework. It seems that, provided the teacher plays this kind of role efficiently, the class will submit to any amount of such spoon-feeding, preferring safe and easy security to the possible pains and uncertainities of learning by their own efforts and mistakes.

However, in time, such a routine produces its own difficulties and frustrations. Where everybody is expected to make the same responses, rivalries are bound to spring up. Not everyone can please the teacher equally. The children find that they cannot easily share his attentions. And so rivalry and mutual antagonisms begin to disrupt the group. Bill Green, who can always answer the teacher's questions, becomes an object of hostility. Maggie Brown, who is more bored and restless than most, and is falling behind in her work, becomes the center of tittering attention. And suddenly, from leaning helplessly on the teacher and competing for his good opinion, the class finds a new kind of unity by combining against him and against the frustrations imposed by his method of teaching. The culture has changed from dependence to something quite different.

Before we look at this new, aggressive and potentially destructive situation, let us consider another kind of pupil-teacher relationship which appears at first sight rather like the dependent one but turns out to be something else. Probably many teachers would agree that the ideal teaching-learning situation is one in which the teacher works with the one pupil. For the master teaching the pupil we substitute two scholars, one more experienced than the other, but both partners in an enterprise of which the outcome remains unknown. This pairing relationship or working partnership is the essence of the university tutorial situation. But it has its counterpart, certainly in the sixth form, and less obviously in classrooms lower down in the school. Every time a teacher sits down by a child to work through a mathematical problem, or to talk with him about a picture he is painting or a poem he is writing, or to discuss what is happening in a scientific experiment, he is using a pairing relationship. But, since he cannot do this with more than a handful of members of a class in any one lesson, he must also make it possible for the children to pair off with each other.

Clearly this procedure, if work goals are unclear to the children, can degenerate quickly into chaos and confusion. For in a group that has broken up into pairs there is no visible and tangible leader. The controlling factor is something in the future—the hope of a worthwhile product from each pair. The danger is that the situation becomes too competitive, or that the group will settle into lethargy, leaving it to one pair to do the real work. And so the success of the pairing activity is likely to depend on the teacher's ability to make his class feel that the contribution of each pair is essential to the success of the final product. This product may be the creation of a wall newspaper or a magazine, or the mounting of an exhibition, or the staging of a dramatic sequence; or it may be something as abstract as the mastery of a new kind of mathematical problem or of a new scientific concept or the greater understanding of the human problems in a novel.

I have been trying to apply to the classroom situation a theory of group behavior that was worked out in the late 1940s and early 1950s by Dr. W.R. Bion on the basis of intensive experimental work with small groups. Some of these were groups of patients in a therapeutic situation at the Tavistock Clinic in London; others were training groups at the Tavistock Institute of Human Relations—people in responsible positions in industry and education, including some members of the staff of the Tavistock Institute itself. Unlike many other psychiatrists doing pioneer work in the field of group therapy, Bion strove to avoid the temptation of merely treating his patients as individuals in the group. Similarly, with the training groups, he avoided personal contacts or exchanges with any individual members and confined his interpretative observations to matters that concerned the group as a whole. Over and over again he found that the underlying emotional processes in the group were both antagonistic to and essential to the conscious and sophisticated purposes of its individual members (Bion, 1961).

At times his groups were dominated by their need for one person on whom to depend, and they would try to set up this person as omniscient and infallible. At other times they appeared to be relying on a pair, as if in the hope that this pair might produce the new magical leader in the future. And at other times they were concerned only to preserve their own identity by fighting something or running away from it. The real problem for every group seemed to be to learn to recognize these unconscious needs, or 'basic assumptions', and to become capable of mobilizing the one that was most appropriate for the task they were meant to perform.

Now we can, I think, find parallels to these kinds of phenomena in our school classrooms. Bion's theory helps us to understand the difference between the helpless dependence that saps real work and the intelligent use of the basically dependable teacher. It helps us to see the difference between the group that escapes into fruitless pairing situations and the group that consciously uses pairs to bring a planned project to fruition. It helps us to see the difference between the destructive fight-flight culture that leads to anarchy or to apathy, and the healthily aggressive relationship between teacher and class that promotes learning through the dialectic of discussion and argument.

The fight-flight culture can take one of two forms. If antagonism is open, it will take the form of noisy rebellion, and the leader will be the most openly aggressive boy or girl in the class. If the antagonism is concealed, it will take the form of a massed flight—not necessarily a physical flight, though this frequently happens when the bell rings at the end of a tedious lesson, but more probably a flight into silence and apathy. In such a situation it is hard to detect where the leadership lies. The one certain thing is that it is no longer invested in the teacher, however strenuously he goes on trying to teach. And apathy can be just as hostile and nearly as exhausting in its effect on the teacher as open rebellion.

From the point of view of the group, the fight-flight culture is no more satisfactory than the dependent culture. If the leader of the dependent group has to be infallible and omniscient—the perfect teacher in the classroom, who never puts a foot wrong—the leader of the fight-flight group must be invincible, or so swift in retreat that no one can catch either him or the group that follows him. So the hostile class, which is trying to ensure its survival by fighting or running away from the teacher, needs a child who is brave enought to defeat the teacher or cunning enough to lead the group right out of the situation. This may be possible in fantasy. But in reality the whole organization of the school, and of the society that the school serves, is there to prevent the success of either fight or flight. Moreover, any child who leads such a fight exposes others as well as himself to the punitive powers of the institution. And as casualties mount, it becomes more and more evident that this culture will not ensure the survival of the group either. And the class may collapse suddenly into its former docility, returning helplessly to the dependent culture.

A vivid example of this kind of abrupt switch of the emotional temperature from aggression to submission was brought back some years ago to a tutorial-group discussion by a graduate student after the term of school practice. Mr. K. told us how he found himself teaching a first form that had had a succession of teachers, of whom he was the eighth, for French. It was regarded as a difficult form; and there was in it one particular boy who was a persistent troublemaker. After a long series of lessons in which this boy had been thoroughly disruptive, Mr. K. gave him some lines as a punishment. When he brought them the next day, Mr. K. noticed that he had written 'ABK is mad' across the paper. He decided to ignore this and merely dropped the paper into the wastepaper basket. About half-way through the lesson the boy started misbehaving again, so he brought him out to the front, and presently noticed that he had written 'ABK is mad' on the blackboard. He then sent him outside the door, and subsequently discovered that he was writing the same message on the dusty corridor window, to the great amusement of those still inside the room. Mr. K. told this story with considerable humor, but without disguising the difficulty he had been faced with in trying to deal with the boy. It was also evident that, exasperated as he had been, he had found the boy attractive.

This part of his story had a distinctly comic flavor; the sequel, which he divulged later in the tutorial-group session, was unexpectedly moving. Asked what further steps he had taken, he replied sadly: 'Well, I pushed it still further out.' He had finally reported the boy to his form master, with the result that he was given a beating. Mr. K. added even more sadly: 'This had a shattering effect on the class. For a whole week they were struck dumb. So I was able to get on with my teaching. But they were quite unable to learn.' The group received this in a stunned silence, evidently as much affected by Mr. K's complete honesty as by his concern about the effect his action had had on the class.

The discussion that arose in the tutorial group after Mr. K. had told us this story threw an interesting light on the problem. One member of the group remarked that perhaps this boy had only been putting into words something that most children feel at times about most teachers. From that it was an easy step to consider that the tutorial group had sometimes regarded me as slightly mad, and indeed sometimes still held this opinion. They agreed, but Mr. K. reminded me with a smile that the message had not yet been written on my carpet.

Reflecting on this incident from the safe distance of a private study, one wonders whether it might have been possible to treat it as a group phenomen rather than as a personal display of impertinence to a teacher. For in a sense, this particular boy was acting as a spokesman of the group. By throwing the impertinent comment back to the class, almost as a counter-joke, and asking whether the rest agreed with his opinion, the teacher could have taken the sting out of the attack and at the same time made a little legalized aggression against him possible.

It is a question of distinguishing between behavior that springs from a personality defect in the child and behavior that is expressing something on behalf of the group. It may be that a child's persistently aggressive behavior can best be met by recognizing that he is being allowed to carry a good deal of the aggression for the group, and by trying to use this group aggression in some positive way. Most teachers come to recognize, as Mr. K. did, that sending the fight-flight leader out of the room is very rarely a solution to the problem. Too often the rest metaphorically accompany the banished offender, even if he does not find such a vivid way of keeping attention focused on himself as this particular boy did. If, on the other hand, the punishment, or the sequel to the punishment, is too drastic, the form is crushed to the point of helplessness.

There is, however, a form of retaliation that is a great deal more dangerous to the group than the removal and punishment of a ringleader; and that is for the teacher himself to walk out. By doing this, he himself becomes the victim of the aggression he arouses in the group, leaving behind him as an uneasy sense of loss and guilt. It occasionally happens that a teacher who has antagonized a class of children allows himself to be driven out in this way. If ever a class provokes a teacher to these lengths, its members are left feeling that they have been collectively guilty of a sort of murder. If their mood turns to remorse they will seek to make amends. If their mood turns to ridicule the damage to themselves may be very much greater, since they may set out to test all subsequent teachers to the limits, and may come to boast of their talent in destroying their teachers in this way.

The ultimate test of any members's ability to take the group's hostility, whether this member is the teacher or one of the pupils, is his willingness to stay in the group. Now in the classroom the teacher is both more free and less free to leave than anyone else. He is more free because he is an adult. But he is less free because he is bound to the group by ties of duty and responsibility; and the pupils know this. And so, if he leaves for no reason except to punish them, he is abandoning them. The primitive fear of the loss of the supporting mother is thus reactivated in the pupils. And so, surprisingly, such an exit is likely to be marked not with a howl of delight but with a sudden shocked silence. The expected triumph turns abruptly to dismay. When the class fools the teacher to the top of his bent, what they are really testing is his ultimate concern for them. If he cares for them more than for his own dignity, he will stay. If he 'teaches them a lesson' by leaving he expresses his ultimate, perhaps irredeemable, hostility: he abandons them.

In such a withdrawal, there is also for the teacher, an element of defeat and even perhaps of self-punishment. He himself is bound to be left with an overwhelming sense of inadequacy, which will have to be lived through when he next encounters these same people, and even others who, he feels, may have heard about the incident. His pupils will probably sense his predicament too. And so, along with their own feelings of guilt, there is the anxiety arising out of his defeat. For they need to feel that he is somehow indestructible.

A class who, in Bion's terminology, is dominated by the fight-flight basic assumption, needs to be helped to face and master its own dangerous aggression. It may be that children who find themselves in this situation consciously fear their leaders even while they allow them to lead. Teachers who are prepared to admit that they have been faced by such group behavior will sometimes report that individual children have said to them privately, or even openly in class: 'Why don't you keep us in order, Sir?' Perhaps the real plea is: 'Why won't you help *us* to keep *ourselves* in order, Sir?' The difference in wording is significant.

Certain members of the class begin to dislike the anarchy that is created by their own disruptive leaders. They find themselves longing for a teacher who will establish himself as a dictator and bring order out of chaos. Yet merely to substitute an authoritarian regime is not really a solution to the problem. For the group will just as easily fall a prey to the next disruptive leader that comes along. The aggression has to be used rather than merely suppressed for the time being.

I suggested earlier that the group that has taken flight into apathy is just as hostile as the openly rebellious group and can be nearly as exhausting to the teacher. In the hostile class, the object of attack is the teacher, and his best solution is somehow to direct the aggression against the difficulties in the work situation. In the apathetic class, everyone is trying to run away from the demands of the work situation; and the problem is to bring the disguised hostility out into the open in such a way that fight, in the form of attack on difficulties, takes the place of the wish to run away from the difficulties.

Again, an example may make the point more clearly. It is 11:20 a.m. I am sitting at the back of the classroom in a girls' grammar school. Miss L. is reading a selection of Keats' poems with a fourth-year class—the A stream. Nothing she can tell these girls about Keats' life, no question she can ask them about the poems they are reading succeeds in bringing a flicker of a human expression to their faces, let alone a spontaneous comment to their lips. They watch her politely, appear to be listening, or stare unseeing at the books in front of them. What are they really thinking? What sort of revelations would the teacher get if she threw her prepared lesson aside and challenged three or four of them to say what was really in their minds or what they would consider a reasonable topic for poetry in the 1960s? How might their attitude change, I wonder, if she were to come down from the teacher's high desk that dominates the room from one corner, and if, for once, the school convention that compels even these tall, well-developed girls to stand every time they answer a question or offer a comment could be waived.

Afterwards we discuss the problem. Miss L. is in despair about this class, for she knows that the girls are intelligent and is perceptive enough to realize that although in her lessons their faces may look empty their minds certainly are not. She decides to try shock tactics. In her next lessons she asks them what they would consider important enough to be subject for poetry—what they themselves would choose to write about if they had to write poetry. At first, suspecting a trap, they give her the answers they think she wants them to give. Challenged further, they begin to bring real enthusiasms out into the open, and they also begin to test her out by trying very mildly to shock her.

Now this lesson, although at the time it could not have been said to have much advanced the cause of Keats versus the current pop star, did ultimately affect their whole attitude to poetry. They found that they did not have to pretend with this teacher that they liked everything she read them; at the same time they found that, if she was prepared to allow them to be aggressive in expressing their opinions, she also expected them to produce reasons for those opinions. When eventually I saw this class again, Miss L. began by reading with them a poem by Robert Frost, with a few preliminary remarks to put it into a context. The girls discussed it with some heat, and then, with the help of provocative interjections from the teacher, began to thrash out what it was that made poetry distinguishable from prose. What astonished me was the way in which this roomful of extremely reserved young women, whose thoughts could have not been guessed at from the mask-like faces they had showed before to their teacher, had been transformed into a number of vivid and distinct personalities, expressing at first quite crude and naive ideas, but gradually, under the pressure not only of the teacher but also of the group, tightening up their choice of words and phrases and trying to communicate clearly to one another what they were struggling to think out.

During the weeks that had intervened between the two lessons I saw, Miss L. had been able by degrees to dispense with all the meaningless formalities I had noted in the earlier lesson. The girls now spoke spontaneously, without raising their hands; they did not stand while speaking, but sat as any group of adults would sit while conducting this kind of discussion; and they addressed each other, turning around in their chairs to do so, almost as often as they addressed the teacher. Yet there was order in the proceedings. They were sensitive to one another's impulses and were prepared to listen as well as talk.

This teacher had succeeded in turning a situation which had degenerated into a flight from the task into something more like a pairing culture. She had effected this change by first bringing out the hostility concealed behind the politely bored, resolutely expressionless faces in her classroom, inviting the girls first to direct this against herself in the form of an open rejection of the materials she had been using with them, and then channeling it into the intellectual task of determining what really constituted poetic expression in any age.

LEADERSHIP RE-EXAMINED

Let us now try to put Bion's ideas together in the framework of the school classroom.

In the dependent culture the danger for the group is that it relies too implicitly on the leader and becomes frustrated because the leader cannot rise to the expectations people have of him. And so the teacher, as the dependent leader, must contrive to be reliable while continually urging the class to question his omniscience, challenge his opinions and realistically accept his human limitations. And at times he will create situations in which members of his class take his role, and become accepted as alternative leaders in a basically dependent culture, using their own expertise as he uses his when he is the accepted leader.

In the pairing culture, the danger is that the group rests in the lazy hope that two members will continue indefinitely to carry responsibility; individuals then become frustrated because their hope of some perfect product from these two is never realized. Here the teacher's role is to break up the task and give each pair or small group a manageable part of it to tackle. In this way achievement becomes possible, because no one any longer supposes that one pair can be left to produce the magic solution.

In the fight-flight culture the danger is that the group will either destroy the teacher or itself by the unleashing of its own hostile impulses or withdraw from the situation altogether. And so the role of the teacher is to channel the aggression into an attack on ignorance and apathy, so that the class rediscovers its powers of cooperation in a learning situation and uses it leaders in a constructive way.

Thus when one kind of basic assumption threatens to overwhelm the group and make work unproductive, the teacher has to try to find ways of mobilizing another, so that new forces can come into play and be used by the group in an increasingly mature and responsible fashion.

The leadership of the children or young people in changing classroom situations now comes to be seen as intimately bound up with the kind of leadership the teacher himself chooses to use. And as the class grows more mature as a group, and better able to handle its emotional needs, so its members will discover that leadership can be exercised in many different ways and by many different individuals.

13.

GROUP DYNAMICS TRAINING

F.C. Redlich and Boris M. Astrachan

Educational opportunities which allow for some understanding of the importance and functioning of small groups have been until very recently, conspicuously absent in psychiatric training. Since 1965, the department of psychiatry at Yale has conducted a formal group training program in which residents experience and study the behavior of groups. Prior to this a number of faculty members participated in such sessions and also in residential group relations conferences conducted jointly by the Tavistock Institute of London, the Washington School of Psychiatry, and Yale's department of psychiatry. More recently several faculty members have participated in conferences sponsored by the National Training Laboratories. In general, students and faculty found such training stimulating and useful.

The importance of knowledge about groups is quite obvious. Man is a social animal. He has inherited the capacity and propensity for social behavior from his primate ancestors and has learned group behavior during the long process of education in family and peer groups. To be a committed member of several groups and at the same time assert one's own individuality is a basic dilemma of the human condition.

During the 20th century living in groups has become more complex. The population increase, crowding in cities, greater mobility of migrating groups, and the creation of huge technocracies have contributed to this complexity. More than ever we need to understand the psychology of groups and intergroup behavior.

In psychiatry, knowledge of group relations has become important for both diagnosis and therapy. The observation of individuals in groups teaches us much about their adaptive or nonadaptive functioning. Obviously group therapy must be based on a solid knowledge of group relations. It is less appreciated that psychiatric therapy in institutional and community settings also requires fundamental and practical knowledge of groups and the transactions between such groups as patients, their families and peers, and the different groups of mental health workers.

Theoretical and practical knowledge about groups is derived from a great variety of sources. First there are the contributions of social psychology, sociology, and anthropology (Cartwright and Zander, 1953; Etzioni, 1961; Gaster, 1959; Katz and Kahn,

1966; Lewin, 1951; Linton, 1956; Mills, 1967; Parsons, 1951 and 1964). Then there are the fascinating observations of group behavior by ethologists (Ardrey, 1966; Jolly, 1966; Lorenz, 1963) and, finally scant but significant works by psychoanalysts and psychiatrists (Ezriel, 1952; Foulkes and Anthony, 1964; Freud, 1949; Kelman, 1963; Redl, 1942; Slavson, 1964; Sutherland, 1952; Whitaker and Lieberman, 1965). An important segment of our knowledge derives from the observations of experiments carried out in controlled settings. This includes the so-called laboratory training, stimulated by the work of Kurt Lewin and described by Schein and Bennis (1964; 1965) and others (Lewin, 1951; Lewin et al, 1938; Thomas et al, 1963; Tuckman, 1965). Another, although related, approach was evolved by social scientists and psychoanalysts of the Tavistock Institute. Most of the theoretical constructs were developed by W.R. Bion (1961), Ken Rice (1964; 1965), and Erick Trist (1959).

The work at Yale has been based primarily on the theoretical and practical work of the Tavistock group. Ken Rice and Pierre Turquet played an important part in the training of our faculty during their visits to Yale University and in the three group relations conferences conducted jointly by the Tavistock Institute, the Washington School of Psychiatry, and Yale's department of psychiatry. In its own training program Yale's department of psychiatry has incorporated other views and concepts suggested by Argyris (1964), Berne (1966), Mills (1965; 1967), Slater (1964), Schein and Bennis (1964; 1965), although the austere, disciplined, and intellectually stimulating approach of the Tavistock group continued to appeal to us.

A basic premise of our training program is that the task of training in group relations is educative and not therapeutic. This applies whether the groups meet daily or only weekly and whether they are conducted within our own institutional setting or in a residential conference. Our primary intention is to provide our students with opportunities to learn about group behavior. In this process they should learn a good deal about individual behavior in the group setting, and perhaps even something about their own behavior. However, our groups do not have as their primary concern the development of interpersonal competence. In the "study group," emphasis is placed upon understanding the preconscious aspects of group behavior, particularly the preconscious feelings and ideas centering around leadership.

Our formal training program in group dynamics begins with a two-week, daily "study group" experience[1]. This is followed by application groups and then a year-long seminar in group and organizational dynamics held for psychiatric residents. The small study groups consist of 11 to 13 members and a faculty or staff member who functions as a group leader. The latter is referred

---

[1] In the past, residents were introduced to group dynamics through weekly group sessions organized by some of the subunits of the department of psychiatry. A few isolated "marathon" sessions were also held.

to as a consultant because he does not carry out ordinary leadership functions but rather serves the group as a stimulant and catalyst for its own interpretative and clarifying work. He sets the boundaries and general tone in which the sessions are conducted. His "leadership" remains undefined and he does not tell the group how to behave. Without clear instructions other than the open-ended request to explore its own behavior, the group consequently falls back on primitive, previously acquired behavior patterns. The understanding of such behavior—which in our opinion occurs in all groups—is the most important gain in this type of group work.

Our small study group sessions last for 90 minutes. Group members are selected from different professions. The consultant facilitates the elaboration and expression of fantasies about leadership and the group. It is therefore important that he not have close professional or personal relationships with any of the members. He must also safeguard the confidentiality of the group process. With the cooperation of the group members, efforts must be made to see that any material produced in the group will be held confidential and information obtained in group transactions will not be used to the detriment of group members.

The application groups focus on the relation of the study group experience to the work situation. During this exercise the trainer is much more directly involved with the group members, directly responding to their questions and focusing more on the content than upon the group processes. Although many group members have the wish to "wrap up" the experience, the trainer, while directly gratifying member's wishes to learn more about groups by presenting some theoretical material, continues to insist that much remains to be learned.

The intent of the group training we have conducted is to provide an opportunity to study the essential aspects of group behavior. Tentatively, we define a small group as a structured face-to-face aggregate of transacting persons who are bound together by a task, culture, and image of the group. It should be kept in mind that there are other aggregates of people, such as the crowd, which is an unstructured mass without boundaries, and the large group, a structured group in which it is impossible for all members to engage in face-to-face relationships at the same time.

In the remainder of our presentation, we shall limit ourselves to a didactic exploration of small face-to-face groups. Although the distinction is an obviously artificial one, we shall discuss separately the essential characteristics of groups (boundary, structure, tasks, group culture, and group image) and the influence of the group on the individual (authority relationships, establishment of membership, and transactions).

GROUP CHARACTERISTICS

BOUNDARIES

The fact that groups have boundaries is one of the most important characteristics that students of group relations experience and study. We distinguish three types of boundaries: spatial, temporal, and psychological.

The spatial boundary is the most obvious one. Usually the study group meets in a room with chairs arranged in a circle; the group begins to function when the consultant enters and closes the door. The group begins to consider the room its own territory and is often willing to safeguard it against strangers[2]. Within the group territorial arrangements are observed; seating arrangements are important to the group, particularly who sits next to the consultant. During the application group meetings the discussion of spatial boundaries is extended to the relevance of territories occupied by patients', psychiatrists', and nurses' groups. This territoriality is apparent even in modern psychiatric hospitals where strict rules about "territory" are still enforced, either explicitly (defined nursing or medical areas) or implicitly (areas of the day room where only patients sit, etc.). The uniting of professional, subprofessional, and patient groups, as in the cafeteria of a modern hospital, is often an uncomfortable experience that is strongly resisted by staff and even at times by patients.

The study group learns to appreciate time boundaries. This is experienced quite vividly when—out of a group of strangers—a cohesive and distinctive group emerges and ends quite abruptly at a given time. The "death" of the group is usually experienced with anxiety, anger, and most of all with some grief, expressed overtly and covertly. Often arrangements are made, under one pretext or the other, to prolong the life of the group. It is also noted by group members that the consultant plays a powerful role in determining time boundaries by punctually starting and ending the group sessions.

The most important boundaries are the psychological boundaries of the groups, which define who belongs to the group and who does not. We distinguish external boundaries, separating members from non-members, and internal boundaries, which we will discuss later in the context of the influence of the group on the individual. External psychological boundaries are expressed by appearance and behavior. Study groups often develop some language that defines membership and excludes outsiders. In the application group, members may discuss this further. In many settings, such as hospitals, prisons, and military organizations, membership in groups is indicated by

---

2 In residential conferences this may be directly explored in intergroup exercises (Higgins and Bridger, 1964) Territorial arrangements are also of significance in defining behavior. Behaviors in the work group at a residential conference, corresponding to what Goffman (1958) calls the "front room," are different from behaviors in the "back room," such as lounges, bars, bedrooms, and washrooms.

uniforms and insignia. Behavior, language, special jargons and vocabularies, and gestures denote and connote membership in a group. In a psychiatric hospital a patient may act "crazy," a therapist may not. In some groups such as in adolescent peer groups, a certain appearance, conduct, and language are indicative of membership in a given group.

STRUCTURE

The study groups provide an excellent opportunity to examine group structure. By structure we mean the hierarchical organization of a group. Practically all human groups—including the groups of patients in the back wards of mental hospitals—have structure. Usually we distinguish between the official or proclaimed structure, the assumed or fantasy structure, and the real structure which may become obvious only after careful study. Status (one's position in a hierarchy) may be fixed or changing. It may be, as Parsons (1964) pointed out, ascribed or achieved. The status of members in study groups is essentially achieved status, although the status that a group member occupies in society also has impact on his group status. All this may be observed and analyzed in study groups and further explored in application sessions.

The status of leader is highly important. As we have already mentioned, in study groups leadership remains undefined. This permits members of the group to project their fantasies about leaders and leadership onto the consultant and to act out old identifications with previously encountered leaders. Individuals and cliques in the group aspire to take over leadership in fact or fantasy. Many of the transactions in the group deal with the dynamics of such feuds.

The group learns from this about different types of good and bad leadership: about powerful and powerless leaders, about figureheads and "the power behind the throne," and about executive and spiritual leaders. Group members learn about overestimation and underestimation of leaders. They become cognizant of the difficult and complex tasks that most leaders face.

Study groups permit the study of mobility because any member may become or cease to be a leader for longer or shorter periods of time. Yet the consultant remains, under ordinary circumstances, the head of the group. This allows members to additionally study a system that has certain relatively fixed, immobile elements. Within these broad limits the tendency toward conformity—so-called consonance—and the forces which destroy the group, such as decay or rebellion, may be studied under relatively controlled circumstances.

GROUP TASK

All groups have tasks, one of which may be designated as primary, since it is the most necessary for group survival. A.K.

Rice (1964) has described the need of the group to explicitly define its primary task. Secondary tasks may impose constraints on the primary task.

The primary task of the study group is to examine its own behavior. In order to do this it must insure that certain group boundaries will be erected, that membership will be maintained, and that a number of other secondary tasks will be defined and attended to. In the application group, members may discuss, for example, the primacy of tasks in a teaching hospital. Such a hospital must teach to survive, but adequate service and research must be carried out lest the teaching function deteriorate. At times the service and research demands may then almost assume primacy. An important task of the group leader is the definition and reiteration of the primary task.

Groups that are primarily oriented to their external work are described as "work oriented," and groups oriented to inner processes are described as "process oriented." Both tasks are obviously necessary and must balance and complement each other. The treatment task of a therapeutic team in a psychiatric hospital might be described as that team's external task. The internal task consists of producing and maintaining group cohesion, communication, and motivation.

GROUP CULTURE

Each group and each organization has a certain code of ideology and values, which states what behaviors of the group and its individual members are rewarded or punished. Another code states how a group is supposed to use its possessions, particularly its tools and instruments. These codes have been referred to as the ideological and instrumental aspects of the culture (Wheelis, 1958). Students of small groups have the opportunity to study the codes of the total group and subgroups.

In our study groups the members, representing a variety of mental health professions, have the extraordinary opportunity to examine the values of other disciplines. Our groups also frequently examine sexual roles within groups and, less frequently, racial and religious difference. The culture developing in these groups arises from the values, attitudes, and ideologies brought into the group by each member. The style of leadership undoubtedly influences group culture, and group members often compare their groups and their consultants to others.

GROUP IMAGE

Each group forms multiple images of itself. The group projects an image to others, the "official image." It may have another conscious image of itself which is not to be shared with others, as well as an unperceived, unconscious image. These images are not constant but change continually. The group images are interpreted, influenced, modified, and at times "officially" stated by the group leaders.

The study groups are generally quite aware of the behavior of other groups and, while recognizing the irrationality of needing to project a "good image" in an educational exercise, often go to great lengths to do so and to internally convince themselves and their own group of its value. This phenomenon can be studied in such groups and further explored in application groups.

Berne calls great past leaders who have created powerful groups and group images *euhemeri*. This is a Greek word roughly synonymous with mythical heroes, demigods, or saints. Euhemeri are often invoked and quoted by the group. Psychiatrists will invoke and quote Pinel, Rush, Freud, Kraepelin, or Meyer, for example, thus justifying or condoning the group's principles or actions. Study groups permit the exploration of group idealization and denigration and the motivations of such processes.

THE INDIVIDUAL IN THE GROUP
AUTHORITY RELATIONS

The study group experience stimulates and fosters the exploration of authority relations (Astrachan & Redlich, 1967). An investigation of authority relations is not only basic to an understanding of therapeutic relationships but also critical for an appreciation of the role of leadership in therapeutic hospital settings and the role of "expert" in consultative work and community work. In the study group the consultant's group-centered, theme-centered comments and his air of detached awareness focus initial member responses on leadership and allow for the elaboration of fantasies about authority. Each member, to a greater or lesser degree, participates in this process and can explore the shared responses to leadership, as well as (to the degree that the individual wishes to share this with the group) his own individual responses to authority.

In the application group members have the opportunity to relate their own study group experiences about authority to their experiences at work with patients, supervisors, and teachers.

MEMBERSHIP

The establishment of one's membership in the group is explored both individually and collectively in the study group. The evolving structure of the group has a significant impact on the individual experiences and intrapsychic life of each member, Slater (1966) has described this process for similarly oriented groups, noting that the initial identification with leadership must, to some extent, be overcome before the group members can begin the process of defining the relationship of member to member. In this later process the members explore the limits of toleration they will have for one another's behavior. It is, of course, possible to focus on member-member interaction at the very beginning of a group's formation, but in our experience this occurs only when group leadership clearly defines this behavior as basic to group functioning and when this exercise of authority by leadership is unchallenged.

The phenomenon of scapegoating is frequently observed in groups, and the acceptance and rejection of group members is related to the development of inner psychological boundaries. A member of a group may, for short or long periods of time, be severely rejected but not expelled and still remain a member of the group. This rejected or alienated member also differs from an outsider or stranger. In application groups, the function of the deviant (Dentler et al, 1959) can be explored, as can the participation of the total group in the deviant behavior.

GROUP TRANSACTIONS

The study group is primarily concerned with the exploration of transactions within the group. One fundamental assumption about groups states that any transactions between any members of the group affect the whole group. This deceivingly simple fact has been overlooked for a long time, and indeed we believe that many psychiatrists are not cognizant of it.

Many transactions are strongly correlated with the status of the actors. We refer to such relatively stable patterns of action as role behavior (Levinson, 1959), which is prescribed behavior or, stated differently, behavior that may be expected in a given situation and in a given group. We are particularly interested in the ability or inability of individuals to shift roles. Certain roles occur frequently in most groups: the various types of leaders; the spiritual leader or "party philosopher"; the overt or latent anti-leader, who exists in all groups that produce leaders; the conformist, or yeasayer; the nonconformist, or naysayer; the victims, martyrs, and scapegoats; the jesters and buffoons.

In the study group one can observe the overt, conscious, rational or irrational transactions and get some indication of covert, irrational, preconscious transactions. Berne (1966) has described a transactional theory of group behavior, describing a number of games (including ceremonials and pastimes) that are "played" by group members in their attempts to avoid work and change. In the examination of such transactions in the study group setting, the individual is able to understand the manner in which group themes influence member-member behavior. Bion (1961) has identified the most important irrational and defensive forms of group behavior that disrupt the behavior of the work group as: the fight-flight group in which the members destroy or escape; the dependency group in which members helplessly try to follow a leader without assuming responsibility; and the pairing group in which members form irrationally determined subgroups or cliques with unconscious fantasies of producing a new group leader.

The work of groups is often impeded by the group's indulgence in immature and infantile behavior. It is appropriate to speak of such infantile group behavior, usually characterized by irrational anxiety, rage, and depression, as group regression. All groups under stress become regressive. In the study group such regression is produced by the difficulty of the assignment to study one's own behavior and by the ambiguous role of the consultant.

Another fundamental group dynamism that may be explored in study groups is the tendency toward conformity or consonance. The basic forces underlying it are conscious imitation or unconscious identification. The last basic dynamism we mention is projection, or the irrational assumption of the existence of one's own experiences in others. It is true that without identification or projection no group formation could take place; unchecked identification and projection, however, lead to fundamental distortion of communications and actions of group members. The experiencing and exploration of these precon-scious group processes have received much attention in the study groups we have conducted.

ADVANTAGES AND DISADVANTAGES OF TRAINING IN GROUP RELATIONS

We believe that the small study groups, as well as other exercises provided in group relations conferences, provide an interesting opportunity for participants to learn about the many aspects of group behavior we have mentioned. Such an experience usually is far from neutral or casual. Quite frequently a number of participants become upset in this process; a few individuals whom we observed have become temporarily so upset that we had reason to call their behavior psychotic. Such responses in themselves testify vividly to the powerful processes that occur in groups. Little is known so far about these upsets. In most cases, we believe that a strong latent predisposition toward such disturbed behavior existed. Fortunately the upsets are, in our experience, of short duration and do not justify the opposition to participation in study groups and group relations conferences voiced by some conservative psychiatrists.

In general, we believe that the opportunity to learn about group behavior and its relevance for the work of psychiatrists and other mental health workers outweighs the risks. Obviously more experience with these new methods, their benefits, and risks must be gained. Sound research-based evaluations will ultimately tell us how to proceed best.

14.

STRANGE ENCOUNTERS: The Use of Study Groups with Graduate Students in History

David F. Musto and Boris M. Astrachan

Historians have been increasingly interested in the use of psychology for the understanding of historical events. This broadened application has come during a period in which historical tools have multiplied to include the methodology of sociologists and political scientists and such technical devices as the computer. In company with these newer methods, psychology has become somewhat respectable in the historical profession. The significant studies by William Willcox (1964) and by Donald David (1960) are of value not only historically but also psychologically, although written by historians. That both these studies are biographies reflects the fact that published research and theory in individual psychology remain more readily available for the historian than the study of group dynamics.

Confronted with the difficulty of using psychological concepts when he is not familiar with their value and limitations, the historian — however friendly to psychological explanation — generally either uses more familiar methods which circumvent psychological data or relies on a commonsense psychology which could be shared by most of his readers. Psychological factors in history, whether individual, group, or cultural, are occasionally ignored, sometimes because the historian is unaware of their presence, but more often because he encounters difficulty in analyzing them solely with his historical training. Attempts by historians to gain for themselves the facility they want have by and large been frustrating. Theories and abstractions, usually their only contact with psychology, cannot be critically evaluated or meaningfully employed without some knowledge of the data on which they are based — and this knowledge is not imparted in the traditional education of the historian.

The historian's problem, then, is to acquire the ability of creatively adapting psychological theory to a particular person or group. The difficulty in acquiring a facility from articles or books, coupled with a widening conviction that historians must come to grips with the psychological aspects of past events, has led to an interest in more direct contact with psychology.

But a barrier which must be overcome is the historian's lack of close and examined contact with others, such as a psychiatrist has in his training. Depth studies of living persons from whom, for example, the relevance of childhood years can be more clearly seen and evaluated, are not on the agenda for graduate students in history. The experience of repeatedly examining actions of ongoing groups, of coming to some judgment of what groups do and what remarkable power a group has, simply cannot be properly appreciated from any document. Of course, historians, like anyone else, can form opinions about groups and people from their own experience and judgment, which may be extensive and sound or otherwise. But clinicians, focusing more on groups and individuals in the here and now, can make theoretical contributions or call attention to data which their specialized, intensive study has indicated may be relevant. It is difficult, however, for clinicians to transmit this information in an assimilable form; theory separated from its bases or primary sources cannot be very easily applied.

For the working historian, familiarity with psychology means a sensitivity to the appropriate data and an awareness of which concepts might be relevant. In investigations in which these data and concepts are pertinent, psychology is a tool of some value, but it is, of course, not the only tool and it is only infrequently the chief tool. Furthermore, there are areas in history which offer little possibility for the application of psychological knowledge. But to the extent that direct, examined contact with others is missing from graduate education, historians who could benefit from it are hampered.

A major gap in communication, then, results from the fact that clinical literature and the clinician begin with an examined experience of close interpersonal relationships which historians have not had. Little basis for balanced discussion exist in the presence of this disparity. Of course, equal training is not a practicable counsel; without some direct, examined contact with others, however, it is difficult to see how one can very easily appreciate the subject matter of psychology in proper perspective and consider investigating it.

Yet clinical psychology and psychiatry and history have a similarity extending beyond their common subject. Both are taught by that venerable technique for conveying an art—the apprentice system. A graduate student studies primary sources; his work is criticized and evaluated over a period of some years and he begins to get a feel for the analysis of data. The same is true of the clinical student of psychological principles. The articles, books, and lectures are important, but the essential element in the preparation of a clinician consists of his treating many patients with detailed supervision, at the same time checking assumptions which may or may not be accurate; immersion in this procedure hopefully results in his internalizing meaningful conclusions about the dynamics of human behavior. This familiar method tends to convince the apprentice that his way of analyzing man is the one that any objective observer would choose. The kinds of data that are considered acceptable evidence for important generalizations differ in the two apprentice-trained groups, and there is, therefore, an emotional collision when representatives of the groups meet. But when the two meet on common ground, after the incompleteness of their respective disciplines has been accepted, there is an exhilarating widening of perspective.

A "STUDY GROUP" FOR HISTORIANS

To those attempting to improve communication between the groups, it seemed that historians should have some contact with the raw data—the "primary source material" of psychology—followed by an opportunity to conceptualize it and to hear and to question clinicians abstracting from it. After considering the various methods of contemporary psychology, experience in a small group setting appeared to be a possible way to meet these criteria. Because within groups powerful, unrecognized psychological forces are continually in operation, the "study group" model, developed at the Centre for Applied Social Research, Tavistock Institute of Human Relations, was chosen as the vehicle for the study of these forces. This type of group has as its major task the study of its own behavior as a group. There is no desire, nor is it part of any agreement with the students, to help the group members learn more about their own behavior in groups so that they might become more "effective" group members. The aim is learning, not therapy.

Briefly, study groups are composed of about ten members, including a consultant who is experienced in group functioning. Our group met for one and a half hours, five days a week, for two weeks; two weeks is a typical length for such groups, but some of them meet all day during that period. There is no agenda. The task is to study the interaction of the group as it occurs. The role of the consultant is to comment on the functioning of the group as it appears to him; the group can do what it wishes about his comments.

This description of a study group's functioning is usually greeted with a doubtful shaking of the head by someone not familiar with its operation. How can such a loosely organized group form? What does it do? How can it be like any group in history? But the group does quickly form, attains great cohesion, and is remarkably similar to other groups with more traditional organization and tasks. It has an advantage in not having the cover of a more specific task or organization to obscure the members' interaction.

Such groups have had a variety of applications and modifications. They have been described as providing a valuable experience in the training of group therapists, but they have also helped business and government executives and community organizers learn about the functioning of groups.

237

The relation of the group to its leadership provides the basic data out of which theoretical formulations about these groups have been constructed[1]. The Tavistockian study-group leader attempts to define carefully his own boundaries and to maintain his separateness from the members. He can, however, function effectively only if he is in the group sufficiently to share in the common feelings and attitudes, while being separate enough to observe the group, himself, and his own feelings. From this position he can investigate his impact on the group. He has no political power to lead the group, save, initially, the power resident in the fantasied expectations of him. His real power comes from his definition of the group task and his devotion to this task. Yet by insisting on his separateness and by attending to his task, he defines himself as leader and the group is by implication encouraged to elaborate even more fantasies about him (Slater, 1966).

The members experience the group as a tremendous threat to their wishes to remain separate individuals and, at the same time, as a seductive invitation to them to be part of a mass. The threat to individuality is intensified by the sanctioned behavior of one group member, the leader-consultant, who insists on separateness and is feared and given power by the group. Others begin to respond to him with hostility almost as the very first group meeting begins.

In order to cope with the demands of this situation the members must begin to engage one another, to define their relations to each other. Using a variety of roles, they discover, for example, how an individual may serve the group and yet remain almost apart from the group. Of course, as the leader-consultant interprets the roles, he reinforces his separateness and places the others back in the group. His behavior obviously makes him unique; at the same time that he manifests his separateness from the group, he also insists upon his membership in the group, since he cannot make a valid interpretation unless he has obtained his evidence from being in the group.[2] The members grow insistent that they will allow no other person to separate and be beyond the group. Thus the groups will first unite and then either seduce the leader into the group or overthrow him (usually only symbolically). Here the group may examine the processes of consensus, group revolt, and group power, and the manner in which legitimate succession is established. After the group either

---

1 Rice (1965) has described the use of these groups, elaborating the theoretical work of W. Bion, *Experiences in Groups;* London, Tavistock Publications, 1961.

2 Paul Watzlawick, J.H. Beavin, and Don D. Jackson, in their monograph, *The Pragmatics of Human Communication* (New York, Norton, 1967), describe how difficult it is to adequately communicate in this type of situation. A higher level of abstraction is needed to deal with this "bind," and to achieve that higher level one would have to metacommunicate. However, when one metacommunicates in the group, he takes a boundary or leadership position, a position resisted by other group members.

has attempted to change, or has successfully changed leader behavior, the opportunity exists for the members to reexamine relations to leadership and the development of peer relations, and, since such groups are finite, to examine issues relating to the death of the group and to the tremendous power of a group to perpetuate itself.

The question lying behind this particular experiment was whether study groups would promote sensitivity to psychological data and increase appreciation of covert group activity. One hope was that the sensitivity to group processes could be applied to groups of which only records remain. It was believed that experience with the "raw data" would be more valuable if the students were also given an opportunity to appraise critically psychiatrists' interpretations of that same data. Discussion of the group meetings was planned for several weekly seminars after the study-group experience. This phase would be followed by presentation of the members' own historical work or of questions concerning historical subjects, now viewed in the light of what they may have learned from this experience.

A proposal combining these elements was made by one of the authors (DFM) in a lecture on psychiatry and history at the University of Washington in October, 1966. Both historians and psychiatrists responded favorably to the idea, and upon the author's return to New Haven, he presented it to members of the history and psychiatry departments at Yale. The chairmen of these departments agreed to the encounter with considerable interest and support. The co-author accepted the invitation to lead the study group and participate in the subsequent seminars. The final step was to obtain volunteers.

Explaining to the graduate students the nature and purpose of the meetings was difficult. Because of our primary affiliations, the proposal for interdepartmental contact seemed to come from the Department of Psychiatry. Presentation of the program to the history graduate student association was greeted with embarrassed laughter and derision. Two of the 80 or so students afterwards said they they would be interested. The group pressure for conformity was too great, we felt, to permit more widespread interest from being voiced, so form letters were written to the approximately 100 graduate students in residence. In the privacy of their rooms somewhat over 30 replied.

We then held a large group meeting in which we attempted to anticipate and openly face the interested students' reactions. They were quite suspicious of what the Department of Psychiatry was planning to do to them. They wondered what our *real* motives were. We said we were trying to provide history graduate student with an experience in group functioning which might be useful to their history research. But, many asked, were we not really trying to find out how historians worked as compared to, say, (shudder) sociologists? Several students had been deceived by another department conducting research. They were not prepared to accept as true our avowed intentions. We explained that we expected to benefit by learning more about groups, and perhaps by writing a paper about the experience. Many of the students had questions about whether the experience would be applicable to their own areas of study and we indicated our inability to guarantee direct applicability. We arranged further individual interviews with interested students to help them clarify their interest and to allow us some flexibility in selection. The number meanwhile decreased because some students lost interest and others could not attend during the hours the study group would be held.

Of the 22 finally interviewed, we selected eleven, which was the maximum number we had decided upon for the group. Our criteria for selection included relevance of psychological concepts to the individual's research, no current or recently terminated psychotherapy, and no obvious emotional instability. We could easily have formed two groups of, say, nine each from the number fitting these criteria. Without design, the group was composed almost totally of persons who had no exposure to psychiatry or courses in psychology (other than brief exposure in social science or biological science surveys). The average year in graduate school was the third, but ranged from first to seventh. We do not know how typical these factors are for history graduate students, but the members' ability to participate in the group meetings and the seminar afterwards seemed satisfactory.

THE STUDY GROUP EXPERIENCE

A brief outline of the study-group meetings will give some idea of their course, although, in a fundamental sense, it cannot replace the experience itself. The purpose of the experience was to provide living data so that the process of abstracting or describing could be studied. The italicized comments summarize our conception of the dynamics of a session and represent, of course, only one way of understanding the group.

The meetings began in the first week of the second semester. A few days before we began, one of the eleven selected students withdrew because of a teaching assignment conflict, which left ten group members; of these, one came for the first time on the fourth day because his invitation had arrived late. Therefore, there were 97 possible attendance hours and of these 94 were filled. The meetings were held in an elegant Yale-Gothic conference room in the Hall of Graduate Studies. Chairs were set in a circle for the consultant and the participants; one chair was set just outside the circle for the observer.

At 10:30 on a February morning, nine graduate students assembled. Most were strangers to one another. Several members carried something to help while away the time—a note pad, the New York Times, a pipe; three who knew one another spoke quietly about shared classes. Silence prevailed for the first five minutes. Then the consultant remarked, "It does seem the group has a hard time beginning." And from then on for 15 hours there was hardly a break in the exchanges. A few questions were immediately asked. Why the empty chair? One member, Albert, asked for introductions and, moving around the circle, the members gave their names and areas of study, and a few gave their seniority in graduate school. Charles pointed out the largest subgroup, the "China lobby" — students of Chinese culture; it consisted of the three who were sitting together, including Charles. Charles began jockeying for leadership of the "China lobby." The struggle continued and increased as the consultant refused to take the expected role of group leader, but discussion of the struggle did not occur until the consultant repeatedly emphasized its presence.

In this first session the direct focus on the consultant was much less than anticipated. When the members commented on the consultant in this session or defined his role, they spoke of such leadership functions as setting an agenda or calling the meeting to order. When they commented on the person of the consultant, they focused on their distrust of psychiatrists, who had "hidden motives" and who might experimentally manipulate or "trick" the group. When the consultant commented on the manner in which the group avoided examining its relation to him, this was responded to with "Do you want to be in the group, fella?"—as though the members, all from a different discipline from the consultant's, saw themselves as initially sharing something from which the consultant was excluded. There was additionally a wish to define leadership as residing not in a person, but in an office.

The second meeting occurred during a blizzard. Seven of the nine present the previous day appeared, some having walked for over half an hour through driving snow. Considerable discussion focused on the absent pair, one of whom, Albert, had been competing for leadership the day before. Was he "assassinated"? The danger of leadership was both felt within the group and discussed. The seven had a difficult time, however, examining their own bids for leadership and observing their own interaction. Charles increasingly led the group although he denied that he was doing so or that he even wanted to do so. He was attacked strongly but he held off the wolves, and quieted opposition with a moving anecdote of how he had no desire to be leader because he had once failed as a leader.

Much of the group's behavior was interpreted by the consultant as focusing on leadership issues. Concern with the consultant's leadership style and his "abdication of power" was mirrored in group discussions. The members ambivalently explored the attractions and dangers of leadership. Competing "leaders" felt it necessary to deny the intense group competition for leadership. For example, when one student was caught in parapraxis about wishing to lead he responded by saying that as an educator his function would be "to lead forth, from the Latin 'educo', " and that he had not wished for "any other form of leadership."

The next day the nine were again present. Hostility was shown to the pair who were absent the day before, Donald and Albert. Inside jokes about them and refusal to give much information about the previous meeting characterized the response of the seven. The lack of the sharing involved in the previous day's experience rather than anything now said by the two prodigals seemed to be the reason for their exclusion. More open hositility appeared between the contending leaders. Donald was generally quiet, but Albert was active in exchange with other group members. The group also explored some of the fantasies about the consultant and his "power".

A mythical quality arose about the meeting on the previous day, as if it had been particularly moving and important. This served to significantly isolate Albert. He was "elected" to serve the role of impotent group critic and outsider. The group's behavior implied that he was allowed to have some of the attributes of a leader—that is, he could be separate and might comment on the group as a whole—but that he was defined as being out of the group.

In the fourth meeting the group successfully changed the behavior of the consultant. For one day in each of the two weeks that the study group met (the fourth and ninth sessions), the room in which it usually convened was scheduled for occupancy by others, and another, much larger room was used for the meetings. On the fourth day, metal folding-chairs had been set up in the usual circle, but a number of the group members objected to the use of these chairs when heavy, plush armchairs were distributed throughout the room. With great rapidity, these members constructed a second circle of armchairs, and invited the consultant to leave his circle and join them. He did so. Shortly thereafter, Albert launched an attack against the fundamental assumption of the group. With considerable angry feeling he declared that the group was poorly set up, since without structure it resembled almost no recorded group; that the members would learn nothing; and that the time was, in fact, wasted. He concluded by dramatically announcing that he might stop attending the meetings. The group's response was a strong verbal assault on Albert. The consultant suggested that Albert was speaking, in a way, for those other members who also doubted the worth of the group; the consultant pointed out that the process of extruding a group member from the group tended to mobilize his doubt and to localize group doubt in him. He further pointed out that conditions were beginning to be placed on how group members might act so that, for example, disbelief in the study group's efficacy was not tolerated. Also on that day, Ernest, the member with the delayed invitation, joined the group. He was generally silent. At one point the group considered turning to him as to another consultant, but then decided that this desire arose because they were less interested in working to find out how the group functioned than in having a consultant who would give interpretations to them. The discussion led to considering the difficulties of reconstructing or understanding the group. Chiefly, Charles continued to lead the group. The group asked whether the consultant could be trusted, commented on his fallibility, and almost completely disregarded his attempts to focus on the work of the group.

The group acted effectively to bring the consultant more into its midst, but was then faced with the need to reexamine its relationship to him and to the other special person in the group, Albert. The consultant's efforts to help the group examine the symbolic meaning of Albert's role as isolate and scapegoat were ignored by the group.

The last meeting of the first week seemed to combine an attempt to incorporate the consultant as a buddy (which would end his special role), and the continued attack on Albert (who continued to attend). The group insisted that Albert come up with an alternative plan, which he could not do. As the group members viewed the consultant less as an authority, they increasingly attacked one another, which suggested to some members that a recognized leader protected group members from one another. The group commented on the pleasure of jointly "bumping someone off", of "seeing blood on the sand", but also on how dangerous this made the assumption of, or the attempt to assume, leadership. One member noted that he had seen the consultant smoke a cigar after the group, and wished that the consultant "felt comfortable enough" to smoke in the group.

With increasing vigor the group moved to bring the consultant in, and to extrude the "impotent critic," Albert. The testing of the consultant's "power" seemed to have at least two functions. First, it allowed for some exploration of the destructive potential of the group. As one member stated to the consultant when the latter tried to interpret some of the group's behavior, "I disposed of you on the second day." There followed considerable struggling over the primitive impulses directed from member to member. Second, this testing seemed to be an attempt to force the consultant into the position of "political leader," someone who might take action to forestall the group's destructive behavior.

On Monday of the second week there was further elaboration on how difficult it was for one person to stand out from the group, to change the status quo. There seemed to be a sense of discomfort within the group as well as a feeling of no movement. The less talkative and less dominant members of the group

243

banded together to vote on whether to have a voting procedure to choose topics. Albert supported the idea. The group consensus uncomfortably stifled individuality, and a primitive political structure evolved, apparently to restrain the dominant members of the group. The vote was taken, approved, and interpreted by the members as removing Charles's power.

The group worked intently to avoid work. After finally voting to vote, the group stopping voting. The consultant was not being listened to, Albert was defined as impotent, and Charles was given his "comeuppance." Having deposed leadership, the group was unwilling to allow the rise of other leaders, and, furthermore, was unwilling to allow individuals any degree of freedom in the group [one could be free only be getting out of the group].

Charles began Day 7 with a strong attack on the consultant, asserting that he had failed the group, had lost control of the group, and was desperately grasping at straws with "interpretations." Others wondered about their decision to allow voting. Was the decision aimed at independence or was it perhaps an attempt to establish a leadership of precedent? The consultant reflected that the group members were afraid of exposing and examining leadership and its power. They then considered voting on whether to exclude the consultant from the group. The group, said the consultant, anticipated that in a few weeks all would be explained so that it was not necessary for them to work now. Everyone sensed that the character of transactions had become more "gentlemanly" and that almost no group member had been "put down" for several days. Several members volunteered that the decision to vote had taken "life" out of the group.

On the eighth day the meeting opened slowly with the requests for the consultant "to come down and speak more clearly." The members began to discuss their individual roles, the power of the generally silent member, and the irritation created by various styles of bidding for leadership. An attempt to extrude or "kill" Albert led to expressions of guilt. Someone complained that whatever was being learned in the group could not be footnoted or described. More expressions of boredom came forth. The consultant suggested that the group's impending death was the preoccupation of the meeting. Leadership was again discussed along with the nature of charisma or leader-myth. Some thought that what was comforting or attractive about the myth was that it created a conviction that the leader would not let the group die.

The next to the last day saw a great increase in the discussion of individual roles during the past sessions and a general neglect of the consultant's presence. Albert was absent and this stimulated considerable talk. What was it about Albert that led the group to extrude him? The consultant suggested that the life of the group was so valuable that to preserve it the group had to get rid of Albert. Members exchanged ideas on how to preserve the group. Suggestions included publishing an "alumni directory" and making arrangements to meet again. Ernest, who had joined on Day 4, expressed wonderment at how solid the group seemed and asked how it had ever formed like this from so many strangers. Discussion again centered on Albert and how "picking him apart" on Day 2 seemed to help group spirit. But then it was noted that his fellow absentee, Donald, had now reentered the group. What was the difference between them? Gradually discussion turned to other members and why they were selected. What was it about their personality or lives which was important to the arrangers of the meetings? The group began focusing more on knowing something about one another toward the end of the meeting.

During these three meetings, the consultant felt continually confused and impotent within the group. He continued in his attempts to focus on the group work, but the group paid only limited attention to his words while magnifying his position. In one session, members eliminated his chair from the group and indulged in fantasies of placing it on a table ["our monarch"]. When post-study-group meetings were discussed, the consultant felt himself as having been set apart, deified, and ignored. The vote was seen by the members as having ended the group ["the involvement is gone"], but the group continued and began to approach termination. Historical topics were introduced into the group [such as intrigues in the British Foreign Office and how difficult it was to understand from memoranda what really went on], members began to discuss how they saw the group, and there was some discussion of the roles individuals played on the group.

On the last day Charles started out by describing how he had sized up the group on Day 1, but he elicited only mild interest from the other members. Rather soon they moved into planning a party for everyone. The consultant commented that the group could deal with death in a variety of ways, whereupon he was told to "shut up." One member suggested that those who were really out of the group were the consultant and Albert, who was again present. Then the group returned to the question of how to remain unified. Should members write brief autobiographies and distribute them to one another? Should the wives attend the party although they were not in the group? Someone remarked about the difficulty of planning a party by consensus. The consultant suggested that the group wanted to act as if the meetings has already ended. As the meeting moved on, bursts of laughter at minor witticisms occurred fairly often. One member said that he had to leave early in order to walk to a distant class, but Albert quickly offered to give him a ride so that he could stay until the end of the meeting. The last half-hour the group presented the consultant with ten cigars, each with the name of a member on it, and suggested that the consultant might enjoy seeing each of the members vanish in smoke. Then Charles lighted another cigar, took a few puffs, and passed it around the circle, excluding the consultant and observer; some members conspicuously licked the cigar before smoking, and all but one took a few puffs. The members then presented the observer with a box of pencils.

The meeting drew to a close with a discussion colored with sexual symbolism. There were further suggestions that an alumni song be written, and someone wondered whether the door should be locked to prevent the consultant from leaving.

The last meeting began again with the members seeking to avoid the work of the group, to recapitulate but not to examine the processes of the group. By giving the consultants the ten cigars with members' names on them, and by sharing a ceremonial cigar, the group ended with the fantasy of continuing. The members discussed the symbolic significance of their behavior, noting wishes to take part of others into themselves. Wishes to have an orgiastic experience, however, were modified by overt concern that such an orgy would have to be homosexual. The group ended as if it were continuing.

THE SEMINAR

Nine conventional seminar meetings were held after the study group. They began with a review of the meetings and an attempt at conceptualizing what had happened. This took two forms: specific questions about study-group events and, later, detailed review of the observer's notes on Day 2.

After four seminars we turned to the members' research; their presentations, arising from the study group and its review, either related psychological concepts to their own studies or raised other general questions about group and individual psychology.

Early questions in the first seminars were aimed at clarifying the interaction of personality and role. Members expressed great interest in examining how each individual sought some stable role or was assigned some other role by the group. The development of cohesion was discussed, and this led into discussion of the inhibition of individuality in the group by the developing cohesion. A number of factors were mentioned as possible contributors to the cohesion. These included not only psychological factors but also such things as environmental stress. The consultant suggested that the blizzard had been important in the history of the group. Several members disagreed, maintaining that there was only a gradual increase in cohesion over the first several days; some thought there was no cohesiveness on the second day. Then Ernest mentioned his amazement at how compact and intense the group appeared when he joined it (Day 4). Donald talked about how isolated he felt after missing Day 2, and how in various ways he was excluded or put down on Day 3. Others began to recall these events; they gave examples of other groups which seemed to have solidified after a time of trouble, and of the process through which the "faithful" become an elite, as in the later development of the Chinese Communist and Nazi parties. The discussion then moved into an appreciation of the tremendous power of groups to maintain boundaries between members and outsiders—of how the survivors of the 'blizzard day' felt united and could extend courtesies only with difficulty to the apostates. One of the students of contemporary Chinese culture commented that he had not previously experienced for himself how "artificial" groups can decrease individuality and determine behavior. He had felt that by exercising will power he could preserve his individuality fairly easily, but had failed to do so. He said that the fantasies of the study group were related to the realities of land reform in Chinese villages, as illustrated in a book he had recently read. (Hinton, 1966)

For the intensive examination of the second study-group meeting, each member of the seminar was supplied with photocopies of the notes for the "blizzard day." The problem was now to agree on a description of the meeting from the record and to try to conceptualize it. Battle broke out as participants tried to justify their positions or clarify their recorded statements. The veracity of the record was attacked, but after detailed discussion, no significant errors were found. The group was able to examine its own strong negative reaction and to relate it to the observer's taking an important leadership role for the first time.

The observer's notes described the effective leadership steps taken by Charles, who had denied throughout the blizzard day that he was leading. Since each member had a different view of what had happened, an attempt was made to harmonize the histories. Most members saw "something special" about Charles and agreed that he had led the group and had heroically held off attacks on his leadership in a variety of ways. Donald, who had missed the blizzard day, described his reaction to Charles on Day 3: Charles already seemed to have an "aura" about him and a special role in the group, with members deferring to him on many issues. But Charles did not see it that way. He felt that he had been defending a point of view, and had believed at the time that after it was adopted, leadership would pass to someone with another popular point of view. The group then expressed surprise that Charles, who had led them, didn't "know" what he had been doing. Surely, they felt, he must have known best of all.

The relation of the group to the leader was studied at greater length in the next meeting. The "myths" surrounding leaders, and the disaster that meets leaders who do not live up to "myths" that might not be at all evident to them, were discussed. The psychiatrists outlined various methods of analyzing group processes, such as the contributions of Bion, Slater, and Freud. They also mentioned the early group need for cohesiveness and the later attempts at individuation.

At subsequent meetings, when we had turned to presentations of individual research topics and their relation to psychological concepts, freer discussion developed between the members and the psychiatrists. General questions about issues in other seminars and a variety of research problems were brought up as students sought individual appointments with the instructors.

The rather long period of time that passed before any free interchange occurred was one of the most striking circumstances of the whole experience. It seemed necessary for the members to decide that the psychiatrists were not trying to explain history as a part of psychology, or that psychiatrists did not claim to know the answers although they were interested in the problems. Like most intergroup tensions, unrealistic attitudes toward one another decreased through further contact. But another feeling, perhaps related to the first, was that the psychiatrists did not provide dazzling insights into historical problems—that revelation of the core explanation of history (which some of the members had sought, consciously or unconsciously) was not to be obtained in this way.

To the psychiatrists, the members seemed at times rigid in their desire to avoid discussion of irrational motivation. If the motive or explanation of behavior could not be traced to a recorded statement, they seemed to become disinclined to open the problem to exchange of opinion. But when it was possible to clearly identify the members' distortions, both negative and positive, open discussion of common problems was possible. The experience of the study group was a major influence in breaking barriers and in providing appropriate illustrations for concepts.

CONCLUSIONS

Since the meetings ended we have had an opportunity to review our original anticipations and contemplate further alterations. Some of the initial problems have been reduced by the experience. Hindrances to participation included fear of emotional stress in the group, a refusal to believe any useful help for historians could come from psychiatry, and the uneasy feeling that study groups were gimmicks—"something for business executives." The strength of these deterrents has been reduced, we hope, by the evidence provided by this experience.

Some of the positive attitudes which prompted eager participation were also diminished. The expectations that brilliant psychological syntheses would emerge, that a working knowledge of the use of psychology in history would be acquired, or that an easy additional chapter for the thesis could be written, were all shattered. The study group and the seminars opened an area for consideration and further work. By destroying the myth that psychology had the answers—and also the myth that psychology claimed it had the answer—and by providing some understanding of the level at which psychological theories and insights enter into the explanation of past events, the study group, we believe, helped the members to achieve a more realistic estimate of the value of psychology.

The participants studied the relationship between a record and the event, and investigated the many ways in which an event can be described or perceived by observers of the same occasion. Although record-event discrepancy and observer bias are new concepts for very few students, this kind of experience is of special value in graduate education because of the impact of the "having lived it" quality.

In our attempts to communicate between disciplines within the study group, we were impressed with the difficulty in undertaking and understanding such transactions. The inter-group difficulties modified the study group because the language and constructs of the two groups (psychiatry and history) differ and because the consultant was so easily identified as being part of one of the groups and the members part of the other. The consultant at times had some difficulty in knowing whether he ought to be directing his comments to the small group (the graduate students) or the intergroup (consultant and graduate students). One quality of the meetings which exemplified the difficulty of communication was the group's response to the consultant not so much as a person but as a representative of another group. These qualities of an intergroup experience within the study group suggest the various levels of discourse which must be examined and elucidated before effective exchange is possible. The establishment of formal intergroup exercises between study groups of graduate students may be a way to make intergroup phenomena more explicit and relevant to historical problems.

In our discussion of this work with historians and behavioral scientists, we have been repeatedly impressed with the barely polite attention given by each professional group to what the members of one discipline might learn from another discipline. In general, psychiatrists and psychologists have seemed most interested in what they might learn about small groups and not in what historical perspective might contribute to their discipline. Historians have been primarily interested in how this technique might further the general problem of teaching historical methodology to graduate students, but less interested in looking at psychological theory in relation to the writing of history. The fact that both groups wish to expand the bases for their discipline's familiar outlook, coupled with a distrust of the value of the other's theories, limits the benefits either group derives from exposure to the other.

Our overall impression of the semester is mixed. It was painful to disabuse the anticipation that psychology might explain all: One felt so warmly appreciated at first. When it became clear that psychology's application to history was limited, disappointment followed.

The disappointment, however, gradually evolved to a more open exchange on the value of psychology in the writing of history. With the little training in social sciences that most history graduate students have, the importance or relevance of psychological data is not generally accepted. As a result, we were often speaking on what would be thought of as lower levels of sophistication than those in a social science seminar. At times this was frustrating but it was also beneficial. Our own reflex to explain events in psychological modes is no more constructive than that which ignores their presence. The most profitable exchanges of the meetings did not come until the original uneasiness, which was present even among the members inclined to recognize the value of psychological factors, was replaced with mutual respect.

15.

GROUP PROCESSES IN ENVIRONMENTAL DESIGN: Exposing Architects and Planners to the Study of Group Relations

W. Harold Bexton[1]

With the growth of consumerism stressing social concerns and user orientations, the professions of architecture and planning are developing in directions that require more work in and with groups. The complexity of space planning for most institutional or private organizational clients requires close work with users to insure that the building will function adequately. In some cases the physical design may be expected to contribute to social or organizational goals. Citizens groups in some cities now interview and hire the architects for schools; parents, teachers, students, and administrators expect to work closely with the design teams to program and plan new buildings. Planning in cities requires the close coordination of many diverse groups, decisions often being made in the context of committee meetings. Special interest groups, neighborhood coalitions, environmentalists, politicians and others are concerned about regional as well as local planning decisions and are demanding to be part of the process.

There has been little professional training to meet the group relations needs of modern practice. The field of design or planning "methodologies" has attempted to cover the need with such approaches as rational decision making methods or various systems that purport to allow users to design buildings for themselves. Few of the methods are based on an understanding of how groups function or how to deal with the covert, non task related behavior that is common in these situations.

To experiment with methods of filling the gap in education, a graduate course was offered at the University of California at Berkeley for students with design or planning experience. This course was first titled "Group Relations and Environmental Design," and later, "Irrational Group Processes in Design." The

1 The courses described in this paper were in part supported by a National Institute of Mental Health grant in Behavioral Factors in Architecture at the University of California, Berkeley, and were developed in collaboration with Dr. Arthur D. Colman.

goal was to provide situations for learning that would sensitize the students to the dynamics that occur in small groups and to help them apply the knowledge to their own experience. It was intended to help them recognize the roles they play and to develop awareness of the extent of their responsibilities in complex situations. The focus was on interpersonal problems related to the function of leadership and exercise of authority, as well as task definition and an exploration of the nature of boundaries and the consequence of their absence. Expectations were that specific applications would range from early stages of contract definition, when many of the reasons for hiring might not be explicit, to more effective work with groups to collect and structure information such as user needs.

COURSE DESIGN

The course was divided into two parts. The first portion consisted of Tavistock type study groups composed of twelve members each. These groups would study their own behavior with the help of a consultant who would intervene only to facilitate learning by pointing out the "basic assumptions" operating (see Bion, 1961). In this case the consultant was also the class instructor. Small groups were to meet once a week for two 1¼ hour sessions with a short break in between, this phase continuing for a period of five weeks. The second half of the course was labelled "application groups." Individuals were to submit a short written description of the project they would present for discussion and analysis, and two application groups were to be formed according to the type of project and area of interest. The situations described by the students were to be used as vehicles to examine the small group experience and their own roles, with particular emphasis on problems encountered by architects and planners. The final product was to be a written paper analysing and interpreting the group situation presented in class and relating it to the learning that took place in the study groups.

APPLIED DESIGN

At the College of Environmental Design, U.C. Berkeley, course offerings are treated with a "supermarket" approach. Students decide what courses to attend by reviewing notices, asking other students what subject matter is covered, and learning what the professor is like. Some students pre-enroll but many prefer to sit in on the first lectures of several classes and then decide which to take.

To control the number of students to be admitted, facilitate planning, and screen out students with emotional problems, pre-enrollment interviews were required. Interviews were held the week prior to the first class meeting and course bulletins were given out clearly stating objectives, limits, meeting times, and other conditions applying to the class.

The ideal number of students was set at 30, allowing for two study groups and giving leeway for some inevitable loss between the start of class and the deadline for filing study lists. The two group arrangement would allow students to be assigned to consultants they did not already know and make possible a study of intergroup relations. A different grouping would be used in application work to prevent a continued focus on small group relations and emphasize the change of task and boundaries.

DEALING WITH THE ANXIETIES AND RESPONSIBILITIES OF A NEW COURSE

The number of students selected in the pre-enrollment interviews was a little large for one small group but too small for two. Since more students were expected at the first class meeting, limitation of enrollment was delayed. The atmostphere in the room for the first meeting was one of nervous expectation. Many students were making comments about being unsure whether or not they would take the class, in a loud enough voice for the instructors to hear. When it was announced that the class would be limited to those who had pre-enrolled, a howl of disapproval went up. Every student in the room stated that he was determined to take the class and would not leave. Several of those who had pre-enrolled made impassioned pleas for all those present to be accepted. The reasons given for the size boundaries were discounted; students suggested changing the focus of the study to a group the size of the one present, even though this would subvert the expressed purpose of the course.

Some of the class members had brought friends along for support. They continued to appeal for these students who had not pre-enrolled, hoping to induce the instructors to demonstrate that they were concerned enough to look after the class, comfort them and help them avoid the nagging anxieties they felt about the unknown course. It was suggested that if they were so concerned, they could give up their places to make room for their friends but no one came forward. It was then announced that a second section might be formed in the future but that the first study group would begin after a short break, as planned.

The imminent start of the study group was met by a panicky reaction. Suddenly everyone seemed to have an excuse for not attending. The class was told that all who could not attend that morning would have to give up their places to those on the waiting list. Everyone began talking at once, explaining excuses for not attending the first session, in some cases wanting personal exceptions to be made. One student even pleaded to be ordered what to do, not wanting to assume the responsibility for chosing between this session and another meeting. The final response of many was to come late to the study group. One student, among the most insistent in her demands to be excused without losing her place, never did return.

Section two was subsequently formed. Although the ability to carefully compose the two groups ahead of time was lost and resulted in a situation where one or two in each section knew the consultant well, the racial and sexual mix in each section was about equal.

SMALL GROUP MEETINGS AND THEMES

Section two began with an organizational meeting. Several students indicated that they had a conflict with another class but could manage if the starting time was half an hour later. Since everyone agreed, the instructor consented to the change, the time was finally set and extra small group sessions scheduled to keep pace with section one. This boundary change seemed rational but actually increased course conflicts.

One of the early topics of discussion in both small groups was the difference between the consultants. A number of students appealed to the section two consultant (the author, an architect and Ph.D. candidate) not to "abandon them." They asked if he couldn't "do something about" their consultant (Arthur Colman, a psychiatrist with extensive experience in group relations work). The fantasized ideal was to have the class as one group with two consultants. On one hand, the section one consultant was seen as the villainous task master forcing them to take responsibility, while section two consultant was the protector who would look after their social and emotional needs. The consultants could be played off against each other or they could be paired to carry on a dialogue between themselves, giving the class predigested learning and solving their problems for them. On the other hand, section one consultant was seen as most desirable, a doctor and psychiatrist who could provide therapy for the class. Section two consultant could then be a spokesman and defender, protecting them from the frightening aspects of the knowledge of group relations and the responsibility this implies.

SACRIFICING THE MINORITY MEMBERS

The next stage of the group scenario involved offering "sick" members of the group to each consultant to draw out of them the care they were failing to provide. In each case one female member who was uniquely appropriate, felt compelled to see the consultant outside of class. In section one the female member repeatedly tried to obtain direct personal help from the consultant for herself and others in the group. In section two, the group kept pairing a female Ph. D. student with the consultant. She finally told the consultant that she could not take the pressure of her role and felt that the others could not work by themselves and should just be told what to do. When the consultant's behavior did not change even after this communication, the woman left at a coffee break and did not return. Guilt about her loss consumed the group, who reviewed in meticulous detail all the incidents they felt had led to her departure and explored how she had been acting on their behalf to help them maintain a child-like lack of responsibility.

Pleas to the consultants for help in the groups soon turned to expressions of anger and hostility. The section one consultant was called the "Sphinx" or the "Oracle" and was at times drowned out when he tried to consult. Section two felt less able to directly express hostility toward their consultant, perhaps because he was "an architect like themselves". Instead they created surrogate consultants or scapegoats on which to vent their feelings, a pattern which apparently mirrored what was happening in the department of architecture. After the group maneuvered three consecutive women into position to be sacrifices, they began to realize the extent to which they were repeating the institutional pattern, where women were often manipulated by a class to confront the professors and put into a position to be singled out for ridicule, or else paired with the professor to take the focus off the rest of the class.

THE BLACK MINSTREL SHOW

For several sessions, the one black member in section two began to come late to the study group. He was the most physically imposing male in the group and had been playing a dominant role in the discussions. Until he arrived, the group did virtually nothing. When he entered the room, he talked at top speed, paced around and made interpretations while the others enjoyed the show and urged him on. After several incidents of this sort, he came to the consultant outside of class to plead for help. He wanted to take a dominant and effective leadership position but felt impotent to do so. He would try to make interpretations but lacked information and thus kept making a fool of himself and "just jiving" the group. He asked for material to read, as well as outside counselling so that he could learn to manipulate the group as he felt manipulated and actually fill the role he felt they were offering him. Clearly his valency [2] fit the dependent basic assumption in which the group was operating. As interpretations focussed on these phenomena, the class explored how they had projected their frustrations and feelings of inadequacy onto the black student, tried to use him to challenge and then obtain sympathy from the consultant and finally rejected him as a failure, making him feel sacrificed. Whenever he tried to make a comment after that he was accused of "just jiving them again".

CONTINUING DEPENDENCY: A REPLACEMENT
PAIR OF PARENTS

Dependent themes predominated as regression in the small groups continued. Periods of silliness when they "acted crazy"

2 Valency refers to the tendency a person has to participate in certain basic assumption behavior in groups (Bion, 1961, p. 175).

were called by the class their "comedy acts" or "song and dance routines". When interpretations regarding this behavior were made, the class was able to individuate and work for short intense periods of time, discussing how they were using the "crazy action" to show their helplessness and lack of ability to take responsibility, and the more ritualized "song and dance routines" as a way of expressing their feeling that the consultant was putting on an act for them to dupe or otherwise fool them. Fear of damage they might do each other in competition for leadership had led to the sacrificing of minority members of the group to remove them as a threat (women are included as a minority since architecture is still predominantly a male profession and the threat was real in that the university was giving preferential status to women and racial minorities in hiring, to meet H.E.W. guidelines) and was resulting in fear of taking responsibility to avoid competition among the white male members. Any leadership within the group had to be kept at a very covert level. Now that the women and minority members had been "killed off", neutralized, or silenced, a homosexual group was left to vie for leadership.

Section two had dealt with the loss of the original female leader, who had been protecting the group from the consultant and interpreting his comments for them, by seating the remaining two female members on either side of him. At this point one of the male members declared that he found men as sexually interesting as women and proceeded to tell each person in the group what he found interesting about them, excluding the consultant and the woman to his left. The group had felt relaxed and able to ignore the consultant after he had been seated between the two women, and now it was being suggested that no male in the group was anything more than a sex object, like the women. If the males were sex objects then they were to be similarly fought over and protected and could remove themselves from the leadership struggles. A double pairing then began to take place.

The woman who was sitting on the consultant's left was acting in a caring way, interpreting his comments and acting as a mother who would like to protect her children from the wrath of the father. The younger woman on the consultant's right described that she also found both men and women interesting; she rapidly became paired with the male member who had made similar statements, actually moving to sit with him, opposite the consultant. The parental pair was thus reinforced and a competing pair was created.

The competing pair were not yet ready to challenge the authority of the parental pair; both gave up their sex and clung to a stance of bisexuality, making themselves less serious and less threatening to the rest of the group, who now proceeded to indulge in childish play, under the direction of the young pair. This double pairing continued until the end of the study groups.

The young pair actually became involved in a sexual affair outside the group. A menage a trois developed, with another member of their group playing the role of child. The child was loved but excluded from sex, and at the same time acted as a voyeur and spy for the rest of the group to keep them filled in on the activities of the pair they had created. This secret affair began once the pairing occurred and ended when the small group phase of the course ended. Apparently since the pair had been created by the group any need to exist disappeared when the group ceased to exist.

RELATIONS BETWEEN THE TWO STUDY GROUP SECTIONS: FEAR OF MERGER

Throughout the sessions, comments by each group about the other were very guarded and almost a taboo topic. It was as if the other group had ceased to exist for them and each section itself had become the whole class. As the merging of the two sections became imminent, they talked about fears that the other section had done better and that they would soon have to mix with a lot of strangers for the second half of the course. In fact they were not strangers and all had regularly compared notes about progress and thus knew that both groups were in parallel positions. The end of the small group sessions became a dreaded event. Both groups talked about continuing to meet even after the official end.

APPLICATION PHASE

Between the end of the last small group meeting and the joint meeting to choose applications groups, each member of the class was to write a paragraph describing the project he would present for analysis. Application groups were to be formed around related topics. By this stage, however, the class was in such a dependent state that a simple statement of their projects had become an insurmountable task. The class was so deskilled by the small groups that less than half turned in a project description and of these less than one quarter were intelligible.

To determine application groups, the clearest project descriptions were categorized into four distinct areas. Pairs of these areas were related in content, forming two groups. The remaining class members indicated which topics interested them most and then each consultant took the group whose subject areas were closest to his interests and expertise. This resulted in a good mix of members from each of the previous sections.

The application phase of the course had several sub-goals. As well as learning to apply the processes they had been experiencing, the class had to be brought to the point where they could once again see the consultants as instructors and colleagues with whom they could work, as opposed to "sphinx-like" authority figures giving them "bolts from the blue". Normally, at group relations conferences no other work activities are planned with members and small group consultants. In this case, however, the consultants had to work with many of the students outside the class and thus had to form a working relationship of a different kind with them.

Although members usually carefully avoided the consultants outside the small groups, one or two special trips were taken to see them in their offices. When these incidents were recalled, the students involved spoke of the relief they felt when they found out the consultants were "really human after all" and behaved "more naturally" outside the study groups.

To begin the application phase a short lecture was given, outlining the history of the study group and the development of the body of theory. The two application groups then began meeting in the same rooms that had previously been used for the small groups.

A LAST ATTEMPT AT RETURNING TO THE SMALL GROUPS

A student in one of the application groups acted very shocked and withdrawn during the first session. He came to see the instructor/consultant after the first meeting and described how he felt very strange being in a strange room (the room that the other section had used) with students he didn't know, and added that he must be the only one from his section in that application group. In fact there were seven members from his group and only four from the other section. The new consultant, different environment, and changed group composition made even the members he knew well seem different. He maintained he had no topic for application, although the instructor knew he had one suitable for presentation and praised its value. This student never did return to class.

SERIOUS APPLICATION WORK AT LAST

The students seemed relieved to find the consultants taking a more familiar role in the application phase. As each project was discussed, interpreted, and related to the small group experiences, there were many "aha" reactions. Interest became more intense as the sessions continued. Students who had been hesitant about presenting their projects suddenly became enthusiastic to describe and discuss them. Most were quite able to make interpretations on a fairly superficial covert political level,[3] and several displayed a real depth of understanding, discussing the dynamics at the unacknowledged basic assumption level.

The papers demonstrated the positive value of group relations training for designers and planners, both to improve their work with groups and to better understand the situations in which they

---

3 Colman differentiates "covert politics" which are acknowledged but secret, from the basic assumptions which not only are not discussed but are unconscious (1973, p. 1).

find themselves. The papers documented cases of the use of minorities in professional offices to deal with community groups while giving them no real power to actually help the community or affect the design, the irrational growth mania of some cities and the seeds of such behavior, and the decision making processes of teams of architects using different design methodologies.

THE PROBLEM OF BOUNDARY CLARIFICATION

In the university setting, as a regular class, it can be difficult to get the kind of commitment that is needed for study groups, particularly when compared to the group relations conferences as a temporary educational institution. At the university, students are not required to take the course, and study lists can be changed until late in the quarter. Although this seldom becomes a problem in most courses, it creates a dilemma if the study group is given during class sessions. If students are required to attend each session, an element of coercion is added that is undesirable, especially since the only device for enforcing attendance is the mark that will be given.

External psychological boundaries were similarly difficult to control in the university setting. Students were interviewed by the professor who later became a consultant. In some cases students knew the professors from other courses and seeing them in the unaccustomed role of consultant made the small group experience seem artificial, staged and game-like, reducing the impact. Shortly after they were established, these boundaries had to be broken down for the application phase, to enable the students and instructors to work together. Expected role relations can also interfere through the expectation of a lecture from the instructor. If a mutual sharing of the experience and its application is expected among group members, special steps will have to be taken. Members of the application groups who had the same consultants they had for the study groups tended to be less vocal and more controlled than the others, making a more definite boundary change seem desirable.

Finally, it is difficult to separate members and non-members in the university. While the shared experience, special language and descriptions of behavior characteristic of the group relations work tends to set the class apart, they are at the same time immersed in other classes with other groups. When the study group sessions are spread out over a period of time with students remaining in their usual work environment and undergoing pressures from other courses conflicting for their time, the experience tends to be somewhat diluted.

Internal group boundaries are even more difficult to deal with. If the professor is also the consultant to the study group, the inevitable situation exists where the consultant is also the person the student depends on for grades. Although it was stated that the experiential part of the small group would not "count toward grades", this was easily discounted by the students. This confuses the fantasy and reality distinction in the study group as well as the psychological boundary between the small group and the application group.

REVISED COURSE STRUCTURE

To deal with some of the problems inherent in the university setting, the course structure was altered when it was offered at a later date. Pre-enrollment interviews were held the week before class, but there was no enrollment cut-off until the first class, which was used as an introduction and organizational meeting. The class was to focus on behavior in organizations in a way that would have direct application in planning and architectural programming. It was to start with lectures and seminars on group relations work, including reading assignments. The students would then attend a regularly scheduled local non-residential weekend conference. Class sessions would become a continuation of conference application groups, and finally the students would present their own application topics.

In this class, the first issue that came up was the conference application forms and fees. Some students could not afford the fees, so the class worked together, shared scholarship funds and sought additional financial assistance until everyone in the class ended up paying an equal amount — half the regular fee. This process gave the class a feeling of sharing and produced cohesion.

As the conference approached, the amount of material covered in each seminar decreased, while anxiety about the impending group relations exercises, with strangers in an unfamiliar setting, increased. By the last class before the conference, work on assigned topics was virtually impossible; all questions related to "what exactly" was going to happen in the group events.

CONFERENCE ISSUES

The weekend conference included large group and intergroup events. Throughout the weekend the class from the department of architecture stayed together, actively experimenting with different chair locations and seating arrangements in the intergroup sessions and generally instigating and participating in a great deal of acting out behavior. In fact, the class spoke later about their efforts to subvert the conference and their rage at what they called the authoritarian element that manipulated the membership.

The first group meeting after the conference was held at the office of the course sponsor who had directed the conference. A recurrent theme was the feeling that the knowledge they were to acquire was predetermined and the conference manipulated. The angry discussion around these points was interpreted as anxiety and fear, springing from a dependent position and directed at the sponsor, the course, and the instructor. Another theme that continued to dominate subsequent class meetings was the loss of innocence. The students felt their new awareness, learned from the conference, was a burden that changed their whole view of group situations.

Since the class was still missing the small group exercise, a study group was arranged by using an outside consultant and combining the class from the Department of Architecture with one from the Department of Psychology. The small group consultant was a black man who had experience with consultation to groups in many models including Tavistock; formally however, this was a supervised training experience as a group relations consultant for him.

After the first small group session, the consultant talked enthusiastically about some of the themes emerging. At subsequent meetings between sessions, he spoke less and less about the small groups and instead recounted all his previous experience with groups. At the second to last break he said he was "really on to something" because one of the members had admitted he was homosexual and they were exploring the homosexual themes in the group. He did not come to the last supervision meeting.

At the time the application group was to start, the instructor entered the room alone to find the small group still in session. The consultant was nervous and uneasy; he had shifted to a more individual oriented approach, more like a sensitivity group, and had forgotten the time. It was as if the class had conspired under the lead of a black, female member to fight the consultant and keep him from following through on the group relations model. Their hostile attitude toward the instructor indicated that they felt they had protected themselves from this threatening black consultant with no help from him.

THE DIFFICULTY OF ANALYSING OUTSIDE TOPICS AFTER SUCH AN INTENSE EXPERIENCE

In the remaining classes, application topics were to be presented and discussed; however, it was extremely difficult to get away from the personal changes and personal learning that had taken place. The result was that in spite of excellent classroom work, only one student handed in his paper on time. Other members of the class were so involved in personal changes that they did not want to analyse a past event or experience and instead switched to either on-going experiences or focussed on personal growth and the implications of the model in this sense. Half the papers dealt with personal growth and life changes due to expanded awareness and knowledge. The class had been an intense personal learning experience but some of the goals of the preset task were not met.

CONCLUSIONS

Architects and planners seem to respond with more dramatic action and try to manipulate and change their groups more than most members of groups relations conferences. Considering the creative and manipulative aspects of the profession, this is not a surprising result. As the graduate students in history, described by Musto and Astrachan (1968), moved rapidly into problems of leadership and organized themselves into a legitimate government, so the architects and planners of the first group relations course offered at Berkeley moved rapidly into problems of leadership but resolved them through elaborately designed and structured routines. This is very like the familiar tendency of architecture as a profession to bind up process and the emotionally charged aspects of decision making through the control of physical and space boundaries and the technological parameters of economics, materials and aesthetics.

An important lack in the perspective of both course designs was allowing room for the personal changes the intense experience provoked. This is an important goal of all university education and was especially prized in such an atmosphere as Berkeley. While our major stress had been on institutional or whole group analysis, the student's focus was the personal growth components of the learning. Perhaps this was yet another challenge to the authority, but it is difficult to label it as this within the boundaries of a great university. While the conference events themselves must focus on the group as a whole, the personal knowledge that results is an important first step that must be assimilated if students are going to use the learning to make profound changes in their professional work.

In terms of the students themselves, the first myth that had to be overcome was the expectation that a precise set of instructions about how to deal with group processes would be provided. Students soon realized that the courses provided an opportunity to learn firsthand about the processes that operate in groups and created an environment in which these issues could be discussed. Individuals would have to take the responsibility for applying the knowledge which would provide no direct rules but rather new insights for understanding the situations with which they were confronted.

In most professional work experienced by the students, an individual's chances of making many changes were fairly limited. Change could always be made within the boundaries for which the individual was responsible, however, including his own contract definition, but this took a great deal of honesty and courage. To confront changes in the personal sphere of influence meant recognizing the anxieties and fears that each individual felt and finding mature methods for dealing with these. The more intensive second course forced a focus on the self as a starting point for change, differentiating personal action and intentions from group action, and led to the introspection that predominated in the application phase. Follow up work with students showed that the second class was more profoundly affected by the experience and were continuing to do more work in or related to the field of group relations as it affected their professional work than the first class. This would suggest that the more intensive group relations experience, with more carefully controlled boundaries, had more impact in the long range.

A final conclusion is that the group relations classes were very successful even in the seemingly unlikely fields of architecture and planning. In fact they helped educate students to realize 1) many of the problems on which these professions tend to focus are not the real issues concerned but rather substitutes for covert feelings and agendas, and 2) environment is a complex interaction between social-psychological and physical factors that are interdependent with the system in which they exist. It not only provides many new directions for architects and planners to explore and enriches and clarifies existing directions, but the experience points out the multitude of applications that are possible in many different professions.

C
Organizational Consultation

16.

THE IMPACT OF GROUP RELATIONS CONFERENCES ON ORGANIZATIONAL GROWTH

Roy W. Menninger

For six years, The Menninger Foundation has participated in the Tavistock-Washington School of Psychiatry group relations conferences, having now sent some 60 people to one or more conferences. Such intensive experience on the part of so many psychiatrists, psychologists, social workers, activities therapists, nurses and aides, teachers and child care workers from a single psychiatric institution has had an impact on our organization in a variety of major and minor ways; this paper is an attempt to describe some of the consequences of this program for our staff, for the groups with which and in which they work, and for the administrative structures and the management of the organization.

The material on which this paper is based was collected from written summaries requested of those who attended the conferences. These summaries were supplemented with selected interviews.

BACKGROUND — CONTEXT

The Menninger Foundation is a non-profit institution committed to goals of treatment, education, research and prevention in psychiatry. It is perhaps best known for its application of psychoanalytic principles to the hospital treatment of persons with severe psychiatric illnesses and for the development of one of the largest psychiatric training programs in the country, now having trained more than 1,000 psychiatrists.

Profoundly affecting the development of the intellectual and psychological climate of the organization was the fact that its progress, direction and pace were essentially set by the brothers Menninger, who with their father, began a group practice of psychiatry in Topeka in 1919. Challenged by the vision of Doctor Karl and moderated by the managerial talents of Doctor Will, the whole staff of the organization reflected an excitement and vigor which brought The Menninger Foundation to national public and professional prominence during the two decades after World War II.

In a manner similar to the experience of other organizations directed and shaped by charismatic leaders, this growth was achieved at a subtle and only subsequently recognized cost: the failure to develop strong secondary leadership. As a consequence, the organization was ill-prepared for the abrupt transition which occurred in 1966 with the partial retirement of one founding brother and the death of the other. Suddenly bereft of both its president and chief of staff, the organization was thrown back upon itself, confronted with a mammoth and unfamiliar task of determining its course and choosing its leaders. In this transition, the organization experienced innumerable stresses as previously unexpressed feelings surged to the surface demanding recognition and satisfaction. Multiple groups organized around sentient needs, vying for influence and control.

The lack of sophisticated understanding about group behavior reinforced the prevailing perspective which sought to explain the behavior of a particular individual exclusively in terms of his psychology and the political issues dividing staff. Groups were thought to be mere aggregations of individuals, the group behavior therefore the expression of cumulative individual behaviors, or the consequence of several "strong" or "sick" persons.

The result was a climate of anxiety and helplessness, punctuated by crises focusing on part of the organization with intense scapegoating attacks on the "integrity" or "pathology" of the individuals most prominently identified with the crisis group or issue. This ad hominem approach to organizational problems intensified the helplessness and fear of all those involved, and nearly always obscured the underlying institutional problem which desperately needed resolution.

With the choice of a new president in 1967, work on the reestablishment of a strong structure began, and with considerable effort and struggle, often painful and occasionally unsuccessful, a new management philosophy was gradually developed. The initial management groups were limited by their inexperience as collaborative managers, by an insufficient understanding of group process and dynamics and by some romantic assumptions of the president that unstructured groups could be effective if they were just composed of well-meaning idealistic mental health professionals.

From a perspective which emphasized the collective nature of our organizational problems, and the collective responsibility of all those involved to work at solving them, we gradually have evolved a pattern of participative management. In the process of sharing the responsibility for developing an organization-wide annual budget, a move toward departmental decentralization was inititated and—over a period of several years—substantially strengthened. Through this approach, a new concept of responsibility emerged: an awareness that a single person or group at the top would not solve every problem, and its corollary, that program and department directors had the means, the authority, the responsibility and, gradually, the know-how to decide many programmatic issues themselves. Because of a heavy reliance on groups and committees for the implementation and management of virtually every aspect of the organization's business, the need to learn more about the psychology of groups became increasingly evident. This need was underscored by frequent failures of some group efforts, with the unfortunate return to ad hominem attacks on others as a discharge for the frustration and anger that failure had produced.

The experience of several staff members in the Tavistock-Washington School of Psychiatry Group Relations Conference suggested that this approach offered some promise of providing experiential learning and training in groups and group process which we appeared to need so desperately.

The Tavistock model is well described in a paper by Margaret Rioch (1970) published in the International Journal of Group Psychotherapy, to which the reader is referred. Briefly, these conferences use unstructured small and large groups as contexts in which to study the nature of group behavior. A special characteristic of these conferences is the use of specially constructed intergroup exercises, which dramatically illustrate the problems of representation, i.e., of exercising authority on behalf of others, of managing conflicts between groups, and of drawing and crossing boundaries as groups interact with each other.

The conference concludes with a series of application groups, in which the intensive experience of the conference is examined for its relevance to the "back-home" settings of the participants.

By its use of unstructured groups, the conference makes visible for study the covert processes which operate in and among all groups, particularly unspoken attitudes and behavior patterns which may hinder or further the work of the group. What stands out for those who participate is the useful contrast between groups whose behavior and performance is dominated by intense, emotionally charged, irrational basic assumptions, and the ideal effectively functioning, work-oriented task group. The prevalence of the former and the remarkable difficulties of achieving the latter in the conference itself provide powerful new insights about group processes in organizational life elsewhere.

Because the consequences of a decision to participate extensively in a series of group relations conferences are inevitably fused with other growth and development processes at work at The Menninger Foundation, it is of course arbitrary and potentially inaccurate to single out changes in organizational functioning and assume they have come from the group relations experiences. This is especially true because the group principles which become so experientially evident in the group relations conference are consonant with the evolving philosophy of management of the president, whose value system (based upon these principles) predated our experiences with group relations conferences. The comments which follow must be understood therefore as currently observable characteristics of parts of our organization, many groups within it, and individuals in positions of responsibility who have been at least influenced by our extensive group relations experience.

OBSERVATIONS

Most easily described are the reported changes: changes in what people say about what they see, think, feel and understand. Harder, but not impossible to document are the behavioral changes which are less clear-cut, less impressive and dramatic, and more difficult to attribute directly to the impact of a group relations conference experience.

The most common discovery of those who have attended is the appreciation and, for some, the dramatic dawning of a new awareness that groups themselves are something more than a sum of parts, that they can become entities with collective characteristics which are not just ascribable to the various individuals comprising them, and that they can behave in definable, recognizable ways that cannot be characterized by simple, or useful, resort to the language or concepts of individual psychology.

The realization that groups have definable patterns qua groups relatively independent of the particular personalities which comprise them had led to new appreciation of group phenomena in many contexts other than the conference in which the discovery took place, and to a new basis for examining the interaction between the personality of a particular individual and the group for which he is a part.

For example, the prominence of strong dependent wishes as an emotional current in every group and the extensive and persistent efforts of the group to protect and maintain a dependency culture have impressed most staff members who have attended the conferences. In the back-home setting, it is now clearer how the demands upon the leader to tell the group what to do, how to do it, when to do it and why, and then to reward the members, or protect them, although partly legitimate, are also expressions of an infantile need for dependency and operate in the back-home groups to interfere with effective work on the ostensible task of the group.

Staff members have begun to examine the extent to which the nature of a large organization induces a dependency culture among its members, a culture which acts to retard initiative and discourage much risk-taking. In addition, the insidious costs of excessive dependency—erosion of self-esteem, chronic feelings of helplessness and depression—are often hidden from those who are paying it. Paradoxically, this unsatisfactory balance is maintained by silent acceptance of it, with justifying references to the (supposed) limits of one's authority. For example, a common statement, actually incorrect and sometimes even expressed by department directors, alleged that, "I do not have authority to fire a staff member who is not competent or who cannot perform adequately."

A scrutiny of dependency patterns within an organization makes it clear that a degree of dependency of members on each other and on the leader is necessary if it is to function effectively. Task groups are dependent upon the leader for direction and guidance. Large groups require a structure, clear leadership and an agenda to function well. Team members need an understanding of the ground rules and objectives of the team, and these must be provided by the leader. This appropriate use of dependency, however, must be distinguished from the infantile, fantasy-based dependency patterns of basic assumption groups which deskill the members and prevent them from working effectively.

The group relations conference particularly illuminated the extent to which members of a group actively collude (often merely by being passive) in the maintenance of the very oppression they complain of. As a result of this learning, group members are no longer quite so easily able to sit quietly through a discussion of an issue with which they strongly disagree; no longer is the easy displacement of the "cause" of a problem to a mythical "they" somewhere up above so readily available—if only because increasing numbers of one's colleagues here will point out that an expectation of a "solution" from above is yet another expression of a basic assumption of dependency.

There is a growing realization that each member of a group, and hence of the organization, does have a degree of authority to work at the task to which he is assigned, and the authority to work at changing the circumstances which limit his effectiveness. People here now speak of a new "freedom" to speak up in groups, to express disagreement or differing perspectives, to point out the collusive patterns of passivity and dependency in the group and committees in which they are working. But particularly is there a perceptible increase in the dedication to the task at hand, and a capacity to regard the group as a work group rather than merely a vehicle for expressing or mobilizing the cumulative frustrations arising from a chronic acceptance of a dependency stance.

A number of individuals in leadership positions—seminar leaders, committee chairmen, or leaders of administrative units—have reported new zest in approaching the challenge of working with their groups. They are much more willing to challenge and confront their groups (particularly with evidence of passivity or inertia) and have reported positive and exciting changes stemming from this more active and responsible stance. One administrative unit leader reported that he no longer waits for his task group to work simply out of its inhibitions; he actively attempts to diagnose the group's hangups, and thereby enables them to return to the work task. A major subcommittee of the management group has for the first year worked successfully on the difficult task of developing a basic budget, when this same work in previous years tended to be a means for engaging in a wide variety of covert conflicts over program priorities that should have been settled in or by other groups.

Staff efforts to establish Half-Way House living facilities for patients in transition from long-term hospitalization to community life have existed in this organization since 1959. At least four different interdisciplinary committees, occurring at two to four year intervals during these twelve years, prepared thoughtful and clinically sound proposals supporting the establishment of Half-Way House resources. Staff interest and clinical need were clearly present. Each proposal was "handed up," and each committee waited in silence, eventually assuming that a Half-Way House was not possible because no decision to implement the proposals had "come down". Basic assumptions were rampant and passivity reigned.

In mid 1971, a Half-Way House proposal was approved and the facility opened five months later. Two major factors are seen as having made the difference. One was the effective plan of participative management practices which had been put into practice by the President. Second, several members of the committee had attended group relations conferences and had acquired a vast new awareness of the power of the group processes as well as the basic assumptions which interfere with the performance of a task. Risk taking, working through of some philosophical splits and a willingness to tackle the many boundary issues characterized the work on the committee, enabling it to develop a plan which had a high probability for success.

A second discovery of great moment is an awareness of a powerful tendency of members of groups to use individuals both inside and outside the group as targets or depositories for unacceptable feelings and attitudes. Because this transfer (projective) process is unconscious, and because the person selected for scapegoating usually has assisted in his nomination by his own provocative behavior, members of groups in the organization seldom are able to see the relationship between the parts of their feelings being denied and the individual who appears to epitomize those same feelings. The realization from the group relations conference experience that scapegoating always involves projection now has promoted a quicker recognition of occasions when group members are using others in the illegitimate service of their own unacknowledged needs. The immediate consequence is that working groups are more able to treat scapegoating as a symptom of an unrecognized group problem whose solution is necessary if the group is to proceed with its work task.

> One senior staff member reported a recent experience in a group psychotherapy study seminar. He was presenting certain ideas about combined individual and group therapy to his colleagues for their reactions. To his great surprise the newest member of our group, and one with the least amount of group experience, began to engage him in a rather vehement debate about the validity of his position. He responded unwisely to the bait and found himself becoming increasingly exasperated with his challenger, not only because of the younger colleague's naivete but also because his senior colleagues sat by quietly, seemingly enjoying the contest. He was able to retrieve the situation by offering his interpretation of the group's competitive, anti-authority feelings towards him as the department director making the presentation.

A third observation is the frequency of reports of personal learning accompanying the conference experience. Often characterized as having a tremendous impact (''...not even all of my years of a personal analysis showed me the parts of myself I saw there...''). This learning occurred in spite of the fact that the primary task of a group relations conference is to study the behavior of groups rather than individual styles, in contrast to other well known group programs.

Many reported discovering new aspects of their own behavior. A senior staff member responsible for several task groups commented on his new awareness of a previously unrecognized tendency to smooth over conflict the moment it appeared; with this realization, he has found himself better able to tolerate emerging conflict well enough to use it to sharpen the issue in question.

> Thus, in a meeting of a training committee a difference of opinion was expressed among the committee members regarding how stringent the requirements should be for

promotion to supervisory rank. Strong feelings were beginning to emerge in the group and the chairman, checking his tendency to move on to another subject, laughingly remarked that he had learned from the group relations conference that he tends to pour oil on troubled waters "and that's helpful to no one,"; he then proceeded to draw the conflict into the open, to the material benefit of the group and the issue under discussion.

Others have discovered an unperceived blending with others in groups in ways apparently intended to reduce anxiety and maintain a coalition in the face of anticipated trouble or disagreement. The tendency to withdraw into silence, justified by statements of "I'm listening and learning from others," is now recognized as a means of protecting a dependent, passive role. "Typical" behaviors emerged in the group relations conferences in forms that betrayed their anxious origins. One staff member commented on his recurrent "peacemaker" role; others remarked on a new awareness of their ambivalence about leadership: angry with it, disappointed with it, eager for it and resentful when it emerged.

The capacity of groups to evoke atypical behaviors from its members—the "role suction" described by Fritz Redl (1951)—was a startling discovery, and dramatically illustrated the reality of a group psychology which could not be explained by a limited intrapsychic frame of reference.

In the conference experience, persons who considered themselves "leaders" were surprised to find themselves quiet and passive, immobilized and feeling stupid. At the same time, persons found unpleasant consequences from their "ordinary" modes of relating to others that were quite unexpected. Women accustomed to a quietly seductive mode of relating to men found themselves attacked for allegedly expressing blatant sexuality far in excess of their intentions. Mildly disputatious men experienced a sense of being "loaded" by the group with a pressure to be the spearhead of attack on the leader for his "failure" to meet various expectations (usually of a dependent sort) of the group, and often responded to an extent that later caused them wonder and surprise for such "atypical" behavior. In a dozen other ways, individuals found paradoxes in their own and other behaviors that forced intense examination of themselves and stimulated efforts to make these contradictions understandable.

Most important from the point of view of these remarks, the juxtaposition of data from the inner and outer worlds has served to induce a new willingness to look at the behavior of individuals in groups as jointly determined, with the new assumption that an acknowledgement of the group psychological forces could make the behavior both more understandable and more manageable.

The fourth major perceptual change is in turn related to the other three. This is the change in perceptions of and attitudes about authority. In a manner recognized as virtually universal (however irrational it may be), "authority" at The Menninger Foundation (i.e., management) has been the target of many projected assumptions. It is often assumed to be indifferent at least and malignant at worst. The discovery that every person, at every level, has the authority he needs to work at the task he has, has opened up a new awareness of the frequent irrational use of authority figures as displacement targets. Such use of authority figures has enabled those at lower levels to justify failure, explain their dissatisfaction, and complain about their helplessness.

After the group relations conference, many staff members reported amazement at their unwitting collusion first to install a leader of the group, then to undermine him or unseat him in ways felt at the time to be entirely "reasonable" and "appropriate". Repeatedly, those named to the role of leader were then carefully denied real power to make decisions; persons asked to represent the group in its dealings with other groups were often so restricted in their mandate as to be ineffective. Over and over again, the alternative wish to be led and the refusal to permit it reenacted itself in the life of the conference. As a consequence, the participants returned with a new awareness of the many ways groups can operate to emasculate or weaken its leadership, while stolidly maintaining innocence and ignorance of its actions.

Some of those who have participated report an increase in their tolerance for the vicissitudes and responsibilites of the leader's role, in that they expect less in regard to wishes now recognized as inappropriately dependent (and hence antithetical to the task). Parallel to the new freedom in groups, there is less fear that initiatives taken to accomplish a task will lead to retaliation or covert punishment.

At the same time, there is a clearer recognition of what the responsibilities of the leaders are, or should be: to establish the agenda, to keep the group focussed on the task, to establish and maintain the boundaries, to define roles and functions (including his own) within the group clearly and unequivocally, to maintain the operating structure of the group as it works on its task, to delegate authority clearly, and to make decisions in the absence of consensus. This additional understanding has not only helped many persons function more effectively as chairmen and group leaders, but it has sharpened our expectations of those who have accepted the role of leadership. There is now sophisticated pressure on leaders to perform adequately; casual, unclear, sloppy direction is much less willingly (i.e., passively) tolerated.

In sum, the effect of the many new perceptions about groups has been to generate a new broader perspective on the complex relationships between the individual and his group, among group members, and between groups. The outstanding characteristics of this newer perspective is a greater psychological distance: a greater capacity of the participating individual to observe even as he experiences. In a manner similar to the phenomena attributed to the observing ego in relation to intrapsychic conflict, the post-conference individual sees individual-group-intergroup phenomena in a more objective light. He no longer feels the impact of group behaviors in quite the same, affectively loaded, personalized way that previously provoked a variety of intense, irrational reactions which inhibited clear thinking and prevented wise action.

He is, of course, still capable of being caught up in the powerful swings of group emotion, but no longer as mindlessly. Many participants have reported a kind of deja vu experience after their return from a conference, observing in their task groups here phenomena similar to what had occurred in the unstructured groups of the group relations conference.

> Thus, during a difficult organizational meeting in which the year's agenda and the group's primary task were being reviewed, one group became quite anxious about leadership and authority. One of the factors contributing to this situation was some ambiguity regarding the tenure of its current leader whose term of office was vaguely thought to be coming to an end, although this time boundary had never been clearly spelled out. The conversation in the group became chaotic and frenetic with each contribution being almost totally unrelated to the preceding comment. Finally, someone remarked that this meeting "is as crazy as a large group exercise," and the group was able then to begin ferreting out the sources of its anxiety and confusion.

The ability to note the parallel between the irrational aspects of the conference experience and the intrusion of irrationality into a task-oriented group here is probably the major mechanism by which the conference learning becomes translated into new, more efficient behaviors.

There has been an almost unanimous recognition that irrationality is an inevitable part of group life. A greater appreciation of this fact arises in the conference experience from one's opportunity to perceive hostility and mistrust being directed at the leadership, irrational fears concerning their retaliative powers, as well as paranoid fantasies regarding alien subgroups in the intergroup exercise. This increased sensitivity to the proneness of groups to become inefficient and to be detoured from the task by these "basic assumptions" has led a number of staff members to report a considerable increase in patience and tolerance towards such deviations when they occur. Some have even instituted special techniques to help them attend to these possible interferences. One leader of a clinical team now holds a weekly unstructured meeting in order to encourage his staff to ventilate their feelings about their work and their relationships with each other. One committee sets aside the last 10 minutes of its weekly meeting for a rehash of the emotional currents which may have been interfering with the group's task.

The program has not been without some negative consequences. The group relations conference experience has been responsible for a kind of "awakening" that has set in train rather intensive searching re-examinations of personal and professional goals for some who have attended. Although this scrutiny has been ultimately constructive, it also brought several staff members to the point of leaving the organization. A sudden new awareness of long-standing patterns of personal behavior indirectly led to a disruptive shift within one department because the new insights required the staff member to seek a substantially different role outside the department.

It has been easy for some of us to fall into magical thinking about the cumulative experience of having so many staff people attend the conferences, as if their doing so would somehow make the all-too-familiar problems of groups "go away." We have tended to expect too much new knowledge and new skill, too much change, too much "mature behavior" from those who have gone, and the discovery that change is neither that easy nor that dramatic has led to some disillusionment with the program. Those who have participated have come back as "veterans," prone to talk in the jargon of the conference and occasionally given to using their insights about groups as a new form of oneupmanship. There has been a perceptible tendency to develop an "in-group" feeling among those who have gone, and more than one person has commented resentfully about being excluded from the fraternity.

The excitement of the experience and the recognition of its potency as a learning opportunity have contributed to a current tendency of some to view all human interactions as aspects of an extended group relations conference. The swing of the intellectual pendulum away from its previous exclusive focus on intrapsychic conflict to a new preoccupation with social systems and intergroup processes has created misunderstandings and new charges of over-simplification. Although it is probable that this is a passing phase, it has created secondary problems. These problems, however painful and discomforting, have not diminished the substantial gains which the experience has provided.

ORGANIZATIONAL CONSEQUENCES

Out of a broader, more rational perspective about group process has come a new way of relating the parts of our complex organization to each other. Even as the context of the group contributes additional understanding of individual behavior, understanding the processes operating between groups contributes to an understanding of the organization, of which the groups are a part. Management then comes to be seen as a collection of individuals playing leadership roles and comprising a group in its own right that interacts with other groups throughout the organization. From this vantage point, management philosophy, especially in an organization committed to a decentralized structure operating in a participative management mode, influences and is affected by inter-group dynamics, down to and including the therapeutic climate of the patient himself, and outward as far as the influence of the organization reaches.

In any organization, a great deal of what happens is a consequence of actions initiated by individuals representative of groups, and implemented by groups or representatives of groups. The interplay between groups as represented by these individuals, and the individuals within their group, is a realm of phenomena deserving better conceptualization than is now available.

For us, a beginning has been established in a systems approach with the recognition of the usefulness of concepts developed by the late A.K. Rice (1963, 1965). From him, and reinforced by the group relations conference experience, we have begun to recognize the role which boundaries play in the life of all groups and the problems of boundary crossing which develop as one group interacts with another. The compelling problems of simultaneously maintaining and managing these boundaries, i.e., regulating the intercourse of a group with another, while trying to organize the functions and structure within the group have become evident.

Recognition of the dual nature of this task has severely challenged those professionals who need administrative skills which are not generally part of the world or life experience of the mental health professional. Each finds now that he must represent the interests of his group while also participating in the management group planning overall objectives and policy; if he fails to communicate the consequences of this higher-level group planning to his constituency (his own group), he will have failed the vital boundary function in a way that produces isolation and paranoia within his group, and retards the introduction of data from his group into the planning and thinking of the management group.

A former director of our nursing service saw herself as a strong leader defending the importance of nurses within a traditionally doctor-controlled hospital. She communicated to the nurses her frustrations with hospital administration. At the same time, in the administrative meetings of the hospital (Hospital Council) she was rather passive and communicated only privately to other hospital council members that she felt nurses were being neglected. As a result, frustration and suspiciousness toward hospital administration increased among nurses, and frustration and suspiciousness toward the nursing staff increased among hospital administration. Only after this breakdown of the boundary functions of the Director of Nurses was diagnosed and resolved by opening up the channels of communication between the nursing service and hospital administration, could the irrational nature of many of these frustrations, complaints, and suspiciousness be resolved.

In other circumstances, a failure to recognize the importance of properly managed boundary functions may result in serious intergroup conflict. Thoughtlessly proceeding with a plan which crosses the boundary of one or more groups is regarded by them as territorial intrusion quite properly deserving forceful resistance and even ejection, if possible. The consequences of non-cooperation are evident, and , again, erroneously attributed to the authority "up there"' rather than recognized as a consequence of the failure of the leader to ensure that boundary functions between two groups were properly managed.

Aware of the need for a special training program in research for psychologists, the Director of Research developed a plan and had firm promises of financial support before the Chief Psychologist and his Director of Training had been fully consulted about the impact of the plan on the structure and function of the psychology discipline. A rather acrimonious confrontation discharged the feelings that had been built up but did little to resolve the impasse, and both groups were quite convinced they had been "sold out" by their leaders and unsupported by the President.

A general recognition throughout the organization of the hazards of intergroup operations, and the fact that many issues require consideration by groups which do not regularly relate to each other through ordinary management structure, or which involve more than one group, has led to the development of a concept of "arenas"—the creation of ad hoc groups whose members are authoritative representative of subgroups with an interest in or concern about the specific issue or problem at hand. Thus described, this move will hardly justify a label of "new"; what is new is the realization of how very much more frequent the creation of such temporary "arenas" must be than is generally appreciated, and how specifically an "arena" approach may be a method for managing the universal problem of intergroup conflict, itself a phenomenon given insufficient attention in most organizations.

The episodic need for new office space as one program shrinks, another expands, and new trainees arrive previously has precipitated eleventh-hour crises in which each party involved felt aggrieved and misunderstood. With the creation of a "space commissioner," the problems are anticipated long enough in advance to permit him to call together representatives of the groups involved to negotiate changes in the most equitable and smoothest way. Problems around office assignments have now virtually disappeared.

This kind of approach to organizational problem-solving, currently characterized as a move toward "ad-hocracy" as a kind of organizational style beyond bureaucracy, best fits the changing character of many problems which a more rigid hierarchial structure simply cannot manage without become increasingly centralized and autocractic. It warrants considerable further testing and development.

Programmatic developments within the organization which appear to reflect an influence of group relations conferences on us have been several. The rise in interest in and expansion of group psychotherapy and family therapy programs has been encouraging. A review of the history of these programs at The Menninger Foundation shows them to have struggled along limply, supported by verbal messages of interest, but in fact severely handicapped by a steadfast and exclusive commitment of most professionals to the individual, one-to-one structure of treatment. With the progressive increase in numbers of staff members who attended group relations conferences, the group programs have begun to grow.

An awareness of the conference model as a method which teaches by allowing confrontation and then integration of different perceptions of interpersonal experience moved us to try a form of it for internal planning and problem-solving purposes. As changes in hospital administration led to greater section (ward) autonomy and decentralization, the centrally organized Activities Therapy Department found itself in severe conflict about its purposes and methods, both within itself, and vis-a-vis the professional treatment staff of the hospital. Utilizing a series of small groups involving all the staff of the Activities Therapy Department, supplemented with intergroup meetings and meetings of small group plenipotentiaries, assisted by consultants, and lasting over a period of six months, a new and more explicit conception of the professional role and function of the activities therapist worker was elaborated and ultimately introduced successfully into the hospital treatment system.

Stimulated by the group relations experience, the growth of the therapeutic community concept has rapidly accelerated, having languished in a setting dominated by a dyadic concept of therapy undiluted by much awareness of the importance and usefulness of group process. Arising from similar roots has been the realization that the hospital patients themselves constitute a group whose boundaries need to be defined and recognized by the professional and management groups in the interest of better treatment and better hospital management.

More recently, and still in process, the increasingly sensitive and difficult role and function conflict between the nurses and aides has been channeled into specially designed conferences of these two groups. All members of each group will meet among themselves in small groups first, in order to develop the whole range of opinions and issues. Subsequently, we will proceed to a series of intergroup meetings between the nurses and aides groups that will enable the participants to learn about the role and function alternatives which have been developed by each group. Consultants assigned to the nurse and aide groups will help the participants to learn experientially from the group and intergroup process as well.

The emphasis of this specialized conference is on the resolution of intradepartmental tensions and conflicts, and in this way differs from a group relations conference, which keeps its focus on the study of "here and now" experiences within and between groups. However, the structure of group and intergroup meetings, and the use of consultants playing specific roles are features of a group relations conference which we are incorporating in our conference structure.

At the highest organizational level, the infusion of a better understanding of group and intergroup process has substantially promoted our collective efforts to develop adequate budgets which promote programmatic growth while conforming to the very realistic limits of our resources, and has enormously facilitated really effective longer range planning. In part, these spurts in organizational effectiveness also reflect the growth of the President as he has worked at the difficult task of reconciling groups and individuals, parts to wholes, and of defining leadership and followership roles.

In summary, our experience with the group relations conferences has given our organization a kind of "observing ego": a new perspective and a new conceptual framework that has enabled us to grapple more effectively with the inevitable problems of organizational life. It has provided the means of reducing the grip of the irrational upon us, freed time and energy for the more important job of moving our organization toward its objectives, and will permit us to include this rich experience as part of our expanding educational thrust. The group relations program has unequivocally demonstrated its worth to us many times over.

17.

A CASE-STUDY IN THE FUNCTIONING OF SOCIAL SYSTEMS AS A DEFENSE AGAINST ANXIETY

A Report on a Study of the Nursing Service of a General Hospital

Isabel E.P. Menzies

INTRODUCTION

The study was initiated by the hospital, which sought help in developing new methods of carrying out a task in nursing organization. The research data were, therefore, collected within a socio-therapeutic relationship in which the aim was to facilitate desired social change.

The hospital is a general teaching hospital in London. This implies that, in addition to the normal task of patient-care, the hospital teaches undergraduate medical students. Like all British hospitals of its type, it is also a nurse-training school. The hospital has about 700 beds for in-patients and provides a number of out-patient services. Although referred to as 'the hospital', it is, in fact, a group of hospitals, which, at the time of the study, included a general hospital of 500 beds, three small specialist hospitals, and a convalescent home. The group of hospitals has an integrated nursing service run by a matron located in the main hospital. Nursing staff and students are interchangeable between hospitals.

The nursing personnel of the hospital number about 700. Of these, about 150 are fully trained staff and the remainder are students. The nurse-training course lasts four years. For the first three years, the student nurse is an 'under-graduate'. At the end of the third year she takes the examination which leads to 'state-registration', effectively her nursing qualification and licence to practice. In the fourth year, she is a postgraduate student.

The trained nursing staff are entirely deployed in administrative, teaching, and supervisory roles, although those who are deployed in operational units working with patients also carry out a certain amount of direct patient-care. Student nurses are, in effect, the nursing staff of the hospital at the operational level with patients, and carry out most of the relevant tasks. From this point of view, it is necessary that student nurses be deployed so as to meet the nurse-staffing requirements of the hospital. The student nurse spends comparatively little time undergoing formal instruction. She spends three months in the Preliminary Training School before she starts nursing practice, and six weeks in the nursing school in each of the second and third years of training. For the rest of the time, she is in 'practical training', i.e. acquiring and practicing nursing skills by carrying out full-time nursing duties within the limits of her competence. The practical training must be so arranged that the student has the minimal experience of different types of nursing prescribed by the General Nursing Council.[1] The hospital offers, and likes nurses to have, certain additional experience available in specialist units in the hospital. The hospital's training policy is that the student nurse has aproximately three months' continuous duty in each of the different types of nursing. Each student nurse must be deployed in a way that fulfills these training requirements. The possibilities of conflict in this situation are many. The nursing establishment of the hospital is not primarily determined by training needs, which take second place to patient-centered needs and the needs of the medical school. For some considerable time before the start of the study, the senior nursing staff had been finding it increasingly difficult to reconcile effectively staffing needs and training needs. Pressures from patient-care demanded that priority be given to staffing, and constant training crises developed. The policy of three-month training tours had in effect been abandoned and many tours were very short;[2] some nurses came almost to the end of their training without having had all the necessary experience, and others had a serious imbalance owing to too much of the same kind of practice. These crises created the more acute distress because senior staff wished to give increasing priority to training and to raise the status of the nurse as a student.

The senior staff began to feel that there was a danger of complete breakdown in the system of allocation to practical work and sought our help in revising their methods. My purpose in writing this paper is not, however, to follow the ramifications of this problem. I will make some reference to it at relevant points, and will consider later why the existing method persisted so long without effective modification in spite of its inefficiency.

The therapeutic relationship with the hospital was to some extent based on the belief that we would be wise to regard the problem of student-nurse allocation as a 'presenting symptom'

1 The nursing body that controls nurse-training.

2 A sample check of actual duration showed that 30 percent of student moves took place less than 3 weeks after the previous move and 44 percent less than 7 weeks.

and to reserve judgment on the real nature of the difficulties and the best form of treatment until we had done further diagnostic work. We began, therefore, with a fairly intensive interviewing program. We held formal interviews with about 70 nurses, individually and in small groups, and with senior medical and lay staff; we carried out some observational studies of operational units; and we had many informal contacts with nurses and other staff. Respondents knew the problem we were formally studying, but were invited to raise in interview any other issue that they considered central to their occupational experience. Much further research material was collected in the later meetings with senior staff as we worked together on the findings from the interviewing program.[3]

As our diagnostic work went on, our attention was repeatedly drawn to the high level of tension, distress, and anxiety among the nurses. We found it hard to understand how nurses could tolerate so much anxiety, and, indeed, we found much evidence that they could not. In one form or another, withdrawal from duty was common. About one-third of student nurses did not complete their training. The majority of these left at their own request, and not because of failure in examinations or practical training. Senior staff changed their jobs appreciably more frequently than workers at similar levels in other professions and were unusually prone to seek postgraduate training. Sickness rates were high, especially for minor illnesses requiring only a few days' absence from duty.[4]

As the study proceeded we came to attach increasing importance to understanding the nature of the anxiety and the reasons for its intensity. The relief of the anxiety seemed to us an important therapeutic task and, moreover, proved to have a close connection with the development of more effective techniques of student-nurse allocation. The remainder of this paper is concerned to consider the causes and the effects of the anxiety level in the hospital.

NATURE OF THE ANXIETY

A hospital accepts and cares for ill people who cannot be cared for in their own homes. This is the task the hospital is created to perform, its 'primary task'. The major responsibility for the performance of that primary task lies with the nursing service,

3 It is a feature of a therapeutic study of this kind that much of the most significant research material emerges in its later stages when the emphasis of the work shifts from diagnosis to therapy. Presentation and interpretation of data, and work done on resistances to their acceptance, facilitate the growth of insight into the nature of the problem. This extends the range of information seen to be relevant to its solution, and helps overcome personal resistances to the disclosure of information. An impressive feature of the study here reported was the way in which, after a spell of working on the data, the senior nursing staff themselves were able to produce and execute plans directed towards dealing with their problems.

4 There is much evidence from other fields that such phenomena express a disturbed relation with the work situation and are connected with a high level of tension. See, for example, Hill & Trist (1953).

which must provide continuous care for patients, day and night, all the year round.[5]   The nursing service, therefore, bears the full, immediate, and concentrated impact of stresses arising from patient-care.

The situations likely to evoke stress in nurses are familiar. Nurses are in constant contact with people who are physically ill or injured, often seriously. The recovery of patients is not certain and will not always be complete. Nursing patients who have incurable diseases is one of the nurse's most distressing tasks. Nurses are confronted with the threat and the reality of suffering and death as few lay people are. Their work involves carrying out tasks which, by ordinary standards, are distasteful, disgusting, and frightening. Intimate physical contact with patients arouses strong libidinal and erotic wishes and impulses that may be difficult to control. The work situation arouses very strong and mixed feelings in the nurse: pity, compassion, and love; guilt and anxiety; hatred and resentment of the patients who arouse these strong feeling; envy of the care given the patient.

The objective situation confronting the nurse bears a striking resemblance to the phantasy[6] situations that exist in every individual in the deepest and most primitive levels of the mind. The intensity and complexity of the nurse's anxieties are to be attributed primarily to the peculiar capacity of the objective features of her work situation to stimulate afresh these early situations and their accompanying emotions. I will comment briefly on the main relevant features of these phantasy situations.[7]

The elements of these phantasies may be traced back to earliest infancy. The infant experiences two opposing sets of feelings and impulses, libidinal and aggressive. These stem from instinctual sources and are described by the constructs of the life-instinct and the death-instinct. The infant feels omnipotent and attributes dynamic reality to these feelings and impulses. He believes that the libidinal impulses are literally life-giving and the aggressive impulses death-dealing. The infant attributes similar feelings, impulses, and powers to the other people and to important parts of people. The objects and the instruments of the

---

5 My colleague, G. F. Hutton, in analyzing the data from another hospital study, drew attention to the descent of modern hospitals from orders of nursing sisters. These early hospitals were entirely administered by the nurses. Doctors and priests were necessary and important visitors, but visitors only. They met special needs of patients but had no administrative responsibility. The tradition of what Hutton called "nurse-directed communities" remains strong, in spite of the complexity of organization of modern hospitals and the number and diversity of patient-centered staff.

6 Throughout this paper I follow the convention of using fantasy to mean conscious fantasy, and phantasy to mean unconscious phantasy.

7 In my description of infantile psychic life, I follow the work of Freud, particularly as developed and elaborated by Melanie Klein. A brief but comprehensive summary of her views may be found in her papers "Some Theoretical Conclusions Regarding the Emotional Life of the Infant,' Klein (1952b) and 'Our Adult World and its Roots in Infancy', Klein (1959).

libidinal and aggressive impulses are felt to be the infant's own and other people's bodies and bodily products. Physical and psychic experiences are very intimately interwoven at this time. The infant's psychic experience of objective reality is greatly influenced by his own feelings and phantasies, moods and wishes.

Through his psychic experience the infant builds up an inner world peopled by himself and the objects of his feelings and impulses.[8] In the inner world, they exist in a form and condition largely determined by his phantasies. Because of the operation of aggressive forces, the inner world contains many damaged, injured, or dead objects. The atmosphere is charged with death and destruction. This gives rise to great anxiety. The infant fears for the effect of aggressive forces on the people he loves and on himself. He grieves and mourns over their suffering and experiences depression and despair about his inadequate ability to put right their wrongs. He fears the demands that will be made on him for reparation and the punishment and revenge that may fall on him. He fears that his libidinal impulses and those of other people cannot control the aggressive impulses sufficiently to prevent utter chaos and destruction. The poignancy of the situation is increased because love and longing themselves are felt to be so close to aggression. Greed, frustration, and envy so easily replace a loving relationship. This phantasy world is characterized by a violence and intensity of feeling quite foreign to the emotional life of the normal adult.

The direct impact on the nurse of physical illness is intensified by her task of meeting and dealing with psychological stress in other people, including her own colleagues. It is by no means easy to tolerate such stress even if one is not under similar stress oneself. Quite short conversations with patients or relatives showed that their conscious concept of illness and treatment is a rich intermixture of objective knowledge, logical deduction, and fantasy[9]. The degree of stress is heavily conditioned by the fantasy, which is, in turn, conditioned, as in nurses, by the early fantasy-situations. Unconsciously, the nurse associates the patients' and relatives' distress with that experienced by the people in her phantasy-world, which increases her own anxiety and difficulty in handling it.

Patients and relatives have very complicated feelings towards the hospital, which are expressed particularly and most directly to nurses, and often puzzle and distress them. Patients and relatives show appreciation, gratitude, affection, respect; a touching relief that the hospital copes; helpfulness and concern for nurses in their difficult task. But patients often resent their

8 For a further description of the process of building the inner world see Klein (1952b and 1959).

9 For a description of some patients' concepts of illness see Janis (1958) where there is also an account of how working through the fantasy may relieve the anxiety.

dependence; accept grudgingly the discipline imposed by treatment and hospital routine; envy nurses their health and skills; are demanding, possessive, and jealous. Patients, like nurses, find strong libidinal and erotic feelings stimulated by nursing care, and sometimes behave in ways that increase the nurses' difficulties, e.g. by unnecessary physical exposure. Relatives may also be demanding and critical, the more so because they resent the feeling that hospitalization implies inadequacies in themselves. They envy nurses their skill and jealously resent the nurse's intimate contact with 'their' patient .

In a more subtle way, both patients and relatives make psychological demands on nurses which increase their experience of stress. The hospital is expected to do more than accept the ill patient, care for his physical needs, and help realistically with his psychological stress. The hospital is implicitly expected to accept and, by so doing, free patients and relatives from certain aspects of the emotional problems aroused by the patient and his illness. The hospital, particularly the nurses, must allow the projection into them of such feelings as depression and anxiety, fear of the patient and his illness, disgust at the illness and necessary nursing tasks. Patients and relatives treat the staff in such a way as to ensure that the nurses experience these feelings instead of, or partly instead of, they themselves, e.g. by refusing or trying to refuse to participate in important decisions about the patient and so forcing responsibility and anxiety back on the hospital. Thus, to the nurses' own deep and intense anxieties are psychically added those of the other people concerned. As we became familiar with the work of the hospital, we were struck by the number of patients whose physical condition alone did not warrant hospitalization. In some cases, it was clear that they had been hospitalized because they and their relatives could not tolerate the stress of their being ill at home.

The nurse projects infantile phantasy-situations into current work-situations and experiences the objective situations as a mixture of objective reality and phantasy. She then re-experiences painfully and vividly in relation to current objective reality many of the feelings appropriate to the phantasies. In thus projecting her phantasy-situations into objective reality, the nurse is using an important and universal technique for mastering anxiety and modifying the phantasy-situations in the objective situations that come to symbolize the phantasy-situations [10] Successful mastery of the objective situations gives reassurance about the mastery of the phantasy-situations. To be effective, such symbolization requires that the symbol *represents* the phantasy object, but *is not equated* with it. Its own distinctive, objective characteristics must also be recognized and

10 Klein (1948b) stresses the importance of anxiety in leading to the development of symbol-formation and sublimation.

used. If, for any reason, the symbol and the phantasy object become almost or completely equated, the anxieties aroused by the phantasy object are aroused in full intensity by the symbolic object. The symbol then ceases to perform its function in containing and modifying anxiety[11]. The close resemblance of the phantasy and objective situations in nursing constitutes a threat that symbolic representation will degenerate into symbolic equation and that nurses will consequently experience the full force of their primitive infantile anxieties in consciousness. Modified examples of this phenomenon were not uncommon in this hospital. For example, a nurse whose mother had had several gynecological operations broke down and had to give up nursing shortly after beginning her tour of duty on the gynecological ward.

By the nature of her profession the nurse is at considerable risk of being flooded by intense and unmanageable anxiety. That factor alone, however, cannot account for the high level of anxiety so apparent in nurses. It becomes necessary to direct attention to the other facet of the problem, that is to the techniques used in nursing service to contain and modify anxiety.

DEFENSIVE TECHNIQUES IN THE NURSING SERVICE

In developing a structure, culture, and mode of functioning, a social organization is influenced by a number of interacting factors, crucial among which are its primary task, including such environmental relationships and pressures as that involves; the technologies available for performing the task; and the needs of the members of the organization for social and psychological satisfaction, and, above all, for support in the task of dealing with anxiety[12]. In my opinion, the influence of the primary task and technology can easily be exaggerated. Indeed, I would prefer to regard them as limiting factors, i.e. the need to ensure viability through the efficient performance of the primary task and the types of technology available to do this set limits to

11 Segal (1957) uses the terms symbolic representation and symbolic equation. In developing this distinction, she stresses the acute anxieties experienced by patients in whom the symbol does not merely represent the phantasy object but is equated with it. She illustrates from the material of two patients for both of whom a violin was a phallic symbol. For one patient the violin *represented* the phallus and violin-playing was an important sublimation through which he could master anxiety. For the other more deeply disturbed patient, the violin was *felt to be* the phallus and he had had to stop playing because he could not touch a violin in public.

12 Bion (1955) has put forward a similar concept in distinguishing between the sophisticated or work group concerned with a realistic task and the basic-assumption group dominated by primitive psychological phenomena; the two 'groups' being simultaneously operative aspects of the same aggregation of people.

The importance of anxiety and defenses against it have been much stressed in psychoanalytical theories of personality development. Freud's earliest works show his interest and he develops his theory in later work (Freud, 1955, 1948). The central developmental role of anxiety and defenses has, more recently, been much stressed by Melanie Klein and her colleagues (Klein, 1952b, 1948b).

For a fuller discussion of the primary task and related factors see Rice (1958).

possible organization. Within these limits, the culture, structure, and mode of functioning are determined by the psychological needs of the members[13].

The needs of the members of the organization to use it in the struggle against anxiety leads to the development of socially structured defense mechanisms, which appear as elements in the structure, culture, and mode of functioning of the organization[14]. An important aspect of such socially structured defense mechanisms is an attempt by individuals to externalize and give substance in objective reality to their characteristic psychic defense mechanisms. A social defense system develops over time as the result of collusive interaction and agreement, often unconscious, between members of the organization as to what form it shall take. The socially structured defense mechanisms then tend to become an aspect of external reality with which old and new members of the institution must come to terms.

In what follows I shall discuss some of the social defenses that the nursing service has developed in the long course of the hospital's history and currently operates. It is impossible here to describe the social system fully, so I shall illustrate only a few of the more striking and typical examples of the operation of the service as a social defense. I shall confine myself mainly to techniques used within the nursing service and refer minimally to ways in which the nursing service makes use of other people, notably patients and doctors, in operating socially structured mechanisms for defense. For convenience of exposition, I shall list the defenses as if they are separate, although, in operation, they function simultaneously and interact with and support each other.

Splitting up the nurse-patient relationship. The core of the anxiety situation for the nurse lies in her relation with the patient. The closer and more concentrated this relationship, the more the nurse is likely to experience the impact of anxiety. The nursing service attempts to protect her from the anxiety by splitting up her contact with patients. It is hardly too much to say that the nurse does not nurse patients. The total work-load of a ward or department is broken down into lists of tasks, each of which is allocated to a particular nurse. She performs her patient-centered tasks for a large number of patients, perhaps as many as all the patients in the ward, often 30 or more in number. As a corollary, she performs only a few tasks for, and has restricted contact with, any one patient. This prevents her from coming effectively into contact with the totality of any one patient

13 The different social systems that have developed under long-wall coal-mining conditions, using the same basic technology, are a good example of how the same primary task may be performed differently using the same technology when social and psychological conditions are different. They have been discussed by Trist & Bamforth (1951).

14 Jaques (1955) has described and illustrated the operation of such socially structured defense mechanisms in an industrial organization. The term is his.

and his illness and offers some protection from the anxiety this arouses.

Depersonalization, categorization, and denial of the significance of the individual. The protection afforded by the task-list system is reinforced by a number of other devices that inhibit the development of a full person-to-person relationship between nurse and patient, with its consequent anxiety. The implicit aim of such devices, which operate both structurally and culturally, may be described as a kind of depersonalizaton or elimination of individual distinctiveness in both nurse and patient. For example, nurses often talk about patient, not by name, but by bed numbers or by their disease or a diseased organ, 'the liver in bed 10' or 'the pneumonia in bed 15'. Nurses themselves deprecate this practice, but it persists. Nor should one underestimate the difficulties of remembering the names of say 30 patients on a ward, especially the high-turnover wards. There is an almost explicit 'ethic' that any patient must be the same as any other patient. It must not matter to the nurse whom she nurses or what illness. Nurses find it extraordinarily difficult to express preferences even for types of patients or for men or women patients. If pressed to do so, they tend to add rather guiltily some remark like 'You can't help it'. Conversely, it should not matter to the patient which nurse attends him or, indeed, how many different nurses do. By implication it is the duty as well as the need and privilege of the patient to be nursed and of the nurse to nurse, regardless of the fact that a patient may greatly need to 'nurse' a distressed nurse and nurses may sometimes need to be 'nursed'. Outside the specific requirements of his physical illness and treatment, the way a patient is nursed is determined largely by his membership of the category patient and minimally by his idiosyncratic wants and needs. For example, there is one way only of bed-making, except when the physical illness requires another; only one time to wash all patients in the morning.

The nurses' uniforms are a symbol of an expected inner and behavioral uniformity; a nurse becomes a kind of agglomeration of nursing skills, without individuality; each is thus perfectly interchangeable with another of the same skill-level. Socially permitted differences between nurses tend to be restricted to a few major categories, outwardly differentiated by minor differences in insignia on the same basic uniform, an arm stripe for a second-year nurse, a slightly different cap for a third-year nurse. This attempts to create an operational identity between all nurses in the same category [15] To an extent indicating clearly the need for 'blanket' decisions, duties and privileges are accorded to categories of people and not to individuals according to their personal capacities and needs. This also helps to eliminate

15 In practice it is not possible to carry out these prescriptions literally, since a whole category of nurses may temporarily be absent from practical duties on formal instruction in the nursing school or on leave

painful and difficult decisions, e.g. about which duties and privileges should fall to each individual. Something of the same reduction of individual distinctiveness exists between operational sub-units. Attempts are made to standardize all equipment and layout to the limits allowed by their different nursing tasks, but disregarding the idiosyncratic social and psychological resources and needs of each unit.

Detachment and denial of feelings. A necessary psychological task for the entrant into any profession that works with people is the development of adequate professional detachment. He must learn, for example, to control his feelings, refrain from excessive involvement, avoid disturbing identifications, maintain his professional independence against manipulation and demands for unprofessional behavior. To some extent the reduction of individual distinctiveness aids detachment by minimizing the mutual interaction of personalities, which might lead to 'attachment'. It is reinforced by an implicit operational policy of 'detachment'. 'A good nurse doesn't mind moving.' A 'good nurse' is willing and able without disturbance to move from ward to ward or even hospital to hospital at a moment's notice. Such moves are frequent and often sudden, particularly for student nurses. The implicit rationale appears to be that a student nurse will learn to be detached psychologically if she has sufficient experience of being detached literally and physically. Most senior nurses do not subscribe personally to this implicit rationale. They are aware of the personal distress as well as the operational disturbance caused by overfrequent moves. Indeed this was a major factor in the decision to initiate our study. However, in their formal roles in the hierachy they continue to initiate frequent moves and make little other training provision for developing genuine professional detachment. The pain and distress of breaking relationships and the importance of stable and continuing relationships are implicitly denied by the system, although they are often stressed personally, i.e. non-professionally, by people in the system.

This implicit denial is reinforced by the denial of the disturbing feelings that arise within relationships. Interpersonal repressive techniques are culturally required and typically used to deal with emotional stress. Both student nurses and staff show panic about emotional outbursts. Brisk, reassuring behavior and advice of the 'stiff upper lip', 'pull yourself together' variety are characteristic. Student nurses suffer most severely from emotional strain and habitually complain that the senior staff do not understand and make no effort to help them. Indeed, when the emotional stress arises from the nurse's having made a mistake, she is usually reprimanded instead of being helped. A student nurse told me that she had made a mistake that hastened the death of a dying patient. She was reprimanded separately by four senior nurses. Only the headmistress of her former school tried to help her as a person who was severely distressed, guilty, and frightened. However, students are wrong when they say that senior nurses do not understand or feel for their distress. In personal conversation with us, seniors showed considerable understanding and sympathy and often remembered surprisingly vividly some of the agonies of their own training. But they lacked confidence in their ability to handle emotional stress in any way other than by repressive techniques, and often said, 'In any case, the students won't come and talk to us.' Kindly, sympathetic handling of emotional stress between staff and student nurses is, in any case, inconsistent with traditional nursing roles and relationships, which require repression, discipline, and reprimand from senior to junior[16]

The attempt to eliminate decisions by ritual task-performance. Making a decision implies making a choice between different possible courses of action and committing oneself to one of them; the choice being made in the absence of full factual information about the effects of the choice. If the facts were fully known, no decision need be made; the proper course of action would be self-evident. All decisions are thus necessarily attended by some uncertainty about their outcome and consequently by some conflict and anxiety, which will last until the outcome is known. The anxiety consequent on decision-making is likely to be acute if a decision affects the treatment and welfare of patients. To spare staff this anxiety, the nursing service attempts to minimize the number and variety of decisions that must be made. For example, the student nurse is instructed to perform her task-list in a way reminiscent of performing a ritual. Precise instructions are given about the way each task must be performed, the order of the tasks, and the time for their performance, although such precise instructions are not objectively necessary, or even wholly desirable[17].

If several efficient methods of performing a task exist, e.g. for bed-making or lifting a patient, one is selected and exclusively used. Much time and effort are expended in standardizing nursing procedures in cases where there are a number of effective alternatives. Both teachers and practical-work supervisors impress on the student nurse from the beginning of her training the importance of carrying out the 'ritual'. They reinforce this by fostering an attitude to work that regards every task as almost a matter of life and death, to be treated with appropriate seriousness. This applies even to those tasks that could be effectively performed by an unskilled lay person. As a corollary, the student nurse is actively discouraged from using her own discretion and initiative to plan her work realistically in

16 See above, p 290, for an account of how these roles and relationships arise

17 Bion (1955), in describing the behavior of groups where the need to be dependent is dominant, has commented on the group s need for what he calls a 'bible'. It is not perhaps surprising to find that, in the hospital, whose primary task is to meet the dependency needs of patients, there should be a marked need for just such definitive prescription of behavior

relation to the objective situation, e.g. at times of crisis to discriminate between tasks on the grounds of urgency or relative importance and to act accordingly. Student nurses are the 'staff' most affected by 'rituals', since ritualization is easy to apply to their roles and tasks, but attempts are also made to ritualize the task-structure of the more complex senior staff roles and to standardize the task-performance.

Reducing the weight of responsibility in decision-making by checks and counter-checks. The psychological burden of anxiety arising from a final, committing decision by a single person is dissipated in a number of ways, so that its impact is reduced. The final act of commitment is postponed by a common practice of checking and re-checking decisions for validity and postponing action as long as possible. Executive action following decisions is also checked and re-checked habitually at intervening stages. Individuals spend much time in private rumination over decisions and actions. Whenever possible, they involve other nurses in decision-making and in reviewing actions. The nursing procedures prescribe considerable checking between individuals, but it is also a strongly developed habit among nurses outside areas of prescribed behavior. The practice of checking and counter-checking is applied not only to situations where mistakes may have serious consequences, such as in giving dangerous drugs, but to many situations where the implications of a decisions are of only the slightest consequence, e.g. on one occasion a decision about which of several rooms, all equally available, should be used for a research interview. Nurses consult not only their immediate seniors but also their juniors and nurses or other staff with whom they have no functional relationship but who just happen to be available.

Collusive social redistribution of responsibility and irresponsibility. Each nurse must face and, in some way, resolve a painful conflict over accepting the responsibilities of her role. The nursing task tends to evoke a strong sense of responsibility in nurses, and nurses often discharge their duties at considerable personal cost. On the other hand, the heavy burden of responsibility is difficult to bear consistently, and nurses are tempted to give it up. In addition, each nurse has wishes and impulses that would lead to irresponsible action, e.g. to scamp boring, repetitive tasks or to become libidinally or emotionally attached to patients. The balance of opposing forces in the conflict varies between individuals, i.e. some are naturally 'more responsible' than others, but the conflict is always present. To experience this conflict fully and intrapsychically would be extremely stressful. The intrapsychic conflict is alleviated, at least as far as the conscious experiences of nurses are concerned, by a technique that partly converts it into an interpersonal conflict. People in certain roles tend to be described as 'responsible' by themselves and to some extent by others, and in other roles people are described as 'irresponsible'. Nurses habitually complain that other nurses are irresponsible, behave carelessly and impulsively, and in consequence must be ceaselessly supervised and disciplined. The complaints commonly refer not to individuals or to specific incidents but to whole categories of nurses, usually a category junior to the speaker. The implication is that the juniors are not only less responsible now than the speaker, but also less responsible than she was when she was in the same junior position. Few nurses recognize or admit such tendencies. Only the most junior nurses are likely to admit these tendencies in themselves and then justify them on the grounds that everybody treats them as though they were irresponsible. On the other hand, many people complain that their seniors as a category impose unnecessarily strict and repressive discipline, and treat them as though they have no sense of responsibility[18] Few senior staff seem able to recognize such features in their own behavior to subordinates. Those 'juniors' and 'seniors' are, with few exceptions, the same people viewed from above or below, as the case may be.

We came to realize that the complaints stem from a collusive system of denial, splitting, and projection that is culturally acceptable to, indeed culturally required of, nurses. Each nurse tends to split off aspects of herself from her conscious personality and to project them into other nurses. Her irresponsible impulses, which she fears she cannot control, are attributed to her juniors. Her painfully severe attitude to these impulses and burdensome sense of responsibility are attributed to her seniors. Consequently, she identifies juniors with her irresponsible self and treats them with the severity that self is felt to deserve. Similarly, she identifies seniors with her own harsh disciplinary attitude to her irresponsible self and expects harsh discipline. There is psychic truth in the assertion that juniors are irresponsible and seniors harsh disciplinarians. These are the roles assigned to them. There is also objective truth, since people act objectively on the psychic roles assigned to them. Discipline is often harsh and sometimes unfair, since the multiple projection also leads the senior to identify all juniors with her irresponsible self and so with each other. Thus, she fails to discriminate between them sufficiently. Nurses complain about being reprimanded for other people's mistakes while no serious effort is made to find the real culprit. A staff nurse[19] said, 'If a mistake has been made, you must reprimand someone, even if you don't know who really did it.' Irresponsible behavior was also quite common, mainly in tasks remote from direct patient-care. The interpersonal conflict is painful, as the complaints show, but is less so than experiencing the conflict

18 This has long been a familiar complaint in British hospitals and emerged as a central finding in a number of nursing studies

19 A staff nurse is a fully qualified nurse who is the sister's deputy

fully intrapsychically, and it can more easily be evaded. The disciplining eye of seniors cannot follow juniors all the time, nor does the junior confront her senior with irresponsibility all the time.

Purposeful obscurity in the formal distribution of responsibility. Additional protection from the impact of specific responsibility for specific tasks is given by the fact that the formal structure and role sysem fail to define fully enough who is responsible for what and to whom. This matches and objectifies the obscurity about the location of psychic responsibility that inevitably arises from the massive system of projection described above. The content of roles and the boundaries of roles are very obscure, especially at senior levels. The responsibilities are more onerous at this level so that protection is felt as very necessary. Also the more complex roles and role-relationships make it easier to evade definition. As described above (p. 288), the content of the role of the student nurse is rigidly prescribed by her task-list. However, in practice, she is unlikely to have the same task-list for any length of time. She may, and frequently does, have two completely different task-lists in a single day[20] There is therefore a lack of stable person-role constellations, and it becomes very difficult to assign responsibility finally to a person, a role, or a person-role constellation. We experienced this obscurity frequently in our work in the hospital, finding a great difficulty, for example, in learning who should make arrangements or give permission for nurses to participate in various research activities.

Responsibility and authority on wards are generalized in a way that makes them non-specific and prevents them from falling firmly on one person, even the sister. Each nurse is held to be responsible for the work of every nurse junior to her. Junior, in this context, implies no hierarchical relationship, and is determined only by the length of time a student nurse has been in training, and all students are 'junior' to trained staff. A student nurse in the fourth quarter of her fourth year is by implication responsible for all other student nurses on the ward; a student nurse in the third quarter of her fourth year for all student nurses except the previous one, and so on. Every nurse is expected to initiate disciplinary action in relation to any failure by any junior nurse. Such diffused responsibility means, of course, that responsibility is not generally experienced specifically or seriously.

The reduction of the impact of responsibility by delegation to superiors. The ordinary usage of the word 'delegation' in relation to tasks implies that a superior hands over a task and the direct responsibility for its detailed performance to subordinates, while he retains a general, supervisory responsibility. In the hospital, almost the opposite seems to happen frequently, i.e. tasks are

20 There are usually 3 different lists of tasks in a ward, numbered 1,2, and 3, and a student nurse may well be Number 1 in the morning and Number 2 in the afternoon, e.g. if the Number 2 of the morning goes off duty in the afternoon.

frequently forced upwards in the hierarchy, so that all responsibility for their performance can be disclaimed. In so far as this happens, the heavy burden of responsibility on the individual is reduced.

The results of many years of this practice are visible in the nursing service. We were struck repeatedly by their low level of tasks carried out by nursing staff and students in relation to their personal ability, skill, and position in the hierachy. Formally and informally, tasks are assigned to staff at a level well above that at which one finds comparable tasks in other institutions, while the tasks are organized so as effectively to prevent their delegation to an appropriate lower level, e.g. by clarifying policy. The task of allocating student nurses to practical duties was a case in point. The detailed work of allocating student nurses was carried out by the first and second assistant matrons[21] and took up a considerable proportion of their working-time. In our opinion, the task is, in fact, such that, if policy were clearly defined and the task appropriately organized, it could be efficiently performed by a competent clerk part-time under the supervision of a senior nurse, who need spend little time on it.[22] We were able to watch this 'delegation upwards' in operation a number of times as new tasks developed for nurses out of changes resulting from our study. For example, the senior staff decided to change the practical training for our fourth-year nurses so that they might have better training than formerly in administration and supervision. This implied, among other things, that they should spend six months continuously in one operational unit during which time they would act as understudy-cum-shadow to the sister or the staff nurse. In the circumstances, personal compatibility was felt to be very important, and it was suggested that the sisters should take part in the selection of the fourth-year students for their own wards. At first, there was enthusiasm for the proposal, but as definite plans were made and the intermediate staff began to feel that they had no developed skill for selection, they requested that, after all, senior staff should continue to select for them as they had always done. The senior staff, although already overburdened, willingly accepted the task.

The repeated occurrence of such incidents by mutual collusive agreement between superiors and subordinates is hardly surprising considering the mutual projection system described above (p. 290). Nurses as subordinates tend to feel very dependent on their superiors in whom they psychically vest by projection some of the best and most competent parts of themselves. They feel that their projections give them the right to expect their superiors to undertake their tasks and make decisions for them. On the other hand, nurses, as superiors, do

21 The nurses third and fourth in seniority in administration

22 Arrangements are almost complete for the re-structuring of the task along such lines

not feel they can fully trust their subordinates in whom they psychically vest the irresponsible and incompetent parts of themselves. Their acceptance of their subordinates' projections also conveys a sense of duty to accept their subordinates' responsibilities.

Idealization and underestimation of personal development possibilities. In order to reduce anxiety about the continuous efficient performance of nursing tasks, nurses seek assurance that the nursing service is staffed with responsible, competent people. To a considerable extent, the hospital deals with this problem by an attempt to recruit and select 'staff', i.e. student nurses, who are already highly mature and responsible people. This is reflected in phrases like 'nurses are born not made' or 'nursing is a vocation.' This amounts to a kind of idealization of the potential nursing recruit, and implies a belief that responsibility and personal maturity cannot be 'taught' or even greatly developed. As a corollary, the training system is mainly orientated to the communication of essential facts and techniques, and pays minimal attention to teaching events oriented to personal maturation within the professional setting[23]. There is no individual supervision of student nurses, and no small group teaching event concerned specifically to help student nurses work over the impact of their first essays in nursing practice and handle more effectively their relations with patients and their own emotional reactions. The nursing service must face the dilemma that, while a strong sense of responsibility and discipline are felt to be necessary for the welfare of patients, a considerable proportion of actual nursing tasks are extremely simple. This hospital, in common with most similar British hospitals, has attempted to solve this dilemma by the recruitment of large numbers of high-level student nurses who, it is hoped, are prepared to accept the temporary lowering of their operational level because they are in training.

This throws new light on the problem of the 30 percent to 50 percent wastage of student nurses in this and other Bristish hospitals. It has long been treated as a serious problem and much effort has been expended on trying to solve it. In fact, it can be seen as an *essential* element in the social defense system. The need for responsible semi-skilled staff greatly exceeds the need for fully trained staff, e.g. by almost four to one in this hospital. If a large number of student nurses do *not* fail to finish their training, the nursing profession risks being flooded with trained staff for whom there are no jobs. The wastage is, therefore, an unconscious device to maintain the balance between staff of different levels of skill while all are at high personal level. It is understandable that apparently determined

23 This is connected also with the attempt to eliminate decision-making as far as possible. If there are no decisions to be made, the worker simply needs to *know* what to do and how to do it.

efforts to reduce wastage have so far failed, except in one or two hospitals.

Avoidance of change. Change is inevitably to some extent an excursion into the unknown. It implies a commitment to future events that are not entirely predictable and to their consequences, and inevitably provokes doubt and anxiety. Any significant change within a social system implies changes in existing social relationships and in social structure. It follows that any significant social change implies a change in the operation of the social system as a defense system. While this change is proceeding, i.e. while social defenses are being re-structured, anxiety is likely to be more open and intense [24] Jaques (1955) has stressed that resistance to social change can be better understood if it is seen as the resistance of groups of people unconsciously clinging to existing institutions because changes threaten existing social defenses against deep and intense anxieties.

It is understandable that the nursing service, whose tasks stimulate such primitive and intense anxieties, should anticipate change with unusually severe anxiety. In order to avoid this anxiety, the service tries to avoid change wherever possible, almost, one might say, at all cost, and tends to cling to the familiar even when the familiar has obviously ceased to be appropriate or relevant. Changes tend to be initiated only at the point of crisis. The presenting problem was a good example of this difficulty in initiating and carrying through change. Staff and student nurses had for long felt that the methods in operation were unsatisfactory and had wanted to change them. They had, however, been unable to do so. The anxieties and uncertainties about possible changes and their consequences inhibited constructive and realistic planning and decision. At least, the present difficulties were familiar and they had some ability to handle them. The problem was approaching the point of breakdown and the limits of the capacities of the people concerned when we were called in. Many other examples of this clinging to the inappropriate familiar could be observed. For example, changes in medical practice and the initiation of the National Health Service have led to more rapid patient turnover, an increase in the proportion of acutely ill patients, a wider range of illness to be nursed in each ward, and greater variation in the work-load of a ward from day to day. These changes all point to the need for increasing flexibility in the work organization of nurses in wards. In fact, no such increase in flexibility has taken place in this hospital. Indeed, the difficulty inherent in trying to deal with a fluctuating work-load by the rather rigid system described above has tended to be handled by increased prescription and rigidity and by reiteration of the familiar. As far as one could gather, the greater the anxiety the greater the

---

[24] This is a familiar experience while the individual's defense are being re-structured in the course of psychoanalytic therapy.

need for such reassurance in rather compulsive repetition.

The changing demands on nurses described above necessitate a growing amount of increasingly technically skilled nursing care. This has not, however, led to any examination of the implicit policy that nursing can be carried out largely by semi-qualified student nurses.

COMMENTARY ON THE SOCIAL DEFENSE SYSTEM

The characteristic feature of the social defense system, as we have described it, is its orientation to helping the individual avoid the experience of anxiety, guilt, doubt, and uncertainty. As far as possible, this is done by eliminating situations, events, tasks, activities, and relationships that cause anxiety or, more correctly, evoke anxieties connected with primitive psychological remnants in the personality. Little attempt is made positively to help the individual confront the anxiety-evoking experiences and, by so doing, to develop her capacity to tolerate and deal more effectively with the anxiety. Basically, the potential anxieties in the nursing situation are felt to be too deep and dangerous for full confrontation, and to threaten personal disruption and social chaos. In fact, of course, the attempt to avoid such confrontation can never be completely successful. A compromise is inevitable between the implicit aims of the social defense system and the demands of reality as expressed in the need to pursue the primary task.

It follows that the psychic defense mechanisms that have, over time, been built into the socially structured defense system of the nursing service are, in the main, those which by evasion give protection from the full experience of anxiety. These are derived from the most primitive psychic defense mechanisms. Those mechanisms are typical of the young infant's attempts to deal, mainly by evasion, with the severe anxieties aroused by the interplay of his own instincts that are intolerable at his immature age[25].

Individuals vary in the extent to which they are able, as they grow older, to modify or abandon their early defense mechanisms and develop other methods of dealing with their anxieties. Notably, these other methods include the ability to confront the anxiety-situations in their original or symbolic forms and to work them over, to approach and tolerate psychic and objective reality, to differentiate between them and to perform constructive and objectively successful activities in relation to them[26]. Every individual is at risk that objective or psychic

25 I will enumerate briefly here some of the most important of these defenses. In doing so, I follow the work of Freud as developed by Melanie Klein (1952b, 1959). The infant makes much use of splitting and projection, denial, idealization, and rigid, omnipotent control of himself and others. These defenses are, at first, massive and violent. Later, as the infant becomes more able to tolerate his anxiety, the same defenses continue to be used but are less violent. They begin to appear also in what are perhaps more familiar forms, e.g. as repression, obsessional rituals, and repetition of the familiar.

26 Or, expressed otherwise, the capacity to undertake sublimatory activities.

events stimulating acute anxiety will lead to partial or complete abandonment of the more mature methods of dealing with anxiety and to regression to the more primitive methods of defense. In our opinion, the intense anxiety evoked by the nursing task has precipitated just such individual regression to primitive types of defense. These have been projected and given objective existence in the social structure and culture of the nursing service, with the result that anxiety is to some extent contained, but that true mastery of anxiety by deep working-through and modification is seriously inhibited. Thus, it is to be expected that nurses will persistently experience a higher degree of anxiety than is justified by the objective situation alone. Consideration in more detail of how the socially structured defense system fails to support the individual in the struggle towards more effective mastery of anxiety may be approached from two different but related points of view.

I will first consider how far the present functioning of the nursing service gives rise to experiences that in themselves reassure nurses or arouse anxiety. In fact, as a direct consequence of the social organization, many situations and incidents arise that clearly arouse anxiety. On the other hand, the social system frequently functions in such a way as to deprive nurses of necessary reassurance and satisfactions. In other words, the social defense system itself arouses a good deal of secondary anxiety as well as failing to alleviate primary anxiety. I shall illustrate these points with some typical examples.

Threat of crisis and operational breakdown. From the operational point of view, the nursing service is cumbersome and inflexible. It cannot easily adapt to short- or long-term changes in conditions. For example, the task-list system and minutely prescribed task-performance make it difficult to adjust work-loads when necessary by postponing or omitting less urgent or important tasks. The total demands on a ward vary considerably and at short notice according to factors like types and number of patients and operating days. The numbers and categories of student nurses also vary considerably and at short notice. Recurrent shortages of second-year or third-year nurses occur while they spend six weeks in the school; sickness or leave frequently reduce numbers. The work/staff ratio, therefore, varies considerably and often suddenly. Since work cannot easily be reduced, this generates considerable pressure, tension, and uncertainty among staff and students. Even when the work/staff ratio is satisfactory, the threat of a sudden increase is always present. The nurses seem to have a constant sense of impending crisis. They are haunted by fear of failing to carry out their duties adequately as pressure of work increases. Conversely, they rarely experience the satisfaction and lessening of anxiety that come from knowing they have the ability to carry out their work realistically and efficiently.

The nursing service is organized in a way that makes it

difficult for one person, or even a close group of people, to make a rapid and effective decision. Diffusion of responsibility prevents adequate and specific concentration of authority for making and implementing decisions. The organization of working groups makes it difficult to achieve adequate concentration of necessary knowledge. For example, the task-list system prevents the breakdown of a ward into units of a size that allows one person to be fully acquainted with what is going on in them and of a number that allows adequate communication between them and to the person responsible for co-ordinating them. In a ward, only the sister and the staff nurse are in a position to collect and coordinate knowledge. However, they must do this for a unit of such size and complexity that it is impossible to do it effectively. They are, inevitably, badly briefed. For example, we came across many cases where the sister did not remember how many nurses were on duty or what each was supposed to do, and had to have recourse to a written list. Such instances cannot be attibuted primarily to individual inadequacy. Decisions tend to be made, therefore, by people who feel that they lack adequate knowledge of relevant and ascertainable facts. This leads to both anxiety and anger. To this anxiety is added the anxiety that decisions will not be taken in time, since decision-making is made so slow and cumbersome by the system of checking and counter-checking and by the obscurity surrounding the localization of responsibility.

Excessive movement of student nurses. The fact that a rise in work/staff ratios can be met only within very narrow limits by a reduction in the work-load means that it is often necessary to have staff reinforcements, usually, to move student nurses. The defense of rigid work organization thus appears as a contributory factor to the presenting problem of student-allocation. The unduly frequent moves cause considerable distress and anxiety. Denial of the importance of relationships and feelings does not adequately protect the nurses, especially since the moves most directly affect student nurses, who have not yet fully developed these defenses. Nurses grieve and mourn over broken relationships with patients and other nurses; they feel they are failing their patients. One nurse felt compelled to return to her previous ward to visit a patient who, she felt, had depended a great deal on her. The nurse feels strange in her new surroundings. She has to learn some new duties and make relationships with new patients and staff. She probably has to nurse types of illness she has never nursed before. Until she gets to know more about the new situation she suffers anxiety, uncertainties, and doubts. Senior staff estimate that it takes a student two weeks to settle down in a new ward. We regard this as an underestimate. The suddenness of many moves increases the difficulty. It does not allow adequate time for preparing for parting and makes the parting more traumatic. Patients cannot be handed over properly to other nurses. Sudden transfers to a different ward allow little opportunity for psychological preparation for what is to come. Nurses tend to feel acutely deprived by this lack of preparation. As one girl said, 'If only I had known a bit sooner that I was going to the diabetic ward, I would have read up about diabetics and that would have helped a lot.' Janis (1958) has described how the effects of anticipated traumatic events can be alleviated if an advance opportunity is provided to work over the anxieties. He has described this as the 'work of worrying', a parallel concept to Freud's concept of the 'work of mourning' (Freud, 1949). The opportunity to work over the anticipated traumata of separation is, in the present circumstances, denied to nurses. This adds greatly to stress and anxiety.

This situation does indeed help to produce a defensive psychological detachment. Students protect themselves against the pain and anxiety of transfers, or the threat of transfers, by limiting their psychological involvement in any situation, with patients or other staff. This reduces their interest and sense of responsibility and fosters a 'don't care' attitude of which nurses and patients complain bitterly. Nurses feel anxious and guilty when they detect such feelings in themselves, and angry, hurt, and disappointed when they find them in others. 'Nobody cares how we are getting on, there is no team spirit, no one helps us.' The resulting detachment also reduces the possibility of satisfaction from work well done in a job one deeply cares about.

Under-employment of student nurses. Understandably, since work-loads are so variable and it is difficult to adjust tasks, the nursing service tries to plan its establishments to meet peak rather than average loads. As a result, student nurses quite often have too little work. They hardly ever complain of overwork and a number complained of not having enough work, although they still complained of stress. We observed obvious under-employment as we moved about the wards, in spite of the fact that student nurses are apt to make themselves look busy doing something and talk of having to look busy to avoid censure from the sister. Senior staff often seemed to feel it necessary to explain why their students were not busier, and would say they were 'having a slack day' or they 'had an extra nurse today'.

Student nurses are also chronically under-employed in terms of level of work. A number of elements in the defense system contribute to this. Consider, for example, the assignment of duties to whole categories of student nurses. Since nurses find it so difficult to tolerate inefficiency and mistakes, the level of duties for each category is pitched low, i.e. near to the expected level of the least competent nurse in the category. In addition, the policy that makes student nurses the effective nursing staff of the hospital condemns them to the repetitive performance of simple tasks to an extent far beyond that necessary for their training. The performance of simple tasks need not of itself imply that the student nurse's role is at a low level. The level depends also on how much opportunity is given for the use of discretion and judgment in the organization of the tasks — which, when, and how. It is theoretically possible to have a role in which a high level of discretion is required to organize tasks that are in themselves quite simple. In fact, the social defense system specifically minimizes the exercise of discretion and judgment in the student nurse's organization of her tasks, e.g. through the task-list system. This ultimately determines the under-employment of many student nurses who are capable of exercising a good deal of judgment and could quickly be trained to use it effectively in their work. Similar under-employment is obvious in senior staff connected, for example, with the practice of delegating upwards.

Under-employment of this kind stimulates anxiety and guilt, which are particularly acute when under-employment implies failing to use one's capacities fully in the service of other people in need. Nurses find the limitations on their performance very frustrating. They often experience a painful sense of failure when they have faithfully performed their prescribed tasks, and express guilt and concern about incidents in which they have carried out instructions to the letter, but, in so doing, have practiced what they consider to be bad nursing. For example, a nurse had been told to give a patient who had been sleeping badly a sleeping-draught at a certain time. In the interval he had fallen into a deep natural sleep. Obeying her orders, she woke him up to give him the medicine. Her common sense and judgment told her to leave him asleep and she felt very guilty that she had disturbed him. One frequently hears nurses complain that they 'have' to waken patients early in the morning to have their faces washed when they feel that the patients would benefit more by being left asleep. Patients also make strong complaints. But 'all faces must be washed' before the consultant medical staff arrive in the wards in the morning. The nurses feel they are being forced to abandon common-sense principles of good nursing, and they resent it.

Jaques (1956) has discussed the use of discretion and has come to the conclusion that the level of responsibility experienced in a job is related solely to the exercise of discretion and not to carrying out the prescribed elements. Following that statement, we may say that the level of responsibility in the nurse's job is minimized by the attempt to eliminate the use of discretion. Many student nurses complain bitterly that, while ostensibly in a very responsible job, they have less responsibility than they had as senior schoolgirls. They feel insulted, indeed almost assaulted, by being deprived of the opportunity to be more responsible. They feel, and are, devalued by the social system. They are intuitively aware that the further development of their capacity for responsibility is being inhibited by the work and training situation and they greatly resent this. The bitterness of the experience is intensified because they are constantly being exhorted to behave responsibly, which, in the ordinary usage of the word in a work-situation, they can hardly do. In fact, we came to the conclusion that senior staff tend to use the word 'responsibility' differently from ordinary usage. For them, a 'responsible' nurse is one who carried out prescriptions to the letter. There is an essential conflict between staff and students that greatly adds to stress and bitterness on both sides. Jaques (1956) has stated that workers in industry cannot rest content until they have reached a level of work that deploys to the full their capacity for discretionary responsibility. Student nurses, who are, in effect, 'workers' in the hospital for most of their time, are certainly not content.

Deprivation of personal satisfactions. The nursing service seems to provide unusually little in the way of direct satisfaction for staff and students. Although the dictum 'nursing should be a vocation' implies that nurses should not expect ordinary job satisfaction, its absence adds to stress. Mention has already been made of a number of ways in which nurses are deprived of positive satisfactions potentially existent in the profession, e.g. the satisfaction and reassurance that come from confidence in nursing skill. Satisfaction is also reduced by the attempt to evade anxiety by splitting up the nurse-patient relationship and converting patients who need nursing into tasks that must be performed. Although the nursing *service* has considerable success in nursing patients, the individual nurse has little direct experience of success. Success and satisfaction are dissipated in much the same way as the anxiety. The nurse misses the reassurance of seeing a patient get better in a way she can easily connect with her own efforts. The nurse's longing for this kind of experience is shown in the excitement and pleasure felt by a nurse who is chosen to 'special' a patient, i.e. to give special, individual care to a very ill patient in a crisis situation. The gratitude of patients, an important reward for nurses, is also dissipated. Patients are grateful to the hospital or to 'the nurses' for their treatment and recovery, but they cannot easily express gratitude in any direct way to individual nurses. There are too many and they are too mobile. The poignancy of the situation is increased by the expressed aims of nursing at the present time, i.e. to nurse the whole patient as a person. The nurse is instructed to do that, it is usually what she wants to do, but the functioning of the nursing service makes it impossible.

Sisters, too, are deprived of potential satisfactions in their roles. Many of them would like closer contact with patients and more opportunity to use their nursing skills directly. Much of their time is spent in initiating and training student nurses who come to their wards. The excessive movement of students means that sisters are frequently deprived of the return on that training time and the reward of seeing the nurse develop under their supervision. The reward of their work, like the nurse's, is dissipated and impersonal.

The nursing service inhibits in a number of ways the realization of satisfactions in relationships with colleagues. For example, the traditional relationship between staff and students is such that students are singled out by staff almost solely for reprimand or criticism. Good work is taken for granted and little praise given. Students complain that no one notices when they work well, when they stay late on duty, or when they do some extra task for a patient's comfort. Work-teams are notably impermanent. Even three-monthly moves of student nurses would make it difficult to weld together a strong, cohesive work-team. The more frequent moves, and the threats of moves, make it almost impossible. In such circumstances, it is difficult to build a team that functions effectively on the basis of real knowledge of the strengths and weaknesses of each member, her needs as well as her contribution, and adapts to the way of working and type of relationship each person prefers. Nurses feel hurt and resentful about the lack of importance attached to their personal contribution to the work, and the work itself is less satisfying when it must be done not only in accordance with the task-list system but also with an informal, but rigid, organization. A nurse misses the satisfaction of investing her own personality thoroughly in her work and making a highly personal contribution. The 'depersonalization' used as a defense makes matters worse. The implied disregard of her own needs and capacities is distressing to the nurse, she feels she does not matter and no one cares what happens to her. This is particularly distressing when she is in a situation fraught with risks and difficulty and knows that sooner or later she will have great need of help and support.

Such support for the individual is notably lacking throughout the whole nursing service within working relationships. Compensation is sought in intense relationships with other nurses off-duty[27]. Working-groups are characterized by great isolation of their members. Nurses frequently do not know what other members of their team are doing or even what their formal duties are; indeed, they often do not know whether other members of their team are on duty or not. They pursue their own tasks with minimal regard to colleagues. This leads to frequent difficulties between nurses. For example, one nurse, in carrying out her own tasks correctly by the prescription, may undo work done by another nurse also carrying out her tasks correctly by the prescription, because they do not plan their work together and coordinate it. Bad feeling usually follows. One nurse may be extremely busy while another has not enough to do. Sharing out

---

27 By tradition a nurse finds her closest nurse friends in her set, i.e. the group with which she started training. Friendship between nurses in different sets is culturally unacceptable. But nurses in the same set spend little working time together except in their short spells in formal instruction.

of work is rare. Nurses complain bitterly about this situation. They say 'there is no team spirit, no one helps you, no one cares'. They feel guilty about not helping and angry about not being helped. They feel deprived by the lack of close, responsible, friendly relations with colleagues. The training-system, orientated as it is to information-giving, also deprives the student nurse of support and help. She feels driven to acquire knowledge and pass examinations, to become 'a good nurse', while at the same time she feels few people show real concern for her personal development and her future.

The lack of personal support and help is particularly painful for the student nurse as she watches the care and attention given to patients. It is our impression that a significant number of nurses enter the profession under a certain confusion about their future roles and functions. They perceive the hospital as an organization particularly well-equipped to deal with dependency needs, kind and supportive, and they expect to have the privilege of being very dependent themselves. However, because of the categorization, they find that they are denied the privilege except on very rare occasions, notably when they go sick themselves and are nursed in the hospital.

I go on now to consider the second general approach to the failure of the social defenses to alleviate anxiety. This arises from the direct impact of the social defense system on the individual, regardless of specific experiences, i.e. from the more directly psychological interaction between the social defense system and the individual nurse.

Although, following Jaques, I have used the term 'social defense system' as a construct to describe certain features of the nursing service as a continuing social institution, I wish to make it clear that I do not imply that the nursing service *as an institution* operates the defenses. Defenses are, and can be, operated only by individuals. Their behavior is the link between their psychic defenses and the institution. Membership necessitates an adequate degree of matching between individual and social defense systems. I will not attempt to define the degree but state simply that if the discrepancy between social and individual defense systems is too great, some breakdown in the individual's relation with the institution is inevitable. The form of breakdown varies, but, in our society, it commonly takes the form of a temporary or permanent break in the individual's membership. For example, if the individual continues to use his own defenses and follows his own idiosyncratic behavior patterns, he may become intolerable to other members of the institution who are more adapted to the social defense system. They may then reject him. If he tries to behave in a way consistent with the social defense system rather than his individual defenses, his anxiety will increase and he may find it impossible to continue his membership. Theoretically, matching between social and individual defenses can be achieved by a re-structuring of the social defense system to match the individual, by a restructuring of the individual defense system to match the social, or by a combination of the two. The processes by which an adequate degree of matching is achieved are too complicated to describe here in detail. It must suffice to say that they depend heavily on repeated projection of the psychic defense system into the social defense system and repeated introjection of the social defense system into the psychic defense sytem. This allows continuous testing of match and fit as the individual experiences his own and other people's reactions.[28]

The social defense system of the nursing service has been described as an historical development through collusive interaction between individuals to project and reify relevant elements of their psychic defense systems. However, from the point of view of the new entrant to the nursing service, the social defense system at the time of entry is a datum, an aspect of external reality to which she must react and adapt. Fenichel makes a similar point (1946). He states that social institutions arise through the efforts of human beings to satisfy their needs, but that social institutions then become external realities comparatively independent of individuals which affect the structure of the individual. The student nurse is faced with a particularly difficult task in adapting to the nursing service and developing an adequate match between the social defense system and her psychic defense system. It will have been made clear that the nursing service is very resistant to change, especially change in the functioning of its defense system. For the student nurse, this means that the social defense system is to an unusual extent immutable. In the process of matching between the psychic and social defense systems, the emphasis is heavily on the modification of the individual's psychic defenses. This means in practice that she must incorporate and operate the social defense system more or less as she finds it, restructuring her psychic defenses as necessary to match it.

An earlier section described how the social defense system of the hospital was built of primitive psychic defenses, those characteristic of the earliest phases of infancy. It follows that student nurses, by becoming members of the nursing service, are required to incorporate and use primitive psychic defenses, at least in those areas of their life-space which directly concern their work. The use of such defenses has certain intrapsychic consequences. These are consistent with the social phenomena already referred to in other contexts in this paper. I will describe them briefly to complete the account. These defenses are oriented to the violent, terrifying situations of infancy, and rely heavily on violent splitting which dissipates the anxiety. They avoid the experience of anxiety and effectively prevent the individual from confronting it. Thus, the individual cannot bring

---

28 Paula Heimann (1952) gives a description of these important processes, through which both psychic and external reality are modified.

the content of the phantasy anxiety situations into effective contact with reality. Unrealistic or pathological anxiety cannot be differentiated from realistic anxiety arising from real dangers. Therefore, anxiety tends to remain permanently at a level determined more by the phantasies than by the reality. The forced introjection of the hospital defense system, therefore, perpetuates in the individual a considerable degree of pathological anxiety.

The enforced introjection and use of such defenses also interferes with the capacity for symbol formation. The defenses inhibit the capacity for creative, symbolic thought, for abstract thought and for conceptualization. They inhibit the full development of the individual's understanding, knowledge, and skills that enable reality to be handled effectively and pathological anxiety mastered. Thus the individual feels helpless in the face of new or strange tasks or problems. The development of such capacities presupposes considerable psychic integration, which the social defense system inhibits. It also inhibits self-knowledge and understanding and with them realistic assessment of performance. The deficient reality sense that follows from the defense system also interferes with judgment and provokes mistakes. The individual is confronted with them when it is too late and a sense of failure, increased self-distrust, and anxiety ensue. For example, mistakes, guilt, and anxiety arise from following out the prescriptions rather than applying the principles of good nursing. This situation particularly affects belief and trust in positive impulses and their effectiveness to control and modify aggression. Anxiety about positive aspects of the personality is very marked in nurses, e.g. fear of doing the wrong thing, expectation of mistakes, fear of not being truly responsible. The social defenses prevent the individual from realizing to the full her capacity for concern, compassion, and sympathy; and for action based on these feelings which would strengthen her belief in the good aspects of herself and her capacity to use them. The defense system strikes directly, therefore, at the roots of sublimatory activities in which infantile anxieties are re-worked in symbolic form and modified.

In general, one may say that forced introjection of the defense system prevents the personal defensive maturation that alone allows for the modification of the remnants of infantile anxiety and diminishes the extent to which early anxieties may be re-evoked and projected into current real situations. Indeed, in many cases, it forces the individual to regress to a maturational level below that which she had achieved before she entered the hospital. In this, the nursing service fails its individual members desperately. It seems clear that a major motivational factor in the choice of nursing as a career is the wish to have the opportunity to develop the capacity for sublimatory activities in the nursing of the sick, and through that to achieve better mastery of infantile anxiety situations, modification of pathological anxiety, and personal maturation.

It may be interesting, in view of this, to add one further comment on wastage. It seems more serious than number alone suggests. It appears to be the more mature students who find the conflict between their own and the hospital defense system most acute and are most likely to give up training. Although the research objectives did not permit us to collect statistics, it is our distinct impression that among the students who do not complete training are a significant number of the better student, i.e. those who are personally most mature and most capable of intellectual, professional, and personal development with appropriate training. Nurses often talked of students who had left as 'very good nurses'. No one could understand why they had not wanted to finish their training. We had the opportunity to discuss the matter with some students who were seriously considering leaving. Many said they still wanted to nurse and found it difficult to formulate why they wanted to leave. They suffered from a vague sense of dissatisfaction with their training and the work they were doing and a sense of hopelessness about the future. The general content of the interviews left little doubt that they were distressed about the inhibition of their personal development. There is also a striking difference in the personalities of groups of students at different stages of training. We do not attribute all of this difference to the effects of training. Some of the differences appear to arise from self-selection of students to give up training. If we are correct in this impression, the social defense system impoverishes the nursing service for the future, since it tends to drive away those potential senior staff whose contribution to the development of nursing theory and practice would be greatest. Thus the wheel turns full circle and the difficulty in changing the system is reinforced. It is the tragedy of the system that its inadequacies drive away the very people who might remedy them.

SUMMARY AND CONCLUDING COMMENTS

This paper has presented some data from a study of the nursing service of a general teaching hospital. Its specific purpose was to consider and, if possible, account for the high level of stress and anxiety chronic among nurses. In following through the data, it was suggested that the nature of the nurse's task, in spite of its obvious difficulties, was not enough to account for the level of anxiety and stress. Consequently, an attempt was made to understand and illustrate the nature of the methods the nursing service provided for the alleviation of anxiety, i.e. its social defense system, and to consider in what respects it failed to function adequately. The conclusion reached was that the social defense system represented the institutional-ization of very primitive psychic defense mechanisms, a main characteristic of which is that they facilitate the evasion of anxiety, but contribute little to its true modification and reduction.

In concluding, I wish to touch briefly on a few points that space does not permit me to elaborate. I have considered only incidentally the effect of the defense system on the efficiency of task performance, apart from stating that it does permit the continuing performance of the primary task of the service. It will have been apparent, however, that the nursing service carries out its task inefficiently in many respects, e.g. it keeps the staff/patient ratio unduly high, it leads to a significant amount of bad nursing practice, it leads to excessive staff turnover, and it fails to train students adequately for their real future roles. There are many other examples. Further, the high level of anxiety in nurses adds to the stress of illness and hospitalization for patients and has adverse effects on such factors as recovery rates. A recent investigation (Revans, 1959) has connected recovery rates of patients quite directly with the morale of nursing staff. Thus the social structure of the nursing service is defective not only as a means of handling anxiety, but also as a method of organizing its tasks. These two aspects cannot be regarded as separate. The inefficiency is an inevitable consequence of the chosen defense system.

This leads me to put forward the proposition that the success and viability of a social institution are intimately connected with the techniques it uses to contain anxiety. Analogous hypotheses about the individual have long been widely accepted. Freud put forward such ideas increasingly as his work developed (1948). The work of Melanie Klein and her colleagues has given a central position to anxiety and the defenses in personality development and ego-functioning (1948b). I put forward a second proposition, which is linked with the first, namely, that an understanding of this aspect of the functioning of a social institution is an important diagnostic and therapeutic tool in facilitating social change. Bion (1955) and Jaques (1955) stress the importance of understanding these phenomena and relate difficulties in achieving social change to difficulty in tolerating the anxieties that are released as social defenses are restructured. This appears closely connected with the experiences of people, including many social scientists, who have tried to initiate or facilitate social change. Recommendations or plans for change that seem highly appropriate from a rational point of view are ignored, or do not work in practice. One difficulty seems to be that they do not sufficiently take into account the common anxieties and the social defenses in the institution concerned, nor provide for the therapeutic handling of the situation as change takes place. Jaques (1955) states that 'effective social change is likely to require analysis of the common anxieties and unconscious collusions underlying the social defenses determining phantasy social relationships'.

The nursing service presents these difficulties to a high

degree, since the anxieties are already very acute and the defense system both primitive and ineffectual. Efforts to initiate serious change were often met with acute anxiety and hostility, which conveyed the idea that the people concerned felt very threatened, the threat being of nothing less than social chaos and individual breakdown. To give up known ways of behavior and embark on the unknown were felt to be intolerable. In general, it may be postulated that resistance to social change is likely to be greatest in institutions whose social defense systems are dominated by primitive psychic defense mechanisms, those which have been collectively described by Melanie Klein as the paranoid-schizoid defenses (Klein, 1952a, 1959). One may compare this socio-therapeutic experience with the common experience in psycho-analytic therapy, that the most difficult work is with patients whose defenses are mainly of this kind, or in phases of the analysis when such defenses predominate.

Some therapeutic results were achieved in the hospital, notably in relation to the presenting symptom. A planned set of courses has been prepared for student nurses, which jointly ensures that the student nurses have adequate training and that the hospital is adequately staffed. Interestingly, it was in preparing these courses that objective data were calculated for the first time about discrepancies between training and staffing needs. For example, to give adequate gynecological training the gynecological wards would have to carry four times too many staff; to keep the operating theaters staffed, the nurses would have to have one and a half times too much theater experience for training. Before this time, the existence of such discrepancies was known, but no one had collected reliable statistical data, a simple matter, and no realistic plans had been made to deal with them. To prevent emergencies from interfering with the implementation of the planned courses, a reserve pool of nurses was created whose special duty was to be mobile and deal with them. A number of other similar changes were instituted dealing with other problems that emerged in the course of the investigation . The common features of the changes, however, were that they involved minimal disturbance of the existing defense system. Indeed, it would be more correct to say that they involved reinforcing and strengthening the existing type of defense. Proposals were made for more far-reaching change, involving a restructuring of the social defense system. For example, one suggestion was that a limited experiment be done in ward organization, eliminating the task-list system and substituting some form of patient assignment. However, although the senior staff discussed such proposals with courage and seriousness, they did not feel able to proceed with the plans. This happened in spite of our clearly expressed views that, unless there were some fairly radical changes in the system, the problems of the nursing service might well become extremely serious. The decision seemed· to us quite comprehensible, however, in view of the anxiety and the defense system. These would have made the therapeutic task of accomplishing change very difficult for both the nursing service and the therapist.

The full seriousness of the situation is not perhaps clear without considering this hospital in the context of the general nursing services in the country as a whole. The description of the hospital makes it seem a somewhat serious example of social pathology, but within the context of other general hospital nurse-training schools it is fairly typical. Nothing in our general experience of hospitals and nursing leads us to believe otherwise (Skellern, 1953; Sofer, 1955; Wilson, 1950). There are differences in detail, but the main features of the structure and culture are common to British hospitals of this type and are carried in the general culture and ethic of the nursing profession. The hospital studied has, in fact, high status. It is accepted as being one of the better hospitals of its type.

The nursing services in general have shown a similar resistance to change in the face of great changes in the demands made on them. There can be few professions that have been more studied than nursing, or institutions more studied than hospitals. Nurses have played an active part in initiating and carrying out these studies. Many nurses have an acute and painful awareness that their profession is in a serious state. They eagerly seek solutions, and there have been many changes in the expressed aims and policy of the profession. There have also been many changes in the peripheral areas of nursing, i.e. those which do not impinge very directly or seriously on the essential features of the social defense system. Against that background, one is astonished to find how little basic and dynamic change has taken place. Nurses have tended to receive reports and recommendations with a sense of outrage and to react to them by intensifying current attitudes and reinforcing existing practice.

An example of a general nursing problem that threatens crisis is the recruitment of nurses. Changes in medical practice have increased the number of highly technical tasks for nurses. Consequently, the level of intelligence and competence necessary for a fully trained and efficient nurse is rising. The National Health Service has improved the hospital service and made it necessary to have more nurses. On the other hand, professional opportunities for women are expanding rapidly and the other professions are generally more rewarding than nursing in terms of the opportunity to develop and exercise personal and professional capacities as well as in financial terms. The increasing demand for high-level student nurses is therefore meeting increasing competition from other sources. In fact, recruiting standards are being forced down in order to keep up numbers. This is no real solution, for too many of the recruits will have difficulty in passing the examinations and be unable to deal with the level of the work. Many of them, on the other hand, would make excellent practical nurses on simpler nursing duties.

So far, no successful attempt has been made in the general hospitals to deal with this problem, e.g. by splitting the role of the nurse into different levels with different training and different professional destinations.

It is unfortunately true of the paranoid-schizoid defense systems that they prevent true insight into the nature of problems and realistic appreciation of their seriousness. Thus, only too often, no action can be taken until a crisis is very near or has actually occurred. This is the eventuality we fear in the British general hospital nursing services. Even if there is no acute crisis, there is undoubtedly a chronic state of reduced effectiveness, which in itself is serious enough.

D
Architecture, Design and Planning

18.
IRRATIONAL ASPECTS OF DESIGN

Arthur D. Colman

The purpose of this paper is to explore some irrational processes which influence physical and social design. Irrational process in design is here viewed as interpersonal and interactional events which play a significant role in a design task despite their lack of rational relationship to its overt or its guiding concepts.

Irrational process in design can be divided into two categories:

1. *Basic Assumptions:* those processes which affect the design task by functioning outside of the awareness of the participating individuals or groups: the personal and group unconscious, and the stereotypic cultural archetypes which influence our behavior in subterranean and *unacknowledged* ways.

2. *Covert Politics:* the social field of alliances, pressure groups, and power influences operating within the design process in *unexamined* ways, unrelated to the overtly stated design determinants. The covert political influences are of course not irrational in themselves, for they usually serve the conscious self interest of individuals or groups. They are considered here as irrational in relation to the design task only. However, their influence on a design may be as bizarre as the most primitive basic assumptions in producing a social and physical structure which has little to do with objective plans for the project and the people it is supposed to serve.

These two categories of irrational processes, the Basic Assumptions and Covert Politics, are linked together by their tendency to exert a surreptitious effect on the overt design task and its determinants. That is not to say that their influence on the design process is necessarily negative. But they are unacknowledged and unexamined, and as such can make a mockery of the rational aspects of the design process, as well as undermine the creative use both of the rational and irrational in the design process. Everyone participating in the developing plans and structures has at one time or another *felt* powerful, personal and interactive processes unrelated to the task, which inexorably change the direction of decisions made despite a continued pretence at rational attention to task. They have also felt the impact of unspoken political influencing processes on key decisions despite pretence at social responsibility and task orientation. It is no wonder then that participants in a design process so often finish with a sense of despair and irresponsibility, experiencing themselves as engaging in a fruitless exercise in which the really important influences are viewed as ''beyond their control''.

BASIC ASSUMPTIONS IN DESIGN

Basic assumptions describe those kinds of irrational processes which have begun to be elucidated through the depth psychologies of Freud, Bion, and Jung. Studies uncovered the unconscious personal group and cultural forces, the hidden motives and assumptions underlying human behavior which are projected into man's words, work and creations, though often under the cover of more overt and rational rubrics.

Design tasks are rarely one individual's responsibility; more usually they require the collaboration of a group or a series of groups. For this reason the study of covert dynamics operating (such as covert processes in work groups and between work groups in organizations) is most vital here (Miller and Rice, 1967; Bion, 1959). Bion describes two levels of work group experience: firstly rational, task oriented, behavior such as gathering data, processing information, and decision making, and secondly, ''Basic Assumption'' behavior. Basic Assumption behavior in a group refers to irrational premises shared by the members of the group who operate towards one another and the outside world ''as if'' these premises were true.

For example a Basic Assumption dependency group operates as if there is a leader who is omnipotent and omniscient, someone who will take care of the group and its needs, who will take responsibility for all of the group's actions thereby taking away each member's collective responsibility for what happens. Another Basic Assumption group is the ''fight'' group whose members operate as if integrity and survival is only possible if they can find an enemy ''outside'' their own group boundary to oppose and destroy. The leader of a fight group is chosen for his ability to accept this assumption uncritically and lead them effectively into battle. The group's work task and work related actions are compromised to the extent to which they are dominated by basic assumption thinking and behaving. For example, a dependency group may covertly set its task as protecting and preserving the leader's invulnerability even if he or she is thereby rendered incapable of performing competently as a work leader. Or, a fight group may change its original work task to one of conquering new territory, defending itself, real or imagined, or destroying these "enemies". The most important theoretical point is the assertion that Basic Assumptions operate in the "group as a whole", or in an institution or organization composed of various combinations of interrelating groups. The important practical point is the effect of these assumptions on the process and progress of a group overtly involved in a work task, which may be severely hampered or even subverted by basic assumption behavior no matter what the dedication of the individual members.

Group relations theory spanning such diverse areas as education, industrial management and psychiatric treatment, has extended the assumption of irrationality beyond the "individual unconscious" to include groups, and complex group systems (Richardson, 1967; Astrachan, Flynn, Geller and Harvey, 1970). Application of Basic Assumptions to design seems inevitable and has already begun (Tepper, Duddy and Colman, 1972; Colman, 1971; Colman, 1973). Their impact on the design process can be thought of as beginning in the hidden motivations of involved individuals and extending to groups, organizations and community in an even more complicated matrix of irrational social function.

For example, Basic Assumptions might be reflected in the design process when an individual transforms his fear of lack of personal identity into structural forms emphasizing clearly delineated authority, or concrete enclosures. Basic Assumptions might be displayed when a planning group, unwilling to take individual responsibility, defers and blindly depends on a Leader or Expert who assumes supercompetence. Or, a group might find itself unable to use leadership or expertise available in the group because of lack of trust and fear of delegating authority even if doing so could add to their knowledge and creativity. The basic assumption of intergroup behavior might be reflected in jealousy and distrust among competing subgroups affecting decision-making in community and city planning. More generally cultural myths and belief systems anchored in the structure and language of a society might unknowingly bind imagination and prevent the consideration of a new perspective on a design problem.

The influences of irrational processes, whether on a personal, group, or cultural level, are extremely difficult to study. They happen, by definition, out of continued awareness. Their importance can really only be recognized afterward, a recognition which is often manifested in a feeling of disbelief at the final outcome of the design process. After the fact analysis of a poorly advised group decision, an ugly, inadequate building, or an unworkable social program, all despite the best overt intentions of the participants, sometimes brings the Basic Assumptions into focus and may make the faulty design processes more understandable. And then of course it is too late, both for the people caught in the developed structure and for the scapegoats who are blamed for its design.

COVERT POLITICS IN DESIGN

In all of us there is great resistance to assigning influence to the unknown. Therefore, the existence of Basic Assumptions and their impact on design can be played down easily because they are *unconscious* processes. In this case we know not what we do. Sometimes, however, we influence in a far more disturbing way with *what is known but cannot be said*. So it is with the influence of Covert Politics in social processes including design. It is not as if knowledge about the pervasive influence of factors such as secret personal relationships, sexual intrigues, personal and group "power trips", special economic interests, and factional ideological struggle on the design processes supposedly based on more "rational" grounds is not embarrassingly available to some of those involved. But it is far safer to deal with the more objective work related variables such as technical requirements, economic constraints, aesthetic considerations and even user group inputs than delve openly into the Pandora's Box of informal relationships which *really* determine what happens. Such influences are almost never included in the measurements, surveys and program evaluation although they often determine which studies are done, which consultants are hired, and which data is given influence in the decision making process. (In fact Covert Politics often function through cooperation of technical and scientific personnel and paradigms as both C.P. Snow and Thomas Kuhn have described from different vantage points) (Snow; Kuhn, 1965).

All political influence in design is not hidden from view. *Overt* political force can, and often is used to influence decisions of consequence to varying interest groups. For example, various user groups who will be affected by the building of a new hospital may attempt to pressure directly the planning group or architects who are responsible for the design. The relative importance assigned by the architectural firm to the patients, the medical professionals, community groups or the board of directors in their preliminary programs for the hospital is a very important design determinant. To the extent that such debate is open, some rational consideration can be given to establishing priorities and developing modes of accommodation and compromise between the various concerned factions. Special individuals with great authority can dictate their wishes openly through blatant use of power. In designing their palaces or their prisons, Herod, or Nero, or Hitler could implement their wishes by fiat. Such power is rare in an area which relies heavily on groups and committees for making and ratifying its most important decisions. Now it is the hidden agenda and hidden alliances which serve as a conduit for special groups whose interests are either unrelated or skewed from the most rational design determinants.

To be effective, Covert Politics is absolutely dependent on secretive relationships. Whenever secrets are revealed, be they hidden agendas or clandestine alliances, they lose a great deal of their motive force. When I was in college and medical school in Boston in the late 1950's and early 1960's, each public works project, whether tunnel, freeway or underground parking garage, was punctuated by a scandal, but always after the structural changes were made permanent. Only once can I remember the scandal breaking before construction was begun. The plan had been to remove a picturesque, historic firehouse in Cambridge to add a new road which could have benefited a few well connected merchants. On that occasion the project was halted for fear of overt political action by angry voters.

The influences of Covert Political process on design is as difficult to study as the influence of Basic Assumptions, but for different reasons. The unconscious, out of continued awareness processes of the latter are replaced here with conscious fear of others. Exposure of corruption, of collusion, even of a minor special relationship results in legitimate fear of recriminations from the accused and the more complex fear of self-exposure. And so even the most ''open secrets'' are overlooked. Occasionally the effect of the hidden relationships becomes so detrimental to the work task, that hidden issues no longer can comfortably be ignored. More rarely, a person takes personal responsibility for saying what he knows and usually, unless he is blameless as a Ralph Nader, he is crucified for his bravery.

The figure below is a summary of the general variables affecting design.

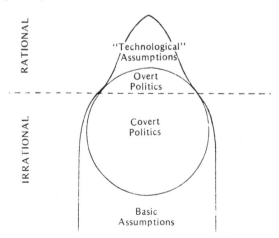

FIGURE 14: Process Model of Components in a Design Task

In any given problem, the irrational behavioral subsystems represented by the categories of Covert Politics and Basic Assumptions are related to each other and to the overt or rational parameters through their effect on the design task. The similarity of this model to the oft quoted iceberg metaphor is deliberate. The rational design parameter such as technical problems, and economic constraints, and the overt politics such as user group considerations, and local and national policy priorities, are the highly visible issues around which the design process evolves. The irrational influences have their effect from behind the scenes and beyond awareness; the extent of this influence changes with the type of design task undertaken. The technical, economic and artistic considerations may become paramount in the simpler conflict-free programs, when territory and power are not at issue. As the stakes are raised and involved individuals or groups vie with each other for control, the surface view of the process no longer adequately describes the design process and "subterranean" variables become more critical.

THE DESIGNER AND THE DESIGN PROCESS

This view of the irrational determinants of the design process may seem both unnecessary and overly vague to the designing professional. The architect and the planner view themselves first and foremost as practical problem solvers. What relevance does this kind of analysis have to a professional already overwhelmed by technical and aesthetic intricacy and change? What is unique about the design process and why is it singled out for an analysis emphasizing irrationality?

My own conviction is that there are unique processes operating in design and on design professionals which make it difficult for them to look beyond the immediate pragmatic and practical variables affecting their work. In other words, they are particularly prone to the impact of the irrational. Related to this functional myopia is the reluctance of many other professionals who design systems to label themselves as "designers" even though they function in this capacity. The first priority in using the process model for an analysis of design functions is a reevaluation of who actually constitute today's design profession, and what are their functions.

The most common usage for the word *design* relates to the rearrangement of physical elements to serve an aesthetic or functional purpose. This is the sense in which it is used in most "Schools of Design" where the design professionals—architects, planners, designers—are trained. Yet the concept of design in most generic sense has traditionally held loftier perspectives.

In theological terms, the Grand Design referred to the belief in a universe that manifested Divine forethought as a proof of the intelligence of a Creator. In other usages, design relates to a conception of a plan or program to be carried out through action according to a preconceived fashion. Design used in this way has had nefarious connotations which perhaps explains the current tendency to limit the word to physical and artistic creations. A design is often thought of as a preconceived plan or *scheme* to be foisted upon unwilling and unconsenting participants. The fear of and fascination with designing environments is related to the juxtaposition of the image of a Grand Design created by Godly forces beyond our control and the cunning Machiavellian schemer whose plans operate despite all thwarting efforts.

Psychiatry is interested in design and the nature of the designing process from the two viewpoints of studying pathogenic environments which reinforce maladaptive behavior, and studying therapeutic environments which reinforce a change to more adaptive behavior. For example, the past decade has seen an enormous amount of research directed towards the family environment and its capacity to support (or create) schizophrenic symptoms in one of its members. These studies have helped move behavioral science beyond direct cause and effect relationships. Concepts which emphasize a pathogenic parent, the much maligned schizophrenic mother, have given way to those which emphasize an interdependent family dynamics, viewing the role of the victim or ''sick one'' as playing an important equilibrating function in the family constellation. For example, if a ''sick'' member of the family leaves this matrix, (to a hospital, or a ''flight into health''), another member may take his or her place as the ''sick one'', thus maintaining the system's stability. There is rarely an overt malice or deliberateness in the behavior of these families or a *conscious design* by family members. These parents often have the best of intentions and most positive goals for their children. The design is not explicit but covert. By teasing out the hidden assumptions and conflicts in family roles and interactions, and by relating these patterns to the stated family aims, the ''design'' process for the current family structure becomes understandable as to its ''products'', no matter how maladaptive.

Studies of attempts in the mental health professions to create therapeutic environments capable of supporting positive changes in the behavior and attitudes of others, have suggested similar complex design mechanisms at work.

To begin with, there is usually a stated therapy model which claims efficacy in accomplishing a treatment goal. This model then determines the design of a treatment system, be it a psychoanalytic emphasis on individual therapy or reinforcement systems based on operant conditioning. There is usually a group of people who openly support the treatment systems proposed and who actively help design the program according to its principles.

However, an observer studying the actual design and operation of the environment usually tells a very different story of how things happened. Often the program's leader is involved in professional or hospital politics. The particular system chosen usually relates more to his personal prestige and power in relationship to his peers than to demonstrated efficacy with a particular group of patients in specific treatment. Staff loyalty might reflect fear for job security or advancement rather than dedication to task or system. Group dependency, the authority structure, and special personality patterns of key individuals may all prominently affect the final shape and structure of the program. The covert politics, personal and group dynamics, and all the irrational elements of the design task play a more critical role in the design of a therapeutic program than the more rational parameters which are openly espoused.

Stripped down to the essential elements, the design process in a family structure, a therapeutic system, a house, or an urban redevelopment project is remarkably similar. Of these four constructions, however, only the architect will agree to be considered *the designer*. Most men and women who begin a family would be very ambivalent indeed about a "family designer" role and the responsibility such a self definition entails. They would feel instead that they were entering into a system whose outlines were already broadly "drawn in" by forces beyond their control. In one sense they would be correct, for the family is a system little open to change by its participants. Behavior and roles are stereotyped both by cultural expectation and by childhood experience. Yet some couples of today (as in every generation) are not willing to accept this "family design". They think of themselves as social engineers and attempt to remodel their own families according to a different program, one of their own making. However, the covert program for family design is not ignored. Despite a new set of overt social ideologies, communes often look and behave like suburbs without walls, and "multiple families" are modern translations of the poverty motivated larger households of two or three generations ago. That is not to say that new forms cannot develop out of generational conflict. But the rarity with which this happens despite hundreds and thousands of attempts attests to the power of the hidden agenda and personal family history over the designers.

Until very recently psychiatrists and other professionals in the mental health field have resisted perceiving their designer role. The role of design professional is hardly consonant with the self image of the therapist whose concern is to fathom and guide the personal communication of Inner Man. Nevertheless, the community mental health movement has forced this perception upon them. To the extent that they have taken this additional role seriously, they too have found the task of designing a different therapeutic system in response to newly defined needs more difficult than first supposed. A good example is the heavily funded Community Mental Health Centers Program, planned to change the forms and control of care to fit the local situation. Most planning boards for these centers realized that a more participatory structure was necessary if the needs of the community were truly to be served. However, the combination of the affinity of physicians for control and the extraordinary dependency needs of the lay world for physician authority, time and again outweighed the best rational plans for a design other than the traditional clinic mode. As a result of these forces miniature "university type" physical and social organizations were transplanted into environments which might have better used a different design. Despite relatively good intentions of the professionals it often took violent means on both sides to change this design.

The same kind of process has been evident among many other professionals involved in design problems. The psychiatrist designing a storefront neighborhood treatment center in an urban slum, the educator planning an experimental college or classroom, the health professional organizing community medical facilties and the architect-planner blueprinting a model city or suburban tract are faced with very much the same process and problems in their design task. In the common aspects of their work, one is little more a "designer" than another, if function rather than historical image or social labeling is considered.

IRRATIONAL PROCESS IN ARCHITECTURAL DESIGN

At the very center of the design process is the creation of new form in space. The form may be social or physical - and usually is both. A new table of organization is reflected in new spatial arrangements both symbolically in terms of interpersonal relationships with each other and in the actual mundane room assignments. A new building creates barriers which include and exclude, creating a caste system controlling rewards and punishments.

Boundaries, both physical and social, emphasize difference with resulting competition and status hierarchies. Boundaries support personal, group, or national identity through a definition of belonging which includes who is in and who is out. This definition is inevitably challenged, sometimes violently, and new boundary relationships are defined. In the animal world, territory and aggression are inextricably bound to one another.

It is no wonder then that the design process, the appropriation and redefinition of space, is particularly prone to the covert, and the irrational. The construction of a 50 story high rise building in Dallas or San Francisco or a new nationwide health system represents an entire new set of power hierarchies and an unleashing of powerful aggressive and competitive feelings. The designer of the system is at the center of these forces.

The enlarged perspective on design suggests a common process involving a variety of professions and is not limited by the parochial technology and constraints unique to a special field or problem. Most previous explorations of the common aspects of design focus mainly on generalities in decision making, information processing, and the logic of planning (Rittel, 1966; Studer and Stea, 1966). The importance of such studies is obvious but they leave out the special links between design and covert process and in so doing rationalize a phenomenon which is far from rational.

I have suggested that designers of social systems find it relatively easy to disclaim direct responsibility for what they build. This is particularly true in large institutions where complicated, diffuse boundaries and authority relationships seem to be the rule. One can blame "bureaucracy" without thereby blaming anyone. Many of these institutions can be understood best by assuming that their primary task is *not* education, medical care or whatever else is named on building facades. Instead, the social system is designed for the irrational primary tasks of self perpetuation and growth as ends in themselves. Responsibility for this design is difficult to trace although its guiding program is built into rules and regulations written by anonymous committees. As Townsend and others pointed out blurred boundary and authority lines prevent definition of the work task and evaluation of performance (Townsend, 1970).

The design professional, particularly the architect, is in a very different position. His products are often clearly bounded in space and time and can easily be defined and evaluated. Irrational process among the groups of people for whom they are designed may be projected directly into the physical structure, symbolically represented through its shape or size, or negatively represented through omission or over-evaluation of one user group's needs relative to another's.

Consider the following example: A physician consulted with me about a problem in his organization around the erection of a new building. He belonged to a group of 50 board certified doctors in one of the Southern States who had joined together in a partnership which had financially prospered. The doctors, their offices and hospital were housed in a group of low ranch style buildings which were suited to the surrounding built environment and the land values. They had added new buildings of similar type as they had grown.

Consultation was sought by Dr. X because of his conflict with Dr. Y, a man of 63 who had initially formed the partnership and had been its elected leader for many years. Dr. Y had proposed that a new building should be in the shape of a tall tower, and had commented on his retirement two years hence at a meeting attended by all of the partners. The message was clear. The new building was to represent a monument to the outgoing founder and leader, a kind of pyramid to his works although presumably ailing patients rather than his last remains would eventually be housed within its walls.

Dr. X emphasized the incredible expense and the impracticability of the tower for effective medical treatment. He perceived the personal aggrandizement implicit in the design but could not understand the passive acceptance of the design by so many of his fellow partners. Only a few "Young Turks" had agreed with Dr. X's strong position against the new building. Dr. X was in his middle forties, relatively young for the group, but was its largest money earner. However, his net proceeds were less than some of the older members whose share was enhanced by their seniority according to organizational by-laws.

During the course of the consultation it became clear that although the economics and medical care effectiveness of the design were the overt issues discussed, they served as cover story for the Covert Politics of the various subgroups involved. The question of succession was paramount reason. Only those who identified with Dr. X's challenge to the current leadership could listen to Dr. X's criticism of the new building. The rest saw him in direct confrontation with the leader and the "old guard" (which he probably was). This "secret" issue (and others of a similar nature) was not articulated at the general meeting of the physicians; rather it dominated countless private meetings and cabals both in and out of the hospital.

Basic Assumption factors common to large group processes and issues of succession and authority were also important in the conflict. Large groups depersonalize their members. Individuals who are used to personal recognition and face to face contact suddenly find themselves unrecognized and isolated. Reactions to this situation vary with the individual and the context. The more anxiety and identity loss are generated by the process, the more the members will search for structure and a leader to whom they can delegate the responsibility for their feelings and for what they perceive might happen if things really got out of control. This delegation process usually proceeds without proper evaluation of its effect on task, program, or the ability of the chosen one. Demagogues in every age have used this large group phenomenon in arenas, forums and sports plazas that decorated their capitals in order to gain the devoted allegiance of the masses irrespective of what personal freedom was given away in the process. Large group process creates Gods and Scapegoats; eventually, all that matters is that an individual belong to a subgroup supported by the leader and not to one that is alien and unprotected.

These processes were very much present in the doctors' group. The partners evaluated statements not by the force of their rational content but by the subgroup they came from and their relationship to pleasing or displeasing the authority. Anxiety in the group was augmented by the competition around succession. The threat posed was to the survival of the group itself, particularly since the leader and the founder were embodied in one person. The pull towards unity and deification (through a monument), a classic pattern large group interaction, was mirrored here too. In their case, it was not only irrational in relation to their overt task but potentially destructive to their more rational self interests, not to speak of the clinical interests of the patients they would treat.

What is the role of the architecture firm plunged into this vortex of unreason? More accurately, how do they avoid being scapegoated for the warring factions? It is likely that they will be only marginally aware (or interested) in the irrational process except as it relates to obtaining the design contract. They may feel obliged to comment on the technical appropriateness of the tower for medical care although doing this with any fervor might jeopardize their position with the leader and his faction. As they become more involved in the social system of the medical partnership it is likely that their design would reflect the covert process of memorialization in various ways throughout the building.

It may seem that this example is unusually slanted to the irrational interests of the participants. How often does a client suggest a particular design for a building? Shouldn't a group of doctors know better than to adopt a design whose symbolism so obviously suggests the irrational needs of the retiring leader? My own observations suggest that the process described is fairly typical of what happens in the course of designing a building. Power struggles that may have simmered on for years will *ordinarily* erupt given the potent stimuli of the design and allocated new space in a definitive structure. The need for building may itself be in part the by-product of intra-organizational conflict. New growth and expansion may provide a panacea for an organization that has lost its sense of purpose or needs to hide internal dissent. Of course, the new territory cannot in itself provide new purpose nor organizational therapy. Internal conflicts are externalized and projected onto the new building which rapidly provides yet another battlefield for warring factions. The architect, wittingly or unwittingly, is frequently in the midst of a conflict from the moment he is consulted. And as a professional he is obligated to take responsibility for what he designs, including the possibility that what he built served irrational purposes which he helped to memorialize permanently in steel and concrete.

This process of scapegoating the architect may be overt and deliberate. Black architects today are often used by those in authority as buffers and screens for the angry demands of their own race. For example, the only black man in an architectural firm was given added authority beyond that of his usual position as a draftsman, to negotiate with a black citizens' group about the design of a school. He recognized the tokenism in this maneuver but nevertheless accepted, feeling that he could help his people get a design which would better suit their needs. The clients took less responsibility for their own input into the new building because of their trust in one of their own in what they viewed to be a leadership position. The architect was seduced by their acceptance of him as "one of them" into not pressing them for their ideas and participation on the assumption that he knew what they wanted. A potentially difficult situation was thus cooled off and the black architect without real authority in the firm or real knowledge of the community he served, was left with little leverage to influence the final design.

On another occasion a prominent black architect was hired to build a large building complex in a racially mixed but predominantly black ghetto. His choice for that position was a conscious attempt by the funding agencies to calm the doubts of the community about the new building in their neighborhood. He himself felt that the money could be more appropriately used for human services rather than buried in a multimillion dollar structure of questionable value. He took the job, however, in part for his own personal aggrandizement and experience and in part to be able to influence the community's ability to get what it wanted later on by involving it in the planning process at government expense. This strategy was shared with the community leaders who agreed to the plan. The building was built and was probably relatively useless in terms of real community needs. On the other hand, leadership skills were evolved from within the neighborhood itself.

It is all but impossible to evaluate the outcome of this blending of Machiavellian politics and irrational individual and group processes. It illustrates the complex relationships between building, power and political process—here made overt by an architect who consciously used a building to design a social process.

Architects may unwittingly be drawn into covert organizational processes which may irrationally alter the programming and design tasks. An example of this kind of a subtle influencing system occurred during an intensive study of the needs of a variety of groups who would be served by a new Children's hospital. The architect spent a great deal of time in the existing hospital personally interviewing and providing questionnaires to all potentially interested groups. The definition of "interested groups" was unusually wide-ranging and included not only physicians, staff and hospital board but also commonly ignored groups, such as nurses, nurse aides, and paraprofessionals of all kinds and even the patients themselves! The selection reflected this particular architect's commitment to designing an environment that served the actual user population and included their objectives and requirements. The one group that was overlooked in the survey was the parent group. Their participation was not elicited in the hospital design and the final design program did not include specifications which particularly served their needs.

The lack of consideration of the parents in the planning of an environment for their children seems a curious oversight especially in such a sophisticated "user oriented" endeavor. Yet this omission has a strong historical background in general hospital culture. It is usual for hospital personnel to resist intrusion from outsiders no matter how relevant they are to the patient's comfort and welfare. It is true that the scientization of medicine over the past 50 years has provided important bacteriological reason for restricting visiting privileges, limiting family participation and so on. Yet technological advances work both ways and in fact where there was a commitment to family oriented medicine, ways have been found to provide significant human contact without sterilization. This kind of commitment is rare and even when programs are begun they seem unusually difficult to maintain. On the surface it is difficult to understand where the reluctance to commit the profession to such values arises and even more difficult to grasp how staff so rapidly communicated "medical" Basic Assumptions to a relatively neutral architect appraising user needs.

One way of gaining further understanding of these uses is to analyze the basic assumptions that are shared by medical organizations. A primary task of health professionals is to care for the sick and dying. In hospital practice this is often translated into presiding over desperate and hopeless situations over which they have little control despite recent advances in medical science. Pediatrics is no exception. There is no more heartbreaking situation in all of medicine than the spectre of a child with a massive birth injury, uncontrollable leukemia, or chronic dehabilitating disease searching for hope in the faces of a staff who know that no hope exists. Menzies has studied the kinds of irrational organizational processes in hospital wards that develop under severe stress (Menzies, 1967). Staff searches for rules of conduct, stereotyped roles, and hyper-professional stance which protect the individual from facing the agonizing emotions of inadequacy, helplessness and despair. They share in an irrational search for an all-knowing healer or all-powerful cure, which explains the tendency to venerate certain physicians who like to be worshipped and to call experimental drugs and procedures "miracle cures". In an effort to escape the responsibility for being unable to help and the inevitable feelings of self blame, they may project the blame elsewhere in the form of anger towards the outside referring agencies or more usually on the parents who have brought in the problems and who have to be told the truth. Excessive politeness of hospital staffs often hides barely contained rage. In the privacy of nursing stations and doctors' staffrooms conversations about how badly a child is treated at home or how erratically medicine is given are a routine part of the hospital culture. Reactive fantasies of omnipotence in the staff are balanced by feelings that everything goes wrong only when the child leaves the hospital. Occasionally this may be true and problems such as the battered child syndrome in which the parents beat their own children causing severe damage to their bodies, support the Basic Assumptions permeating the hospital system.

But assuming the veracity of this analysis, how were these irrational attitudes communicated to the architect? How as the architect "taught" not to include the parents in the user population surveyed. It is not as if the hospital overtly communicated its biases. If it had done so the architect might have been alerted to the omission and corrected it. The attitudes do not surface in ordinary questionnaires or interviews unless they are actively sought. As the architect (or other outsider) entered the hospital matrix the covert process is imbibed through myriads of non-verbal communications and indirect allusions, which can be experienced but rarely consciously processed. The influence of these cues on designers whose job is to understand the indepth requirement of their clients should not be underestimated. The more the social system is penetrated and explored, the more the personal involvement with the irrational biases grows. This process is augmented by the very role of neutral outsider who may be used as a screen for the projection of painful and dangerous feelings which exist within the institutions but are either unacknowledged or unexpressed. The outsiders may find themselves mirroring the conflicts and feelings of the various groups (a process which is used by some organizational consultants to identify core problems). The architect often becomes a scapegoat for the system by expressing its covert processes in his design. So, for example, the architect studying the Children's hospital produced a final program which formalized in design the staff's covert hostility towards the parents and a wish for their absence.

Hospital architecture is permeated by these influencing processes. The power of the physician to invoke dependency feelings around issues of sickness and death tends to diminish critical thinking about design issues. Often the covert needs of the physician rather than the welfare of the patient is best represented. For example, my own interest in the psychology of pregnancy and childbirth has made me aware of how irrational currently accepted constraints on *Birth Environment* really are. Most obstetrician's view of the pregnant woman is as a patient with an illness which he alone can terminate at the end of nine months. Another view of pregnancy is as a life cycle crisis of great impact to both man and woman, culminating in the delivery of a new child and the creation of a new family unit (A.D. Colman and L.L. Colman, 1971). A plastic and steel surgical environment may be necessary to facilitate this event but except in an emergency situation (perhaps 5-10% of pregnancies) could be designed to facilitate participants' control over their experience. The sterile "surgical module" design of the labor rooms, the exclusiveness of the delivery suite, the relative isolation of mother and infant from each other during the lying-in period and the virtual separation of the new father from this unit for several days are all designed primarily for the doctors' and nurses' benefit through the collusion of physician and architect. The language of this agreement is medical and technical but the assumptions represent the covert biases of both parties. Recent changes in the way babies are delivered including participation of the father, his inclusion into the delivery room, rooming in, are generally not supported by the hospital personnel or their technology. Rather they reflect the unwillingness of women and their husbands to accept the physicians' assumptions uncritically and their ability to search for other designs without compromising their medical care. And yet the system is perpetuated by the physical structures whose design continues to be within the hospital's medical assumptions and without the input from pregnant couples as one of the main user groups.

It is clear from these examples that the lines between the rational and irrational influence on design, basic assumptions, covert politics, overt politics, and design technology are often unclear. *Overt social action* tends to expose the covert processes which have dominated the design assumptions. What seemed an unthinkable design in the past is routine in the future. The point is that changes in design not only await new technical achievements, but also a willingness to confront the covert processes that prevent new ideas and solutions from emerging.

In the future all designers, including architects, will become more involved with the irrational aspects of institutions and groups as consultations with user groups become expected (and even legislated). Overall I believe this to be an improvement over the self image of Designer as Tarot Magician, cocky enough to project his conceptions into physical and social space without justifying his underlying motivation or examining the ways in which he is scapegoated. Yet there are disadvantages to giving up this romantic notion of professional independence and artistry. Groups and institutions have a way of sapping personal responsibility and risk taking. They can be ''man eaters''; homogenizing individual skills and holding up consensus rather than creativity as their highest value. Without courageous leadership groups easily become mired in stereotypic irrational process, resulting in excess dependence, feelings of helplessness, chaotic decision making and scapegoating. Rather than exert this kind of leadership in the face of these processes, it is often easier to compromise hardwon professional excellence with mediocrity while placing the blame solely on external factors such as economics or prevailing codes and regulations. The great challenge for the modern Designer, whatever his professional label, is to be willing to risk confronting the demon that is part of the human process of people working together. Success may depend on increasing our knowledge about the irrational processes in design rather than escaping into yet another decade of grand designs and banal structures.

19.
ENVIRONMENTAL DESIGN: REALITIES AND DELUSIONS

Arthur D. Colman

The field of environmental design, particularly the study of the environment-behavior interface, has recently gained some prominence in the academic arena, spurred notably by the media's interest in the subject. As usual, more questions are asked than answered. Can the designer of our environment become more conscious and self-determining? If so, to what goals should the design point without creating an over-planned society? When and if goals can be agreed upon by the user population, what kinds of models exist for translating these goals into physical and social realities which will support them?

The purpose of this chapter is to explore the usefulness of operant conditioning for the field of environmental design. To do this, I will attempt to 1) redefine the field of environmental design so that its behavioral effects and implications are clarified, 2) review the uses of operant conditioning as a design model for a variety of socio-physical systems, 3) explore the inadequacies of this model in its current stage of development, particularly in relationship to the problems of scale and intergroup processes, and 4) suggest some future directions for research by operant conditioners and others in the fields of behavioral sciences relating to the problem of environmental design.

THE FIELD OF ENVIRONMENTAL DESIGN

The concept of environmental design, the word design itself, is most often associated with the rearrangement of physical elements in ways which serve an aesthetic or functional purpose. Yet the concept of design is considerably broader. Webster defines it as "The deliberate and purposeful planning of a settled and coherent program for selection of a means and contriving the elements, steps and procedures, which will adequately satisfy some need" (Webster, 1965). Obviously such a definition applies to a broad range of situations, including the design of a sophisticated treatment environment for psychotics or retarded or autistic individuals, the structuring of superior learning environments for graduate students, the design of a playroom in a suburban cottage, and the design of an apartment high-rise living complex.

The word environment is equally restrictive in its current usage. Environment tends to be thought of as land, ocean, water

329

— the external non-living envelope that encloses our lives and behavior. In this view, man is seen as external to his environment, except insofar as his tools and waste products add to its dimensions. Such a dichotomy is perceptively false. Recent work has introduced the term of *social space* into the vocabulary of the behavioral sciences, a concept which suggests the possibility of a useful comparison between physical and social dimensions of our perceptual reality. The work of Hall (1966) and Sommer (1969) in the use of space in everyday behavior and Calhoun (1966) and DeLauwe (1965) on the psychopathology of crowding to mention some of the more prominent workers in this area, have begun to define a new field. Moreover, human forms are a palpable part of our living space, possibly the most critical "environment" in citified living. Architects are belatedly discovering, for example, that aesthetically pleasing sketches of buildings devoid of human figures bare little relationship to the way that same building will look and function when it is filled with the people for whom it was built. Once people occupy those empty courtyards, offices and hallways, the entire environment changes. The interactional chain between the physical and social elements of our environment is extremely complex. The physical shell constrains the types of social structures that may evolve just as the social structure will in turn affect further informal and formal modifications of the physical space. A consideration of these complexities is making architects and designers more and more aware that in order to succeed in structuring aesthetically pleasing and operatively useful environments, they must consider both the human and non-human elements.

The thin line between the human and non-human elements in an environment and their interactive effects on human behavior is exaggerated by some of the autistic children described by Bettleheim (1950) who think of themselves as machines and often relate more comfortably with machines than with people. Colby's reports (1968) of successful use of "computer therapist" with these children is a logical extension of this aspect of their psychology. Actually the differentiation between our reactivity to "thing" and "person" is becoming increasingly blurred as a function of recent innovations in communication technology. It is only necessary to compare the relevant efficiency of emergency television repair services with medical emergency services to appreciate the intensity that television images have for all of us, especially our children. The more interactive mode that cable TV will soon introduce into our homes will surely increase this relationship. As Sidney Jourard (1971) points out in his book *The Transparent Self*, the exploration of outer space has been our greatest stimulus to the exploration of inner space. Those of us who have recently lived through the great oil spills in Santa Barbara and San Francisco Bay, or other ecological tragedies, will have personal knowledge of the vast emotional impact of the non-human environmental catastrophies on our personal selves.

In fact, the ecology movement and its apparent interest in the preservation of the non-human environment seems to have become a vehicle for the expressions of humanistic concern for the individual's psychological survival.

A functional definition of Environmental Design is necessarily changed by the broader reinterpretation of both design and environment sketched above. A more useful definition of environmental design would relate the planning of a coherent program and set of procedures to effect the total human and nonhuman environment in ways that increase the probability that certain goals or "needs" will be achieved. The goal of environmental design would relate to social behavior, such as planning an education or therapeutic system, as much as to aesthetics such as constructing an awe-inspiring church. Input into environmental design problems must then include knowledge relating to modifing human behavior and social systems as well as structural information from engineering or perceptual psychology. The field would expand towards a new view of man, always powerfully effected by his physical and social environment, now actively developing an environmental design model and methodology which would place the effect of the total environment on his behavior more in his own control, and the responsibility for the design and control of the environment on his behavior, in himself.

Such a new definition was predicted and placed in evolutionary perspective by Julian Huxley (Roe and Simpson, 1958) in the 1955 Arden House Conference on Behavior and Evolution. He said, there, "We are now beginning to see the whole development of man as a unitary process of evolution, and man is the agency by which that process is becoming self-conscious and could become *consciously purposeful.* Evolutionary progress, both in the biological and the human sector, is now seen as a fact that is occurring only rarely and by no means inevitably. We may say that cultural evolution, i.e., evolution in a psycho-social phase, can now be seen as an extension of biological evolution with its own peculiarities of methods and results." In Huxley's view evolution seems to have moved toward creating more self-conscious being — man being the latest product. The inevitable result is that man, with knowledge of his purposes, will now begin to think of how to change his own development by *designing his environment,* including his own processes and himself. The entire field of organ transplantation, genic manipulation, and even behavior modification, is directly anchored into this evolutionary drama.

OPERANT CONDITIONING AS AN
ENVIRONMENTAL DESIGN MODEL

Certainly these ideas are hardly new to those of us who, as behavioral scientists, have worked in analyzing, planning, and structuring, the physical and social space in an effort to control contingencies that modify behavior in predictable direction. The writing of B.F. Skinner (1971) from *Walden Two* to *Beyond Freedom and Dignity*, particularly the chapter entitled "The Design of a Culture" have clearly reflected this broader definition of environmental design. The development of the operant cage, popularly known as "The Skinner Box" is an excellent illustration of a purposefully designed environment whose goal is to affect behavior. Using the technology of operant conditioning, the experimenter can design an enclosure which contains specific functional design elements, such as levers operating food, water and electric shock dispensers, an assortment of lights with super-imposed geometrical patterns, patterned and unpatterned sounds, and so on. These elements can then be pre-programmed to provide precise feedback to the responses of animal subjects. It is even possible to include other behaving animals as part of the design. For example, Boren, Liebold and Colman (1969) showed that in certain monkey pairs, feeding a familiar hungry monkey could be used as a reinforcement. Rice and Gainer (1962) and Masserman, Wechkin and Terris (1964) have shown that certain monkeys would work harder to prevent another monkey from being punished. In a sense the operant conditioner had begun to learn how to design simple environments, including both the physical and social elements, which would support specific predictable behavior in the animal experimental situation.

In the last decade, operant principles have been systematically applied to a wide variety of human situations in an effort to both modify behavioral pathology, and enhance learning behaviors. At first the designs were adapted directly from the laboratory to single individuals with specific problems of behavior, such as stuttering, self-mutilatory behavior in autistic children, poor toilet control in retardates, and psychotic and chronic schizophrenic individuals (Frasner and Ullmann, 1965). Interpersonal reinforcements, such as praise, attention, and affection were added to the armamentarian of reinforcing stimuli to design environments appropriate to extinguishing maladaptive patterns and supporting the behavioral goals. In general, these systems were extremely successful and have challenged more traditional therapeutic modalities to include the operant approaches in standard treatment programs around the country. However this direct translation of laboratory procedures was limited to single subjects in specialized, quasi laboratory setting and did not affect the larger social networks that, if unchanged, continue to reinforce the maladaptive behaviors and fail to support the new learning.

In 1963 Ayllon and Azrin (1965) introduced the token economy concept which has played a critical role in translating operant design principles to technical procedures for redesign of the indigenous environments of hospital wards, nurseries, schools, colleges and communities, in a manner capable of supporting a variety of behavioral goals for specific individual and group needs. Their idea was to pay the patient or student in artificial currency for specified behaviors. The tokens were then exchangeable for privileges within a specifiable environment. Tokens, like money, became a generalized reinforcer linked to the individual's own preference in his environment. This system allowed the professional with authority in a social system (psychiatrists or psychologists on a treatment wards, teacher in a school room, etc.), to decide in conjunction with his staff, which behaviors were appropriate for each individual, and link them to reinforcers available in the environment. Specific behavioral plans could be linked to general reinforcement systems as easily as more general group behavioral goals. The economic structure of the ward could be modified to reflect the changing value system. In addition the token economy provided an easily available direct measure of behavior in the environment—both of goal directed behaviors supported by the reinforcement system and the informal behaviors shown through choices of reinforcers. In other words the token economy provided a technology which allowed comprehensive design of an environment geared to modification of behavior for groups of individuals, according to preset therapeutic goals, together with the feedback of information from that environment so that it could be continuously redesigned to better approximate the behavioral goals.

The token economies sought to expand the actual design potential of the model beyond the limited experimental situations for either animals or humans. It included the complexities of a hospital ward, school room, or even a hospital or school. By fading the stimulus systems and shifting to more variable or long term reinforcement schedules from one environment to another (for example between a chronic hospital ward and a state hospital or half-way house in the community), techniques could be developed for extending its effects beyond these boundaries into more complex inter-environment and intergroup relationships.

As large scale and more complex environments were utilized by the behavior modification programs, environmental design in both a physical and social sense became more of a practical reality. For example, Harold Cohen in 1966, a designer by profession, developed the CASE project at a juvenile federal prison in Washington, D.C., which brilliantly synthesized a token economy and physical design principles for a rehabilitation program aimed at improving the social adjustment of the prisoners when released. Academic behaviors were reinforced by a judicious combination of tokens, social reinforcements, and constantly changing colors and forms of the living and study environments. Mr. Cohen's response to disciplinary problems varied from increasing prices, differential praise of the inmates with better behavior, to redesigning the shape and hue of the study cubicles.

It seems clear that operant conditioning concepts and its technical derivatives such as the token economy are an extremely relevant area to apply environmental design, particularly those design problems in which the modification of social behavior is of major concern. That is one of the realities in the field of environmental design today. Having said this, it is time to turn to the limitations of the model and tempting illusions, even delusions that its current vogue may present to its burgeoning practitioners.

LIMITATIONS OF OPERANT CONDITIONS AS AN ENVIRONMENTAL DESIGN MODEL

I want to use my own work as a basis for discussing some of the problems and limitations of operant conditioning as an environmental design model. In 1966 I developed a point economy program designed to change the behavior of severely limited delinquent soldiers for whom the traditional therapeutic milieu mode had miserably failed (Colman, 1969). The program itself, which I'll describe briefly below, was an overall success as far as our stated goals were concerned. More than two-thirds of the experimental group received an honorable discharge at least nine months after return to duty. Less than one-third were in a stockade AWOL, or dishonorably or administratively discharged after nine months. In the comparison group which had received conventional hospital treatment, the figures were reversed. Less than one-third of the men were in the success category and more than two-thirds were in the failure category. In addition, behavioral measures, within the ward, such as absences, suicide attempts, and psychotic episodes, positive performance in educational tests, and so on were all dramatically improved over the previous ward. However, despite the utility of the point system and other operant techniques in this program, many of the design problems faced in setting up and operating the ward were of the type for which the operant model provided little understanding or practical help.

The work was done at Walter Reed General Hospital. The subjects were soldiers who entered the hospital diagnosed as "character disorders", that is they were not psychotic but were felt to need some kind of treatment or rehabilitation. As a group they were little different than the Army stockade population between 1966 and 1969. These men were not the Vietnam dissenters, on the contrary they were eager to fight "the enemy" but had difficulty handling even the most routine Army assignments, were unpopular with peers, had recurrent fights, and made manipulative suicide gestures, and other upsetting behaviors in order to bypass the more unpleasant aspects of Army and stockade life. Typically these men had enlisted in the Army following difficulty with the court, school, or their families.

Our basic assumptions were that these men had failed in both civilian and military life because of behavioral repertoires which provided inadequate reinforcements when operating legally in social situations. Our curriculum, then, offered opportunities for training in education, occupational, and "group skills" which we felt would be applicable to their usual social and work situations. Details of the treatment program have been given elsewhere (Colman, 1971). Pertinent to this paper is the way in which operant principals were used as a design model for a treatment environment to serve these men's needs. One evening, Doctors Israel Goldiamond and John Boren, the ward's sergeant David Collins and psychiatric resident James Rumbaugh, who was trained in operant conditioning principles, and myself sat down and designed the framework of a ward which has continued for more than six years. We identified the *treatment goals*, the *behavioral requirements* necessary to achieve these goals, the *social and institutional reinforcement system*, and designed a *measurement system* capable of providing internal and external feedback on the ward's success rate. Educational opportunities and events such as classes, behavioral contracts, tutoring, and so on were linked by a point economy to the ward institutional reinforcers such as TV passes, and special classes. We planned the room arrangement, the dress, the posting of signs, the activity schedules; in essence we attempted to design the total environment based on the operant technology.

Designing a point economy based on the institutional reinforcers and the relevant educational program was an important step in controlling the environment of the men and modifying their behavior in constructive directions in relationship to the goals of the ward. However, designing the *social* reinforcement system to achieve similar ends was considerably more difficult particularly since analysis of this group of men suggested that the pre-eminent social reinforcers was approval from their own peer group. This meant that their value system, in operant terms the discriminative stimuli for reinforcement within this group, had somehow to be changed in order for the program to run at all. One approach to this problem was the development of a *phase two* program which offered certain men who had functioned well on the ward for ten weeks access to most of the ward's reinforcements without the use of points in return for their performing general leadership duties such as teaching courses, running the unit at night, and supervising the work program. In other words, leadership within the peer group was offered to those men who learned behavior appropriate to the ward's goals. By this means, potential "anti-leaders" within the group were converted to leaders supporting the ward's goals and their informal social behaviors, was thereby placed in the service of the treatment program. Since leadership skills and improved methods for handling authority was one of the key required behaviors of the program, becoming a phase two member also had learning value aside from this critical restructuring of the peer reinforcements.

It is possible now in retrospect to describe the restructuring of peer group values in operant language. What I want to emphasize here is that except for the most general formulation of the problem we faced, operant concepts and technology was of little use in developing this part of the treatment program. What is at issue is the difference between operant conditioning as an analytic and descriptive system versus operant conditioning as a design model. The analytic system requires only the most general application of operant concepts to an on-going series of interactions. However, the design model requires a much higher degree of specificity resting as it does on the availability of a carefully worked out technology based on experimentation. There was simply no applicable technology that we could apply to the complex issues involved in reshaping the value system of this group of men. It required the sergeant's grasp of the military culture together with an understanding of a complex operation of a late adolescent group to provide the framework necessary to develop a workable phase two program. Clearly further study of leadership of group functioning from an operant point of view would be of value in the future program of this kind. Our own work on the ward was a contribution in this direction. However, at the time the ward was designed, the research in the field was too general and simplified to be of much practical value and the same information deficit exists today.

Let me provide what I hope is an even more telling example of the present limitations of the operant model. As difficult as it was to gain control of the authority hierarchy of the delinquent peer group, staff did have control of contingencies important to the patient group. However, even as leader of the ward in an authoritarian Army hospital structure, I had considerably less control over my own staff. The realities of the Army personnel structure did not allow manipulation of staff's institutional rewards (pay, time off, discipline, etc.) as a function of how well they performed in their tasks, except in the case of the most blatant wrong doing or superb positive effort. Furthermore, the staff represented several different professional and nonprofessional disciplines within the hospital, each with their own values and preferred behavior and each with their own sentient group. In other words, all of the ward staff except the psychiatric residents also belonged to other groups with a different chain of command. This meant that my control of the staff—and the crux of the success of the program rested on that control—could not be based on an institutional reinforcement structure using pay, time off or promotion. Rather I had to rely on "softer" factors such as educational opportunities, commitment to the treatment staff, esprit, or rapport, in order to develop appropriate behavior and discriminations in staff interactions with patients. It was also necessary to become involved in the politics of the hospital and even at times in the politics of the other parts of the Army system to make sure that my goals with the staff were not actively opposed by reinforcement systems outside of my immediate control.

It would be fair criticism at this point to suggest that without stronger control over staff, the behavior modification program should not have begun. Unfortunately, except for those lucky individuals who could staff their programs with graduate students whose reward structure is singularly well tied to graduate department politics, the luxury of a committed and controllable staff is very rare indeed. For example, in hospitals it is almost always true that the nursing administrator controls more of the rewards of the nurses and aides working on the treatment ward than does the head of that ward. The same rewards on which we base our token economy program with such success are exactly those rewards that are particularly subject to organizational influence such as bargaining, pressure groups, and unions. This means that the head of the treatment program must almost always work through a larger social system, beyond the boundaries of the ward, and therefore beyond his immediate authority and control, if the program is to succeed.

In 1968 I spent three weeks observing some 20 of the best known behavior modification programs across the country. I was particularly interested in what factors led to 1) successful outcome for patients or students and, 2) the project survival itself. In almost all cases the internal design, that is the operant techniques used to control patient behavior, was well thought out and workable. The design of individual behavior plans or token economies was rarely the critical factor in either outcome or survival. We seem to have considerable design competence in that area. What distinguished successful and long lived programs from less successful and short lived ones, was the extent to which the program leader had taken into account the social and physical boundary relationships between the treatment ward and the surrounding environment, to what extent the program leader had been effective in dealing with factors such as the ward's relationship with other wards in that particular institution, the relationship between critical personnel on the ward and their professional peers in nearby environments, the program leader's relationship with other program leaders and with his administrative superior. For example, I visited a ward which had functioned effectively according to sophisticated operant principles but which was soon closing because no patients were being referred to it. This was blamed on the threat which the ward's success with difficult patients presented to the other more conventional treatment programs in the hospital. Another excellent program was closing because of some well meaning but uninformed protest about the use of punishment. Not unexpectedly, the protest was inspired by local treating professionals in the community. A nursery school program was on the rocks because the school board was holding up its accreditation on the advice of ''prominent'' mental health consultants. Yet another program the staff refused to carry out an operant design for which they had been trained for three months previously because their supervisor refused to count their training towards a status pay raise and because the education team had given special status to those who worked with the operant principles best irrespective of previous hierarchical differences based on experience and time on the job. On the other hand, many programs were working because effective relationships had been forged with administrators, peer professionals, staff, and the community. What was most dramatic to me was the extent to which these factors were almost never dealt with as ''design'' issues, variables capable of analysis and control. Rather they were thought of as serendipitous happenings subsumed under demeaning terms such as ''politics'', or ''administrative crap.'' I began to wonder whether these larger system boundary issues were not in fact critically important program design issues. If they were, then their exclusion in design schema was probably not simply an oversight but more likely a tacit admission that the operant principles were not yet a relevant technology to utilize in their analysis or manipulation.

It is clear to me now that insofar as these administrative and political factors in part determine success or failure of the program's outcome, they are relevant independent variables and must be included in the design model. Yet there are almost no studies of how to work with these variables from the operant perspective. Descriptions of utopias in which goals, behavior, reinforcement, are logically related to one another will not help to bring this about and, until our studies can demonstrate otherwise, there is always the possibility that inter-relating human groups do not operate according to our rules.

If we were to conceptualize our operant concepts and behavior modification techniques as important but limited input into complex environmental design situations, I believe we would have better perspective into the relevant variables affecting the success and failure of our programs. In the laboratory, this perspective is not as necessary because that is one institution designed precisely to allow small and carefully delimited design projects or experiments to proceed under a high degree of control. Even this utopian vision of the experimental situation is breaking down in the face of an omnivorous and intrusive media and the increasing politicalization of the scientific enterprise. Once we remove ourselves from the laboratory, our technical skill will become a relatively small factor in our effectiveness compared to covert and overt inter-group variables.

For the past two years I have been working in the College of Environmental Design at the University of California in Berkeley. My initial reason for this association was that in many areas of my work, particularly in the ward design project, I was in fact acting as an architect and designer of social systems. Yet I had little expertise in the design process except for my intuition and my knowledge of operant conditioning and of other relevant behavioral sciences. Working with a concentration of professional architects, city and regional planners, public health and public policy planners, has made me painfully aware that behavioral sciences as a group has almost no expertise and even less real experience in the field of design. Except for the design of experiments in the laboratory, most of us will be lucky indeed to take part in the design of a few programs of limited scope. This must be contrasted to the above professionals who spend their lifetimes designing and planning physical and social systems, spanning microscopic to macroscopic scales. There is much to be learned from them about the effects and interactions of physical factors with social forces and group and individual behavior. What has been most striking to me is that despite their fund of expertise in working with large scale complex social and physical systems their critical problem is similar to ours; that is the disparity between the technological capability and know-how and their limited knowledge in preventing this knowledge from being blunted and subverted by the very systems they serve. The parallel of this group with the operant conditioners is very striking. The designer has skills which now enable him to translate the most fanciful designs into realities of steel, plastic and glass. They are becoming more aware of the importance of ascertaining these requirements in programs and the need for building in behavioral as well as aesthetic goals in the final design. Yet they find themselves frustrated by the political and social institutions they must work with in order to implement their ideas. Because the physical environment, buildings, space, and territory, is so often equated with personal and political power by human groups, their problems in this regard are considerably more serious than our own. They often end up designing structures which fit the irrational or impractical needs of boards of directors or community power groups rather than the needs of the people who will use and are most affected by the buildings. Behavior modifers need be less involved by such influences since hospitals for the chronically ill and schools for the socially deprived are hardly symbols of power compared to a new 50-story high rise in the financial district of New York, San Francisco or Dallas. When faced with the eroding effects of these inter-group forces on our programs most of us can simply retreat to the laboratory and search for more controlled, smaller scaled settings in which to work.

It is at this point of retreat that the construction of macroscopic design models for entire cultures is most satisfying. Even in these utopian delusions, we have much in common with other designers. For example, Solari, a disciple of Frank Lloyd Wright, is working on new physical models for cities of incredibly high densities which he feels will not only solve our population and space problem but will also somehow create a unique interactional system which will support and create a truly different type of man, a breed free of the anger, competition, strife that current groups of men seem to compulsively reinact.

When I began working at the College of Environmental Design I was more optimistic about the applications of the operant model into larger areas of environmental design. I soon found that although the model had some use in situations where contingencies could be reliably controlled, most design problems began in context in which indeterminant variables are the rule. Recently I have begun studying the process by which complex socio-physical structures are designed, for example a college campus and a medical care system, in the hope of isolating some of the control factors. In each case I have tried to examine the extent to which the acknowledged design model affected the outcome. Thus far I have been impressed by how unimportant the overt design model is in shaping what happened. For example, in the case of the college campus, although the architect firmly believed in the importance of student and faculty participation in the designing processes so that their needs could be adequately represented, the outcome most clearly reflected the prejudices of the planners and the administrators towards youth, intellectuals and the educational process. Similarly although the designers of the abortion care system I studied, planned their program to serve the physical and psychological needs of the women users, the final dehumanized and fragmented system that developed mirrored the providers' unspoken, but active, prejudices about the secret and shady role of the abortionist in their own past history. The process by which objective, clear design guidelines are undercut by less reasoned individual and group motives is obscure. As the scale and complexity of the environmental design situation increases, it apparently becomes more and more difficult for the primary design task to be implemented and for the other contingencies to take over.

What are the implications of these remarks for behavior modification? Some in the field may use them as a further rationale for only designing environments where control is available. However, as I have tried to suggest earlier in the paper, no behavior modification is really immune from the same forces that maladaptively modify the design of a building or a medical care delivery system. We need to study and investigate in larger scale and more complex systems if only to develop strategies and techniques for controlling some of the covert factors which may undermine our best designed programs. More importantly if we view our disciplines, as I do, as a theoretical and methodological resource for the field of environmental design, I believe we might play an important part in explicating these complexities through our own analytical model.

One approach might be to methodically analyze existing social systems using the operant model in the way that Ferster (unpublished) and Goldiamond and Dyrud (1968) have recently analyzed complex therapeutic systems. Marshall and I (in press) have recently begun to look at the encounter group from an operant model, not only to understand its intra-group processes, but also to study the development of satellite groups in reaction to the discontinuous stimuli and reinforcement systems at the boundary between the encounter group culture and everyday social interactions. These kinds of analysis tend to be more difficult than studying more enclosed, controllable situations. Yet they are necessary if we are to fully test and implement the operant model in more complex environmental design issues.

20.

THE ARCHITECT AND PLANNER: Change Agent or Scapegoat?

A discussion of the nature of the relationship with complex clients and the growing need for organizational and process consultation.

W. Harold Bexton

INTRODUCTION

Hardly a week goes by without a newpaper article on some planned enterprise that has turned into a fiasco, generated a scandal, or at least had disappointing results. Whether these are regional plans, urban redevelopment, or building designs for large organizations or institutions, there seems to be a common lack of ability to undertake plans that take into account the various interest groups involved in such a way that satisfactory results will be produced. Inevitably personal accusations are hurled about whenever a problem is publicized, but it seems unlikely that individuals alone can account for the apparent patterns of failure. To better understand such situations a more generalizable approach is needed that takes into account the group and organizational dynamics involved. This chapter will focus on the nature of the relationship between complex clients and outside consultants, architects or planners who are hired to plan projects or make changes in existing facilities.

One thing most projects have in common today is that they involve large numbers of people, both groups who will be affected by the planning and large complex organizations. How well the facilities respond to the needs of these groups is likely to be the criteria by which success will be ultimately measured. Yet when discussing different projects of this type with the environmental professionals involved, feelings of helplessness and being scapegoated are often expressed. Frequently these feelings are displayed in uneasy jokes about the experience or comments such as, "There I was gradually being pinned to the wall so everyone could take pot shots at me..." Many of the situations arise when there is a lack of clarity about the job the architect or planner is expected to do.

CONTRACTUAL LIMITATIONS

There are often covert aspects of a job which it is hoped will respond to environmental change. Although it may not be explicitly stated in the contract, the architect or planner may be expected to contribute to solving organizational problems, instituting new teaching methods, creating social interaction, promoting work efficiency or job satisfaction, improving treatment programs, reducing crime, or increasing business. This problem is compounded by the fact that architects and planners tend to see themselves as important agents in affecting behavior and thus are likely to accept readily such a mandate without adequate knowledge or the authority to intervene in the system.[1]

The real needs may be in the area of organizational change — an anxiety provoking subject to deal with. While the physical environment may not require much change at all, new facilities may be hailed as the answer since such changes are seen as easier to handle and the results may even help obscure other needs that the organization would prefer to ignore. On the other hand, organizational needs may be recognized but kept undercover as a hidden agenda that will be covertly "worked out" in the planning process. Seldom are issues of this type explicitly stated in contractual agreements, and even when they are, the environmental professional is unlikely to be given the power or necessary means to carry out such tasks. In fact, he may be saddled with many early decisions over which he has no control and which may affect the nature of the project, sometimes insuring failure.

ENVIRONMENTAL CHANGE DEALS WITH BOUNDARIES

Whether or not the architect has any power to effect change in the organization he is dealing with, he must certainly gather information and manipulate various parts to achieve some goal, improve function from some point of view or create some form he desires. By the very nature of the design task, the architect tends to take a wholistic view, from determining how outside pressures will affect the institution's building program (even if this is only at the level of minimum standards and fire safety codes), down to details of putting a price tag on space demands and helping determine priorities. In this way he often becomes a coordinator of many diverse parts of the organization, particularly if it is large, with many departments and little communication between them. The job then deals to a great extent with determining boundaries and the nature of transactions across them. These affect people's territories and role relations, and thus tend to raise and become the focus of disputes.

In the planning process while the disputes center on physical issues, the real points in question are often emotional, social and territorial.

For example, a waterfront development was proposed in the

1 A study by Howard Boughey showed that 92% of the architects sampled believed that they had an effect on behavior and the social interaction in their buildings (Boughey, 1968).

San Francisco Bay area. A large proportion of the waterfront had been bought up by an out of state developer who commissioned a local well known architect to draw up plans for a high income development. The developer claimed that rents had to be high or the project would not be feasible, and every effort was made to cater to this desire. The existing users of the waterfront, however, vary across the whole range of the social scale. If the project were built as originally planned, it would wipe out most of the local houseboat community, many craft businesses and small industries located in the area. Since special planning commission approval was needed, a great dispute arose around such issues as the adequacy of the structure, the potential for added pollution, the impact of greater traffic and other technical points. While the technical planning was satisfactory, the architects and engineers were told in effect that their plans were inadequate for reasons centered elsewhere and never overtly discussed. The planners solved all the problems they were allowed to, but the real controversy was over social and territorial issues of control.

COVERT ISSUES IN PLANNING

When new space is being planned and needs are being surveyed, the architect can find himself collecting information on people's dreams. He is unavoidably plunged into the fantasy life of the groups he is dealing with. Since his job involves whose dreams get built and whether or not they are appropriate or suitable to the task system and goals of the institution, the architect is often involved in making decisions that appear rational but turn out to be incredibly dysfunctional and irrational[2] when viewed from outside the organization. Arthur Colman suggests that these irrational processes can be divided into two categories: basic assumptions and covert politics (Colman, 1973).

The basic assumptions are unconscious personal, group and cultural forces, hidden motives and assumptions that are projected into group work as irrational premises shared by members. While the basic assumption life of the group is irrational and will not stand up to objective analysis, the group operates ''as if'' these premises were true. The basic assumptions that operate in the groups were adnumbrated by Wilfred Bion as dependency, fight-flight and pairing. The assumptions that operate in the groups were adumbrated by attain security through and have its members protected by the leader who, being seen as omnipotent and omniscient, is expected to take responsibility for them. Action is essential for the fight-flight group, whose members may feel paranoiac and assume that they have met to fight or flee from something. A

2 Throughout this paper ''irrational'' refers to processes that are not related to the primary task of the group. While some actions may be rational in terms of some personal goal, such as relief of anxiety, they are still considered irrational in this paper unless they relate positively to the task.

major function of its leader is to recognize danger; individuals have secondary importance to the group. When operating in the basic assumption pairing, the group assumes it has met for the purposes of reproduction and that two people will get together on behalf of the group to carry on the task of creating something, such as a plan that will be their savior.[3]

CONSCIOUS BUT UNDERCOVER PROCESSES

Covert politics refers to the social field of alliances, pressure groups and power influences operating within the design process in unexamined ways, unrelated to overtly stated design determinants. Colman notes that the covert political influences are not irrational in themselves, in that they serve the conscious self-interest of individuals or groups, but they are irrational in relation to the design task (Colman, 1973). While the basic assumptions are unconscious and unacknowledged, covert politics are acknowledged but are not discussed openly. Both covert politics and basic assumptions have a surreptitious effect on the overt task and its determinants. While their influence on the process is not necessarily negative, since they are unexamined and at least partially unconscious, they can make a mockery of the rational design process. The more complex and vague a design task, the more these factors will affect the outcome.

The effect of covert politics can be illustrated by the planning of an institution on the west coast. This institution ran special programs for children with neurological learning problems. They operated out of old houses and a portion of an old hospital where some physical therapy was carried on. The programs they were using were based on Gestalt methods and were achieving a high degree of success. It was unanimously agreed that the form their new building should take, to best achieve treatment and educational goals, was a decentralized plan with small scale schools located in the neighborhoods to insure parental involvement. When funds became available, however, this plan could not be followed because the politicians responsible for the approval stated that a centralized facility was the only acceptable form. In private they admitted that a centralized facility would provide a monument to their short terms in office and would have more impact for the purpose of furthering their political careers. The architect's response in the final form was a large centralized institutional building with smaller scale units expressed within it. This was a superficial and unsuccessful way of providing the type of space that was considered optimum for the program, and results in the new building did not equal earlier work in the old facilities. Perhaps the requirement of a centralized large scale monument also fit in with the architect's view of the type of building that was most likely to help his career.

3 For a full discussion of the basic assumptions, related emotional states and discussions of the processes that take place when these assumptions are in operation, see Bion (1961) and Rioch (1970).

UNCONSCIOUS GROUP PROCESSES

When dealing with a group of users, an architect tends to assume a leadership role at meetings since he must structure the information he requires. If the group is operating in the basic assumption dependency, they may feel that the architect, as an expert, has all the answers to their problems or can find them out himself and they have few skills or opinions that are of any use in this task. Many an architect or planner has been told that all the user's (or community's or organization's) hopes are resting with him and he had better not let them down—yet they are helpless to assist him. Thus he is in a double bind, because without the help and expert assistance of the group, adequate planning can not be done, yet if it is not done the architect will be characterized as having let them down. The group will have ambivalent feelings in that they want to be dependent and be looked after and feel frustrated that the architect has let them down, yet at the same time they hate the architect for making them feel deskilled and dependent. Although the architect cannot obtain the necessary information and guidance from the group to do his job, he is felt to have abandoned them, and attempts are likely to be made to subvert his work and challenge his authority and competence. In such situations usually the architect falls quickly into the role demanded by the group and provides leadership and direction in terms of plans. These plans will invariably be hotly disputed, and the architect could risk being scapegoated for not fully understanding the needs. There will be much vying for position by more dominant members as they try to step into a leadership position—perhaps by showing the architect how to reorganize his plans. These changes will inevitably meet opposition, and disagreements will occur. The plans, however, may be quite irrelevant to the issues at stake, which may be jealousies, dominance struggles, prestige, succession or other irrational (as far as the task is concerned) ends.

In the basic assumption pairing, the group may push its own director or leader and the architect together to come up with a savior in the form of a plan. Meetings would tend to focus on getting the two together to solve the problems for the group. Any plan presented would likely be rejected, and some version of the process described above would occur.

In the basic assumption fight-flight, on the other hand, the group would act as if there were an outside enemy that must be opposed or thwarted. Action would be so essential that options could not be explored and needs could not be adequately surveyed. The enemy could be an outside agency that perhaps controls funds, or it could be a portion of their own organization, but in any case the architect risks being drawn into the process. The result could be that key needs are passed over or some group left out, even if it means the design will result in a building that will not adequately function as intended.

MAINTAINING AND REINFORCING EXISTING BOUNDARIES: THE ARCHITECT AS "SOFT COP"

The architect could be given responsibility for maintaining boundaries and positions of present leaders in an organization, since they hired him or because he is more attuned to their needs. Such requests need not always be explicitly stated. Colman suggests they can be "taught" to outsiders through a myriad of non-verbal communications and indirect allusions, which are experienced but rarely consciously processed (Colman, 1973). Where this teaching involves maintaining existing status hierarchies, the architect has been characterized as a "soft cop" (Goodman, 1971). When existing rigid or dysfunctional aspects of an organization are being constructed in steel and concrete, the architect stands to be scapegoated by users, who may vent their feelings on him and the building as an agent of the oppressors. In such cases users will have a stake in making the design look bad.

Even when the architect is not acting solely on behalf of superiors, users could have a stake in making the building look bad if they feel they have been left out of the planning process. Perhaps they feel that their input would have provided better solutions or their input may in fact have been presented and ignored. In any case the result can be a self-fulfilling prophesy, as users insure that the inadequacies they feel the scheme possesses are borne out in reality.

Another possibility is that a preconceived form, whether from the architect or from management, was "sold" to the users. This may have been done by using processes that apparently involve users in decisions, when the actual building form was decided before the process began. This can happen inadvertently and in good faith, when the architect, confronted with the irrational processes in the groups he must deal with falls back on something he is sure of—a rough plan he preconceived at the outset or worked out with management. In these cases, whether their input was put to best use or not, the users involved may feel they had a part in the design and may be hesitant to criticize it, even when parts are obviously dysfunctional. Users change however, and newcomers having had no stake in the planning are more likely to spot and point out deficiencies, which are likely to be blamed on the architect.

CO-OPTION BY SUBGROUPS WITHIN THE SYSTEM

On the other hand, if the planner or architect pays too much attention to a group with little power in the system, he may find himself being used by a subgroup that is disenfranchised. This could lead to the loss of the job due to antagonizing the administration which hired him or it could lead to a different series of irrational decisions. The subgroup could be a group of "young turks" who are intent on challenging the authority structure for the sake of their own personal power and advancement. These could be a group of young doctors in a hospital or executives in a corporation, for example. The architect may find that his plans are only a vehicle for disputes over territory, power and authority, and once again he stands to be the scapegoat, since he is the outside person who is causing the tensions.

As well as introducing anomalies that might insure failure, groups can conspire to produce an idealized form that, within the realities of daily operation, cannot be used in the manner intended. Perhaps this could be due to overlooking available evidence and information or once again due to failure to include a key group of users. This result could also be due to a lack of clarity of boundaries on the design task itself.

An example to illustrate some of the above points is the design of a children's hospital by a large departmentalized architectural office. A senior, very experienced programmer who was committed to user needs was assigned to the job. The programmer polled all hospital staff and worked extensively on the job, becoming very friendly with top ranking doctors in that institution. In the resulting space program several key but low ranking groups were left out, even though they were critical to the type of service desired by the hospital. The building had in effect formalized the staff's covert hostility and wish for absence of the rather stress provoking or low status groups that were left out—parents[4], interns and nurses aides.

THE ARCHITECT'S AGENDA: SPATIAL OPPORTUNITIES

Another factor which can create unexpected results, both good and bad, is the characteristic of architects to be "spatial opportunists". That is, they can see the potential possibilities and unexploited advantages of which others may be oblivious. Comments such as, "This is a depressing space now, but if we took out those walls and opened up another window, etc., it could be...", are common in this regard. This process can be very productive and is one of the reasons an architect is hired. In a meeting with various warring factions of users, however, the various possible spatial delights often become the hidden agenda of the architect, and he may favor schemes that support this end, in spite of functional consequences (consequences of which the group may have kept him ignorant). The architect can then be used as an ally by someone in the organization, even though the architect's reasons for his choice may be quite personal and even fleeting, and perhaps, given all the facts, he would change his mind.

4 For a description of some of the dynamics and anxieties inherent in children's hospitals, see Colman, 1973, p. 13

GAPS BETWEEN IDEALIZED GOALS AND THE REALITY OF DAY TO DAY ADMINISTRATION

The manner in which an institution is administered is a key part of the environment. If administrative prerogatives are not included as design criteria or are not altered to match design goals, the physical environment may not be able to function as intended. In fact, the way the space is administered has a dramatic effect on behavior and the way the space is used. This brings to mind such examples as student lounge areas in schools, envisioned by idealistic designers as the exclusive territories of students and harboring a wide variety of activities, when in reality these spaces are policed by teachers who enforce a rigid and limited use of the space. Or recall public housing, designed with separate front yards for the row houses so that the tenants can individualize their plots with little fences and flowers, when in reality the housing authority intends to mow all front yards (to insure that they look tended) in one sweep with large mechanized grass cutters.

An example of the effect on the environment of the attitudes and approach of administration and the resulting social system is a study of two nursing homes for the aged. The two buildings, virtually identical in design and furnishing, were evaluated along with other buildings by a group of gerontologists. The most noteworthy first impression was the vast difference in atmosphere between the two buildings. At one the majority of the patients were bed-ridden and seemed sickly. They had little control over their personal boundaries; the nurses running the institution washed and fed them, thereby controlling most dimensions of their lives. When questioned, the head nurse stated that people came there to die and the staff was not going to stand in their way. This could be characterized as a "warehousing" model of care, as described by Miller and Gwynne in their study of residential institutions for the physically handicapped (Miller and Gwynne, 1972). In the other nursing home, although the residents had entered at a similar age and state of health, the atmosphere was bright and cheerful. Residents greeted visitors at the door and could be seen busily cleaning and raking leaves, planning activities and generally making full use of the environment. The head nurse in this home stated that it should not be considered an institution, but rather it was the home of the residents and they should feel responsible for it. She felt the nursing staff should be available when requested, but that residents should control the boundaries.[5]

MEETING ORGANIZATIONAL GOALS: MAKING UNCERTAINTY TOLERABLE

Organizational goals must be known if a building or plan is to

5. This example was recounted by Leonard Gottesman of the Philadelphia Geriatric Center at a Gerontological Society Conference, in Puerto Rico, December 1971, entitled "Housing and Environments for the Elderly."

be produced that satisfies all needs, yet there are often many unstated goals. An obvious example is the need all organizations have to maintain themselves. This is logical and desirable as long as it is necessary for the accomplishment of the task. However, at times insuring survival may take priority even when it adversely affects the functioning of the organization. While an institution's goals may be stated to be education or medical care, for example, the social system may be such that the primary task becomes self perpetuation and growth as ends in themselves. At the same time, details of social interaction and corresponding territories and environments tend to be structured to reduce anxieties and uncertainties.

If we consider the open systems model proposed by Miller and Rice (1967), we can discuss organizations in terms of systems of activities which involve an exchange with the environment: intake, boundary regulation, conversion process, boundary regulation, and output. Around the operating activities, or conversion process, exists a boundary control function and that monitors transactions between inside and outside. The boundary regulation in organizations thus is a leadership or management function, and as such it is more administrative than technical in nature. The boundaries are to protect the task system from interference, and the leader or manager is given the authority to play this role. In large organizations or institutions, however, complicated and diffuse boundary and authority relationships tend to be the rule. In such situations it is difficult to assign responsibility for decisions; guidance comes through rules and regulations written by anonymous committees, the work task is difficult to define, and evaluation of performance is often impossible. Controls in these cases are sometimes imposed not to protect the task system from interference but to protect management against anxiety. Parameters may be controlled not because they are relevant in such a case but because they are measurable. Their function then is to create an illusion of certainty as a means of coping with uncertainty.

Unfortunately, when faced with an uncertain situation where there is pressure to produce a plan, identifiable and apparently stable elements are seized upon by the architect as areas that are able to be planned. These may even determine the form of the building where other factors fail to surface or remain uncertain. If the formative factors are defenses against anxiety that hinder task performance, the result will be a structure that is incapable of functioning adequately, and the architect's job will be seen as a failure.

THE ARCHITECT'S SYSTEM

Not only are environmental professionals confronted with defensive behavior in the organizations they are planning for, but there are anxieties associated with their own organizations as well. Architects, for example, have many stresses to deal with. Each job the architect takes on carries with it the fear of failure. Among these are failure to satisfy the client, leading to loss of the job and possibly professional reputation or failure to produce a well functioning building, resulting in bad publicity and loss of future jobs. At the same time there are personal design standards and values which must be met or compromised. Also important are the opinions of peers and colleagues, partners, and office employees, since these people will have to cooperate to complete the job. Approvals must also be sought from planning and building authorities and perhaps from neighborhood or local political groups; finally, the standards of the profession as a whole, including current design preferences are factors to be considered.

Architects deal with these stresses in a number of ways, some productive and others detrimental to the tasks. In recent years the trend has been toward the departmentalization of most large offices. The overt reasons for this approach are easy to discuss but rather unconvincing, many of the reasons being not only covert but unacknowledged. Usual arguments are efficiency and specialization possible in departmentalized offices. To a certain extent this is rational and productive; yet specialization can still occur in a job team approach to office organization without the detriment of departmental boundaries to deal with, boundaries instead being related to the actual project as a whole. In a profession where coordination and communication between different phases of the job are vital, frequently with no clear cut-off point possible (even in the best interests of the task), departmentalization leads to many complaints about designers not understanding the programming that was done (and that often has to be cut off prematurely so that the job can be passed to the next department). Correspondingly, designers complain that working drawing departments did not fully understand their intentions, and working drawing departments complain that site decisions are not made in keeping with their pristine detailing.

In a profession where following a job through and seeing the results of work done is so important for personal satisfaction, departmentalization tends to preclude much involvement by forcing repetition of similar details on many different jobs, usually in a standardized procedure. The act of processing the work then tends to become more important than the jobs themselves, just as departmental boundaries become more important than job boundaries. Departmentalization relieves anxieties by diffusing responsibility and decision making. Nobody becomes sufficiently involved in a job to feel much personal stake in it, design or functional mistakes cannot be blamed on any one person, and change or development within the office is easy to avoid.

BALANCE BETWEEN TASK PERFORMANCE
AND TOLERABLE ANXIETY

While the characteristic feature of socially structured defenses is the orientation to helping individuals avoid the experience of guilt, anxiety, doubt, and uncertainty, the attempt to avoid such confrontations is never completely successful. These attempts can be seen as a desire to eliminate events that evoke anxieties connected with primitive psychological remnants in the personality. In the nursing service, for example, the dramatic situations in reality bear a striking resemblance to the fantasy situations that exist in every individual in the deepest, most primitive levels of the mind. Even less exaggerated circumstances, however, are subject to some extent to the intrusion of the remnants of the fantasy world of the infant, peopled by himself and the objects of his feelings and impulses.[6] In the attempts to avoid such confrontations a compromise is inevitable between the aims of the social defense system and the demands of reality as expressed by the need to perform the task in an atmosphere with a tolerable level of anxiety.

This can be illustrated by imagining an organization to be a hanging mobile of wires and strings, so that a three-dimensional structure is obtained, as shown in figure 15. On one side is the task system — this side represents the rational, task-related behavior. The task carries with it certain inherent anxieties however, which are reflected by corresponding weights on the other side. On this other side are the basic assumption life of the groups involved, socially structured defenses against anxiety, and other irrational elements such as covert political issues which balance off and sometimes weigh down that side, thwarting the task. While the unconscious irrational aspects cannot be eliminated, they can at least be balanced by mechanisms to deal with them in a productive way on the rational side, hopefully to use these aspects of group functioning as an advantage. Unfortunately in most institutional settings we have too few devices to deal with the irrational side, which, because it is composed mainly of unacknowledged processes, is denied, even when rationally conceived plans unexplainedly continue to go awry. It is important to remember that conscious attention must be paid to the irrational side which deals with emotional needs and anxieties in order for the task to be accomplished, even though the result may be a system that is apparently less efficient.

HOW THE ARCHITECT AND PLANNER AFFECT
ORGANIZATIONAL EQUILIBRIUM

If we go back to the involvement of an architect or planner in the organization, it is clear that any change to improve task

6 This theory relates to the psychoanalytic position of Melanie Klein. See Klein, 1952 and 1959.

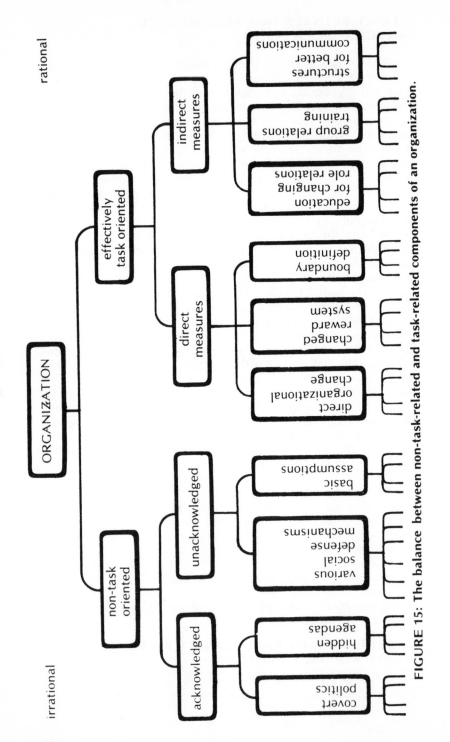

FIGURE 15: The balance between non-task-related and task-related components of an organization.

performance will upset the balance that exists and will cause stress in the system. While these issues are difficult to deal with, since they are outside the conscious awareness of those involved, clues can be discerned that will give an indication what is occurring. Comments by members of the organization tend to mirror various aspects of the collective anxiety. Similarly, each subgroup voices unconscious tensions and anxieties which collectively form the legacy of the organization which they all share. The difficulty of working without knowledge of the processes taking place is that changes or movements in one part of an organization are mirrored in all the other parts to the extent that the individuals involved perceive the changes as affecting their lives. Therefore, any change in any part of the system tends to change all the other parts; the extent to which the parts are affected is determined by the boundaries of the parts or subgroups. Each individual and subgroup behaves in such a manner that tensions will be reduced, equilibrium restored and status quo maintained. Since they occur at a covert and unacknowledge level, these efforts to restore balance can occur despite a conscious desire for change and innovation.[7]

Maintaining the status quo involves stabilizing the allocation of time, resources, priorities, power and security, and spatial needs express all of these. When planning is attempted then, boundaries may be altered; even defining them may be seen as a threat to stability, since they determine how changes in one part will be mirrored in other parts of the system. This means that boundaries are likely to appear threatened as soon as the environmental professional starts to work, with the result that greater group cohesiveness occurs, often accompanied by feelings that confidentiality is very important, although the reason why is seldom explicitly stated or even rationally considered. In this state threats to members by non-members are avoided, and the "outsider" position of the architect or planner can seriously affect his ability to do his job. He runs the risk of being excluded and denied information. More commonly he is drawn into collusion with the group, acting out their denial of the stressful realities, or there is pressure on the architect to be co-opted by one or another subgroup, although this may be counter to his task. If he sticks closely to the task, he may be treated as an irritant; the group will employ various means to divert him from the task.

THE ARCHITECT AS A PRIME MOVER FOR CHANGE AND SYMBOLIC CHANGE AGENT

When he begins programming, the architect attempts to determine in detail how various activities take place and how he can best accommodate these functions. All factors must be

---

7 A more complete description of mirroring in this context can be found in Miller and Rice, 1967. The theory that comments by members relate to the group as a whole was described in Bion, 1961.

woven into a design that will not only solve all functional problems but will be considered a work of art in its own right. Because he sees all parts of the organization and must fit these into some framework, taking cognizance of relations between them and priorities within given constraints, the architect develops an overview of the problem. He may have supplemented his information from the users with research of his own on the method of operation of a portion of the organization in question, since he takes his task seriously, and this research may have unearthed some new or alternate way of performing the activity. Or simply, the architect's explicit definition of relationships that were previously implicit and taken for granted may lead to a new view of how they can be organized. He is then in a position to see inefficiencies or illogical arrangements or assumptions that might interfere with the tasks.

By pursuing in an innocent and honest way, the goals and objectives of the organization and the best methods of achieving these, the architect can find that *he has inadvertently become the one who is most concerned with the institution's stated primary task.* He is, however, dependent on the knowledge and cooperation of those who occupy and operate in the space, and they are the people he must satisfy if the design is to be accepted and function satisfactorily. This means that although he is armed with inadequate information about how the organization functions or may have a great deal of information on the wrong issues (usually technical or physical problems, when the key issues to understand the system are often social and unacknowledged), the architect becomes the prime mover for change. He may also become symbolic of change to many of the subgroups within the organization. He has caused stresses in the system and appears to have a powerful voice in affecting the future, especially when he meets often with top administrators who hired him and must approve all plans. He is then likely to become the focus of fantasies toward authority and leadership. When preliminary approvals are obtained for portions of his work, usually by the highest authorities in the organization or by outside agencies, the architect or planner tends to be seen by some as a change agent who is gathering support to destroy the comfortable system, by others as an agent of conservatism. At this point even those who considered him fairly powerless and of little threat tend to fear lest he become the one who is able to open a ''Pandora's Box'' of uncontrollable and frightening possibilities.

When a new space is created and people define what they want, they tend to choose a space that will reduce their anxieties, fitting into some of the social defenses described above. Elizabeth Richardson describes an example in her analysis of the school system. She describes an English teacher who, in an attempt to induce his secondary school class to discuss the literature among themselves instead of through him, had moved them from their standard class to a university type of seminar room, with chairs around a table. Instead of responding positively to the change to a less school-like environment, the students saw the changes as menacing and openly complained that they did not like the room. While they wanted to be treated like grown-ups, they felt ambivalent and feared leaving their dependent child-like positions. The change of room arrangement created anxiety because it reminded them of their near adult status requiring more responsible action. Since the teacher had manipulated the change it was feared as permanent and had to be fought before childhood was forever lost. Richardson also describes a similar English class in which previous attempts to change the room had failed. One day, however, the class was forced to use the library unexpectedly. As it happened the seating arrangement was accidently like the one the teacher had been attempting to adapt them to. The class turned out to be the best of the year (Richardson, 1967). Perhaps the temporary and sudden change avoided triggering the defensive resistance of the class.

Another example is the design of a new building on one of the campuses of the University of California. A leading architectural office researched the problem and produced a preliminary design incorporating allowances for the changing modes of teaching, the growing independence on the part of students, and other innovations aimed at improving the university teaching environment. This design was displayed at the university to invite comments. The result was a series of outraged student meetings that criticized the plans, saying they did not respond to student needs and would not work. As a result a series of student forums were held to incorporate student input into the design. The final scheme was far more conventional than the original but the student protest was calmed. On visiting the completed building, the architect sadly recounted how disappointed he was. He felt the building did not function as well as intended and he felt that the original plan would have been far superior. Change was avoided and familiar defenses maintained at the expense of the task.

CONCLUSIONS

If maximum benefit is to be received from new environments for existing organizations, intervention must be very carefully planned. Changes may need to be instituted while still allowing users to maintain familiar and comfortable areas of competence and role relations. If more acute shifts are required, users may require training to prepare them for the new roles and to help them develop competence and self-confidence in changed or changing situations. If the methods are not carefully thought out, intervention in the system, which is necessary to do the job, may increase resistance to desirable and needed changes. By the wrong kind of intervention, then, the architect or planner can make his job more difficult and feel that he is being scapegoated.

Organizational consultation, based on theories discussed in this volume, shows great promise in the ability to deal with these concerns, and one is tempted to suggest that a group relations and organizational consultant should be the first person hired when dealing with any complex institution, organization or urban complex. There is very little in the way of documentation of such applications, however. The area is ripe for further work.

Certainly there can be little doubt that aptitude for organizational analysis and ability to intervene in a productive way would be extremely useful to any planner. As stress on evaluation of buildings and planning decisions continues, documentation of processes by which the groups arrived at decisions will begin to be kept in more detail, both as an aid in deciding criteria for evaluation and to see where the processes went wrong or where they were successful. With growth no longer a cultural given, architects must be able to determine which jobs they would be advised to refuse or restructure, or when to recommend that no new building be built. The planner must void entanglement in physical or environmental issues that are being fought as substitutes for other issues which are not explicitly stated. As this type of knowledge becomes more widely used, not only could the success of plans be improved but also planning and design funding could be much more effectively allocated to obtain maximum results.

21.

THE GROUP, PHENOMENON AND PHILOSOPHY: A Look at the Historical Emergence of Cities

Dennis Williams

One of the most profoundly mystical aspects of urban history is its very basis. What is a city? How did cities or dense urban living evolve? These questions have not been answered. That is not to say that answers have not been given—they have. But, no answer has been advanced that gives peace to the inquisitive mind. The mind has only been placated by the abstraction of socio-economic externals; development of occupational specialization, growth of trade, emergence of class structure; or through proposals of broad generalizations, as a city emerges when 40,000 people live in a physically limited space.

Gideon Sjorberg, in *The Preindustrial City*, lists some of the abstracted criteria that characterize the emergence of the city (Sjorberg, 1960 pp. 27-31). He designates three prerequisites: (1) a favorable "ecological" basis, (2) an advanced technology, both in agricultural and non-agricultural spheres, and (3) a complex social organization. The first prerequisite demands a favorable climate, productive soil and an adequate water supply. The advanced agricultural technology would provide the necessary food surplus to support large concentrations of people and to create trade. An advanced industrial technology would provide the means of trade transportation and improve the means of agricultural production; plows, irrigation principles, etc. Distribution of the agricultural surplus for trade and community subsistence necessitates the development of an economic system; also the development of specific occupational groups that would complete certain complex tasks. Some social order must simultaneously evolve so that labor is distributed among the workers and for the regulation of economic commodities. These prerequisites help one *to view* the conditions preceding the emergence of urban environments but they do not help one to *understand* the process. The most important aspect of the phenomenon, that of the relationships of the individual to the groups that make up the city, is ignored. The complexity of the urban evolution process is simplified by ignoring the inhabitants of the urban environment who initiate it.

Lewis Mumford has attempted *to understand* the city-emergence process through a more "human" orientation. Quoting from *The City in History:*

> That urban transformation was accompanied, perhaps preceded by...outpourings from the collective unconscious... The local chieftain turned into the towering king, and became likewise the chief priestly guardian of the shrine... The village neighbors would now be kept at a distance: no longer familiars and equals, they were reduced to subjects... When all this happened, the archaic village culture yielded to urban civilization...whose outward manifestation has been the historic city (Mumford, 1961, p.30).

> The city was the chief fruit of the union between neolithic and a more archaic paleolithic culture. In the new proto-urban milieu, the male became the leading figure...Man's strength now lay in feats of aggression and force...in forcing his will on other men (Mumford, 1961, p.27).

and from *The City Invincible:*

> (Reference to the quiet village life of the Neolithic period that followed the society of the male hunter)...Did agriculture push back the hunter permanently, or did the growing scarcity of game make him feel that his own predatory life was becoming too insecure as long as he depended upon killing other predators? Was he perhaps lured by the comforts and sociabilities of the villages? Before the city springs into being the hunter's camp turns into a permanent stronghold, held by someone a little too vaguely described as the "local chieftain"...Similarly, although the hunter had a function in the village economy, he had to be bought off; and, since he was in a minority, probably the function of his castle or fortress was as a holding point— not a protective retreat for the villagers but as a means of defense against them...(Mumford, 1960).

In spite of the Jungian Connotations, the Freudian allusions, an understanding of the process of urbanity is only suggested, hinted at in a fluidity of language. What Lewis Mumford only touches upon is again that which one would assume would transform urban expressionism into urban understanding—the relationships of the groups and individuals that make up the city or the potential city. Perhaps an understanding of the group process can be applied to the emergence of the city.

What Bion thought was perhaps only an interesting phenomenon in his analysis of the group process as the co-existence of the work group and basic assumption group was developed by Slater as not only an approach to viewing group formation and development, but as a philosophical approach in utilizing the group-individual boundary process as a model for understanding social situations. In his own words:

It might be objected that the many parallels drawn merely reflect a kind of grandiosity on our part, an attempt to crowd all of life and history into the tiny shell of one particular and even atypical variety of a contemporary group experience (Slater, 1966, p. 234).

Perhaps Slater does indulge in a kind of grandiosity, but the product is a model that can be utilized in understanding urban development. For, as even presented in the poetic rapture of Lewis Mumford, the transition from neolithic serenity to chieftain citadel is the transition from dependency assumption group to fight-flight assumption group. Or, in applicable Slater terminology, the birth of the consciousness of the individual from the ''mother'' image of society—the strengthening of the ego (Slater, 1966, pp. 219-250). In physical terms, the gradual revolt from the dependency period is marked by the dominance of man over his environment. Because the dependency revolt is a slow process, the growth consciousness is characterized by repetitive episodes of infatuation with the dependency situation. Eventually, a fight-flight condition results from this dependency — this realization of the impotency of the situation. In other terms, the individualism that is emerging within the group becomes identifiable with some central person who becomes the fight-flight leader.

Using the evolution of Athens for an example, the fight-flight group builds the walled citadel during the Mycenaean Period (1300 B.C.) in Greece. The fight-flight leader develops the paranoia of the neolithic dependency group by designating external enemies from whom the community must be protected. The wall that is constructed around the citadel is not simply, thus, an architectural feature that develops with the citadel; it is the physical representation of the paranoia of the fight-flight group—the attempt at independence from the dependency situation. The wall is simply in Sjorberg's words, a "physical aspect" of the city (Sjorberg, 1960, p. 35). It is a physical aspect of the citadel that reflects the individual-group boundary awareness of the (potential) city.

The citadel becomes not only the home of the fight-flight leader but also that of the group god. The megaron contains a hearth and altar in addition to the throne of the leader. Eventually the consciousness or ego must be separated from the leader who helped build it as the religion must grow from one which centers about a weak distinction between self and world, between religion and other roles, to a religion which emphasizes more characterization of mythical beings and more distinction of roles (priesthood).

The megaron is also the banquet hall of the leader and is thus symbolically the cannibalistic ritual place of his disposal. As ritual and religious connotations cannot secure the position of the fight-flight leader, the transition to loving pair takes place. The king marries to produce the messiah. This period lasted in Athens from 800 to 500 B.C. But, it cannot continue perpetually. The growing independency of the population is marked by the increasing role they play in politics; assemblies meet, lawcourts are appointed. As the religion grows from the almost all earth mother of the citadel to the humanized gods and goddesses of Classical Greece, the king moves from the citadel and the citadel becomes the home of the patron god—Athena in Athens.

The palace of the fight-flight leader becomes the temple and the walls that once represented fight-flight paranoia become symbols transmitted through generations that now define the sanctuary of the acropolis. Public buildings are constructed outside the acropolis to reflect the emergence of individuality. The public buildings are erected in the public square, the agora. There they become the physical realities of the revolt from the fight-flight leaders. This last step takes us to the Athens of 450 B.C.

In this process, from 1300 B.C. to 450 B.C., Athens became a city. Perhaps, for Athens, what designated that it had become an urban environment was not the density of the population (which is unknown in ancient times) or the development of trade or the evolution of social structure, but the point at which the fight-flight situation dissolved so that the urban group became more consciously aware of its responsibility to itself and to a place. Athens then shifted from its designation as the citadel inhabited by the fight-flight leader to an inhabited city.

Since group processes are so heavily embedded with mythological symbolism and sexual overtones, in interpreting the evolution of an urban environment by means of the "group" process, the mythological interpretation is almost inherently included. In addition, the socio-economic view can be used to augment the group-individual understanding of urban evolution. All that is asserted is that people, individuals in groups, preceded the socio-economic patterns that describe the city environment. And, that what is learned from the development and formation of groups can help explain the evolution of the city — that which began as a group.

Bibliography

Allaway, A. J. 1959. "Introduction." In *Exploration in Group Relations*. Leicester: Leicester University Press.

Almond, R. and B. M. Astrachan. 1969. "Social systems training for psychiatric residents." *Psychiatry*, 32, 277-291.

Ardrey, R. 1966. *The Territorial Imperative*. New York: Atheneum.

Argyris, C. 1962. *Interpersonal Competence and Organizational Effectiveness*. Homewood, Illinois: Dorsey Press; London: Tavistock Publications.

Argyris, C. 1964. *Integrating the Individual and the Organization*. New York: John Wiley & Sons

Astrachan, B.M., H.R. Flynn, J.D. Geller, and H.H. Harvey. 1970. "Systems approach to day hospitalization." *Archives of General Psychiatry*, 22, 550-559. *Group Relations Reader*, p. 193.

Astrachan, B.M. and F.C. Redlich. 1967. "Leadership ambiguity and its effect on residents' study groups." New York: Mid-winter meeting of the American Academy of Psychoanalysis.

Ayllon, T. and N.H. Azrin. 1969. "The measurement and reinforcement of behaviors of psychotics." *Journal of Applied Behavior Analysis*, 2, 207-214.

Babayan, E. A. 1965. "The organization of psychiatric services in the USSR." *International Journal of Psychiatry*, 1, 31-35.

Bennis, W.G. 1959. "Leadership theory and administrative behaviour." *Administrative Science Quarterly*, 4, 259-301.

Bennis, W.G. and E.H. Schein. 1964. *Interpersonal Dynamics*. Homewood, Illinois: Richard D. Irwin.

Bennis, W.G. and H.A. Shepard. 1956. "A theory of group development." *Human Relations*, 9, 415-457 (Republished in W.G. Bennis, K.D. Benne, & R. Chin, eds. *The Planning of Change*. New York: Holt, Rinehart, and Winston, 1961, 321-340.)

Benoit, H. 1955. *The Supreme Doctrine*. New York: Pantheon Books.

Berne, E. 1966. *Principles of Group Treatment*. New York: Oxford University Press.

Bettleheim, B. 1950. *Love is Not Enough*. Glencoe: The Free Press.

Bexton, W. H. 1975. "Group Processes in Environmental Design: exposing architects and planners to the study of group relations." *Group Relations Reader*, p. 251.

Bexton, W.H. 1975. "The architect and planner: change agent or scapegoat?" *Group Relations Reader*, p. 343.

Bion, W.R. 1955. "Group dynamics: a review." in M. Klein, P. Heimann, and R.E. Money-Kyrle, eds. *New Directions in Psycho-analysis*. London: Tavistock Publications; New York: Basic Books.

Bion, W.R. 1961. *Experiences in Groups*. London: Tavistock Publications; New York: Basic Books. Selections in *Group Relations Reader*, p. 11.

Boughey, H N. Jr. 1968. *Blueprints for Behavior: The Intentions of Architects to Influence Social Action*. Ph.D. dissertation, Princeton University.

Bradford, L.P. and J.R. Gibb, eds. 1964. *Theories of T-group Training*. New York: John Wiley & Sons

Brown, T. McP. 1969. Personal communication.

Buckley, W. 1968. *Modern Systems Research for the Behavioral Scientist.* Chicago: Aldine Press.

Burke, R.L. and W.G. Bennis. 1961. "Changes in perception of self and others during human relations training." *Human Relations*, 14, 165-182.

Calhoun, J.B. 1966. "The role of space in animal sociology." *Journal of Social Issues*, 22, 46-58.

Cartwright, D. and A. Zander, eds. 1953. *Group Dynamics.* Evanston, Illinois: Row, Peterson.

Cohen, K.M., J.A. Tilepezak, and J.S. Bis. 1966. *Contingencies Applicable to Special Education of Delinquents.* Silver Spring: Institute of Behavioral Research Press.

Colby, K.M. 1968. "Computer-ordered language development in non-speaking children." *Archives of General Psychiatry*, 19, 641-651.

Colman, A.D. 1971. *The Planned Environment in Psychiatric Treatment: a Manual for Ward Design.* Springfield: Thomas.

Colman, A.D. 1973. "Irrational Aspects of Design." *Man-Environment Systems*, 3, 161-176, *Group Relations Reader*, p. 313.

Colman, A.D. 1975a. "Environmental design: realities and delusions." *Group Relations Reader*, p. 329.

Colman, A.D. 1975b. "Group consciousness as a developmental phase." *Group Relations Reader*, p. 35.

Colman, A.D. and S.L. Baker. 1969. "Utilization of an operant conditioning model for the treatment of character and behavior disorders in military setting." *American Journal of Psychiatry*, 125, 1395-1403.

Colman, A.D. and J.J. Boren. 1969. "An information system for measuring patient behavior and its use by staff." *Journal of Applied Behavior Analysis*, 2, 207-214.

Colman, A.D. and L.L. Colman. 1975. *Love and Ecstasy.* New York: Seabury.

Colman, A.D., K.E. Liebold, and J.J. Boren. 1969. "A method for studying altruism in monkeys." *Psychological Record*, 19, 401-405.

DeLauwe, C. 1965. *Des Hommes et Des Villes.* Paris: Payot.

Dentler, R.A. and K.T. Erikson. 1959. "The functions of deviance in groups." *Social Problems*, 7, 98-107.

David, D. 1960. *Charles Sumner and the Coming of the Civil War.* New York: Knopf.

Dohrenwent, B.P. and B.S. Dohrenwend. 1965. "The problem of validity in field studies of psychological disorder." *Journal of Abnormal Psychology*, 70, 52-69.

Duddy, J.H., 315, 364

Edelson, M. 1970a. *The Practice of Sociotherapy.* New Haven: Yale University Press.

Edelson, M. 1970b. *Sociotherapy and Psychotherapy.* Chicago: University of Chicago Press.

Eissler, K.R. 1953. "The effect of the structure of the ego on psychoanalytic technique." *Journal of the American Psychoanalytic Association*, 50, 104-143.

Eliade, M. 1959. *The Sacred and the Profane.* translated by Willard R. Trask. New York: Harcourt, Brace & World.

Etzioni, A., ed. 1961. *Complex Organizations: A Sociological Reader.* New York: Holt, Rinehart and Winston.

Ezriel, H. 1951. "Notes on psychoanalytic group therapy: II. Interpretation and research." *Psychiatry*, 15, 119-126.

Farndale, J. 1961. *The Day Hospital Movement in Great Britain.* London: Pergamon Press.

Federn, P. 1961. *Ego Psychology and the Psychoses.* New York: Basic Books.

Fenichel, O. 1946. *The Psychoanalytic Theory of the Neuroses*. New York: Norton.

Ferster, C.B. 1972. "An experimental analysis of clinical phenomena."

Fichelet, R., Meignier, R., G. Michelat, and L.F. Yaun. 1963. "Comments about an intervention on real environment." Milan: Third International Conference on Group Psychotherapy.

Fischer, C. 1960. "Preconscious stimulation in dreams, associations, and images." *Psychological Issues*, 2(3). New York: International Universities Press.

Foulkes, S. R. and E. J. Anthony. 1964. *Group Psychotherapy*. Baltimore: Penguin Books (revised edition).

Fowles. J. 1967. *The Magus*. New York: Dell.

Frasner, L. and L.P. Ullman, eds. 1965. *Research Behavior Modifications: New Developments and Implications*. New York: Holt, Rinehart, and Winston.

Freeman, P. 1962. "Treatment of chronic schizophrenia in a day center." *Archives of General Psychiatry*, 7, 259-265.

Freud, A. 1937. "The ego and the mechanizms of defence." In *The International Psycho-analytical Library*, No. 30. London: The Hogarth Press, 1969 (Fifth impression).

Freud, S. 1865. "Studies on hysteria." *Complete Psychological Works of Sigmund Freud*. Vol. II. London: Hogarth Press, 1950/Pp. 1-251.

Freud, S. 1911. "Formulations on the two principles of mental functioning." *Complete Psychological Works of Sigmund Freud*. Vol. 12. London: Hogarth Press. 1950.

Freud, S. 1913. "Totem and Taboo." *Complete Psychological Works of Sigmund Freud*. Vol. 13. London: Hogarth Press, 1950.

Freud, S. 1917. "Mourning and melancholia." *Collected Papers of Sigmund Freud*, Vol. IV. New York: Basic Books, 1959. Pp. 152-170.

Freud, S. 1919. "Lines of advance in psycho-analytic therapy." *Complete Psychological Works of Sigmund Freud*. London: Hogarth Press, 1950.

Freud, S. 1921. "Group psychology and the analysis of the ego." *Complete Psychological Works of Sigmund Freud*. London: Hogarth Press, 1950.

Freud, S. 1921. "Group psychology and the analysis of the ego." *Complete Psychological Works of Sigmund Freud*. Vol. 18. London: Hogarth Press, 1950.

Freud, S. 1926. "Inhibitions, symptoms and anxiety." *Complete Psychological Works of Sigmund Freud*. London: Hogarth Press, 1950.

Gainer, P., 332, 365

Gaster, T.H., ed. 1959. *Frazer's The New Golden Bough*. New York: Criterion Books.

Gibbard, G.S., J.J. Hartman, and R.D. Mann, eds. 1974. "Group Process and development." In *Analysis of Groups*. San Francisco: Jossey-Bass. P. 90.

Glascote, R.M., A.M. Kraft, S.M. Glassman, et al. 1969. *Partial Hospitalization of the Mentally Ill*. Washington, D.C.: Joint Information Service, American Psychiatric Association, American Association for Mental Health.

Glidewell, J.C., M.B. Kantor, L.M. Smith, and L.A. Stringer. 1966. "Socialization and social structure in the classroom." In L.W. Hoffman and M.L. Hoffman, eds. *Review of Child Development Research*. New York: Russell Sage Foundation, 2, 221-256.

Goffman, E. 1958. "The characteristics of total institutions." In *Symposium on Preventive and Social Psychiatry* sponsored by Walter Reed Army Institute of Research and the National Research Council. P. 43-84.

Goldiamond, I. and J.E. Dyrud. 1968. "Some applications and implications of behavioral analysis for psychotherapy." *Research in Psychotherapy*, 3, 54-89.

Golding, W. 1958. *Lord of the Flies*. London: Faber & Faber.

Goodman, R. 1971. *After the Planners*. New York: Simon and Schuster.

Goshen, C. 1959. "New concepts of psychiatric care with special reference to the day hospital." *American Journal of Psychiatry*, 115, 808-811.

Gosling, R. and P. Turquet. 1964. "The training of general practitioners: the use of group method." Paper at conference on group methods. London: Tavistock Institute of Human Relations.

Guy, W.M. Gross, G.H. Hogarty, et al. 1969. "A controlled evaluation of day hospital effectiveness. " *Archives of General Psychiatry*, 20, 329-338.

Hall, E.T. 1966. *The Hidden Dimension*. New York: Doubleday.

Hausman, W. 1975a. "The application of group relations methods and concepts to the psychiatric clinic." *Group Relations Reader*, p. 181.

Hausman, W. In press. "Reorganization of a department of psychiatry." In E.J. Miller, ed. *Task and Organization*. London: John Wiley & Sons.

Heimann. P. 1952. "Certain functions of introjection and projection in earliest infancy." In *Developments in Psycho-analysis*. London: Hogarth Press & Institute of Psycho-analysis.

Higgins. G.W. and H. Bridger. 1964. "The psychodynamics of an inter-group experience." *Human Relations*, 17, 391-446. And as Tavistock Pamphlet No. 10. London: Tavistock Publications, 1965.

Hill, J.M.M. and E.L. Trist. 1953. "A consideration of industrial accidents as a means of withdrawal from the work situation." *Human Relations*, 6, 357-380.

Hinton, W. 1966. *Fanshen*. New York: Monthly Review Press.

Hogarty, G.E., H. Dennis, W. Guy, et al. 1968. " 'Who goes there': a critical evaluation of admission to a psychiatric day hospital." *American Journal of Psychiatry*, 124, 94-104.

Hutton, G. 1962. "Management in a changing mental hospital." *Human Relationships*, 15, 283-310. And "Managing systems in hospitals." *Human Relations* 15, 311-333.

James. W. 1890. *The Principles of Psychology*. London: Macmillan; New York: Holt.

Janis, I.L. 1950. *Psychological Stress: Psycho-analytic and Behavioural Studies of Surgical Patients*. London: Chapman & Hall.

Jaques, E. 1955. "Social systems as a defence against persecutory and depressive anxiety." In *New Directions in Psycho-analysis*. London: Tavistock Publications; New York: Basic Books.

Jaques, E. 1956. *Measurement of Responsibility: A Study of Work, Payment, and Individual Capacity*. London: Tavistock Publications; Cambridge, Mass.: Harvard University Press.

Joffee, W.G. and J. Sandler. 1965. "Notes on Pain, Depression and Individuation." *Psychoanalytic Study of the Child*, 2, 395-424.

Jolly, A. 1966. "Lemur Social Behavior and Primate Intelligence." *Science*. 153, 501-506.

Jones, A.L., G. Cormack, and L. Bow. 1963. "Whither the day hospital." *American Journal of Psychiatry*, 119, 973-977.

Jourard, S. 1971. *The Transparent Self*. New York: Van Nostrand Reinhold

Illing, H.A. 1957. "C.G. Jung on the present trends in group psychotherapy." *Human Relations*, 10, 77-83.

Katz, D. and R.L. Kahn. 1966. *The Social Psychology of Organizations*. New York: John Wiley & Sons.

Kelman, H.C. 1963. "The role of the group in the induction of therapeutic change." *International Journal of Group Psychotherapy*, 13, 399-432.

Klein, E.B. and L. J. Gould. 1973. "Boundary issues and organizational dynamics: a case study." *Social Psychiatry*, 8, 204-211.

Klein, M. 1930. "The importance of symbol formation in the development of the ego." *Contributions to Psycho-analysis [1921-1945]*. London: Hogarth Press, 1948. Pp. 236-250.

Klein, M. 1935. "The psychogenesis of manic-depressive states." In *Contributions to Psycho-analysis [1921-1945]*. London: Hogarth Press, 1948. Pp. 282-310.

Klein, M. 1946. "Notes on some schizoid mechanisms." In Klein et al, eds. *Developments in Psycho-analysis*. London: Hogarth Press, 1952.

Klein, M. 1952. "Some theoretical conclusions regarding the emotional life of the infant." In Klein et al, eds. *Developments in Psycho-analysis*. London: Hogarth Press.

Klein, M. 1959. "Our adult world and its roots in infancy." *Human Relations*, 12, 291-303. Reprinted as Tavistock Pamphlet No. 2. London: Tavistock Publications, 1960.

Kramer, B.M. 1962. *Day Hospital: A Study of Partial Hospitalization in Psychiatry*. New York: Grune & Stratton Inc.

Kuhn, T. S. 1965. *The Structure of the Scientific Revolution*. Chicago, University of Chicago Press.

Langsley, D.G., F.S. Pittman, P. Machotka, et al. 1968. "Family crisis therapy: results and implications." *Family Process*, 7, 145-158.

Levinson, D.J. 1959. "Role, personality, and social structure in the organizational setting." *Journal of Abnormal Social Psychology*, 58, 170-180.

Lewin, K. 1951. *Field Theory in Social Science*. New York: Harper.

Lewin, K. and R. Lippitt. 1938. "An experimental approach to the study of autocracy and democracy: a preliminary note." *Sociometry*, 1, 292-300.

Likert, R. 1961. *New Patterns of Management*. New York: McGraw-Hill.

Linton, R. 1956. *Culture and Mental Disorders*. Springfield: Thomas.

Lofgren. L.B. In press. "Organizational design and therapeutic effect." In E.J. Miller ed. *Task and Organization*. London: Wiley & Sons. *Group Relations Reader*, p. 185.

Lorenz, K. 1963. *On Agression*. New York: Harcourt, Brace & World.

Losen, S.M. "The school psychologist — psychotherapist or consultant?" *Psychology in the Schools*, 1, 13-17.

Mahler, M.S. 1963. "Thoughts about development and individuation." *The Psychoanalytic Study of the Child*, 18. New York: International Universities Press, Inc.

Mahler, M.S. 1972. "On the first three subphases of the separation-individuation process" *International Journal of Psychoanalysis*, 53, 333-338.

Mann, T. 1930. *Mario und der Zauberer*. Berlin: S. Rischer. (Excerpts trans. by Margaret Rioch.)

Marshall, K.E. and A.D. Colman. 1974. "Operant analysis of encounter groups." *International Journal of Group Psychotherapy*, 24, 42-54.

Masserman, J.H., S. Wechkin, and W. Terris. 1962. "Altruism in Monkeys." *American Journal of Psychiatry*, 55, 123-125.

Mayo, E. 1945. *The Social Problems of an Industrial Civilization*. Cambridge: Harvard University Press; London: Routledge & Kegan Paul.

McCaffree, K.M. 1968. "The economic basis for the development of community mental health programs." *Medical Care*, 6(4).

McGregor, D. 1960. *The Human Side of Enterprise*. New York: McGraw Hill.

Menninger, R. In press. "The impact of group relations conferences on organizational growth." *International Journal of Group Psychotherapy. Group Relations Reader*, p. 265.

Menzies, I.E.P. 1951. *Technical Report on a Working Conference for Public Health Nurses, Noordwijk, the Netherlands, 1950*. World Health Organization, 1951.

Menzies, I.E. P. 1960. "A case-study in the functioning of social systems as a defense against anxiety." *Human Relations* 13, 95-121. Reprinted as Tavistock Pamphlet No. 3 London: Tavistock Publication, 1961 and *Group Relations Reader*, p. 281.

Menzies, I.E.P. 1961. "Some psychological consequences of belonging to an organization." Paper given at the Group Relations Training Conference, Leicester University/Tavistock Institute.

Miller, E.J. 1959. "Technology, territory, and time: the internal differentiation of complex production systems." *Human Relations*, 12, 243-272.

Miller, E.J. and G.V. Gwynne. 1972. *A Life Apart*. London: Tavistock Publications.

Miller, E.J. and A.K. Rice. 1967. *Systems of Organization*. London: Tavistock Publications. Selections in *Group Relations Reader*, p. 43.

Mills, T.M. 1965. *Group Transformation*. Englewood Cliffs, N.J.: Prentice-Hall.

Mills, T.M. 1967. *The Sociology of Small Groups*. Englewood Cliffs, N.J.: Prentice-Hall.

Mumford, L. 1960. *The City Invincible*. Eds. Carl H. Kraeling and Robert M. Adams. Chicago: The University Press, pp. 230-231.

Mumford, L. 1961. *The City in History*. New York: Harcourt, Brace and World, Inc.

Musto, D.F. and B.M. Astrachan, 1968. "Strange encounter: the use of study groups with graduate students in history." *Psychiatry*, 31, 264-276. Selections in *Group Relations Reader*, p. 235

National Training Laboratory 1953. *Human Relations Training: Assessment of Experience, 1947-1953*. Washington: National Education Association.

Newman, R. 1967. *Psychological Consultation in the Schools*. New York: Basic Books

Parsons, T. 1951. *The Social System*. Glencoe, Illinois: Free Press.

Parsons, T. 1964. *Social Structure and Personality*. New York: Free Press of Glencoe.

Pascal, B. *Pensees*. New York: Dutton, 1958.

Redl, F. 1942. "Group emotion and leadership." *Psychiatry*, 5, 573-596.

Redl, F. and D. Wineman. 1951. *Children who Hate*. Glencoe, Illinois: Free Press.

Redlich, F.C. and B.M. Astrachan. 1969. "Group dynamics training." *American Journal of Psychiatry*, 125, 1501-1507. *Group Relations Reader*, p 225

Revans, R.W. 1959. *The Hospital as an Organism: a Study in Communications and Morale*. Preprint No. 7 of a paper presented at the 6th Annual International Meeting of the Institute of Management Sciences, September 1959, Paris. London: Pergamon Press

Rice, A.K. 1951. "The use of unrecognized cultural mechanisms in an expanding machine shop." *Human Relations*, 4, 143-160.

368

Rice, A K 1958 *Productivity and Social Organization: the Ahmedabad Experiment.* London Tavistock Publications

Rice, A K 1963 *The Enterprise and its Environment* London Tavistock Publications.

Rice, A K 1965 *Learning for Leadership* London Tavistock Publication. Selections in *Group Relations Reader*, p 71

Rice, A K and E L Trist 1952 "Institutional and sub-institutional determinants of change in labour turnover." *Human Relations*, 5, 347-371.

Rice, G E and Gainer, P 1962 "Altruism in the Albino Rat" *Journal of Comparative and Physical Psychology*, 55 123-125

Rittel, H 1966 "Some Principles for the Design of an Educational System For Design In Passoneau, J " (Ed) *Educational For Architectural Technology* St Louis AIA Research Projects

Richardson, Elizabeth 1967 *The Environment of Learning.* London Thomas Nelson and Sons Ltd Selections in *Group Relations Reader*, p. 215.

Rickman, J 1951 "Methodology and research in psychological pathology." *British Journal of Medical Psychology*, 24 (Part 1), 1-7

Rioch, M J 1970a "The work of Wilfred Bion on groups" *Psychiatry*, 56-65 *Group Relations Reader*, p 21

Rioch, M J 1970b "Group relations rationale and technique." *International Journal of Group Psychotherapy*, 20, 340-355. *Group Relations Reader*, p 3

Rioch, M J 1971 " 'All we like sheep' (Isaiah 53 6) followers and leaders " *Psychiatry*, 34, 258-273 *Group Relations Reader*, p 159

Robinson, R and M Roman 1966 "New directions for the psychiatric aide." *Nursing Outlook*, 14, 27-30

Roe, A and Simpson, G 1958 (Ed) *Behavior and Evaluation* New Haven, Yale University Press

Sarason, S B , M Levine, I I Goldenbero, D L Cherlin and E M Bennett. 1966 *Psychology in Community Settings.* New York Wiley & Sons

Schein, E H and W G Bennis, eds 1965 *Personal and Organizational Change Through Group Methods.* New York Wiley & Sons.

Segal, H 1957 "Notes on symbol formation." *International Journal of Psycho-analysis*, 38, 391-397.

Selznick, P 1957 *Leadership in Administration.* Evanston, Illinois Row, Peterson

Singer, D L , M B Whiton and M L Fried 1970 "An alternative to traditional mental health services and consultation in schools a social systems and group process approach." *Journal of School Psychology*, 8, 172-178 *Group Relations Reader*, p 207

Sjorberg, G 1960 *The Preindustrial City* Illinois The Free Press

Skellern, E 1953 *Report on the practical Application to Ward Administration of Modern Methods in the Instruction and Handling of Staff and Student Nurses* London Royal College of Nursing

Skinner, B F 1948 *Walden Two* New York MacMillan

Skinner, B F 1971 *Beyond Freedom and Dignity.* New York Knopf

Slater, P E 1961 "Displacement in groups." In W G Bennis, K D Benne, and R Chin, eds *The Planning of Change* New York Holt, Rinehart, & Winston Pp 725-736.

Slater, P E 1966 *Microcosm.* New York Wiley & Sons

Slavson, S R 1964 *A Textbook in Analytic Group Psychotherapy* New York International Universities Press

Snow, C P Series of novels on scientific politics

Sofer, C 1955 "Reactions to administrative change a study of staff relations in three Bristish hospitals" *Human Relations*, 8, 291-316

Sofer, C 1961 *The Organization from Within* London Tavistock Publications; Chicago Quadrangle

Sommer , R. 1969 *Personal Space* New Jersey Prentice-Hall, 1969

Studer, R. G. and Stea, D. 1966. "Architectural Programming, Environmental Design and Human Behavior." *Journal of Social Issues*, 22: 127-136.

Sutherland, J. D. 1952. "Notes on Psychoanalytic Group Therapy: I. Therapy and Training." *Psychiatry*, 15, 111-117.

Sutherland, J. D. 1959. "Appendix" to *Explorations in Group Relations*. Leicester: Leicester University Press.

Tannenbaum, R., I.R. Weschler, and F. Massarik. 1961. *Leadership and Organization: A Behavioral Science Approach*. New York: McGraw Hill.

Tart, C.T. ed. 1969. *Altered States of Consciousness*. New York: Wiley & Sons.

Tepper, G., Duddy, J H., and Colman, A D. 1972. "Boundary Crossing at SEA-TAC: A view of the International Arrivals Facility at Seattle-Tacoma International Airport." *Proceedings of the Human Factor Society*.

Thomas, C.S. and G. Weisman. "Emergency planning: the practical and theoretical backdrop to an emergency treatment unit." *International Journal of Social Psychiatry*.

Thomas, E J. and C.F. Fink. 1963. "Effects of group size." *Psychological Bulletin*, 60, 371-384.

Tolstoy, L. *War and Peace*, trans. Louise and Aylmer Maude. New York: Simon & Schuster, 1942.

Townsend, R 1970 *Up the Organization*. New York, Knopf.

Trist, E L. and K W. Bamforth. 1951. "Some social and psychological consequences of the longwall method of coal-getting." *Human Relations*, 4, 3-38.

Trist, B.L., G.W. Higgins, H. Murray, and A.B. Pollack. 1963. *Organizational Choice: Capabilities of Groups at the Coal Face under Changing Technologies*. London: Tavistock Publications.

Trist, E.L. and C. Sofer. 1959. *Explorations in Group Relations*. Leicester: Leicester University Press.

Trotter, W. 1916. *Instincts of the Herd in Peace and War*. London.

Tuckman, B.W. 1965. "Developmental sequence in small groups." *Psychological Bulletin*, 63, 384-399.

Von Bertalanffy, I. 1968. *General Systems Theory*. New York: George Braziller.

Watzlawick, P., Beaven, J H and Jackson, D D 1967 *Progmatics of Human Communication*. New York, Norton

Webster's Third New Dictionary. 1965. Springfield: Merrima.

Weschler, I.R. and B.H. Schein, eds. 1962. *Issues in Training*. Washington: National Education Association.

Wheelis, A. 1958, *The Quest for Identity*. New York: W.W. Norton & co.

Whitaker, D.S. and M.A. Lieberman. 1965. *Psychotherapy Through the Group Process*. New York: Atherton Press.

Wilder, J F., G. Levin, and I. Zwerling. 1966. "A two year follow-up evaluation of acute psychiatric patients treated in a day hospital." *American Journal of Psychiatry*, 122, 1095-1101.

Willcox, W.B. 1964. *Portrait of a General: Sir Henry Clinton in the War of Independence*. New York: Knopf.

Williams, Dennis, 1975. "The group, phenomenon and philosophy: a look at the historical emergence of cities." *Group Relations Reader*, p. 359.

Wilson, A.T.M. 1950. "Hospital nursing auxiliaries." *Human Relations*, 3, 1-32.

Winnicott, D.W. 1953. "Transitional objects and transitional phenomena." *International Journal of Psychoanalysis*, 24, 89-97.

Zwerling, I. and J.F. Wilder. 1964. "An evaluation of the applicability of the day hospital in treatment of acutely disturbed patients." *Israel Annuls of Psychiatry* 2, 162-185.

Author Index

372

Subject Index

W

Y